W9-DEO-721

ISRAEL AT THE POLLS

Alma College
Monteith Library

SIGILLUM ALMAE COLLEGII.
IN NOMINE DEI, AMEN.
INCORPORATED A.D. 1886.

ISRAEL AT THE POLLS

The Knesset Elections of 1977

Edited by Howard R. Penniman

American Enterprise Institute for Public Policy Research
Washington, D.C.

Library of Congress Cataloging in Publication Data

Main entry under title:
Israel at the polls.

    (AEI studies ; 203)
    Includes index.
    1. Israel. Knesset—Elections, 1977-Addresses,
essays, lectures. 2. Elections—Israel—
Addresses, essays, lectures. I. Penniman,
Howard Rae, 1916– II. Series: American
Enterprise Institute for Public Policy Research.
AEI studies ; 203.
JQ1825.P365I82   329'.023'569405   78–22059
ISBN 0–8447–3305–9

AEI studies 203

© 1979 by American Enterprise Institute for Public Policy Research,
Washington, D.C. Permission to quote from or to reproduce materials in
this publication is granted when due acknowledgment is made.
The views expressed in the publications of the American Enterprise Institute
are those of the authors and do not necessarily reflect the views of the staff,
advisory panels, officers, or trustees of AEI.

Printed in the United States of America

CONTENTS

793129

LIBRARY
ALMA COLLEGE
ALMA, MICHIGAN

PREFACE

Israel at the Polls: The Knesset Elections of 1977 is another of the studies of national elections in selected democratic countries published by the American Enterprise Institute for Public Policy Research (AEI). Books already in print examine presidential elections in France and parliamentary elections in such diverse countries as the United Kingdom, India, Ireland, Italy, Japan, three Scandinavian countries (Denmark, Norway, and Sweden), and Canada. Studies of elections in seventeen countries on five continents have been published or are in process. At least two elections will be covered in each country, providing opportunities for comparisons through time in individual countries as well as comparisons among countries. The series will also examine the direct election of representatives from nine countries to the European Parliament in 1979.

In the 1977 Knesset elections the Labor Alignment, which with its predecessor Mapai had dominated Israeli politics for more than half a century, was defeated by the Likud, another coalition of parties most of which antedated the foundation of the state of Israel. The Likud, led by Menachem Begin, won 33.4 percent of the popular vote and forty-three Knesset seats. By contrast Labor's popular vote dropped from 39.6 percent in 1973 to an all time low of 24.6 percent in 1977, and its representation in the Knesset slid from fifty-one to thirty-two members, one of whom, Moshe Dayan, resigned from the party even before the new legislature took office. Behind the two leading coalitions came the Democratic Movement for Change (DMC), with 11.6 percent of the vote and fifteen seats, and the National Religious party, with 9.2 percent of the vote and twelve seats. Nine lesser parties shared 18.7 percent of the votes and eighteen seats, while another nine failed to win the 1 percent of the vote that is the legal minimum required for representation in the Knesset.

The Labor party, as Myron J. Aronoff points out in Chapter 5, was the chief political architect of modern Israel. It played a significant "role in the creation and shaping of the major socioeconomic and political institutions of the pre-independence *yishuv* (the Jewish community in Palestine)." In turn most members of the trade unions, the agricultural cooperatives, and other organizations developed by Labor regularly supported that party's candidates at the polls.

It is not surprising then that nearly all Israeli political analysts expected another Labor victory in 1977. Any government long in office is a good bet to continue its winning ways and a party that has led a nation for so long and controls so many public services must seem virtually invincible. Judith Elizur and Elihu Katz report in Chapter 9 that just one opinion poll published during the campaign predicted a Likud victory, and it was largely ignored. Even on election night when national television spokesmen reported that both a survey of persons leaving the voting places and a computer analysis of the early returns pointed to a major Likud victory, many voters insisted that the projections must be wrong and that later figures would show Labor back in power.

Immediate reasons for the Labor party's loss of support were not difficult to find. The election had been called six months earlier than required after Prime Minister Yitzhak Rabin had dismissed three National Religious party ministers from the cabinet. A succession of major scandals that reached even to the level of the prime minister himself had plagued the party. Labor activists, according to Aronoff, felt they had little or no influence on party decisions. Israeli voters regularly rated the increasing cost of living as the nation's most pressing problem, but inflation continued to grow at an annual rate of about 35 percent.

In fact, signs of Labor's declining popularity had been evident at least four years earlier. Many in the country blamed government blundering for the nation's early problems in the unexpected Yom Kippur War, which cost the lives of nearly 3,000 Israeli soldiers. In the December 1973 elections, which had been postponed three months by the war, Labor's shares of the vote and of Knesset seats fell sharply from their 1969 levels. Likud by contrast was the one party to register significant gains both in votes and in seats. Asher Arian points out in Chapter 3 that while the nation favored Labor over Likud by eleven percentage points in 1973, the vote in the Israeli army, which is made up largely of young men, gave Likud a slight edge over Labor. This margin in the military was to increase sharply in the 1977 peacetime elections, when soldiers gave Begin and Likud 46 percent of their votes, Labor 22 percent, and the DMC 16 percent. Arian's research further shows that Likud's support among young people was not confined to the military. Likud picked up greater support in all age groups between 1969 and 1977, but the rate of increase was greatest among eighteen to twenty-four year old voters. In that group in 1977 some 51 percent supported Likud while only 20 percent backed the Labor slate.

Other sources of support for the Likud augur well for the party's future. Oriental Jews—those born in Asia or Africa, mainly in Arab countries—constitute 22.1 percent of Israel's population. In 1977 they gave almost exactly one-half of their votes to Likud and 30 percent to the Labor party. Israeli-born citizens, who now make up slightly more than half of the nation's population, backed Likud with 40 percent of their votes in 1977 while giving Labor only 16 percent. Oriental Jews and the Israeli-born as a group are younger than the European-born Jews who were once the great majority of the Israeli citizens but who now constitute about 27 percent of the population. The European-born Jews were the one major ethnic sector of the community to support the Labor party in 1977. In Arian's words, this "demographic composition of the electorate is an important key to the upsurge of the Likud and offers us an insight into likely trends in the future."

The changing character of Israel's electorate is also reflected in the makeup of recent cabinets. Five months after the 1973 elections Golda Meir put together a new cabinet with twenty-three members, roughly two-thirds of whom were born in either Europe or America while less than one-fifth were born in Israel. Four years later Begin's smaller cabinet included ten ministers born in Israel, five in Europe, and two in Morocco.

The Democratic Movement for Change, one of half a dozen new parties contesting the 1977 elections, contributed to the magnitude of Labor's defeat. A majority of its leaders and voters had previously been identified with Labor. Efraim Torgovnik estimates in Chapter 6 that at least ten of the fifteen DMC candidates elected to the Knesset were put there by the votes of former Labor party supporters. Led by Yigael Yadin, a war hero and a distinguished archeologist, the Labor dissidents hoped to become a more powerful force in government as an independent party than as a faction within Labor. The election results, however, damaged the DMC's bargaining position. Likud began with forty-five members (including the 2 newcomers from the Shlomzion party) and then added 12 votes from the National Religious party and 5 more from two smaller religious parties, to give Prime Minister Begin 62 votes and a clear, if not comfortable, majority in the 120 member Knesset. Likud could also count on the support of

Dayan, officially an independent, who was named minister of foreign affairs in the new government. Under these circumstances Torgovnik argues that the DMC's 15 votes were not needed to give Likud a working majority but only offered insurance against unforeseen catastrophe. After months of negotiations the DMC joined the government. Yadin was named deputy prime minister and three others received cabinet posts, but the party gained little in the way of policy concessions. The influence that DMC leaders had hoped to wield as an independent part of a ruling coalition simply was not available to them in the Likud government.

If the DMC met with less political success than its leaders had anticipated, its creation and subsequent career illustrate several interesting characteristics of the Israeli political system. First, new parties abound in each election. Avraham Brichta in Chapter 2 says that the profusion of parties is due to their emphasis on ideology. Aronoff makes somewhat the same point when he states that the Israeli "political system has been characterized throughout its history by a process of fission and fusion." The electoral rules accommodate these political developments by requiring only 750 signatures and a deposit of 40,000 Israeli pounds (approximately $2,500 in 1977) for a party to qualify for the election. The deposit is forfeited if the party wins no seats in the Knesset.

Second, the proportional-representation system followed in Israel provides for the election of 120 legislators from a single national district and allocates seats on the basis of the "highest-average formula" which slightly favors the larger parties. Still, as the following figures show, the Knesset closely mirrors the popular support received by the parties: Likud won 33.4 percent of the popular vote and 35.8 percent of the Knesset seats; Labor's share was 24.6 percent of the votes and 26.7 percent of the seats; the DMC received 11.6 percent and 12.5 percent; and the National Religious party 9.2 percent and 10 percent.

The DMC campaigned hard for a major reform of the electoral system that it claimed would bring voters closer to their government by instituting the election of two-thirds of the members from smaller districts and another third nationally. The impact of various proposed versions of the electoral reform on representation in the Knesset illustrates some of the political consequences of electoral laws. Brichta provides tables in Chapter 2 to show that under five different reform systems the votes cast for Likud in 1977 would have given the party as few as forty or as many as fifty-three Knesset seats while Labor's seats would have ranged from thirty-two to forty-three. Each reform would have reduced somewhat the number of parties receiving seats in the Knesset.

Third, a traditional aspect of the Israeli political system has been the extreme centralization of control over candidate selection. In the Labor party, according to Aronoff, candidates have usually been selected by "a small committee . . . appointed by the top party leadership, who generally choose their most trusted lieutenants from the secondary echelon of leaders." The DMC criticized this centralization and argued for the selection of candidates by all members of the party somewhat in the manner of American primary elections. In selecting its own candidates, however, the DMC gave its better-known leaders a considerable advantage by prohibiting campaigning in the internal party election. Decentralization, it became clear, creates its own problems. The DMC's members were generally of European background, over forty years of age, and better educated and more wealthy than the supporters of the other parties, and most of the candidates they chose reflected these characteristics. Instead of increasing the demographic representativeness of the party, the open nominating process decreased it. Torgovnik points out that at a time when opinion polls were predicting that the DMC would win twelve seats, the party members selected only one Oriental candidate to run in the first fourteen places on its list. Labor party spokesmen were quick to claim that this result showed up the DMC as the "party of the whites and the rich." What in fact the DMC had demonstrated was that while a highly centralized party seeking votes from many segments of the population can include nominees from many ethnic groups, a party with a decentralized nominating process may find that its leaders' plans are frustrated by well-intentioned followers who simply vote for the candidates they prefer or the best-known contenders, not for the strongest overall slate.

Finally, the DMC's experience points up the problem of reform parties in many political systems. Some leaders in the party placed reform above all else. Others saw the party as a vehicle for gaining influence that had been denied them in other political organizations. Torgovnik notes that in the negotiations with Begin the reformers in the DMC were at a disadvantage and that "once it became apparent that the DMC could not bring its principles into the [Begin] government . . . seasoned politicians led the move to leave the principles outside; thus, the DMC became a party of expediency."

The Likud government was expected by observers in Israel and elsewhere to make its most important policy changes in foreign affairs. Benjamin Akzin says in Chapter 4 that the policies of Herut, the largest party in the Likud coalition, stressed "the claim of the Jewish state to the whole of historic Palestine." Herut also argued that, while "Israel should not resort to war to acquire [new] territory," it could legitimately "extend Israeli rule to any further part of historic Palestine through agreement or should Israel come to occupy any part of it in the course of a war forced upon it." This view of Israel's relation to the territories fitted well with those of members of the National Religious party, some of whom, according to Akzin, bypassed their previous party allegiance to vote directly for Likud. The new government's foreign policy has approximated that advocated by Herut and Likud. While the government's line has been less flexible than that followed by the Labor party, it has probably reflected public opinion. According to Bernard Reich in Chapter 10, during the summer and fall of 1977 "there developed a wide-ranging consensus on the central issues that seemed to concern the overwhelming majority of the Knesset and of popular opinion: no return to the lines of June 4, 1967, no negotiations with the PLO, and no independent Palestinian state on the West Bank."

Reich suggests that Anwar Sadat's visit to Israel in the late fall of 1977 changed the overall foreign policy situation. He says, "While the foreign policy posture devised in the wake of the 1977 election identified Israel's negotiating position and its basic concerns and demands, the eventual policy would be a variant determined in the negotiating process." Ten months later, that process has not been completed.

Eleven authors, nine of them from Israel, have contributed essays to this volume discussing the issues and events that led up to the election, the parties' backgrounds and campaigns, and the surprising election results and its possible meanings. Daniel J. Elazar introduces the volume with a chapter on the history and general characteristics of modern Israel. Avraham Brichta describes the political and electoral system and analyzes some proposals for electoral reform. Asher Arian contributes two chapters—one discusses the characteristics of the electorate, while the concluding chapter takes an overall look at the election and its consequences. Benjamin Akzin, Myron Aronoff, and Efraim Torgovnik contribute separate chapters on the three largest parties—Likud, Labor, and the DMC. Elyakim Rubinstein describes the National Religious party and the lesser parties that abound in Israel. Leon Boim examines the continuing problem of financing political parties and elections. Judith Elizur and Elihu Katz discuss the media coverage of the campaign and election and comment on possible new and more important roles for the media in later elections.

Bernard Reich analyzes the impact of the election on Israeli foreign policy. Richard M. Scammon supplies the electoral data in Appendix B. Appendix A, prepared by AEI, is a description of the Histadrut, that peculiar Israeli institution whose real functions and importance are barely suggested by its English name, the General Federation of Labor. Finally, the glossary of parties compiled by Myron J. Aronoff briefly identifies more than thirty-five parties, current and defunct, that are mentioned in the book.

I wish to thank a number of people for their assistance while this book was being planned and written. During my stay in Israel Daniel J. Elazar and Ira Sharkansky helped identify excellent contributors and added greatly to my understanding of the nation's government and politics. Asher Arian, drawing on his experience in editing two earlier books on the 1969 and 1973 Israeli elections, offered helpful advice during the planning of this study. Arian expects to publish a book on the 1977 election in his series next year. Herbert Alexander provided necessary specialized help in editing manuscripts. Stephen A. Smith contributed significantly to the project by locating the last-minute information that is so often needed to finish a book.

HOWARD R. PENNIMAN

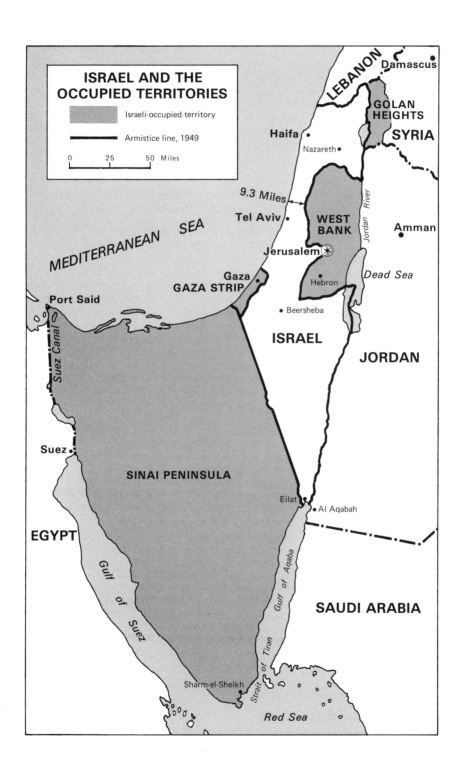

ISRAEL AND THE OCCUPIED TERRITORIES

- Israeli-occupied territory
- Armistice line, 1949

0   25   50 Miles

LEBANON

Damascus

GOLAN HEIGHTS

SYRIA

Haifa

Nazareth

9.3 Miles

Tel Aviv

WEST BANK

Jordan River

Amman

Jerusalem

MEDITERRANEAN SEA

Gaza

GAZA STRIP

Hebron

Dead Sea

Port Said

Beersheba

ISRAEL

JORDAN

Suez Canal

Suez

SINAI PENINSULA

EGYPT

Eilat

Al Aqabah

Gulf of Suez

Gulf of Aqaba

SAUDI ARABIA

Strait of Tiran

Sharm-el-Sheikh

Red Sea

1

Israel's Compound Polity

Daniel J. Elazar

On May 17, 1977, the Israeli electorate voted to turn out a sitting government for the first time since the establishment of the state. Indeed, it was the first serious setback for Labor since the struggle between the Labor camp and its opponents in the late 1920s had led to the ascendancy of the former, culminating in the Labor party victory in the 1931 elections for the Jewish national assembly in Mandatory Palestine. It is not unfair to say that this defeat symbolized the end of the first generation of Israeli statehood. That generation, which had witnessed the founding moments of the state between 1947 and 1949, reached the peak of its power in the Six-Day War of 1967 and entered its final period with the Yom Kippur War in 1973.

The electoral history of the country has paralleled this generational rhythm. The all-inclusive governing coalition that established the state in 1948 gave way to a Labor dominated government in the first elections in 1949. Labor's position was nearly undermined in the 1951 elections as a result of mass immigration, but the Labor camp, using the resources at its disposal and under David Ben-Gurion's leadership, managed to resurrect itself and in the 1955 elections established the clear dominance that it maintained for the next twenty-two years. Beginning in the 1965 elections, however, the groups that were later to become the backbone of Likud support began to defect from the Labor electorate, and by the 1973 elections, in the immediate aftermath of the Yom Kippur War, Likud was moving toward ascendancy. Thus the 1977 electoral results were not simply a fluke or the result of immediate campaign issues but reflected a long-term trend within the Israeli body politic.

This trend is one manifestation of the transition from a polity based on ideological divisions to one in which the expression of public interests is more complex. The initial momentum for the creation of Israel could only have come from people with strong ideological moti-

1

vations; indeed, in the early years ideological divisions permeated the political structure to the point where politics and the benefits thereof were rooted in a system of ideological movements-cum-parties that had coalesced in the 1920s. But Israel's continued existence depends upon a process of "settling in." More and more, this seems to mean adaptation to the exigencies of territorial democracy.[1] In this respect, Israel's development parallels that of other new societies.

Israel as a New Society

Israel is one of the handful of "new societies" in the world, in the select company of the United States, Canada, the Republic of South Africa, Australia, and New Zealand.[2] Therein lies the beginning of an understanding of the politics of the Jewish state. New societies are those founded "from scratch" as a result of migrations to virgin territories (that is, territories essentially uninhabited or perceived to be so by the migrants) since the beginning of the modern era in the mid seventeenth century. Their settlers underwent a frontier experience as a major part of the process of settlement, and each in its own way was from its very beginning a modern society. These new societies stand out in sharp contrast to both traditional societies and those that have undergone modernization, whether from a traditional or a feudal

---

[1] The term territorial democracy was first used by Orestes Brownson in *The American Republic* (1866) to describe noncentralized, American institutions in contrast to centralized, Jacobin ones. It is used in this context as the form of political organization in which the principal expressions of politics and political interest are articulated through territorial political units (for example, states, counties, cities, or towns); territorial political structures (for example, electoral districts); and territorial political organizations (for example, the county medical association, the regional planning society) that possesses real power or influence in the shaping of public policy. See Russell Kirk, "The Prospects for Territorial Democracy in America," in Robert A. Goldwin, ed., *A Nation of States* (Chicago: Rand McNally, 1974), 2nd ed. for one view of territorial democracy. I have elaborated on his definition of the concept in my forthcoming book, *Federal Democracy*, and have applied it to Israel in *Israel: From Ideological to Territorial Democracy* (New York: General Learning Press, 1971).

[2] The concept of "new societies" is based in part on the work of Louis Hartz, *The Founding of New Societies* (New York: Harcourt, Brace & World, 1964). At least some of the Caribbean and Latin American countries, which in some ways meet the primary objective criteria used in determining which are the world's new societies, may have to be added to this list. Though the surface evidence is mixed, I have strong reservations about including them. It bears noting that Israel is the only new society whose founders did not come, in the main, from the British Isles or Northern Europe. The great majority of Israel's settlers came from Asia or Eastern Europe, the Near East and North Africa, bringing with them very different cultural baggage.

base. The key to their birth as modern societies lies in the migration of their founders to frontier environments where they were able to create a social order with a minimum amount of hindrance from entrenched traditional or feudal ways or from existing populations needing to be assimilated.

Traditional or feudal societies are built upon what are generally accepted as organic linkages among tribes, communities, or estates whose origins are lost in history. New societies, in contrast, are constructed upon conscious (and usually historically verifiable) contractual or covenantal relationships among individuals and groups; the sense of common purpose that bound their founders together continues to bind subsequent generations. In almost every case, the dominant founders of a new society—those who set its tone—were motivated by a common sense of vocation based on ideologies or commitments they brought with them and which they tried to apply in the creation of new political and social institutions. In the process of nation building, they forged a sense of vocation that continues to serve as a shared mystique, a future-oriented myth, to inspire or justify the efforts of their heirs.[3] The actual creation of these civil societies was almost invariably manifested through some kind of constituting act, usually one that was expressed in documentary form. Even if no single compact or constitution was involved, the political organization of each new society is based on many "little" compacts necessitated by the realities of having to create new settlements and institutions "overnight" on virgin soil.

While the founders of each new society brought with them a cultural heritage derived from their societies of origin, their motive in migrating was almost invariably a revolutionary one. They sought to create a better society than the one they had left, believing it impossible to do so in the lands of their origin. As part of their efforts, they took what they believed to be the most significant ideas and institutions from their homelands and transplanted them, with appropriate adaptations.

Though Palestine in the nineteenth century was not as empty as North America in the early seventeenth century, for the Zionist pioneers it was effectively empty in that they did not expect to model the society they intended to build upon any indigenous social order,

---

[3] For an examination of mystique as future-oriented myth, see John T. Marcus, "The World Impact of the West: The Mystique and the Sense of Participation in History," in Henry A. Murray, ed., *Myth and Myth Making* (New York: George Braziller, 1960), pp. 221–239.

Arab or Jewish.[4] Even the "old *yishuv*"—the Jewish settlements that antedated the Zionist efforts and did not share the same sense of political vocation, although they, too, sought to build new societies of their own—was strictly off limits as a model. The goal of the pioneers was to replace its way of life, based as it was on traditional Judaism, with a new one that, while in harmony with the highest Jewish ideals, would be fully modern—whether socialist, liberal democratic, or religious.

The Zionist pioneers explicitly and consciously intended to build the kind of society advocated for their countries of origin by their European revolutionary peers, who shared the same modern ideologies. But the very essence of Zionism was that Jews could only build their new society by leaving the lands of the Diaspora and migrating to a new land or, more accurately, by returning to their "old-new land."[5] In the process of implanting their settlements and institutions in the new territory, the Zionist pioneers shaped a sense of national vocation that has become the Israeli mystique.[6] While Zionist theories were based on the ideas of organic nationhood common in nineteenth-century Europe, the organizations and settlements of the pioneers themselves were quite literally based on compacts or covenants linking the dedicated individuals who took upon themselves the burdens of creating the new society.

The construction of the modern Israeli polity began in the last generation of the nineteenth century. The first modern Jewish agricultural settlements were established in the 1870s. By World War I, when that generation came to an end, the well-known second *aliya* (literally, "ascent"—the term used to describe migration to the country) of

---

[4] Early Zionist literature makes few references to an indigenous population in Palestine that would have to be dealt with on a continuing basis. Moreover, in making this assumption about the "emptiness" of the land, the Zionists merely reflected common European notions about non-European populations in that period. See Rufus Learsi, *Fulfillment: The Epic Story of Zionism* (New York: World, 1951); Arthur Hertzberg, ed., *The Zionist Idea* (New York: Doubleday, 1959); and Walter Z. Laqueur, *History of Zionism* (New York: Holt, Rinehart & Winston, 1972).

[5] The term "old-new land" was used by Theodor Herzl himself as the title for his utopian novel (*Altneuland* in the original German), which describes his vision of life in a restored Jewish state. For a broad picture of Zionist thought as a modern ideological system, see Hertzberg, *The Zionist Idea*.

[6] Horace M. Kallen delineates the relationship between Israel and its mystique in *Utopians at Bay* (New York: Theodor Herzl Foundation, 1958). For an Israeli view of the mystique see, for example, David Ben-Gurion, *Rebirth and Destiny of Israel* (New York: Philosophical Library, 1954); Ronald Sanders discusses the development of the mystique in contemporary Israel in *The View from Masada* (New York: Harper & Row, 1966).

1903–1914 had brought in the most important of the future founders of the state who created the first of the institutions that were to give the state its tone.[7] The founders were for the most part imbued with contemporary socialist ideologies; hence, their covenants and compacts were oriented toward a cooperative, rather than an individualistic, model of social and political organization. Later they were to acquire a strong collectivist tinge. This orientation was reinforced by the Jewish political culture of the founders. As a result, when the state of Israel was established as an outgrowth of the Jewish *yishuv* of the pre-state period, it assumed very extensive responsibilities within the polity. Today Israeli society is permeated by governmental activity. Israel may be the only new society developed on the basis of socialist principles.

On another level, Israel is heir to the first identifiable "new society" in history, that of the Jewish people, who, in the ancient Israelite migration to Canaan and settlement there under the aegis of the Abrahamic and Sinai covenants, represented a similar phenomenon approximately three millennia before the opening of the modern era.[8] The biblical account of their experience offers a paradigm of the new society model set forth here. Both the covenantal nature of Jewish political organization and the future-oriented mystique of the Jewish people were institutionalized within ancient Jewish society and, after passing through various permutations in the Land of Israel and in the Diaspora, reappeared in new form in modern Israel.[9] One consequence

---

[7] Laqueur, *History of Zionism.*

[8] There is now reasonable historical evidence to confirm this whether the biblical account is exactly accurate or not. Perhaps more important, the Israelite experience as it is described in the Bible is paradigmatic of all subsequent new societies. Indeed, in its explanation of the origins of the Jewish people the Bible devotes considerable space to discussing and emphasizing precisely those elements that are here identified as being essential to the definition of new societies. The use of covenant forms to create political relationships was an ancient Near Eastern practice as George E. Mendenhall has pointed out in "Covenant Forms in Israelite Tradition," *Biblical Archeologist*, vol. 17, no. 3 (July 1954), pp. 50–76. The Israelites transformed the covenant principle from one used for quasi-feudal purposes between rulers or polities into one used for federal purposes within polities. See, for example, S. J. Mackenzie, *Faith and History in the Old Testament* (New York: Macmillan, 1963), pp. 40–53; and John Bright, *A History of Israel* (Philadelphia: Westminster Press, 1956).

[9] While no one has directly discussed ancient Israel as a new society, Yehezkel Kaufman has laid the groundwork for such a discussion in his monumental *Toldot Ha-Emunah Ha-Yisraelit* [History of the faith of Israel] 4 vols. (Jerusalem and Tel Aviv: Bialik and Dvir, 1937–1960); also available in an abridged English version as *The Religion of Israel* (Chicago: University of Chicago Press, 1960), selected and translated by Moshe Greenberg. See also Henri Frankfort, et al., *Before Philosophy* (London: Pelican Books, 1949) and Harry M. Orlinsky, *Ancient*

of this was that even those Jews who came from distinctly premodern environments had, to some degree, internalized a political culture with "new society" characteristics that, however latent, could be made manifest upon their resettlement in the new territory under new political and social conditions.

Consequently, an understanding of Israel's political and social system is not to be found in the study of modernization. Instead, the crucial questions to be confronted are those revolving around the actualization of a new society: the problems of political and cultural continuity and change, of how the particular cultural baggage brought by Jews returning to their old-new land was subsequently modified by the experience of nation building in the new territory; the impact of the new territory and the confrontation with it (what in the United States has been called "the frontier experience"); and the constitutional problems (in Israel's case, problems of reconstitution) that necessarily accompany the creation of a new society.[10]

Israel has an emergent political culture composed of a number of different elements that exist in somewhat uneasy tension with one another. This tension is evident in a great gap between the formal institutional structure of the polity (which is an expression of European statism) and the actual political behavior and informal institutional arrangements that make it work. Formally, Israel is a highly centralized, hierarchically structured, bureaucratic state on the model of France. In fact, the state and its institutions function on the basis of myriad contractual agreements—actual and tacit—which assume widespread power-sharing on a noncentralized basis. These are enforced through a process of mutual consultation and negotiation in which every individual party to an agreement must be conciliated before action is taken.

Israel (Ithaca: Cornell University Press, 1954). Lincoln Steffens offers some suggestive if unusual confirmations of this hypothesis in "Moses in Red," reprinted in Ella Winter and Herbert Shapiro, eds., *The World of Lincoln Steffens* (New York: Hill & Wang, 1962). Some Zionist thinkers, beginning with Moses Hess, the best of them, did see ancient Israel as the first "nation" in the modern sense, thus coming close to the concept suggested here. Hertzberg, *The Zionist Idea*, discusses them in his introduction. See also Hans Kohn, *The Idea of Nationalism* (New York: Macmillan, 1944), Chapter 1. For a discussion of the continuity of the Jewish political tradition in this respect, see Daniel J. Elazar, *Covenant as the Basis of the Jewish Political Tradition* (Ramat-Gan: Bar-Ilan University and Center for Jewish Community Studies, 1977) and "Kinship and Consent in the Jewish Community," *Tradition*, vol. 14, no. 4 (Fall, 1974), pp. 63–79. See also Salo W. Baron, *The Jewish Community*, 3 vols. (Philadelphia: Jewish Publication Society, 1942).

[10] Daniel J. Elazar, *Israel: From Ideological to Territorial Democracy* (New York: General Learning Press, 1971).

Because Israel is still an emergent society, the precise political-cultural synthesis cannot yet be forecast. So, for example, in 1975 the proportional-representation, party-list electoral system, which has been a feature of modern Israel since the beginning of the Zionist effort was modified to provide for the direct election of mayors independently of their city councils and to endow them with a modest veto power over council actions. This radical departure represents a step away from continental European parliamentarianism, at least on the local plane, and toward a separation of powers model which is more consonant with Jewish political culture.

Finally, Israel is an exceptional phenomenon in the world of modern territorial states in that it is intimately linked to the Jewish people, an entity with political characteristics not confined to a particular territory. Israel itself has still-undetermined boundaries, a condition which is presented to the world as a product of momentary circumstances but which has been characteristic of the polities in the Middle East since the dawn of recorded history. Moreover, a great part of its political life is and will continue to be rooted in confessional, consociational, and ideological divisions that are far more permanent than boundaries have ever proved to be in the Middle East. With all the trend toward territorialization within Israel, territory remains only one of the dimensions which its people and institutions use in organizing space and time for political purposes.

The Compound Structure of the Israeli Polity

For those familiar with Western European, and most particularly American, institutions (where polities are territorially based, where government is organized fairly simply on two or three levels or planes, and where the greatest complexity is found in the overlapping of local governments), the Israeli situation is complex indeed. For those familiar with the American federalist theory of the compound republic, it is of particular interest to note that the Hebrew word used to describe the organization of a polity or government, *leharkiv*, means "to compound."[11] The same word is used to describe complexity, offering etymological testimony to the expectations inherent in the environmental and cultural matrix in which the Jewish people always have been embedded and in which Israel functions today. The fundamentally contractual character of Jewish political life is reflected in the idea that bodies and polities are compounded from different

---

[11] Vincent Ostrom, *The Political Theory of a Compound Republic* (Blacksburg: Virginia Polytechnic Institute Center for the Study of Public Choice, 1971).

entities that retain their respective integrities in the larger whole.[12] Thus the state of Israel can be seen as a republic compounded in a variety of ways.

In formal terms, Israel is a parliamentary democracy in which the 120-member Knesset is the repository of state sovereignty. The Knesset is elected on the basis of proportional representation with the country serving as a single constituency. Parties submit lists of candidates in rank order and voters cast their ballots for an entire party list. Each party is awarded the number of seats equivalent to its percentage of the total valid vote, with excess votes above the number required per seat distributed by a formula designed to reduce the chances of very small parties to obtain a seat or two in the legislature. As a result, Israel has a multiparty system, with no party ever having won a majority of the Knesset seats since statehood; all cabinets, known in Israel as governments, have been formed by coalition. Customarily, the party winning the largest number of seats in the Knesset takes the lead in coalition formation. Until the elections under consideration here, the Labor party or its predecessor, Mapai, had formed every government since the establishment of the state, in every case relying upon a coalition.

The Knesset is elected at least once every four years. While it can be dissolved earlier, this has rarely occurred, and the tendency is for a Knesset to fill out its full term. The government is responsible to the Knesset and sits as long as it enjoys the confidence of the Knesset. Only the prime minister must be a member of the Knesset, although in practice well over half of the ministers usually are. As in other parliamentary democracies in the twentieth century, the government tends to dominate the Knesset rather than vice versa, although the Knesset has developed some means of exerting influence within the government-dominated system, particularly through its standing committees.

The Knesset elects a president for a six-year term to serve as head of state. His powers are quite limited and are in the main symbolic. His principal governmental role is to initiate the coalition-building process so that a government may be formed after the elections.

Israel has an independent judiciary, whose independence is jealously guarded. In accordance with the political doctrine of parliamentary systems, the Knesset is the repository of political sovereignty in the state (a matter not altogether in accord with

---

[12] Elazar, "Kinship and Consent."

Israel's political culture: significantly, the term "sovereignty" is never used in Israeli law) and formally the High Court has no power of judicial review over the constitutionality of Knesset acts. Nevertheless, it has extended its powers of judicial review as far as possible in that direction, at times ruling legislation unenforceable because of procedural inadequacies.

Israel did not adopt a written constitution upon the attainment of statehood. Instead, those who sought one and those who opposed it compromised, agreeing to enact piecemeal a series of basic constitutional laws which would, in the end, amount to a constitutional document. These basic laws require a minimum of sixty-one votes, or half the total Knesset plus one, for enactment, amendment, or repeal, but otherwise there is relatively little distinction between basic laws and ordinary legislation.

The elections for the Knesset are the only countrywide elections in which all Israeli citizens are entitled to participate. Permanent residents as well as citizens may vote in local elections for mayors and councilmen. Until 1975, local councils were elected on a party list basis and the mayor was number one on the leading list; since then, direct election of mayors has been instituted, while councils are still elected on the basis of party lists.

This formal structure can at best serve as a benchmark for understanding Israeli politics. It is perhaps most accurate in matters pertaining to Israeli electoral politics, primarily because its fixed electoral requirements are those most fully implemented as written in law. Even so, their meaning is dependent upon the way in which the Israeli polity is compounded.

The Compound of Ideological Parties. In the first place, the political system of Israel is a compound based upon federal and consociational connections between different Zionist parties or movements. Various groups of socialist Zionists, each with its own ideology, erected their own settlements and institutions in the country, as did Zionists with a liberal (in the European sense) ideology and others whose primary ideology was derived from traditional religion. The latter groups ranged from religious socialists, who based a modern collectivist ideology on ancient religious sources, to the religious right, who saw no reason to allow any kind of secular thinking or behavior in the state to be.

Each of these movements sought to create as comprehensive a range of institutions as it could, a kind of nonterritorial state of its own, but within the framework of the overall Zionist effort. Since

9

they also wanted the overall effort to succeed, they federated to form various umbrella organizations and institutions through which they could pursue the common objective of a Jewish homeland, even while contesting with one another over the shape of the state to come and the vision that would inform it. This federation of movements became the basis for the present Israeli party system. In many respects, it conforms to the models of consociationalism put forth by Lipjhart, Daalder, and others.[13]

Today, as in the past, the country divides into three "camps": labor, liberal or center (the Hebrew term translates as civil, and religious).[14] Contrary to the conventional wisdom, the three camps do not relate to each other on a left-right continuum but stand in something like a triangular relationship to one another, portrayed in Figure 1–1. For a long time, preoccupation with European modes of political thought prevented students of Israeli politics from seeing this, even though there never was a time when Israel was not organized on this basis. What each has staked out for itself is a particular vision of what the Zionist enterprise and its creation, the Jewish state, are all about. At times that vision has taken on ideological form, and at times it has been nonideological. The camps themselves divide into parties, some of which are quite antagonistic to one another within the same camp; it is within the camps that left-right divisions do exist. The size of each camp is not fixed, either in relation to the total Jewish population or in relation to the others, but whatever the fluctuations, the camps themselves persist. Their persistence is reflected in the general stability of Knesset elections in Israel and in the division of offices within the World Zionist Movement.

A governing coalition is formed when major shares of two of the camps can be combined. Until the most recent election, government coalitions generally consisted of some two-thirds of the labor camp, plus two-thirds of the religious camp, plus a small crossover element from the civil camp. In the Begin-led government coalition, the same principle operated but in reverse: virtually the entire civil camp, except for Independent Liberal Gideon Hausner, joined forces with the entire religious camp. This coalition was joined by a significant element from the Labor camp, the Democratic Movement for Change. This, more than any mathematical formula, explains the basis for coalition formation in Israeli politics.

---

[13] K. D. McKae, ed., *Consociational Democracy: Political Accommodation in Segmented Societies* (Toronto: McClelland and Steward, 1974).

[14] S. N. Eisenstadt, *Israeli Society* (London: Weidenfeld & Nicolson, 1967), and Leonard J. Fein, *Politics in Israel* (Boston: Little, Brown, 1967).

Figure 1–1
THE THREE ZIONIST CAMPS

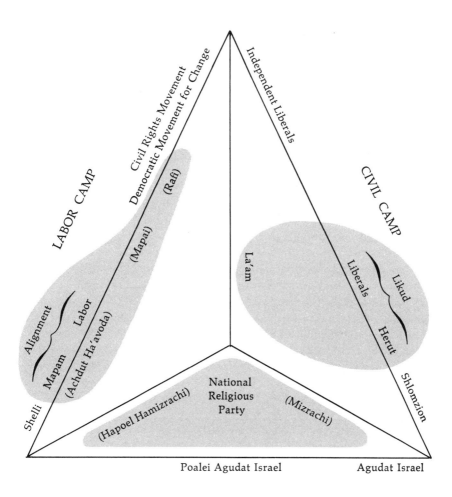

RELIGIOUS CAMP

NOTE: This figure shows the left-right position of the major Israeli parties within the three Zionist camps. Shaded areas show the major party federations for the 1977 elections; in parentheses are the names of important groupings no longer in existence as separate parties. The placement of a party's name on an inside line of the big triangle indicates its ideological affinity with the adjoining camp; thus Hapoel Hamizrachi was ideologically close to the labor camp, Mizrachi to the civil camp. The Democratic Movement for Change, though most of its leaders and supporters came from the labor camp, eventually joined the Likud government. SOURCE: Author.

As the ideologically based party or "movement" federations became institutionalized, they became tighter and more all-embracing. They developed their own settlements, their own newspapers and journals, their own cultural institutions, their own educational systems, their own banks, their own industries, and even their own armies. In pre-state days this was particularly functional, not only as a way of mobilizing energy for the pioneering tasks but as the basis for organizing the incipient Jewish commonwealth within the political context of the British Mandate. The colonial authorities, recognizing that the fundamental aspirations of the Jewish pioneers ran counter to their interests in most respects, did not wish to relinquish any serious governmental powers to the Jewish community. On the other hand, the Palestine in which the pioneers were building their new structure had long been organized on the basis of the millet system, a form of political and social organization that has existed throughout the Middle East for centuries, if not millennia. The millet system provided for the maintenance of quasi-autonomous ethnic communities organized on the basis of ethno-religious (here understood as a form of ideological) ties within the framework of whatever empire was in power at any particular time. This system made it both easy and natural for the colonial authorities to allow the Jewish community to function as what was, in effect, the Jewish millet.[15]

Since imperial policy under the millet system was to severely limit the internal activities of the ruling power and to allow each millet to determine the extent of local services to be provided to its members, the system made it possible for the Jewish community to provide such governmental or quasi-governmental services as it wished without too much reference to the formal governmental structure. Every Jew, simply by virtue of being Jewish, was assigned to the Jewish community as a matter of "citizenship" and was required to adjust himself and his life within the framework of that community, just as Muslims and various Christian groups did in their respective communities.[16]

The ideological basis of the federation of parties was functional in yet another way. The overwhelming majority of the Zionist pioneers came from the countries of Eastern Europe where socialist

---

[15] Eisenstadt, *Israeli Society*.

[16] The status of the Jewish community in Palestine was formalized in law in this manner under both the Ottoman and British regimes. The Palestine Orders in Council of 1922, 1923, and 1939 and the Jewish Communal Ordinance of 1927 set the framework for the internal autonomy of the *yishuv* under the mandatory regime.

and other movements dedicated to radical social change flourished in an atmosphere of the most extreme ideological intensity. Hence they brought with them a strong predisposition toward making ideology the measure of all things and a tendency toward ideological hairsplitting. Indeed, so intensely ideological were they that it is possible to argue that only their common Jewishness, which led them to certain perceptions about the necessity for unity at some point and which gave them a useful cultural inheritance for the promotion of the requisite unity, kept them from going the divisive or repressive way of their non-Jewish peers from the same East European milieu.

Understood in this context, Israel's adoption of the proportional-representation system was quite appropriate. Voters cast their ballots for party lists, and seats in the legislature or on the local councils were distributed among the parties in proportion to the votes they received; thus each constituent unit in the federation of parties was provided with representation according to its strength as a unit. This was no different, in essence, from other kinds of federal arrangements in which the territorial units are represented as such in the federal legislature, but in which the choice of the representatives is left to the units to make internally. As long as all potential citizens could find a home within one of the parties, this system was able to adequately represent the *yishuv*, provide a proper arena for bargaining among the various interests within it, and promote the adoption of policies and courses of action appropriate to the needs of the overall community.

This was the situation inherited by the new state in 1948. The essence of the constitutional history of Israel since then has been a growing conflict between the original ideological basis of Israeli civil society and the new demands of a post-statehood generation. The Israelis' growing perception of the need to modify the existing political order is a response to a convergence of forces that have greatly weakened the degree of commitment to the specific ideologies of the pre-state period while increasing the functionality of territorial units at the expense of existing ideological institutions.

The federation of parties was perpetuated even during the period of mass immigration following the establishment of the state (1948–1951) and subsequently. New immigrants were "allocated" among the various parties for integration purposes in proportion to the parties' existing strength. Each party was given responsibility for settling an appropriate percentage of the new arrivals and integrating them into the life of the country. Each supplied its immigrants in the temporary settlement camps with leaders who provided access to the country's institutions and served as the conduit for transferring state assistance in the settlement process. In return, the immigrants became enmeshed in the parties' own institutional structures and became faithful voters for "their" party in Knesset elections more often than not, thus contributing to the virtually undeviating record of electoral stability that Israel maintained for a generation. Their loyalty also contributed to insuring the perpetuation of the status quo in public policy making, usually by allowing the same people to remain in office for long periods of time and discouraging the introduction of young people (or new faces of any age, for that matter) into the higher levels of political decision making.[17]

Furthermore, because of most of the immigrants' lack of familiarity with popular government, their willingness to conform to the models set before them contributed to the growth of the power of the party professionals. Even in the years before statehood, the parties and their subsidiary institutions had been growing more centralized, partly because of the exigencies of the objective situation in which the pioneers found themselves and partly because of their original socialization into the political life of Eastern Europe where centralization of power was the norm. Still, in those years, when the *yishuv* was small and relatively homogeneous and face-to-face interpersonal relations were still possible among most party members, the impact of the centralizing tendencies was substantially reduced.

Mass immigration changed the scale of political organization in the country and opened up new possibilities for professional politicians to concentrate party decision-making powers in their own hands. For most of the first two decades of statehood, their success in doing just that was virtually unlimited. Thus, within their respective spheres, the parties remained the basic decision makers, and decision making was increasingly concentrated in the hands of the national party leaders.

On the other hand, the role of the parties or their institutional agents (including the Histadrut, the General Federation of Labor, which embraced virtually the entire work force prior to 1948 and continues to embrace the overwhelming majority of both urban and rural workers) in the provision of normal public services was progressively reduced. Though they continued to provide some services that in other political systems are provided by governments, the

---

[17] In turn, the larger parties have introduced a limited system of ethnic "ticket balancing" in the composition of the party lists, which determine who is actually elected to the Knesset once the party's proportion of the total vote is established.

14

transfer of other services, particularly those of military units, elementary schools, and labor exchanges, to the state had the effect of substantially reducing the dependence of the citizenry upon the parties once they had passed through the initial stages of settlement and absorption. This was particularly true in the case of urban dwellers. The parties' role in their daily lives was shifted to the management of "influence" (protektzia) and the distribution of jobs (particularly, but not exclusively, in the public services); the control of ostensibly neutral enterprises (housing projects, industries, and business enterprises, in particular) and government departments was the key to their power.[18] As the parties lost direct control over certain public services, they strengthened their control over public nongovernmental institutions and organizations in compensation, thereby maintaining their overall power even under the changed circumstances.

With the passing of the period of mass immigration, the divergencies between the political and social structures of the country began to develop in earnest. While party governments of the old style remained dominant, especially at the state level, the parties themselves began to lose their meaning. Not only were they losing responsibility for functions, but their ideological bases were deteriorating. The decline in importance of rural pioneering, the changes in the world situation (particularly the growing antagonism of the Soviet Union and its satellites toward Israel and the concomitant increase in Israeli ties with the United States), the disappointments with socialist orthodoxies at home and abroad growing out of their evident disfunctionality for development purposes and their frequent antidemocratic manifestations, combined to move all but the most hardened ideologues out of old grooves.[19] Only in the religious camp do the ideological justifications remain sufficiently strong to create demands as intense as in the early days. These are accommodated by maintaining parallel general and religious institutions in many fields.

Moreover, the great bulk of the population was becoming more or less settled and was developing ties both to the land and to the state that were independent of those fostered by the parties and their ideologies. This was particularly true among the young, whether native-born or reared from early childhood in the country. To them, the land of Israel was "home" in a way that it could not be to their

---

[18] Nadav Safran describes the shift of party control from direct to indirect services in The United States and Israel (Cambridge, Mass.: Harvard University Press, 1967), Part 3.

[19] The political aspects of this are discussed in Fein, Politics in Israel.

immigrant parents.[20] In this respect, the situation in Israel today parallels that of other new societies when the initial ideology of the founders ceased to be all encompassing. Nevertheless, the importance of the compound of parties remains great because it is so highly institutionalized.

The Compound of Economic Sectors. Another means by which Israeli society is compounded is through the division of public activity into what are known in Israel as "sectors": governmental, cooperative, and private along one plane and urban and rural along another. It is not surprising that most enterprises in a government-permeated society like Israel exist by virtue of government assistance, either through direct investment, loan guarantees, or simple sponsorship with appropriate tax benefits, favorable foreign exchange rates, and the like. While the Israeli government has veered sharply away from the strongly socialistic position of its leadership at the beginning of statehood, this has not meant any movement toward laissez-faire. Government's role remains as great as ever in promoting state-permeated social capitalism within a mixed economy. It is enhanced by the fact that Israel's precarious security situation and narrow economic base give political decisions priority over economic ones in most cases.

If the government sector is invariably the strongest, the cooperative or workers' sector is the oldest and most hallowed. It emerged in the 1920s, when the various small collectives of Jewish pioneers were brought together to create the Histadrut[21] and the Hevrat Ovdim (Workers' Society), which was to be the means through which the Labor Federation could establish and maintain its own complex of economic activities. While the cooperative sector has diminished greatly in importance since the establishment of the state, it remains the biggest nongovernmental owner and operator in the country. The largest industries, including the largest conglomerate in the country, are under its ownership. The internal public transportation companies, with the exception of the state railroads and the minuscule internal airline which provide very limited service, are workers' cooperatives. The kibbutzim and moshavim are integral parts of the cooperative sector.[22] The largest department store chain is Histadrut-owned. The

---

[20] Alan Arian (Asher Arian in Israel—the author of Chapters 3 and 11 in this book) has documented and analyzed this in *Ideological Change in Israel* (Cleveland: Case Western Reserve University Press, 1968).

[21] For a fuller discussion of the organization and role of the Histadrut in present-day Israel see Appendix A.

[22] On the kibbutzim and moshavim see below, pp. 17–19.

16

Histadrut operates Kupat Holim (the Workers' Sick Fund), the largest health maintenance organization in the country, which serves over two-thirds of the population, and through it controls a network of hospitals and old-age and rest homes—in other words, the complete apparatus of a socialized health system. In addition, the Histadrut is the great comprehensive labor union in the country.

The Histadrut has become considerably bureaucratized over the years, so that, while it has sought to serve the Zionist mission of rebuilding the state and the public good as interpreted by its leaders, it has also become at least as distant from its own members as the government is from the man in the street, if not more so. This needs to be emphasized so as to gain proper perspective on the workings of that sector.

Finally, there is the private (meaning capitalist and small business) sector, which is growing after having been the weakest of the sectors for many years. Although there has always been private enterprise within the Zionist effort, because the overwhelming majority of the pioneers were socialists, private business was not a very acceptable form of pioneering activity. Only in recent years has the importance of a healthy private sector, both as a countervailing power to the other two sectors and as an element of the economy in its own right, come to be recognized and even encouraged by the government. It is typified by the range of private entrepreneurial activities characteristic of all modern Western societies.

By and large, these three sectors have not developed on a competitive basis; rather, they tend to cooperate with each other as could be expected in a small country with a relatively weak economy and a political culture which emphasizes partnership. Many enterprises have been jointly developed by two or all three sectors. Efforts on the part of private investors—usually from overseas—to "buck" these arrangements have generally come to naught since, unless the government's attitude is favorable, it is very difficult to succeed in any economic enterprise in Israel. What is particularly important is that the government, which is generally assumed to be in the business of providing services, also has a strong economic stake in the society, while the general labor association, which in other countries would be an interest group, plays an even more important role as a supplier of services on a "retail" as well as "wholesale" basis and as an economic developer.

The division between urban and rural sectors is equally important. The rural sector tends to be self-contained in many respects, because almost all agricultural production and rural life are embraced

17

within the framework of the kibbutzim and moshavim. Moreover, the special place which the kibbutzim and moshavim occupy in the Zionist enterprise makes them the arbiters of the rural sector. (The original Zionist vision placed heavy emphasis on Jews' returning to the soil, where they would redeem themselves through cooperative toil in a natural setting.)

Not only are the kibbutzim highly integrated political, social, and economic units, the exact antithesis of fragmented urban society, but in many respects they are more modern than Israeli cities in their culture, behavior, and technological development. Every kibbutz is organized as a cooperative society in which all except the most personal items of property are legally held in common. Social life is necessarily intimate, with a common dining hall and other facilities to enhance the already great likelihood of high social integration that exists in any community of a few hundred to a few thousand people.

The moshav is more individualistic than the kibbutz. In the moshav every family has its own farm and private life, with some work and all major purchasing and marketing done in common. This makes for a cooperative rather than a collectivized atmosphere, but since the moshav is small (usually much smaller than the kibbutz), it tends to be a highly integrated social unit. Like the kibbutz, the moshav is both a cooperative society with shared economic functions and a municipal unit with its own general meeting and local committee.

The particular character of rural settlement in Israel is such that even family farms are concentrated in villages with their own local institutions; the 728 rural settlements that enjoy local governmental autonomy have an average population of under 800. Moreover, rather than confining themselves to limited local government tasks, as those serving populations that small in the United States would do, the kibbutzim and moshavim provide comprehensive economic and social services as well as traditional municipal functions on a level that far exceeds almost anything known among Western local governments. Services which they cannot properly provide are often provided by the regional councils, the federations of settlements to which they belong, which are themselves relatively small, ranging in population from 678 to 20,378, with only four over 10,000.[23]

Because these rural settlements can bring to bear a full range of options—political, economic, social, and commercial—to confront any problem, they are the most autonomous local governments in the

---

[23] Yosef Criden and Saadya Gelb, *The Kibbutz Experience* (New York: Herzl Press, 1974).

country and also the ones with the most effective cooperative arrangements with one another and with the state authorities. The greater internal diversity of the cities and their more limited corporate purposes prevent them from functioning nearly as well. Moreover, since cities are considered to be mere byproducts of the Zionist movement, which, as a back-to-the-land movement, was in many respects anti-urban, they do not have the same claim on the resources or respect of the state that the rural settlements do.[24]

The cities are open to greater permeation by the external society —including the institutions of the state and the cooperative sector— in every respect. While the kibbutzim and moshavim are closely integrated within the cooperative sector, as the elite elements of that sector they can manage their relationships with it. Cities, on the other hand, are often dependent upon decisions taken by the cooperative sector at the higher echelons of its bureaucracy, over which they have minimal influence.

Ethnoreligious Pluralism in Israel. On another level, the state of Israel is compounded of a Jewish majority and several different ethnoreligious minorities: Muslim Arabs (344,000); Christians, mostly Arab (77,300), divided into various churches; Druse (38,000); and small communities of Bahai, Circassians, and Samaritans—each with its own socioreligious structure and legal status. Following the Middle Eastern pattern, all of these groups seek to preserve their corporate identity, and Israel has granted them a legal status and institutional framework through which to do so. Under Israeli law, there is no Israeli nationality as such, only Israeli citizenship. Individuals are Jewish or Arab or Armenian or whatever by nationality.

While the legal status and institutions of each group are adapted to its particular situation, with Muslim Arabs having the most comprehensive among the minorities and Circassians the least, all have certain basic institutions and government support for their activities as corporate entities as well as the normal services provided to all citizens. Since, in Israel, matters of personal status are by law the province of the religious communities (this, too, is a common Middle Eastern pattern), every person must be a member of some religious community if he or she hopes to get married, divorced, or buried. Of course, while an individual may choose to use only these minimal services from his or her religious community, the communities provide many more services and are expected to do so by their faithful.

---

[24] Eric Cohen, *The City in Zionist Ideology* (Jerusalem: Hebrew University Institute of Urban and Regional Studies, 1970).

Each religious community has its own religious courts, whose judges are supported by the state, hold commissions from the state on the basis of qualifications determined by each religious community, and are selected by the appropriate bodies of each religious community under procedures provided for by state law.[25] These courts administer the religious laws of their communities—each of which has its own legal system for matters within its competence. Religious laws stand in relationship to the secular legal system in Israel roughly as state laws stand in relationship to federal law in a federation with a dual legal system.

The principal administrative organs of the religious communities vary from community to community. The Christian communities have no separate administrative bodies other than the church hierarchies, which also handle matters of religious law, because they are essentially in the Catholic tradition; they also play a more limited role in the lives of their citizens. The religious functions of the Muslim communities are administered through the *wakfs*, the Muslim religious trusts; and in the Jewish communities, every locality with a Jewish majority has a local religious council consisting of laymen and rabbis elected through a complex formula and jointly supported by the state and local governments. All of these bodies are, in some respects, subject to oversight by the Ministry of Religions, whose minister is a member of the cabinet and which is the channel through which state funds reach the various religious groups.

Because of the pattern of settlement common in the rural Middle East, where villages are either ethnically homogeneous or shared by perhaps two ethnic groups, local government becomes a major vehicle for the expression of these corporate interests. The Israeli government has made great efforts to encourage villages housing these minorities to acquire full municipal status and to utilize the instrumentalities of local government not only to provide local services but also to express the cultural personalities and values of the groups within them. This represents a partial adaptation to the realities of what was known as the millet system under the Ottoman Empire, whereby every ethnic group was constituted as a millet with its own internal autonomy.[26]

---

[25] M. Jaffe, "The Authority of the Rabbinate in Israel," *Public Administration in Israel and Abroad* (Jerusalem: Israel Institute of Public Administration, 1966).

[26] It must be emphasized that the separations which result are by choice and not by law. While Arabs may go to any school in Israel, they prefer to maintain their own schools, in which the principal language of instruction is Arabic rather than Hebrew and the curriculum reflects Arabic culture and either Muslim or Christian religious beliefs and practices.

From the point of view of the state, these religious groups obtain their powers through state law. From the perspective of each of the religious communities, however, their powers flow directly from heaven and their law represents the divine will. As far as they are concerned, the state has only a minimal role in determining their existence and certainly no legitimate role in determining their powers other than that to which they are willing to acquiesce.[27]

Each of the several communities represents a further compound within its ranks. Every Arab locality is a compound of extended families—really clans—so much so that voting and political office holding, not to speak of decision making and the distribution of political rewards, are dependent upon competition or cooperation among the extended families in each locality. Every so often a group of young people emerges to challenge this arrangement, and it is said that the Arabs are modernizing and will no longer be bound by this kind of familial loyalty. However, all but the most radical of the young usually end up following the lead of their families in these matters. One consequence is that Arab voting patterns originally reflected agreements between each clan and one of the Israeli political parties, based upon political trade-offs rather than principle. This, too, has begun to change. As a result of the radicalization of sectors of the Arab population, increasingly the clans are voting for the Israeli Communist party, more as an expression of Arab identity than for ideological reasons.

Israel as a Jewish State. While by law Israel has no established religion, it is, by self-definition, a Jewish state. This means not only a state with a Jewish majority, but one in which the Jewish people as a corporate entity can express its particular culture, personality, and values and which seeks to foster the expression of that triad as, perhaps, its principal task. It is in this respect that many Israelis, including the leadership, consider the state a part of a larger entity known as the Jewish people. Israel is the only politically "sovereign" state within that entity and, as such, occupies a unique position. It is also, for certain purposes, a Jewish community and maintains relationships with other Jewish communities on what could be considered a federal basis. The Jews of Israel, particularly the most politically conscious among them, see the fostering of this relationship as one of the tasks of the state.

---

[27] It would not be incorrect to estimate that as many as one-third of all Israelis hold the religious law of their respective communities in higher regard than the law of the state, including a small group of Jews (perhaps several hundred) who reject state law altogether.

The principal institutional manifestations of this special relationship between Israel and the Jewish people are found in the "national institutions" functioning within the state's territory. These
institutions are so named because they are considered to belong to
the entire Jewish people (or nation, in Zionist terminology) and not to
the state of Israel alone. Among these are the Jewish Agency and the
World Zionist Organization (WZO), which are responsible for Jewish
immigration, land settlement, and vital social and educational projects
in Israel, and the Zionist education of Jews in Israel and outside; the
Jewish National Fund (JNF), which is responsible for land purchase and
reclamation throughout the country; and the Keren HaYesod (Foundation Fund) which is responsible for fund raising throughout the
world except in North America.[28] Constitutionally, they are linked
with the state by special compacts affirming this unique relationship.[29]

The country's universities are also national institutions. The
Hebrew University is formally designated as such by law. Its library
is the national library and is so named. All other universities in the
country have the same status, de facto, since they have the same
arrangements for governance and funding. The universities' boards
of governors are drawn from the Jewish community worldwide; some
two-thirds of their budgets come from world Jewish sources and only
10 percent from the funds of the state of Israel. Budgeting and policy-
making powers are shared by the state's Council for Higher Education, the university's "national" governing board, and the academic
senate (roughly the equivalent of state, federal, and local bodies, if
one were to translate them into modern political terminology). Even
the political parties themselves are technically national rather than
state bodies tied in with party branches as in other countries. (For
example, ex-Foreign Minister Yigal Allon was recently named chairman of the "national," or worldwide, Labor party while Shimon
Peres, the head of the opposition, remains chairman of its Israeli
"branch.") Although the reality is that officials of the state dominate

---

[28] Lands purchased by the Jewish National Fund are deemed to be the permanent
possession of the entire Jewish people for whom the JNF serves as trustee. They
cannot be alienated through sale but only through long-term lease to those who
work them or who develop them for useful purposes. Virtually all Jewish agricultural settlements, including the kibbutzim and moshavim, are located on JNF
land which they hold by lease. The terms of the leases include social provisions
with regard to proper land use and require the observance of the Sabbath in
matters connected with the property on the part of the leaseholder (many of the
latter provisions have proved legally unenforceable but retain some moral
authority).

[29] See Eisenstadt, *Israeli Society*, p. 299.

the national institutions when they care to (and this is invariably the case with the parties), it does not change the theoretical basis upon which they are structured and which does influence their operations.

Since 1967, these fine points of political theory have taken on a new reality and a new concreteness—so much so that they are now clearly major factors in determining the direction of Israeli political development. A small minority that wishes to dejudaize Israel continues to exist. Far more significant, however, for the mainstream of Israeli political development is the way in which figures such as Moshe Dayan, Yigal Allon, and Yitzhak Rabin—the first sabra generation of leaders—have embraced the idea of Jewish peoplehood, not to speak of the revival of the discussion of the matter of Israeli Jews' connection to both their Diaspora brethren and to Jewish religious tradition that can be found across the length and breadth of the land.[30] Menachem Begin, who is firmly rooted in this sense of Jewish peoplehood and tradition, has become a major articulator of both dimensions and has invariably received a favorable response from his public.

Granted, the aforementioned developments can lead to very serious theoretical, conceptual, and practical problems for Israelis, other Jews, and people attempting to study the Israeli political system. Unfortunately, reality frequently has that effect. What is clear is that Israelis and their institutions are no more (or less) capable of dealing with reality in this regard, or better equipped to do so, than are Diaspora Jews or social scientists.

Finally, the Law of Return, which guarantees every Jew (except those fleeing criminal prosecution of one kind or another) the right of entry into Israel and more rapid naturalization than non-Jewish immigrants, in effect obligates the state and local governments of Israel to provide services to every Jewish immigrant from the moment of his or her settlement in the country.[31] In fact, because of the domi-

---

[30] Since June 1967, *Midstream* has regularly printed speeches and statements by these men and others affirming their reconsideration of this question. Published examples of the Israelis' rediscovery of their Zionist and Jewish connections are cited in Daniel J. Elazar, "The Rediscovered Polity: Selections from the Literature of Jewish Public Affairs, 1967–1968," *American Jewish Year Book*, vol. 70 (Philadelphia: The Jewish Publication Society of America, 1969), pp. 132–237.

[31] There is a great deal of misunderstanding regarding the Law of Return. Israel has immigration laws similar to those of other Western countries, with permits issued upon application and naturalization following in due course. However, since Israel is considered the state of the Jewish people, Jews enter almost as if they were engaging in interstate migration in the American manner. It should be noted that similar laws hold true in other countries with regard to those considered nationals even if born outside their borders.

nant political culture, such services and benefits are extended immediately to all those accepted as residents of the state, without
regard to ethnic, national, or religious distinctions.

Some have suggested that Israel is also compounded on the
basis of the country and region-of-origin groups within the Jewish
population. Certainly these groups exist within the body politic, but
because none of them seek to perpetuate themselves as separate
groups, except for limited cultural, religious, or filio-pietistic purposes,
they lack the legitimacy of the other elements out of which Israel
is compounded. Israeli politics does take these groups into consideration in more or less subtle ways. Overt efforts to give group ties political expression, however, have been discouraged by members of the
groups themselves. Thus, since the early days of the state, no ethnic
lists have been successful as such in state elections or, except for a
few peripheral cases, in local ones. On the other hand, there are
definite efforts to balance tickets, particularly in local elections, and
to provide representation for different groups on tickets in the Knesset
elections. Moreover, some local lists, while claiming to be of a general
orientation, in fact represent predominantly one country-of-origin
group or another. Thus, while the shared ideology of Jewish Israel
is highly integrationist, in fact something akin to what is known as
ethnic politics in the United States exists under the surface.

The tendency toward "ethnic" politics (the term is misleading in
the Israeli context since all Jews are of the same *ethnos* or people)
increasingly overlaps with issue areas since a very large majority of
the least successful families in Israel, from a socioeconomic point of
view, are Jews from North Africa (Morocco, Algeria, Tunisia, Libya,
and Egypt) and West Asia (Iraq, Iran, Syria, Lebanon, Turkey,
Afghanistan, India, and the Soviet Asian Republics) who came to the
country after the establishment of the state. These are the so-called
Oriental Jews, who now form a majority of the state's population.
These Jews are from families that never left the Middle Eastern culture areas, who have lived within the Islamic world since the rise of
Islam, and whose customs reflect that world just as those of Northern
European Jews reflect their world. It should be noted that most of the
Oriental Jewish immigrants have done well enough, but, at the same
time, the bulk of those who have not are drawn from their ranks.
As these have-nots and their advocates have become more militant in
demanding government assistance to improve their lot, their mili-
tancy has taken on "ethnic" overtones.

Manifestations of Territorial Democracy

If ideological democracy places a premium on doctrinal faithfulness (or what passes for it) in the attainment of true citizenship and political influence, territorial democracy places a premium for their attainment on simply living in a particular *place* by right. Territorial democracy has two faces. It can be used as a means for specific communities to secure political power or influence by occupying specific territories or it can be used in a very neutral way to enable any groups that happen to be resident in a particular area at a particular time to secure a voice in the political process. What is common to both is the role of territorial units as the basis for organizing power.

Territorially based polities of the first kind began to develop as a matter of course when the pioneers settled in and staked claims to "turfs" of their own. The first of these were explicitly territorial: the moshavot (private, as distinct from cooperative, farming villages), the kibbutzim, and the moshavim, which came to conceive of themselves as virtually autonomous communities in the pre-state days. Israel's cities, the embodiment of the second face of territorial democracy, began their development at essentially the same time as the first agricultural settlements. The first of them, the "new city" of Jerusalem (that is, the settlement outside the walls of the "old city"), begun in the 1860s, was founded as a synthesis of the two faces, consisting as it did of neighborhoods created as virtually antonomous communities within the city by like-minded householders contracting together to found new settlements within an urban context.

The first city consciously founded as an urban settlement without an ideological base other than the general ideology of Zionism was Tel Aviv—significantly enough, founded in the same year as the first kibbutz, 1909. Tel Aviv represented, from the first, territorial democracy in its most neutral sense. Whoever settled within the city limits was entitled to the rights of local citizenship and could participate in political life to the extent and in the way he desired (within the context and opportunities offered by the political system in general) without having to subscribe to any particular ideological or religious doctrine or formula. One result of this was that Tel Aviv, for years, went counter to the countrywide trend toward socialism; it became a stronghold of the General Zionists (the present Liberals), though as the city grew larger its population became more mixed and diversified and the city lost any particular ideological tinge it might have had.

Tel Aviv became at one and the same time the paradigm and the caricature of the Israeli city as a neutral, democratic, territorial political unit. In the 1920s and 1930s and then at an accelerating rate after 1948, other cities followed its lead. As the country's Jewish population expanded, many of the original moshavot, which had been founded as agricultural colonies in preideological days became citified and were transformed into just such neutral territorial units. After 1948 these were supplemented by more than twenty new towns founded to absorb the new immigrants. Taken together, these cities, which by 1967 encompassed 65.3 percent of the country's total population, have become the major vessels for the assimilation of the waves of mass immigration that came into the country beginning in the 1930s.[32]

Today Israel's cities (which embrace over 85 percent of its population) provide the principal opportunities for nonideological participation in Israeli political life; hence, they are the entry points through which immigrants from Oriental countries and their children have gained political power. Two points illustrate this trend. First, one of the most frequently noted phenomena of politics in Israel is the disproportionately large percentage of leaders drawn from the Russian-Polish-Rumanian groups, particularly from the kibbutzim. Oriental immigrants and their children are particularly notable by their small numbers in the Knesset, the cabinet, and the ministries. This is emphatically not the case at the local level. Slightly more than 50 percent of the Jews of Israel are from North Africa or West Asia by birth or by descent. Approximately 47 percent of the political leaders and public officials (taken together) at the local level are drawn from those groups. Moreover, many have become mayors or deputy mayors (already 37 percent of the total in 1965), giving them concomitant political and social advancement.[33]

The development of nonideological politics within nominally

---

[32] *Statistical Abstract of Israel, 1968* (Jerusalem: Central Bureau of Statistics, 1968). In a significant number of cities and towns, territorial neutrality has led to the development of ethnic neighborhoods, which, however, under the present electoral system, are unable to obtain direct local representation. Perhaps as a result, ethnic ticket-balancing is even more pronounced on the local level than in Knesset elections.

[33] Szewach Weiss, *Hashilton Hamkomi B'Yisrael*, [Local government in Israel: a study of its leadership] (Tel Aviv: Am Oved, 1972), Chapter 10. It should be noted that the recruitment and advancement of Sephardic and Oriental Jews is not spread evenly throughout the system of local government. The older and larger cities have disproportionately fewer officeholders from those backgrounds, while the new towns with their mainly "new immigrant" populations have disproportionately more.

ideological parties has already spread to higher political echelons as well, partly in response to new voter interests as registered by party leaders with their fingers on the public pulse and partly in response to objective conditions that have consistently demanded pragmatic rather than ideological solutions to unanticipated problems. In this way, at least, objective conditions have functioned to reinforce the local consequences of territorial democracy, thereby mitigating the possibilities of conflict inherent in its pressures upon the older ideologically based system.

The precise nature of this movement of Oriental Jews and others who do not fit into the present party establishment into the larger arena of the Knesset and the supralocal party organizations will depend to no little extent on the fate of proposals for electoral change that are presently under consideration as part of the overall movement from ideological to territorial democracy. While electoral reform is far from certain, it is clear that most Israelis are quite eager for changes in the voting system that will introduce territorially based representation, at least to some extent.[34] It is equally clear that the parties themselves are either reluctant or hostile to the idea. They have attempted to blunt the reform effort by broadening the terri-torial basis of representation within their respective party organizations. Should they succeed in this effort, the federation of parties would no doubt survive more or less intact and even gain new strength. Should electoral reform come about, the present system would indeed undergo adjustments.

Whatever the results of the electoral reform effort, all indications are that Israel's political order is at the beginning of a period of change induced by the continuing process of "settling in" in a new society. While the trend right now is away from the ideological patterns of the first generations of pioneers and toward political participation on a territorial basis, in the last analysis, democracy in Israel, as in the other new societies, must develop out of a synthesis between the ideological, territorial, and ethnoreligious dimensions. By their very nature, such societies require the maintenance of a national mystique (with its ideological overtones) as the basis for the consensus that

---

[34] Of the several proposals for district elections under consideration in Israel at the present time, the two most prominent are: the proposal to establish single-member constituencies as in the United Kingdom, which is likely to substantially alter the present party system; and the proposal to elect eighty members from sixteen five-member districts which, with the election of another forty members at large, would guarantee the continued existence of the present party system. On electoral reform, see Chapter 2 in this book.

holds them together, while, simultaneously, the sheer passage of time tends to promote the expression of certain aspects of that mystique through other channels.

The Conflict of Cultural Inheritances

The political culture of contemporary Israel is compounded of a number of elements that have yet to merge into an integrated whole. Three major political cultural strands can be isolated.[35] The most visible of these was imported from Eastern and Central Europe by the majority of the pioneering generation and built into the state's institutions at every turn. Its salient elements, for our purposes, are: a strong statist-bureaucratic orientation, a perception of public officials as standing in a superior relationship to the general public by virtue of their role as servants of the (reified) state, an acceptance of heavy state involvement in the economic and social spheres as normal and even desirable, and a strong tendency toward encouraging the centralization of power wherever power is exercised. Political organization is expected to be centralized, hierarchical, and bureaucratic in character.[36]

The second political cultural strand was also imported. While primarily associated with Jewish immigrants from West Asia and North Africa, it can be found among those European Jews who came to Israel directly from the *shtetl* (the Yiddish term for the East European townlet where the average Jew lived at the turn of the century) or a *shtetl*-like environment and were not previously acculturated to the larger European environment. While this political culture also perceives the governing authority as a powerful force existing outside and independent of the people, it sees government as both more malevolent and more limited, the private preserve of an elite, functioning to serve the interests of that elite. Government is perceived in very personal terms as a ruler with whims rather than as the comprehensive

---

[35] The concept of political culture is discussed in Gabriel A. Almond and Sidney Verba, *The Civic Culture* (Princeton: Princeton University Press, 1963); Lucian Pye and Sidney Verba, eds., *Political Culture* (Princeton: Princeton University Press, 1965); Daniel J. Elazar, *American Federalism: A View from the States* (New York: Thomas Y. Crowell, 1966), Chapter 4; and *Political Culture, Working Kits No. 1 and 2* (Philadelphia: Center for the Study of Federalism, Temple University, 1969). Fein, *Politics in Israel*, presents one picture of Israel's political culture in Chapters 2 and 3.

[36] See Gabriel A. Almond, "Comparative Political Systems," *The Journal of Politics*, vol. 18 (1956), pp. 391–409, for suggestive comments on the political culture of continental Europe. An expanded exposition of his thesis can be found in Almond and Verba, *The Civic Culture*.

and reified state of the first political culture. Individuals imbued with this political culture have no concept of political participation, perceiving themselves as subjects not citizens. Indeed, they perceive the subject's task as being to avoid contact with the government or anyone associated with it, insofar as possible, for safety's sake. When they have to deal with government officials, they generally take a petitionary approach, humbly requesting consideration of their needs and recognizing the superior power of the official without necessarily endorsing his authority. The state is definitely not looked upon as a vehicle for the provision of services or for social improvement. Rather, the hope is that its role will be as limited as possible so that it will interfere in the lives of its subjects as little as possible.[37]

The third political cultural strand grows out of the indigenous political experience of the Jewish people in their own communities. It is civic and republican in its orientation and views the polity as a partnership of its members, who are fundamentally equal as citizens and who are entitled to an equitable share of the benefits resulting from the pooling of common resources. This culture combines the expectation of a high level of citizen participation with that of a clear responsibility on the part of governing authorities to set the polity's overall direction. The concept of the reified state does not exist in this Jewish political culture, nor does the notion of a ruler ruling by whim. Rather, the community is perceived as constituted by its citizens, reflecting the character of the Jewish people as a new society. Individual responsibility to the community is perceived to be of prime importance, and members of the community are held to have civic obligations to fulfill by virtue of their association with it. At the same time the leaders of the community are perceived to be responsible to the community in two ways: to its constitution, which gives it shape as a community, and to its members, who give the leaders their authority. The role of the community in dealing with human needs is perceived to be substantial but never all-embracing. That is, politics is not conceived as the be-all and end-all of life or as its architectonic principle. Rather, politics is perceived as an important means for creating the good society, necessary for living the good life, both of which are defined in other (traditionally religious) terms. Whereas the first two political cultures see authority and power as hierarchical, Jewish political culture sees it as federal, that is, as the product of a series of covenants (or partnership agreements) derived from the great

---

[37] Almond and Verba, in *The Civic Culture*, discuss this. See also Edward Banfield, *The Moral Basis of a Backward Society* (New York: Free Press, 1958).

29

covenant that created the Jewish people and reaching down to the immediate compacts that create specific communities within the Jewish body civic or politic that affirm the essential equality of the partners as well as the authority of the institutions they create.

Though the origins of this strand are as old as the Jewish people itself, the circumstances of Jewish political life since the destruction of Jewish independence some 2,000 years ago, and most particularly since the rise of the modern nation-state in the last 200 years, were such that Jewish communities were not in a position to preserve their own political autonomy unadulterated. Consequently, the Jewish strand is frequently more latent than manifest. At the same time, every Jewish community did maintain an internal political organization of its own, to a greater or lesser extent, which even when not conceived to be political by its members did serve to socialize them into certain specific patterns of political behavior vis-à-vis one another and the community as a whole.

This strand is spread across virtually the entire Jewish population of Israel to a greater or lesser extent, which means that, more than any of the others, it provides common points of reference and possibilities for communication among Jews from widely varying Diaspora environments. While the character and content of Jewish political culture have been less well explored than either of the other two strands, in recent years studies of Jewish political behavior over time have brought us to the point where we can begin to extrapolate certain patterns that seem to be endemic to it.[38]

To some extent, Israeli civil society is already an amalgam of the three strands, with different institutions reflecting one strand more than the others. In other respects, the three stand in tension and even conflict. Thus the Israeli bureaucracy is very European in style as well as in structure, while the army—the most fully Israeli institution in the whole country—comes far closer to the model of authoritative relationships rooted in Jewish political culture.[39] The subject strand,

---

[38] The study of Jewish political culture is still in its infancy. The materials by this author cited above offer a good starting point for examining the subject. More specifically, see Baron, *The Jewish Community*; Irving Agus, "The Rights and Immunities of the Minority," *Jewish Quarterly Review*, vol. 45, pp. 120–129; Gedalia Alon, *Mehkarim B'toldot Yisrael* [Studies in the history of Israel] (Tel Aviv, 1957–1958), vol. 11, pp. 58–74; and Jacob Katz, *Tradition and Crisis* (New York: Free Press, 1961), Chapters 1–5.

[39] Fein, *Politics in Israel*, Chapter 5, describes the bureaucracy. An excellent description of the federal (in its social sense) character of the army is provided by S. L. A. Marshall, "Israel's Citizen Army," in *Swift Sword* (New York: American Heritage, 1967), pp. 132–133. See also Amos Perlmutter, *Military and Politics in Israel* (Totowa, N.J.: Frank Cass, 1969).

whose legitimacy is in doubt everywhere, is particularly visible in the development towns.

Yet underneath all of these, the upward thrust of the previously latent Jewish political culture is becoming increasingly evident, albeit far from unilinear in its progress. Take the role of the Supreme Court in relation to the Knesset. Following European models, the Knesset is formally the highest repository of authority or sovereignty in the state, with its supremacy both specified in law and taken for granted in practice. Parliamentary systems do not give their supreme courts power to declare acts of parliament unconstitutional. Accordingly, Israel makes no formal provision for judicial review of legislative acts of the Knesset.[40]

At the same time, courts have always held very authoritative positions within the framework of Jewish political life, and Jewish political culture has emphasized judicial decision making as being of the highest importance. The Supreme Court of Israel has taken its obligations very seriously and, beginning in 1969, has, in effect, asserted a limited power of judicial review, effectively declaring an act of the Knesset to be unconstitutional by holding that it was unenforceable (98169 *Berman* v. *Minister of Finance and State Comptroller*). Israel's *Marbury* v. *Madison* came about by the action of an individual citizen who filed suit against the implementation of a Knesset act to finance election campaigns out of public funds on the grounds that the act was discriminatory on behalf of existing parties and against new seekers of Knesset seats. The court held that even though Israel's written constitution is not complete, the article dealing with elections had been adopted properly and could be held to be of constitutional validity and that under its terms the act was indeed discriminatory and hence unconstitutional. It enjoined the minister of finance from paying out any funds under the act's provisions. The Knesset accepted the court's ruling and in response passed a revised act designed to accommodate its constitutional objections, thereby effectively affirming at least a limited power of judicial review as part of the country's constitutional mechanism and moving the country a step away from the European models and closer to a model indigenous to the Israeli situation.[41]

---

[40] See Yehoshua Freudenheim, *Government in Israel* (New York: Oceana Publications, 1967). The situation in classic parliamentary democracies is portrayed in John C. Echlke and Alex N. Dragnich, eds., *Government and Politics* (New York: Random House, 1966).

[41] Amnon Rubinstein discusses this question in "Supreme Court vs. The Knesset," *Hadassah Magazine*, vol. 51, no. 7 (March 1970).

Though a common political culture is still in its formative stages, certain elements within it can already be identified. First, there is the strong sense of national unity—one might say embattled national unity—which pervades the country, the effect of Israel's immediate security position and the whole history of Jewish isolation in the larger world. Since the former is simply a continuation of the latter in a particular context, this element is rooted very deeply in the psyches of Israeli Jews.

Similarly, a common sense of vocation is inherited from the larger Jewish political culture. Until the 1950s this sense of vocation was clearly manifested through the Zionist vision of rebuilding Israel to redeem the Jewish people. Since then its precise character has become somewhat less explicit as it has become ideologically simplified and intellectually broadened. The revival of elements of the Zionist mystique after 1967 has given it new life.

The federal element (in the social even more than the political sense) is an important component of Israel's emergent political culture. We have already noted the use of federal principles in the foundation of the state's institutions. These institutional arrangements are simply the most visible manifestions of the federal principles that permeate Israeli society and its political culture from its congregational religious organization to its system of condominium housing, even though it has no acknowledged federal structure. Contractual government, the constitutional diffusion of power, and negotiated collaboration are all elements of the Jewish political culture that are finding expression, albeit imperfectly, in the restored Jewish state.[42]

Constitutionalism, republicanism, and desires for self-government are also deeply rooted in the emergent political culture of Israel. Whatever the problems faced by the country, threats to constitutional legitimacy or the republican form of government are not among them. Indeed, it is precisely because such threats are virtually unthinkable that we know that cultural rather than simply strategic or expediential supports for constitutionalism and republicanism are involved.

---

[42] There is good reason to believe that the federal element is present in all of the new societies, derived, at least in part, from their origins as contractual partnerships. This is true even in those societies where no visible federal structure is involved. Contractural government, the constitutional diffusion of power, and negotiated collaboration seem to be characteristic of their polities. See Daniel J. Elazar, *Studying the Civil Community* (Philadelphia: Center for the Study of Federalism, 1970) and "Federalism" in the *International Encyclopedia of the Social Sciences* (1968).

In other matters, the shape of the emergent Israeli political culture is more equivocal. Impressionistic observation seems to reveal that a change is taking place in the relationship between the bureaucracy and the public. While the bureaucrats may not be becoming more efficient, they are becoming less officious, accepting their role as public servants rather than officials of the state.

The same equivocal situation prevails in regard to the role of the citizens. It is generally assumed that citizens should be concerned with civic matters, and citizen participation in elections as voters is particularly high. At the same time, attempts to develop a widespread "participatory" outlook run into difficulties because of the nature of the party system, where centralized control and adherence to the ideological symbols and forms of an earlier generation act to discourage participation by those who are not "political" in Israeli parlance (that is to say, those who do not make politics the overriding concern in their lives).

In this connection, it is important to note the first signs of the emergence of the "citizen" or "amateur" in politics. The first manifestation of this phenomenon was the abortive attempt by certain former members of the Rafi party (originally founded by Ben-Gurion and his followers in 1965 and subsequently merged with Mapai and Achdut Ha'avoda as the Labor party) in 1969 to reestablish their political coalition through the mobilization of "amateurs." The reform movements stimulated by the Yom Kippur War extended this effort, and the Democratic Movement for Change (DMC), which won fifteen seats in the 1977 elections, represents its most extensive manifestation to date. The difficulties that confront the effort are fully reflected in the organizational problems of the DMC and its history since the election. In addition, local efforts to create similar coalitions occur from time to time and from place to place. All these represent the difficult beginnings of what could become an important trend.

By the same token the public's expectations of politicians are reasonably high. The people demand a high standard of behavior on the part of those they entrust with power, without necessarily being concerned with devising ways to impose sanctions if they do not live up to that standard. Prime Minister Rabin's resignation over his foreign bank account is one reflection of this. Indeed, the question of political morality in this sense was a major issue in the 1977 elections. Here, too, there has been no crystallization of political-cultural patterns, as the events of the past year have revealed.

Political Response

As Israel enters its second generation of statehood and its fifth of pioneering, its political system is still in the process of responding to the demands of state building. This response can be viewed through at least three dimensions: the developing structure of Israel's constitution, the character of republican government in Israel, and the quality of Israeli democracy.

Constitutionalism. We have already noted how the covenant idea, with its underlying premise that civil society is really a partnership among the contracting individuals who form it, is basic to Israel both as a new society in the modern sense and as the heir to the Jewish political tradition. The unbroken line from the Israelite tribal federation through the *kehilot* (the organized Jewish communities) of the Diaspora to the kibbutzim of modern Israel has yet to be established by research, but such probings as have taken place give every indication of revealing its existence. Certainly, what is common to all is the idea of constitutional legitimacy flowing from contractual consensus.

Israel is committed theoretically to the adoption of a formal written constitution and made an initial effort to write one in 1949. The first Knesset was actually elected as a constituent assembly. The series of compromises involved in the decision to postpone the writing of a constitution need not concern us here. Suffice it to say that a reluctance growing out of just those problems of creating a new political-cultural synthesis indigenous to the new society described above lay at the root of the decision. The problems of religion and state, the precise forms of political institutions, the degree of governmental centralization, and the extent to which individual rights needed constitutional safeguards were basic constitutional questions deemed worth deferring on that account.

Instead, a standing Constitutional, Legislative, and Judicial Committee was established as part of the Knesset's committee structure and charged with the responsibility of drafting Basic Laws on a chapter by chapter basis for submission to the Knesset, where approval by an absolute majority (at least sixty-one votes) would give them constitutional status. In line with the political theory under which the state operates, the final document will continue to be called a Basic Law and not a constitution (the latter term apparently is reserved for use by the Jewish people as a whole, whether one takes a religiously orthodox or a secularist approach to the constitutional problem of Jewish peoplehood). By 1978, five Basic Laws, recognized as constitutional in character, had been enacted. They and other materials deemed to have a substantial bearing on constitutional questions have been interpreted by the government and the courts to create the basis of a constitutional tradition in the state.[43] The High Court of Israel has also moved to transform Israel's Declaration of Independence into a constitutional document or to affirm its status as such.[44]

Republicanism and Democracy. In Israel, as we have seen, representative government was originally conceived to be government through representative institutions (that is, parties and movements) rather than representative men. And, as we have also seen, this approach is now under some attack in a developing struggle over the means of representation and the constitution of the institutions themselves.

Republicanism as originally introduced in Israel rested on European models, which meant that its parliamentary institutions were structured as if the ideal were undivided responsibility of the governors to the governed through the legislature. What has emerged, in fact, is a growing concern with and a continuing, if halting, trend toward separation of governmental powers. The government (that is, the cabinet) has taken on an existence increasingly independent of the Knesset and vice versa, even though most members of the government continue to sit in the Knesset.

The ability of the government to achieve independence is not difficult to fathom. Indeed, the central problem in parliamentary systems all over the world is how to make cabinets responsible to their parliaments rather than simply converting the parliaments into routine ratifiers of cabinet proposals. While Israel has not solved this problem, it has developed and institutionalized certain techniques that aid the Knesset in preserving some independence of its own—within the limits dictated by the parliamentary system—and it has also given it real opportunity to help shape government proposals into better legislation. The Knesset has done this by using a very unparliamentary device: standing committees with functional areas of responsibility somewhat akin to the American model and strikingly opposed to the classical parliamentary one. These standing functional committees include representatives of all the party factions sitting in the Knesset. Meeting behind closed doors, they allow members from the opposition

---

[43] Amnon Rubinstein, *Ha-Mishpat Hakonstitutioni Shel Medinat Yisrael* [The constitutional law of the state of Israel] (Jerusalem: Schocken, 1969).

[44] Ibid., Chapter 1. Kallen, *Utopians at Bay*, pp. 15–22 offers a most suggestive analysis of the Declaration of Independence as a statement of the political theory undergirding the state from this perspective.

parties or the minority parties in the government to influence legislation by the use of their talents as individuals in a way that would be impossible if they had to act openly in an arena where their suggestions would be judged on a partisan basis. Thus the opposition parties are able to make substantial contributions to the legislative process through the committee system, where their more able members can participate as individuals rather than simply as spokesmen for their parties, opposing and subject to public opposition from the ruling coalition at every turn.[45]

In this connection, the expansion of the bargaining arena has to be considered another aspect of republicanism in Israel. As befits a society whose origins lie so heavily in contractual arrangements, bargaining and negotiation are important features of Israel's political process, though, as befits a society torn between formal institutions representing the statist-bureaucratic political culture and tendencies reflecting the others, much of the bargaining is conducted despite the formal structure rather than in harmony with it. The Knesset committee system is simply one way in which it has been institutionalized without overt political change. For most matters, the government itself is hardly more than a coalition of ministries, each of which has been delegated broad powers by the Knesset so that it can virtually legislate in its own field. These ministries negotiate with their clients, their local government counterparts, the prime minister, each other, and the corresponding Knesset committees to implement their programs.

Most of the Jews who have settled in Israel came after the state was established and not as pioneers. In general, they had very low expectations regarding government services and even lower expectations regarding their ability to participate in or even influence the shape of government policies. The expectations of the Arabs, on both counts, were even lower. At the same time, many of the Jews were ambivalent in that they saw the new state as a messianic achievement and hence expected its government to solve personal problems of housing and employment in a very paternalistic way.

As the population acquired an understanding of democratic government, their demands intensified; some groups, once passive, became almost unrestrained in their insistence on having their way. With this escalation of demands came an escalation of complaints about the way in which services were delivered. Individuals would seek to influence those responsible for service delivery in specific cases affecting them, relying heavily on personal contacts to do so, but saw

---

[45] Author's interviews with members of the Knesset, 1968–1969.

no general role for themselves as participants in the political process. This is now slowly changing, as more and more native-born Israelis reflect the socialization process of the school system and what we have come to associate with middle-class values in the political sphere.

By and large, there has been no systematic effort on the part of the public or spokesmen for the public to articulate and aggregate public preferences into collective choices that become the expression of demand. Except in a few areas of immediate concern that are tacitly understood as such, matters in Israel have not much passed the grumbling stage.

By the same token, it would be hard to say that there is a conscious effort to organize in response to such demands. That is obvious enough since the demands themselves are hardly felt to exist. Much of what does exist in this regard is a result not of internal pressures in Israel but of the leaders' being cognizant of the trends in the Western world in this direction and seeking to find echoes of them, or perhaps to anticipate such echoes, within their country.

With that initial understanding, it is possible to identify two major sources of the articulation and aggregation of demands. Protest groups have emerged from among the disadvantaged members of Israeli society, that is to say, those immigrants from Oriental countries and their children who have been left behind in the general upward mobility of the population. They have made substantial claims, particularly in the areas of education and housing, upon all the authorities of the state on the grounds that they are suffering from discrimination and lack of equal opportunity. Their demands have followed traditional lines of protest and are only beginning to lead to systematic efforts to transform the present situation.

The other group consists of members of the academic community whose business it is to study policy problems and make recommendations for their resolution. These people have been tempted to follow conventional Western European and American thinking on the subject, accepting the management-oriented reformism of the twentieth century West. However, virtually all of those who have been in responsible positions have, whether for reasons of political prudence or intellectual skepticism, refrained from pursuing those ideas as far as they have been pursued in the West. In general, little attention is paid to them by the government.

Whether these forces are sufficient to overcome bureaucratic inertia and the natural preferences of a people who have grown accustomed to a hierarchical system is an open question. What is clear is that the political culture of Israel acts as a strong bulwark against changes in the present system—a system that balances formally hierarchical and centralized institutional structures against a myriad of implicitly contractual arrangements, with all the bargaining and negotiation that accompany such arrangements and actually inform the system. Perhaps as the Israeli political culture takes on a more consistent and harmonious character, this will prove to be dysfunctional and one aspect or the other will undergo serious modification.

Conclusion

While there has been considerable continuity in the Israeli government despite the election-induced changes, there are already strong signs that the new government is trying to respond to the demands of Israel's second generation of statehood and is attacking certain sacred cows of the Labor camp in an effort to liberate the Israeli citizenry from many of the restraints of the previous generation. In part, this is a reflection of the liberal economic orientation of the Likud. In part, it reflects its political liberalism, which is committed to limiting government intervention into the lives of the citizenry. The Likud's steps to reduce economic regulation and subsidization generally have been well received by a public that seeks greater freedom in these spheres. The new government has also taken some modest steps to recognize the pluralistic character of Israeli society. At the same time, Prime Minister Begin has emphasized the fundamental linkage between Israel and Jewish culture and tradition. All these initiatives reflect trends in the development of Israeli society that are likely to continue to gain strength in the coming generation.

2

1977 Elections and the Future of Electoral Reform in Israel

Avraham Brichta

The Electoral System

The great variety of electoral systems prevailing in Western democracies may be classified according to three criteria: the type of the ballot, the magnitude of the district, and the formula used in the allocation of seats in the parliament.[1] On the basis of these criteria, we may group electoral systems into three categories: those in which the voter chooses a list versus those in which he votes for individual candidates; those with multimember-district constituencies versus those in which the whole country is a single constituency; and majority versus proportional systems.[2] Israel elects its single-chamber parliament, the Knesset, on the basis of the most extreme form of the proportional-representation (P.R.) list system.

The Ballot. While in the United States or Great Britain the voter votes for individual candidates, in Israel he votes for a list of candidates.[3] Any group of 750 eligible voters, as well as any one of the parties represented in the outgoing Knesset, may submit a list of candidates. A new party, in addition to 750 signatures of supporters,

---

I would like to express my gratitude to my colleague, Allan E. Shapiro, for his useful comments on the final draft of this study.

[1] Compare Douglas W. Rae, *The Political Consequences of Electoral Laws* (New Haven and London: Yale University Press, 1967), part 1.

[2] On the importance of a correct classification of electoral systems, see J. K. Pollock, "Next Steps in Research in Comparative Electoral Systems," J. S. Bains, ed., *Studies in Political Science* (London: Asia Publishing House, 1961), p. 134, and Avraham Brichta, *Demokratia U'Bechirot* [Democracy and elections] (Tel Aviv: Am Oved, 1977), Chapters 1 and 2.

[3] For a collection and elaborate discussion of the electoral laws, see Zvi Jaffe, *Habechirot Laknesset Chukei* [Laws of election to the Knesset] (Tel Aviv: Am Oved, 1973).

must deposit IL40,000,* which is forfeited if no candidate is elected. The aim of the deposit is to deter small, politically insignificant groups from contesting elections. However, one may doubt its effectiveness. In spite of the fact that the amount of the deposit was increased from IL5,000 in the elections to the Seventh Knesset to IL15,000 in the elections to the Eighth and IL40,000 in the elections to the Ninth, the number of lists submitted has grown continuously, from sixteen to twenty-one and twenty-two, respectively.

Each list of candidates may contain up to 120 names, and the large parties do, in fact, put up as many candidates as there are Knesset seats. But the actual ballot cast into the box contains only the letter representing the party; no names are inscribed on it. The voter chooses a list of candidates and may neither add the names of new candidates, eliminate candidates, nor change their place on the ballot. He can vote only for the list in toto, or abstain. Israel has thus adopted the most rigid type of list system.

District Size. In the Anglo-American democracies using the simple majority-single ballot system, the country is divided into as many single-member constituencies as there are seats in the Parliament. Even in countries using proportional representation, the country is divided into a number of multimember constituencies. Thus the number of districts in Western European democracies using P.R., varies from four in Luxembourg to fifty-five in Greece.[4] Only in Israel does the whole country function as a single 120-member constituency.

The number and especially the size of the electoral districts is of great importance in determining the distribution of seats in the Parliament. The district magnitude is defined by the average number of members elected in a constituency.[5] As a rule it can be stated that the greater the district magnitude, the more proportional the election outcomes will be—that is, the more nearly proportional to its share of the vote will be each party's share of the seats in Parliament. The great magnitude of the single electoral district accounts, to a large extent, for the near perfect proportionality of the electoral system in Israel.

---

* Editor's note: In June 1977, $1 was worth approximately IL10. Inflation has remained high since then and the value of the pound has been repeatedly adjusted by the Israeli government. In October 1978, $1 was worth roughly IL18.

[4] See Wolfgang Birke, *European Elections by Direct Suffrage* (Leiden: A. W. Sijthoff, 1971), Chapters 7 and 11.

[5] Rae, *Political Consequences*, pp. 19–21.

The Electoral Formula. From the elections to the Second Knesset in 1951 until the elections to the Eighth Knesset in 1973, Israel used the most extreme proportional formula in the allocation of seats to the Knesset. The only obstacle for small splinter groups was the rule that lists obtaining less than *1 percent* of the total of valid votes did not participate in the allocation of seats. After the deduction of invalidated votes and of those cast for lists obtaining less than 1 percent of the total of valid votes, the total number of valid votes was divided by the total number of seats in the Knesset, the resulting number being the Hare quota. Thereafter, the total number of valid votes obtained by each party was divided by the quota, the resulting number defining the total number of seats allocated to each party that had received more than 1 percent of the total valid votes.[6] Thus, for instance, if a party received 409,000 votes and the quota was 10,000, it would get forty seats in the Knesset and would have a remainder of 9,000 votes.

The difficulty in using the Hare formula stems from the fact that a number of seats remain unallocated at the end of this process. Until the elections to the Eighth Knesset in 1973, Israel used the "largest-remainder" formula in allocating the remaining seats. Although the size of the "remainder" is a matter of pure chance, it has been maintained correctly that the largest-remainder formula favors the *small parties*. Since the number of parties participating in the allocation of seats in the Knesset has been usually more than ten and each party, whether small or large, can utilize its remainder only once, it is obvious that the share of the small parties in the allocation of the usually six or seven remaining seats will be greater than that of the large parties.

In 1973 the two largest parties in the Knesset, the Alignment and the Likud (Gahal, the Herut-Liberal bloc, in the Seventh and Eighth Knessets), joined together in an effort to change the electoral formula and succeeded in passing a private members' bill, known as the Bader-Ofer Bill, to reinstitute the highest-average formula used in the elections to the First Knesset and thereafter abandoned. In spite of the small parties' tumultuous outcry against the proposed change, the bill was approved during the last session of the Seventh Knesset, and the highest-average formula was used in the allocation of seats in the Eighth and Ninth Knessets. While it is true that the highest-average formula favors the large parties—this was precisely the intention of its inventor, Victor d'Hondt—its bias in favor of the large

---

[6] For a detailed discussion of electoral formulas, see Enid Lakeman, *How Democracies Vote* (London: Faber and Faber, 1969), Chapters 5 and 6, and Rae, *Political Consequences*, pp. 21–39.

parties in Israel has been counterbalanced by the very large size of the constituency. As Birke has noted, "The distortion [of the d'Hondt formula] is the larger the smaller the constituency is and hence the smaller the number of seats to be filled and the number of times each list number is divided."[7]

In order to demonstrate the rather modest impact of the d'Hondt formula in a constituency as large as 120 members, we have compared the results of the elections to the Ninth Knesset calculated on the basis of the d'Hondt highest-average formula with hypothetical results computed according to the largest-remainder formula. The results of our comparison are presented in Table 2–1. They show that the two largest parties, the Likud and the Alignment, each gained *two* seats as a result of the readoption of the highest-average formula, and the third party, the Democratic Movement for Change (DMC), gained *one* seat. Had the largest-remainder formula been used, the beneficiaries would have been the small parties: Poalei Agudat Israel, Shlomzion, the Movement for Citizens' Rights, the Democratic Front (Rakah) and the Arab list affiliated with the Alignment—each gaining one seat.

We may, therefore, conclude that the larger the district, the lesser the gain for the large parties from the use of the d'Hondt highest-average formula. Since in Israel the whole country is one 120-member constituency, the use of this formula has the effect of transferring less than 5 percent of the total number of seats from the small parties to the three largest parties, the net gain of the single largest party never exceeding two seats, or less than 2 percent of the total number of seats in the Knesset.[8]

The Struggle for Electoral Reform

The present practice of electing the Knesset on the basis of a country-wide list, proportional-representation system has been a subject of debate ever since the establishment of the state of Israel. Various proposals have been made to change the present electoral system. David Ben-Gurion, who was a great admirer of the British electoral system, proposed to divide the country into 120 single-member con-stituencies.[9] His disciples, who in 1965 established the Workers' party

---

[7] Birke, *European Elections*, p. 62.

[8] This has been the case in all elections since the establishment of the state of Israel. For a detailed comparison, see Brichta, *Demokratia U'Bechirot*, Chapter 3.

[9] For a brief account of Ben-Gurion's position on the subject of electoral reform, see David Ben-Gurion, *Medinat Yisrael Hamechudeshet* [The restored state of Israel] (Hebrew), vol. 2 (Tel Aviv: Am Oved, 1969), pp. 575–579.

TABLE 2–1

ALLOCATION OF SEATS IN THE NINTH KNESSET UNDER THE
D'HONDT AND LARGEST-REMAINDER FORMULAS
(in number of seats)

Party	(1) Present allocation, d'Hondt formula	(2) Projected allocation, largest-remainder formula	(3) Difference between (1) and (2)[a]
Likud	43	41	+2
Alignment	32	30	+2
Democratic Movement for Change (DMC)	15	14	+1
National Religious Party (NRP)	12	12	
Democratic Front for Peace and Equality[b]	5	6	−1
Agudat Israel	4	4	
Shlomzion	2	3	−1
Shelli	2	2	
United Arab list[c]	1	2	−1
Independent Liberals	1	1	
Citizens' Rights Movement	1	2	−1
Poalei Agudat Israel	1	2	−1
Flatto-Sharon	1	1	
Total	120	120	

[a] A + indicates gain in seats as a result of the introduction of the d'Hondt formula, a − indicates a loss in seats as a result of the same.
[b] Including the Israel Communist party and the Black Panthers' movement.
[c] Affiliated with the Alignment.
SOURCE: Calculated from *Results of Elections to the Ninth Knesset: First Report*, Central Bureau of Statistics, 1977, p. 6.

(Rafi) and later the State list, adopted his view; and Yigal Hurvitz submitted a private member's bill during the first session of the Eighth Knesset calling for the introduction of a simple-majority single-ballot system in the elections for the Ninth Knesset.[10]

While this proposal was rejected as being too radical, since it would involve the change of an extreme proportional-representation system into an extreme majoritarian system, another proposal, calling for the introduction of a mixed proportional-constituency system, was referred by the Knesset to its Law and Constitution Committee for preparation for the first reading. According to this proposal, the majority of Knesset members would be elected in a number of multi-member constituencies and the rest on the basis of a countrywide list system.[11] However, because of the fierce objections of the National Religious party, Mapam, and various small parties, coupled with the early termination of the Eighth Knesset's term, this proposal never reached the plenum for the required first reading.[12]

The problem of electoral reform attained special importance during the election campaign to the Ninth Knesset. The demand for a change in the electoral law was stressed in the platforms of both the Alignment and the Likud. Herut—the major partner in the Likud —which had continuously opposed a change in the electoral system because it feared that this would strengthen the Labor bloc, accepted for the first time the position of its partner, the Liberal party, and agreed to support a moderate electoral reform. The call for electoral reform has been almost the raison d'être of the Democratic Movement for Change. The DMC insisted that the single most important task of the Ninth Knesset should be the adoption of a new electoral law. Thereafter, it would dissolve and the elections for the Tenth Knesset would be held on the basis of the new electoral system.

In view of the great importance attributed by the main parties to the need for electoral reform, we shall briefly discuss the main arguments of the critics and the supporters of the present electoral system before analyzing in greater detail the changes in the electoral law proposed by the Alignment, the Likud, and the DMC in their platforms for the 1977 election.

---

[10] See *Divrei Ha'knesset* [Official records of the Knesset], session 36 of the Eighth Knesset, pp. 737–751.

[11] *Basic Law–The Knesset* (Amendment), 1977, draft proposal by the Alignment and the Likud in the Eighth Knesset.

[12] The debate on the proposal in the Law and Constitution Committee began in March 1977. The Eighth Knesset dissolved in April 1977.

The Strengths and Weaknesses of the Present Electoral System.[13] In the view of its critics, the present electoral system has the following shortcomings:

1. The list system makes the representative almost entirely dependent on the party leaders and the party machine. His loyalty to the party leaders is of paramount importance in his actions and deliberations. In the Knesset the M.K. is bound by strict party discipline. He may act independently only in matters of minor importance or when the party decides to grant freedom of voting to its representatives.

2. The representative whose career is almost entirely dependent on the party leaders and machine has no incentive to maintain close contact with the voters. The voter has no representative to whom he may appeal to solve his problems and represent his needs and interests or to whom he may voice his opinions. Thus, the present system prevents any meaningful communication between the representative and the represented.

3. The extreme proportional-representation list system concentrates the power of nomination in the hands of a small group of party leaders and thus tends to stress party loyalty as the main quality of a candidate. Consequently, the recruitment of party functionaries is preferred over that of candidates with a greater capacity for independent deliberation and decision making.

4. The supporters of electoral change claim that the great increase in Israel's population due to immigration, and the disper-

---

[13] A great number of articles have been written on this subject. The discussion of the arguments of the critics and the supporters of the present electoral system is based on the following sources, all in Hebrew:

The arguments of the critics: Abba Eban, "Shinui Mishtar Habechirot" [The need to change the electoral system], *Molad* (October 1951), pp. 367–374; Yigal Eilam, "Bechirot U'mishtar Demokrati" [Elections and democracy], *Molad* (June 1962), pp. 175–181; Abraham Weinshel, "Bechirot Yachassiyot o Ezoriyot" [Proportional representation or a district system], *Ha'uma*, vol. 20 (1967); David Bar-Rav-Hai, "Shinui Shitat Habechirot—Keitzad?" [How to change the electoral system?], *Ott*, vol. 1, no. 2 (1967); and two books published more recently, Meir Bareli, *Iyunim B'Shitot Bechirot* [The case against proportional representation] (Tel Aviv: Am Oved, 1971), and Gad Yaacobi and Ehud Gera, *Hachofesh Livchor* [The freedom to choose] (Tel Aviv: Am Oved, 1975).

The arguments of the supporters: Shlomo Avineri, "Shitat Habechirot Hateuna He Shinui?" [Is there a need to change the present system?] *Molad* (April 1962); Moshe Seliger, "Ideologia Ubechirot" [Ideology and elections], *Molad* (October 1960); Ze-ev Sternhal, "Kvutzot Lachatz Ubechirot Rubiyot" [Pressure groups and plurality systems], *Ovnaim*, vol. 2 (1962); Joseph Shofman, "Demokratia Bemivchan Bechirot" [The challenge of democratic elections], *Ha'uma* (June 1963).

sion of the population due to the establishment of new settlements and development towns in various parts of the country, call for the representation and articulation of specific regional interests in the Knesset. Only a division of the country into single or multimember constituencies could meet these needs.

5. The present system, according to its critics, encourages the multiplicity of parties and makes it necessary to establish coalition governments. This undermines the stability and effective functioning of the system.

The supporters of the present electoral system put forward the following arguments explaining their firm opposition to any form of electoral reform.

1. *The structure of the party system.* The political parties in Israel were established as parties of principle, each with a definite ideology and a particular *Weltanschauung.* As Professor Akzin has pointed out, "basically, the profusion of parties [in Israel] results from the strongly ideological character which most of the parties possess and reflects the multiplicity and intensity of views which various sections of the population hold on economic, religious and other matters."[14] In addition to the function of representing various outlooks and ideologies, the political parties in Israel articulate a myriad of ethnic, religious, and socioeconomic interests. Therefore, the Knesset is regarded as a body of ideological spokesmen and group representatives. Since interest articulation and aggregation is based on national and functional considerations, the division of the country into territorial constituencies would create artificial entities.

2. *The size of the country.* In a small country like Israel there is no room for regional representation. Moreover, the adoption of a constituency system, and particularly the division of the country into small constituencies, would bring about the preference of local interests over national interests, increase the pressure of particularistic interests, and consequently damage the efforts made to accelerate the process of integration.

3. *The lack of relevance of close contacts between the representative and the represented in Israeli circumstances.* Israel is a densely populated country. Most of its inhabitants live in the coastal area. More than one-third of the population lives in the vicinity of Tel Aviv.

---

[14] Benjamin Akzin, "The Role of Parties in Israeli Democracy," *Journal of Politics,* vol. 17 (November 1975), p. 508.

It is on the verge of absurdity to claim that the interests of people living on the left side of a street in Tel Aviv are different from the interests of their neighbors on the right side of the same street.[15] Moreover, the claim that there is meaningful contact between the representative and the represented is being questioned even in countries using the single-member-constituency system. Even in Britain the M.P. is dependent on the party and particularly on the selection committee of his local branch for his nomination. This also explains the almost total absence of independent candidates in the British Parliament. As recent studies have shown, even in the single-member constituencies in Britain the voters decide how to vote on the basis of issues, party platforms, and party identification, and only to a very small extent on the basis of the personality of the candidates.

4. *Representativeness.* The present P.R. system is the most effective in enabling the Parliament to fulfill the "mirroring" function.[16] The P.R. system makes the Knesset a truly representative body and prevents a minority in the electorate from attaining a majority of seats in the Knesset.

5. *Stability.* The multiplicity of parties, according to the supporters of the present system, does not necessarily cause governmental instability. The stability of a political system is not to be measured by the number of parties, but by their ability to create relatively stable coalitions. The party system in Israel may be classified as a centripetal rather than a centrifugal system.[17] Since 1965 the tendency has been toward the creation of two major blocs: the Labor Alignment and the center-right Liberal-Herut-Likud bloc. At present, Israel may be regarded as a four-party system, the two major blocs together with the religious parties and the DMC polling together close to 86 percent of the total vote. Furthermore, the rather remarkable stability of the political system in Israel has been attained under the present electoral system. Finally, the supporters of the present system point out that when the voters decided that a realignment of the political forces was necessary, the transfer of power from the Labor party's long-time hegemony to a right-wing liberal government occurred under the present electoral system.

---

[15] N. Nir, *Divrei Haknesset*, The Third Knesset, session 406, p. 896.

[16] For a discussion of the "mirroring" function of parliaments, see Giovanni Sartori, "Representational Systems," *The International Encyclopedia of Social Sciences*, vol. 13 (New York: Macmillan, 1968), p. 466.

[17] See Giovani Sartori, "European Political Parties: The Case of Polarized Pluralism," in Joseph La Palombara and Myron Weiner, eds., *Political Parties and Political Development* (Princeton: Princeton University Press, 1966), p. 160.

The Proposed Changes in the Electoral System

Shortly before the dissolution of the Eighth Knesset, the Alignment and the Likud reached an agreement according to which the present electoral system would be changed into a mixed proportional-district system; the country would be divided into sixteen constituencies, each electing five members to the Knesset, and the remaining forty M.K.s would be elected under a countrywide list system similar to the present one.[18] The aim of the proposed forty-member central list was to ensure the election of some of the party leaders and functionaries without exposing them to the tiresome and risky process of a constituency campaign. The boundaries of the proposed sixteen districts would be drawn by a special committee of three judges, selected by the High Court from among its members. The districts would be divided in such a manner that their territorial integrity and the equal size of their populations would be assured as far as possible.[19]

It is difficult to evaluate the probable consequences of the proposed electoral system, since the agreement between the Alignment and the Likud did not specify the formula according to which the seats would be distributed, either in the districts or on the central list. Furthermore, the proposal hints at, but does not state, what would be the quota barrier, that is, the percentage of votes a party would have to obtain in order to participate in the distribution of seats in the districts and the central list.[20]

The projections shown in Table 2–2 are based on a division of the country into sixteen adjacent constituencies, each electing five members, and a central list electing forty M.K.s.[21] We have chosen

---

[18] *Basic Law—The Knesset* (Amendment), 1977. Draft proposed by the Alignment and the Likud in the Eighth Knesset.

[19] *Basic Law* (Amendment), 1977, Paragraph 1(b).

[20] Ibid., Paragraph 1(e).

[21] Since the final and comprehensive results of the elections to the Ninth Knesset are not yet available, the results of the elections in the nineteen administrative districts and subdistricts have been used as the basis for the division of the country into sixteen five-member constituencies. Thus I was unable to stick to the principle of equal population in the districts. However, the results in principle compare favorably with a more accurate division of the country into eighteen five-member constituencies, calculated on the basis of the results of the election to the Eighth Knesset; see Brichta, *Demokratia U'Bechirot*, p. 91. I should stress that the division of the country into either sixteen or eighteen constituencies is incompatible with the principle of geographically homogeneous and compact districting. I have analyzed their political consequences because both divisions were proposed by the major parties; these consequences do not differ from those of the twenty-four-district division suggested by the geographers. See Stanley Waterman, "On the Problem of Electoral Districting in Israel," *Ir V'Ezor*, vol. 4, no. 1 (July 1977), pp. 15–31, especially Table 2, p. 40.

TABLE 2–2

PROJECTED DISTRIBUTION OF SEATS IN SIXTEEN FIVE-MEMBER
CONSTITUENCIES AND A FORTY-MEMBER CENTRAL LIST BY THE
HARE (H) AND D'HONDT (D) FORMULAS, BASED ON THE
NINTH KNESSET ELECTION RETURNS
(in number of seats)

District or Subdistrict	Likud		Align- ment		DMC		NRP		Demo- cratic Front		United Arab List		Agudat Israel	
	H	D	H	D	H	D	H	D	H	D	H	D	H	D
Jerusalem	2	3	1	1	1	1	1	0						
Safed and Kineret	2	2	2	3	0	0	1	0						
Afula	1	2	2	3	1	0	1	0						
Nazaret	0	0	1	0	0	0	0	0	2	3	2	2		
Akko	1	1	1	2	0	0	0	0	2	2	1	0		
Haifa	2	2	2	2	1	1	0	0						
Hadera	1	2	1	2	1	0	1	0	1	1				
Sharon	1	2	1	2	1	0	1	1	1	0				
Petah Tiqwa	2	2	1	2	1	1	1	0						
Ramla	2	3	1	2	1	0	1	0						
Rehovot	2	3	1	2	1	0	1	0						
Tel Aviv	2	2	1	2	1	1	1	0						
Ramat-Gan	2	2	1	2	1	1	1	0						
Holon	2	3	2	2	1	0	0	0						
Ashkelon	2	2	1	2	1	0	1	1						
Beersheba	2	3	1	2	1	0	1	0						
District total	26	33	20	31	13	5	12	2	6	6	3	2		
Central list	14	19	12	12	5	4	5	3	3	2	0	0	1	0
Grand total	40	52	32	43	18	9	17	5	9	8	3	2	1	0
Actual, 9th Knesset[a]	45[b]		32[c]		15		12		5		1		4	

[a] Four parties—Poalei Agudat Israel, the Independent Liberals, the Civil Rights Movement, and Flatto-Sharon—each represented by one member in the present Knesset, and Shelli with two, would not succeed in electing candidates under the sixteen-district division.

[b] Includes two representatives of Shlomzion who joined the Likud.

[c] Includes Moshe Dayan who was elected on the Alignment list but left his party shortly after the elections and established an independent single-member faction.

SOURCE: Calculations made on the basis of as yet unpublished data supplied by courtesy of the Central Bureau of Statistics.

to use, first, the Hare and largest-remainder formulas and, thereafter, the d'Hondt (Bader-Ofer) formula in order to test the probable consequences of each on election outcomes.

The division of the country into sixteen five-member constituencies and a forty-member central list system using the Hare quota and the largest-remainder formula would weaken the largest party (the Likud) and strengthen predominantly the medium sized parties (the NRP and the DMC) and probably also the Democratic Front (Communist) party. The increase in the power of the Communists would depend on whether the Northern district were divided into small subdistricts (as it is in our projection) or remained a single district in line with the principle of equal sized voting populations.

On the other hand, the d'Hondt (Bader-Ofer) formula would substantially increase the representation of the two largest parties (by more than 15 percent the Likud, and close to 35 percent the Alignment) as well as increase the strength of the Democratic Front and the small Arab party (whose voters are territorially concentrated), while significantly weakening the representation of the medium sized parties (the NRP and the DMC).

It is quite unrealistic to assume that the large parties would accept the first proposal (the Hare quota and the largest-remainder formula) and the medium sized parties—particularly the NRP—the second (d'Hondt formula), but it is conceivable that the use of the largest-remainder formula in the allocation of seats in the districts and the d'Hondt formula in the allocation of the forty seats on the central list would be acceptable to all parties, even though it would increase the representation of the medium sized parties. The outcome under such a system is projected in Table 2–3.

In fact, this proposal was not discussed during the long and procrastinating coalition negotiations between the Likud and the NRP, on the one hand, and the DMC, on the other.[22] Before its final decision to enter the cabinet, the DMC demanded that the country be divided into twenty four-member constituencies, the remaining forty members to be elected on a central list, while the NRP insisted on no more than six constituencies electing a total of eighty members, the rest to be elected on a central list.

Basing themselves on an analysis of the effects of constituency size on election results, researchers agree unanimously that constituencies electing ten or more delegates produce virtually optimal

---

[22] On the rather naive belief of the Democratic Movement for Change in the magic of electoral reform, see A. Shapiro, "The Political Uses of Enchantment," *Jerusalem Post*, July 18, 1977.

TABLE 2–3

Projected Distribution of Seats in Sixteen Five-Member Districts Using the Hare Formula and a Forty-Member Central List Using the d'Hondt Formula, Based on the Ninth Knesset Election Returns
(in number of seats)

Party	Sixteen districts, Hare formula	Central list, D'Hondt formula	Total	Actual, 9th Knesset
Likud	26	19	45	43[a]
Alignment	20	12	32	32[b]
DMC	13	4	17	15
NRP	12	3	15	12
Democratic Front	6	2	8	5
United Arab list	3	0	3	1
Total	80	40	120	108[c]

[a] Does not include two representatives of Shlomzion who joined the Likud shortly after the elections.

[b] Includes Moshe Dayan.

[c] Plus Agudat Israel and Poalei Agudat Israel (5), Moked (2), Shlomzion (2), Independent Liberals (1), Civil Rights (1), and Flatto-Sharon (1), none of which would win seats under this hypothetical electoral system.

Source: See Table 2–2.

proportionality; enlarging such constituencies by adding delegates will do little to increase the proportionality of the results. Furthermore, the majority of experts believe that constituencies sending five to seven delegates to Parliament preserve an acceptable level of proportionality in election results.[23]

In addition to size, the formula used to allocate mandates in each constituency and in the country as a whole has a considerable influence on election results. As a rule, the Hare formula and the allocation of mandate surpluses by the largest-remainder method used in Israel from the Second to the Seventh Knessets give the advantage to the small parties, while the formula known in Israel as the Bader-Ofer

---

[23] On the important impact of district magnitude, see Lakeman, *How Democracies Vote*, p. 122; Rae, *Political Consequences*, pp. 114–125; F. A. Hermens, *Democracy or Anarchy* (South Bend, Ind.: University of Notre Dame Press, 1941), p. 15, and W. J. M. Mackenzie, *Free Elections* (London: Allen and Unwin, 1967), p. 61.

method gives the advantage to the large parties.[24] Since a few large constituencies and the largest-remainder formula tend to favor the small parties, it is no wonder that Agudat Israel and Poalei Agudat Israel would fare better under a division of the country into six constituencies electing eighty delegates, with the remaining forty chosen from a central list, than from a division of the country into sixteen constituencies.[25] The NRP, similarly, would benefit from the former system, judging by the projections shown in Table 2–4.

The outcomes presented in Table 2–4 show that a system dividing the country into six large constituencies and retaining a central list, with seats allocated according to the Hare quota and the largest-remainder formula, would produce almost the same result as the actual outcomes of the elections to the Ninth Knesset. It would eliminate only the very small parties which elected only one or two representatives in the last elections while increasing to some extent the representation of the Democratic Front (the Communists). However, the introduction of the d'Hondt formula within the six-district system would have a substantial impact upon the allocation of seats in the Knesset. As Table 2–5 shows, the Likud would probably increase its power significantly (by almost 25 percent), enabling it to form a stable coalition either with the NRP alone or with the DMC alone. Thus, using the d'Hondt formula would have a stabilizing effect, even within a system of six large constituencies.

We may assume that the NRP would vehemently oppose the introduction of the d'Hondt formula and would demand the application of the largest-remainder formula instead. But the DMC is equally determined to reject any proposal dividing the country into a small number of large constituencies. The agreement that brought the DMC

---

[24] The Hare formula would have almost the same impact on the election results when applied in fifteen districts as it has in one countrywide district; in other words, it would produce virtually the same results as the present electoral system. On the other hand, the d'Hondt formula would bring about very significant changes—similar to those we have found in the application of the sixteen five-member districts (see Table 2–2). For results of the application of the Hare and d'Hondt formulas in fifteen districts on the basis of the elections to the Seventh and Eighth Knesset, see Brichta, *Demokratia U'Bechirot*, pp. 75–86, and on the basis of the results to the Fifth and Sixth Knesset, see Kraft, "The Impact," *Ott*, pp. 175–176.

[25] The division of the country into six constituencies is based on the present administrative division of the country into six districts, five electing thirteen members and the sixth, the largest Tel Aviv district, electing fifteen members—altogether eighty members, as proposed by the NRP. For a similar division on the basis of the results to the Sixth Knesset, see G. Kraft, "Hashpaat Hachaluka L'Ezorei Bechirot Al Totzaot Habechirot" [The impact of electoral districting on the election results], *Ott*, vol. 1, no. 3–4 (November 1967), pp. 172–176.

TABLE 2–4

PROJECTED DISTRIBUTION OF SEATS IN SIX DISTRICTS (D) ELECTING EIGHTY MEMBERS AND ONE CENTRAL LIST (C) ELECTING FORTY MEMBERS, BY THE HARE FORMULA, BASED ON THE NINTH KNESSET ELECTION RETURNS

(in number of seats)

Party	Jerusalem D	Jerusalem C	Northern D	Northern C	Haifa D	Haifa C	Central D	Central C	Tel Aviv D	Tel Aviv C	Southern D	Southern C	Total D	Total C	Grand Total, Hypothetical System	Actual Allocation in 9th Knesset
Likud	6	1	3	1	4	2	5	3	6	5	5	2	29	14	43	43
Alignment	2	1	4	2	4	2	3	2	4	4	4	1	21	12	33	32
DMC	2	1	1		2	1	2	1	2	2	1	1	10	5	15	15
NRP	2		1	1	1	1	2	1	1	1	2		9	5	14	12
Agudat Israel	1								1	1			2	1	3	4
Shlomzion					1				1				2		2	2
Democratic Front			3	1	1	1	1	1					5	3	8	5
United Arab list			1										1		1	1
Flatto-Sharon											1		1		1	1
Total	13	3	13	5	13	7	13	8	15	13	13	4	80	40	120	115[a]

[a] Four small parties—Shelli (2), Poalei Agudat Israel (1), the Civil Rights Movement (1), and the Independent Liberals (1), would not gain any representation under this system.

SOURCE: See Table 2–2.

TABLE 2–5

PROJECTED DISTRIBUTION OF SEATS IN SIX DISTRICTS (D) ELECTING
EIGHTY MEMBERS AND ONE CENTRAL LIST (C) ELECTING FORTY
MEMBERS BY THE D'HONDT FORMULA, BASED ON THE
NINTH KNESSET ELECTION RETURNS
(in number of seats)

| Party | District | | | | | | | | | | | | Total | | Grand Total, Hypothetical System | Actual Allocation in 9th Knesset |
| | Jerusalem | | Northern | | Haifa | | Central | | Tel Aviv | | Southern | | | | | |
	D	C	D	C	D	C	D	C	D	C	D	C	D	C		
Likud	7	2	3	1	5	4	6	4	7	6	6	2	34	19	53	43
Alignment	2	1	4	2	5	2	4	2	4	4	4	1	23	12	35	32
DMC	2	0	1	0	2	1	1	1	3	2	1	0	10	4	14	15
NRP	1	0	1	0	1	0	2	1	1	1	2	1	8	3	11	12
Agudat Israel	1	0											1	0	1	4
Democratic Front			3	2									3	2	5	5
Minorities list			1	0									1	0	1	
Flatto-Sharon															0	1
Total													80	40	120	112[a]

[a] Six small parties—Moked (2), Shlomzion (2), Poalei Agudat Israel (1), the Civil Rights Movement (1), Independent Liberals (1), and Flatto-Sharon (1), would not gain any representative under this system.
SOURCE: As in Table 2–2.

at last into the coalition fold stipulates that a proportional, multi-member district system will be adopted and put into effect for the elections to the Tenth Knesset.

To this end a committee consisting of representatives of the coalition parties has been established. The committee is obliged to finish its work within nine months. The number of districts serving as the basis for the committee's deliberations will range from six to sixteen.[26] It seems to me that the proposal most likely to be acceptable to all parties would divide the country into fifteen constituencies on the basis of the existing regional divisions, combining the two small regions of Safed and the Kinneret and splitting the Tel Aviv region into three. Under this system the number of delegates would be proportional to the number of persons with voting rights in each constituency. The number of delegates would range from four in the smallest constituency to nineteen in the largest (see Table 2–6).[27]

The regional system would have other advantages, too. It would not require an artificial division of constituencies and thus would avert the danger of gerrymandering. It would ensure a fair representation of local interests and closer ties between the voting public and their representatives in the Knesset. It would reduce the control of central party machines over nominations and would make possible the assignment of secure places in large areas such as Tel Aviv, Haifa, and Jerusalem to the political leaders the parties want to have in the Knesset. This is exactly what they are trying to accomplish through the central list. A proportional system of regional, personal elections could serve as the basis for a fair compromise between the religious parties and the DMC, which would at long last make possible a change in the existing system.[28]

It has been maintained that electoral districting is less important in countries using proportional-representation systems than in those using the first-past-the-post, winner-take-all system.[29] Analyzing the

---

[26] The principles of the coalition agreement were published in *Ma'ariv*, October 25, 1977.

[27] The division of the country into fifteen districts is based on the present administrative divisions, each district electing a number of representatives proportional to the number of eligible voters it contains.

[28] See B. Liberman, "Shitat Bechirot Rubiyot Lemaaseh," [The application of majority sytems in Israel], *Molad* (July 1965); A. Wolfenson, "Bechirot Ezoriyot Bimdinat Yisrael" [A district system of elections in Israel], part 2 (Haifa: Halewanon, 1968); Kraft, "Hashpaat," vol. 1, no. 2 (November 1967); Waterman, "On the Problem," *Ir V'Ezor* (July 1977); Yaacobi and Gera, *Hachofesh Livchor*, p. 65; Avraham Brichta, *Demokratia U'Bechirot*.

[29] See P. S. Taylor and G. Gudgin, "The Statistical Basis of Decisionmaking in Electoral Districting," quoted in Waterman, "On the Problem," *Ir V'Ezor*, p. 37.

TABLE 2-6

Projected Distribution of Seats in Fifteen Unequal Districts by the Hare Formula, Based on the Ninth Knesset Election Returns

(in number of seats)

								District								
Party	Jeru-salem (10)	Safed (4)	Yizrael (6)	Akko (6)	Haifa (15)	Naza-ret (4)	Hasha-ron (6)	Petah Tiqwa (8)	Ramla (3)	Re-hovot (6)	Tel Aviv (19)	Ramat Gan (11)	Holon (9)	Ashke-lon (6)	Beer-sheba (7)	Total (120)
Likud	4	1	1	1	5	1	2	3	1	2	7	4	4	2	3	41
Alignment	2	2	3	1	4	1	1	2	1	2	5	3	3	2	2	34
DMC	1			1	3		1	1		1	3	2	1	1	1	16
NRP	1	1			1	1	2	1	1	1	1	1	1	1	1	14
Democratic Front			2	2		1					1					6
Shlomzion					1						1	1				3
Agudat Israel	1							1			1					3
Moked	1															1
United Arab list				1												1
Flatto-Sharon											1					1

Note: The number of seats for each district is stated in parentheses under the district name.
Source: See Table 2–2.

results of the various proposals to change the present electoral system in Israel by dividing the country into between six and twenty-four constituencies, we may conclude that employing the d'Hondt highest-average formula in place of the Hare and largest-remainder formulas in multimember districts would significantly affect electoral outcomes, greatly benefiting the two largest parties.

3

The Electorate: Israel 1977

Asher Arian

Introduction

The composition of Israel's electorate has changed dramatically since independence in 1948 and the first elections in 1949. Then, with about half a million eligible voters, most of the electorate was made up of immigrants from European countries. In 1977 there were over 2.25 million eligible voters, almost a third of them born in Israel. More than 90 percent of the electorate in 1977 was Jewish and many of them were immigrants or the children of immigrants from Asian and African lands.

Demographic change is an important element in understanding the political turnaround that resulted from the 1977 elections. For the first time since establishing its dominance well before independence, the labor movement lost its hegemony in Israeli politics. This was all the more significant since its political power had been based on, and had reinforced, the Labor-Mapam Alignment's control of the country's economy, the bureaucracy, and an extensive patronage system.

But the 1977 elections cannot be seen in isolation from the political system in which they were held or from previous political developments. In fact, the dramatic results of 1977 represented another low point on the downward curve of the Alignment and a high point in the fortunes of the Likud. Twenty-nine years of opposition politics finally ended, and Menachem Begin, the Likud leader who had headed the Herut-Gahal-Likud lists in eight losing elections, was called upon to form a coalition and serve as prime minister.

The emergence of the Democratic Movement for Change (DMC) headed by Yigael Yadin resulted from many of the internal problems that Israel faced—corruption, oligarchical party structures, the heavy bureaucratization of many aspects of life, and a feeling that the system was unresponsive to the challenge of the country's social and ethnic problems. Ultimately the DMC had a powerful influence in determining the outcome, for while it is true that the Likud (excluding Ariel Sharon) increased its total vote by 3.2 percentage points between 1973 and 1977 and the Alignment lost 15 percentage points compared with the 1973 vote, it was the DMC that made a remarkable first-time showing by gaining 11.6 percent of the total vote. (This is a startling achievement in Israeli political history. David Ben-Gurion's Rafi list, which broke away from Mapai for the 1965 elections and featured Moshe Dayan and Shimon Peres along with Ben-Gurion, won only 7.9 percent of the vote.)

Three profound forces for political change coincided with a number of major shocks to the political system in an all but unbelievable sequence, to pry loose the Labor Alignment from power and to install the Likud. The first of these was the slow erosion of the dominance of the Labor party. A generation after independence, the symbols, leaders, and appeal of the Labor party no longer had the impact on the electorate they had had in the past. No less telling, the party's organizational efforts were cumbersome and a crisp leadership style failed to emerge before the elections. A second trend of major importance was the continuing drift to the right of Israeli public opinion, especially on matters of foreign and defense policy. The hard-line consensus which the Golda Meir and Yitzhak Rabin governments had fostered made the switch-over to the Likud that much easier for the country. Third, important demographic changes in the composition of the electorate reinforced the likelihood of the Likud's becoming stronger with each election. A semblance of class-based politics was introduced into Israel for the first time in 1977 with the shattering of Labor's dominance. It is to these themes that we now turn.

The Uniqueness of 1977

The real surprise was not the direction of the 1977 election outcome, but the timing and extent of the Likud's victory. Well before the election it was clear to many observers that the end of Labor's dominance would one day come—the question was when. What pollsters, politicians, reporters, and the man in the street widely believed was that it would *not* happen in 1977. So strong was the concept of the existing dominant-party system that observers tended to analyze events in terms of their preconceptions, selecting data that supported them and ignoring contrary developments. It can even be argued that this lack of sensitivity speeded the erosion of Labor's support, since in an atmosphere where the continued rule of the Labor Alignment

TABLE 3–1
VOTING INTENTIONS, MARCH–MAY 1977
(in percentages)

Party	Date of Survey		
	March 3–9	April 12–14	May 4–5
Alignment	24.9	18.3	19.8
Likud	21.1	18.3	21.4
DMC	15.0	8.9	10.3
Religious parties	6.0	7.2	7.4
Undecided/no answer	27.7	40.5	34.0
N	(1372)	(497)	(485)

NOTE: Because of the exclusion of the minor parties, the columns do not add to 100 percent.
SOURCE: Surveys conducted by the Israel Institute of Applied Social Research using questionnaires designed by the author.

was considered certain, many voters thought they could "afford" to change traditional patterns of support.

Table 3–1 reports the results of three preelection polls and shows the fluctuations in the parties' appeal and the very large undecided/no answer category.[1] This group was of course the key, and those who dared predict voting results tended to assume that they would largely return to the Labor party; this assumption turned out to be exceedingly inaccurate.

The period before the Knesset elections was certainly unique. The country was faced with a series of very disturbing revelations, any one of which might have caused the downfall of another parliamentary government: the trial and conviction for bribery of Asher Yadlin, a power in the Histadrut and Labor party leader and the Rabin government's nominee as head of the Bank of Israel; the suicide of Housing Minister Avraham Ofer, related to investigations concerning his role in financing the Labor party; Prime Minister Yitzhak Rabin's resignation from the number one position on the Alignment list and his leave of absence from the prime ministership after irregularities in his wife's financial affairs were revealed; the state comp-

---

[1] All surveys mentioned in the text are based on samples of the adult urban Jewish population of Israel. The surveys were conducted by the Israel Institute of Applied Social Research using questionnaires designed by the author, who also analyzed the findings.

troller's report that a lack of preparedness had been discovered in the army's emergency depots; and former Foreign Minister Abba Eban's failure to provide proof of permission to hold foreign currency accounts. The severity of these events, the fact that they revealed corruption or mismanagement at the very pinnacle of Labor's leadership, and their timing immediately before the elections all had their effect. The call for change became more pertinent and the feeling of unease more apparent. The poll findings shown in Table 3–2 reflect these changes in mood. The March poll took place shortly after the Labor party conference which chose Rabin by a vote of 1,445 to 1,404 over Peres to head the party list, and shortly before the internal elections held among the DMC membership to determine their election list.

By the time of the April poll Rabin had resigned as number one and had taken an extended leave as prime minister. The undecided total shot up, and the Likud tied with the Alignment in the poll. By May, some two weeks before the election, the Likud was ahead and the number of undecided votes was still very high. Meanwhile, President Carter was making remarks about a Palestinian homeland and the PLO that made Israelis apprehensive; then an army helicopter crashed killing more than fifty soldiers and rumors of carelessness spread. The televised debate between Begin and Peres was considered a stand-off by many but increased the legitimacy of the Likud and Begin in the eyes of the public.

Perhaps only this exceptional convergence of events could have ended Labor's dominance so abruptly. When asked, after the election, about the major factor affecting their voting decision, about half of the Likud and 60 percent of the DMC voters in the sample said they distrusted a government headed by the Alignment. Forty percent of the DMC voters and half of the Likud voters indicated a positive reason for their vote decision: trust in the leadership of the party they voted for. That positive reason accounted for 43 percent of the Alignment's support; another quarter expressed a general desire to support the Alignment, while fear of the Likud's policies motivated 22 percent of the Alignment voters.

The shift away from the Alignment and to the Likud was uneven. While the general tendency is clear, there were identifiable groups within the electorate that shifted to the Likud from the Alignment and others that left the Alignment for the DMC. It was this crystallizing of the electorate that made the 1977 elections potentially so significant for the future of Israeli politics. The catchall nature of the Labor party was diminished, as upper-middle-class voters of European extraction and high levels of education flocked to the DMC, and many lower-

TABLE 3–2

TURNOUT AND VOTE FOR THE MAJOR PARTIES, BY SETTLEMENT TYPE, 1969, 1973, AND 1977

(in percentages)

Settlement Type and Party	1969	1973	1977
Total population			
Turnout	81.7	78.6	79.2
Likud[a]	26.0	30.2	35.3
Alignment	46.2	39.6	24.6
DMC	—	—	11.6
Cities established before 1948			
Turnout	81.1	78.4	79.6
Likud[a]	30.9	34.8	38.9
Alignment	46.0	39.7	23.9
DMC	—	—	13.7
Cities established after 1948			
Turnout	78.3	73.7	75.9
Likud[a]	26.6	32.6	44.0
Alignment	48.7	40.4	23.0
DMC	—	—	7.2
Kibbutz Movement			
Turnout	86.0	87.0	85.9
Likud[a]	2.6	2.5	3.3
Alignment	89.1	85.2	75.7
DMC	—	—	8.4

[a] Includes Gahal, the State list, and the Free Center in 1969 and Ariel Sharon's list in 1977.

SOURCE: Government of Israel, Central Bureau of Statistics.

class workers of Asian or African background left the Alignment to join their cousins who had constituted the bulk of Likud supporters.

These trends can be seen in Table 3–2. Whereas the Likud improved on its 1973 record in all of these settlement groups in 1977, the extent of the swing was not uniform. In the cities established before 1948 the Likud improved its record by only 4.1 percentage points, compared with 11.4 percentage points in newer towns.[2] These new cities, many of them development towns, had traditionally sup-

[2] All election statistics are from the official publications of the Government of Israel's Central Bureau of Statistics.

ported the dominant Labor party, although their demographic characteristics (Asian-African backgrounds, lower levels of education) would have led one to expect that they would support the Likud. In 1977 the break came, and many of them flocked to the Likud. While former Alignment voters in the older cities were also abandoning their previous voting patterns, they tended much more strongly to wind up supporting the DMC. These two categories of urban settlement account for 75 percent of the Israeli electorate, with almost 30 percent living in the three largest cities, Jerusalem, Tel Aviv, and Haifa. Another 13 percent of the population lives in smaller urban settlements, 7 percent of the electorate in kibbutzim and moshavim, and 4 percent in non-Jewish villages and Bedouin tribes.

The kibbutz movement, comprising only some 3 percent of the population but historically a bulwark of the labor movement and a major source of the Labor-Mapam Alignment's ideology and personnel, did not support the Likud in significant numbers, but the figure rose over 1973, and support for the Alignment fell by some ten percentage points. Even within the kibbutz movement and the kibbutz federation the swing was not consistent. The most noticeable trend toward the DMC was in the kibbutz federation affiliated with Mapai (Ihud). Mapai was the main party of the socialist-Zionist left (see Table 3–1) and included among its members David Ben-Gurion, Moshe Sharett, Levi Eshkol, Golda Meir, and Moshe Dayan; the Ihud federation has always been much more powerful in Mapai and Labor party circles than its numerical strength would warrant. And yet in 1977, in Ihud kibbutzim established before the founding of the state, the Alignment support rate fell from 89.4 percent in 1973 to 72.7 percent, and 16.9 percent of the votes went to the DMC. In Ihud kibbutzim founded after 1948, the trend was even stronger, with the Alignment falling some twenty percentage points to 63.4 percent and the DMC winning 18.8 percent.

A different pattern emerged among the members of kibbutzim affiliated with Mapam (Artzi). Mapam is a party that retains a strong Marxist ideology. It joined the Alignment in 1969. Kibbutz Artzi members were much more loyal to the Alignment: in veteran kibbutzim of the movement, Alignment support fell from 90.9 percent to 88.8 percent, while in postindependence Artzi kibbutzim the respective 1973 and 1977 rates were 83.1 and 78.6 percent. In the case of the Kibbutz Artzi, many more votes went to Shelli, a left-wing dovish party, than to the DMC. In the new Artzi kibbutzim the Shelli vote reached 8.6 percent.

Political participation in 1977, as measured by voting turnout, remained high (see Table 3–2). The high and low points occurred in the first two elections: in the first Knesset elections in 1949, 86.8 percent of the eligible population voted, compared with 75.1 percent in the second elections in 1951. The second highest turnout was in 1965, 83.0 percent, and the second lowest in 1973, 78.6 percent. In general, voting participation is not associated with levels of modernization, except perhaps among the Bedouin tribes. Their 1977 voting rate was only 64.3 percent, much lower than that of other groups.

A differential voting rate among the Jewish and non-Jewish voters does have political significance, however. In analyzing the reasons for nonvoting in 1973, Avneri found that very few Jews abstained for political reasons; that is, their reasons were generally technical in nature—illness, improper registration, lack of identification, and so on.[3] Among non-Jews, nonvoting was most often a deliberate choice; 54.6 percent gave purposeful abstention as the reason for their not voting, compared with 12.8 percent of the sample of Jewish nonvoters.

In sum, voting rates are high for all groups within the society. Since much of the nonvoting among Jews occurred for technical reasons, the effective rate of participation is much higher. Among non-Jews, nonvoting often has political significance. But even in Arab cities, where protest is most strongly felt and the antiestablishment New Communist list (Rakah) won 70.8 percent of the vote, the turnout was 77.4 percent.

In summary, while the Likud improved in 1977 over its 1973 performance, its gains were not uniform. Highly educated, upper-class Alignment defectors of European background tended to shift to the DMC, while those of Asian or African extraction tended to shift to the Likud. The floating vote is revealed by the data from the survey conducted after the election (see Table 3–3). In fact, the very high rate of voting change from one election to another was unique in the 1977 election. According to research reported elsewhere, between 1965 and 1969 about a quarter of the population changed its vote; between 1969 and 1973 about a third did so; and between 1973 and 1977, half.[4] Most of the shifts occurred among those who had supported the Alignment in 1973. Of these (44.5 percent of the sample), less than half voted for the Alignment again in 1977, with 20 percent

[3] Uri Avneri, "Voter Participation in the 1973 Elections," in Asher Arian, ed., *The Elections in Israel—1973* (Jerusalem: Jerusalem Academic Press, 1975), pp. 203–218.

[4] Asher Arian, "Were the 1973 Elections in Israel Critical?" *Comparative Politics* (October 1975), pp. 152–165.

TABLE 3–3

The Stable and Floating Votes, 1973 to 1977

(in percentages of the sample; stable votes in italics)

	Vote in 1977						
Vote in 1973	Likud	Align-ment	DMC	Reli-gious	Other	No answer	*Total, 1973*
Likud	*19*	0.5	2	0	0.5	2	24
Alignment	9	*20*	8	0.5	1	6	44.5
Religious	2	0	0	*5*	0	0	7
Other	1	0	2	0	*1*	2	6
No vote	5	0.5	2	0.5	0.5	4	12.5
No answer	0	0	0	0	0	*6*	6
Total, 1977	36	21	14	6	3	20	100.0 (N=465)

Source: See Table 3–1. The 1977 data are from the June survey.

going to the Likud and 18 percent to the DMC. The 1973 Likud voters remained loyal on the whole, with some 8 percent supporting the DMC in 1977. Those who did not vote in 1973 gave the Likud 40 percent of their votes, the DMC 16 percent, and the Alignment a scant 4 percent. Two-thirds of the DMC's support among people who had voted in 1973 came from former Labor supporters, and almost 30 percent of the Likud's came from the same source.

Once the plunge had been taken, however, and the Likud came to power, the populace readjusted quickly. Six weeks after the elections, 12 percent expressed deep dissatisfaction with the election results, but almost two-thirds were satisfied or very satisfied. Moreover, had the elections been "replayed" six weeks after they actually occurred, the Likud would have increased its strength among the sample by four percentage points, the Alignment by one, and the DMC would have lost two. What had seemed so startling six weeks earlier was quickly accepted.

The Histadrut elections held on June 21 produced results more similar to what had been known in the past. The Labor-Mapam Alignment retained its absolute majority, winning 55 percent of the vote. This was a much better showing than five weeks earlier in the Knesset elections, but three percentage points below what had been achieved in 1973. The Likud gained some eight percentage points over its 1973 Histadrut showing, winning nearly 30 percent of the vote, and the DMC ran a poor third with 6 percent.

The five weeks between the Knesset elections and the Histadrut elections brought about a reversal of some of the trends discussed earlier. The Alignment retained almost all of its Knesset voters and in addition won many votes in the Histadrut elections from those who had supported the Likud and the DMC in the Knesset elections. Among Histadrut members who had voted for the Likud in the Knesset election, less than half voted for the Likud in the Histadrut elections, while a quarter either voted for the DMC or avoided the dilemma by abstaining. The DMC figures are even more striking: a third again voted DMC, another third Alignment, with the remainder abstaining.

The Histadrut election results gave back to the Alignment a feeling of power and hope and ratified the transition to a competitive two-plus party system. The Alignment's Histadrut victory and Begin's impressive beginning as prime minister probably made the Knesset election results more acceptable in the minds of many and thus facilitated the relatively rapid adjustment to this major shift of power in Israeli politics.

Political Dominance

The French political scientist Maurice Duverger wrote that "when a left-wing party becomes dominant, its appetite for revolution is dulled. . . . The dominant party wears itself out in office, it loses its vigor, its arteries harden. . . . Every domination bears within itself the seeds of its own destruction."[5] This is an apt description of the plight of the Labor party in the 1970s. It is appropriate to consider Labor's decline, after so long in power, a major factor in the Likud's ascension to power. There is, of course, a danger in presenting a circular argument: the Alignment lost because its dominance ended and its dominance ended because it lost. But in fact both parts of this statement were true in 1977. Technically, if dominance is considered winning a plurality in the elections, controlling the major power resources in the society, and being the pivot in coalition formation, then clearly dominance ended for the Labor party as a result of the 1977 elections.

The decline of Labor in terms of electoral support, leadership, and ideology, however, was a much more drawn out affair. A machine party heavily strengthened by the fact that it had been the major

---

[5] Maurice Duverger, *Political Parties* (New York: Wiley, 1961), p. 312.

force in the efforts to absorb new immigrants before independence and during the early years of statehood, the Labor party provided the leadership of the country and controlled huge amounts of the import capital that flowed into the country through loans, grants, and investment. Certainly in the early periods many individuals were materially dependent on organizations controlled by the party functionaries. Over time, as some functions were nationalized and processes rationalized, direct material dependence may have decreased, but a sense of psychological dependence prevailed. The party was associated with the state's achievements and its leadership with the state. Its ideology, its value system, predominated. The folk hero of the society—once the kibbutz member, later the jet fighter pilot—was likely to be associated in the public mind with the labor movement.

In a very real sense the Yom Kippur War of 1973 was a turning point in Israel's political history. First, much of the psychological dependence on Labor which had sustained the party for twenty-five years was shattered. The 1973 elections, held weeks after the ceasefire, did not reflect the extent of the trauma of Yom Kippur. In 1977, however, after an incubation period of four years, the sense of dissatisfaction with the ruling party erupted into widespread defection from traditional support for the Alignment. This defection was felt on an organizational level as well. First, prominent Labor leaders such as Meir Amit and Aharon Yariv joined the DMC before the election. The former held the post of chairman of Koor, the Histadrut's leading industrial concern, when he joined the DMC; the latter, a former Labor minister, resigned his Labor party seat in the Knesset to become a member of the DMC. Second, many of the votes that allowed the DMC its impressive showing of fifteen Knesset seats came from the Alignment. As mentioned in the previous section, two-thirds of the DMC voters who had voted in 1973 had supported the Alignment. Third, the Labor Alignment had difficulties in gearing up to a full-scale campaign. The Histadrut organization was tardy in throwing in its wholehearted support, the local activists who as a rule are especially active in local elections were less active since it was decided to hold the Knesset elections independently of the municipal elections, and strong organizational whips, exemplified by Pinchas Sapir and Avraham Ofer in the past, did not emerge in these elections.

The underlying dilemma of the Israeli political scene during the period of the 1977 elections was the crisis of political succession the parties were going through. The Likud's crisis was more moderate than those of the other parties because of the continuing presence of Begin, the undisputed leader of the Herut movement and the

Likud, but even there, challenges had been posed in the past by Shmuel Tamir, Ariel Sharon, and Ezer Weizmann. The National Religious party succeeded in ousting its political boss, Yitzhak Raphael, thereby strengthening the leaders of the Youth Faction, Zevulun Hammer and Yehuda Ben-Meir. And the emergence of the DMC can be viewed as an exercise in recruiting new political leaders from among the economic, military, and university elites. Most acute of all was the crisis that faced the Labor party as it entered the second generation of independence. The founding fathers of the second and third *aliyot* (waves of immigration in the first quarter of the century) had not adequately prepared a political cadre to carry on, and after the 1973 war when many of the old-timers left the scene a leadership vacuum was created. It was partially filled by recruiting individuals who had reached the peak of the military power pyramid and by "parachuting" them to the apex of the political pyramid. This led to inevitable conflict between those who had had military careers and those who had devoted themselves to political careers.

Since the Yom Kippur War, a fascinating process of differentiation had begun to develop in the ruling elite of the Labor party. Those cabinet members who had primary responsibility for security and foreign affairs (Rabin, Peres, Yigal Allon, Israel Galili, and earlier Aharon Yariv) tended to be from military backgrounds *and not* historically associated with Mapai—the party of Ben-Gurion, Eshkol, and Golda Meir. Some of those who dealt with internal matters, on the other hand, had been dependent on the Mapai party machine at various points in their political careers (Yehoshua Rabinowitz, Avraham Ofer, Asher Yadlin, and Moshe Baram). A sense of common purpose never developed between these two groups. Rabin's leadership failed to reconcile conflicting interests, styles, and backgrounds. The party's lack of accepted leadership was the backdrop against which the successive acts of the political drama were played out— the competition between Rabin and Peres for the right to head the list (Rabin won), Rabin's resignation from first on the list because of his personal foreign currency problems, and Peres's ascension to first place a month before the election. The crisis of leadership succession was symptomatic of Labor's loss of political dominance.

These themes are revealed in the public's assessment of the various arguments for supporting a given party (see Table 3–4). On the whole, the Alignment leaders were perceived as experienced and yet incapable of dealing with social and economic problems and corruption. The war-scare element seems to have hurt the Likud but was partially balanced by the desire for change in leadership and for

TABLE 3-4

Voters' Reasons for Supporting the Major Parties, March 1977
(in percentages)

Reason	Alignment	Likud	DMC
Experience of leadership[a]	60	58	60
Increase chance for peace	50	29	34
Good leaders	49	40	46
Flexibility/firmness in peace negotiations[b]	48	48	31
Internal democracy	37	37	57
For electoral reform	36	—	57
Least unattractive party	36	29	31
Deal best with economic and social problems	29	42	39
Energetic leaders	28	33	50
Will deal effectively with corruption	28	45	46
Will provide me with job assistance	9	9	5
Will help me solve problems (housing, and so on)	9	8	5
Alignment brought about corruption[c]	—	45	30
Fear of Likud's extremism	41	—	—
DMC is like the Alignment, so why change?	30	—	—
Alignment leaders cannot be believed	—	36	—
Likud and DMC lack experienced leadership	28	—	—
Alignment and DMC lack clear foreign policy	—	30	—
DMC can bring about real change	—	—	35
Likud and Alignment cannot improve things	—	—	28
Alignment and Likud are basically identical	—	—	17

Note: Entries are percentages of the sample who thought the stated reason was "very persuasive" or "persuasive."

[a] For the Alignment, "experienced leadership"; for Likud and DMC, "give new leadership a chance."

[b] For the Alignment, "will show flexibility"; for Likud, "will show firmness"; for DMC, "policy on territories will bring peace."

[c] For DMC, "Alignment and Likud leaders brought about corruption."

Source: See Table 3-2.

a clear, firm foreign policy. It was the DMC that had the most attractive image: energetic leaders, a program of change and democracy, and a commitment to dealing with internal problems and corruption. This was precisely the image that was most likely to succeed among a relatively well educated electorate. And indeed the DMC's success was selective largely on class lines. The dominant Alignment represented stability, economic and military success in the past—and substantial problems in the present. Dominance ended and the Alignment was eclipsed in the 1977 elections.

Ideological Dominance

An important characteristic of a dominant party is that its ideas are in tune with the times; its values and ideology dominate. Over time, it is likely that the ideas of the dominant party will become frozen and allegiance to them hollow, automatic. Passion drains out of politics and pragmatism replaces it.

A good example of this process is the handling of the territories taken in the Six-Day War of 1967. The establishment position had been twofold: willingness to make territorial concessions for real peace (or progress toward that end) and selective settlement in the territories at the same time. The governments of Meir and Rabin tended to emphasize different aspects of this policy, depending on the conditions that existed and the audience being addressed. Settlements in the territories were largely conducted by Alignment-affiliated groups with government approval. Settlements launched outside government policy—such as Kiryat Arba or Kadum near Nablus—were initiated by the religious-nationalist Gush Emunim group and ultimately won begrudging government support or acquiescence.

The point is that the fervor of implementation passed from the establishment groups to those who perceived themselves as outside the establishment, though there were no ultimate policy differences between their positions. A considerable national consensus developed around the hard line. The only real debate between (and sometimes within) the major camps was when it would be tactically advisable to mention territorial concessions. The major dove position in Israel is not "bring the boys home by Passover," but rather a willingness to concede the possibility of territorial concessions in exchange for certain political and diplomatic moves on the part of the Arabs.

The country had moved to the right. Public opinion was in firm support of the hawk position by the spring of 1977 (see Table 3–5). In March and again in June some two-thirds of a survey sample

TABLE 3–5

OPINION ON THE FUTURE OF THE WEST BANK, BY PARTY IDENTIFICATION,
MARCH AND JUNE 1977

(in percentages)

| | March 1977 | | | | | |
| | Party Identification[a] | | | | | June 1977 |
Opinion	Likud	Align-ment	DMC	No answer	Total	Total
Return nothing	63	30	23	42	42	43
Return a small part	19	27	21	25	22	23
Return a certain part	10	30	29	21	21	21
Return almost all	3	8	18	5	7	5
Return all	5	6	8	6	7	8
N	(289)	(321)	(205)	(366)	(1341)	(447)

[a] Figures for the small parties are not included.
SOURCE: See Table 3–1.

supported the hard-line positions of returning nothing or very little. This varied from 82 percent of Likud supporters through 67 percent of those who did not report a vote preference and 57 percent of Alignment voters, to 44 percent of DMC adherents. This distribution was stable before and after the elections. It had become legitimate to perceive the Likud's leadership as a viable alternative for the country since its policy positions were similar to the government's and to public opinion. In the past, "fear" of the Likud had persuaded many voters to remain faithful to the dominant Labor party. In 1977, re-vulsion against the Alignment and the growing acceptability of the Likud changed its fortunes and turned it from perennial opposition into the leader of the government.

This point can be reinforced by considering the role that public opinion has traditionally played in Israeli foreign policy. Rather than being molded by opinion, foreign policy in Israel generates public opinion. Israelis have displayed a large measure of deference to the leadership and have been malleable in their opinions in support of that leadership on these issues.

Deference does not mean uninformed or uninterested acceptance of policies and decisions. On the contrary, what makes this deference remarkable is that the general public is highly interested in foreign and defense matters. All newspapers give them extensive coverage, both as news stories and in sections devoted to opinion and commentary. Moreover, the Israeli public is relatively well informed about foreign and defense matters. Discrete diplomatic moves, as well as political or bureaucratic debates, usually find their way into the press. The alertness and sensitivity of the public and the small size and integrated character of Israeli society facilitate the rapid circulation of news, political gossip, and rumors. Moreover, foreign and defense matters are the subject of a constant public debate, often lively and sometimes also bitter, in the press, in political speeches, and in the Knesset. Thus, deference does not mean lack of interest, lack of emotional involvement, or lack of criticism.

Public opinion in Israel tends to react to situations rather than to shape them. In this manner, deference supports centralization. This is seen in popularity polls about politicians. Although a politician's career is determined in the party's inner sanctum and although public opinion has little influence over the matter, the public has been supportive and even permissive regarding party decisions. Before he assumes a post and after he relinquishes it, the officeholder's popularity is usually much lower than during his tenure of office. For example, in the March survey 29 percent wanted Rabin to be prime minister, 20 percent wanted Begin, and 18 percent wanted Peres; after the elections, 47 percent wanted Begin to be prime minister, 13 percent Peres, and 11 percent Rabin. Public opinion tends to flow in the direction of the incumbent leader.

Israeli public opinion is quite malleable when leaders of stature attempt to change its course. The results of the opinion polls tend to change in accordance with the arguments of the dominant leadership. In the Israeli situation, this ability to appeal to and win the support of the population is a characteristic of the leadership that the dominant-party type of democracy has fostered. But politics is played by the party elite, and the populace is rarely brought into the action. Public opinion enters the political arena, on the whole, only when it is mobilized by one of the political actors. Since there are very few points of access to the decision-making process, the role of public opinion is limited and few appeals are made to the public. Leaders lead.

In light of this it is easier to understand the role that foreign policy played in the 1977 campaign. The issue was under the surface at all times and even emerged occasionally, but on the whole the campaign did not center on a public debate over foreign affairs. When asked about the most pressing issue the government should deal with,

TABLE 3–6

SURVEY FINDINGS ON THE MOST IMPORTANT PROBLEM FACING ISRAEL,
MAY 1973–MAY 1977
(in percentages)

| | Most Important Problem | | | | | |
	Se-curity	The econ-omy	Social in-equal-ity	Peace	N	All Respond-ents
Date of Survey						
May 1973	41	18	14	8	1,939	
November 1973	54	5	1	37	642	
December 1973	44	2	4	44	530	
March 1977	25	38	13	9	1,372	
April 1977	35	31	13	10	497	
May 1977	27	32	12	11	485	
Respondent's voting intention, March 1977						
Alignment	33	30	13	12		25
Likud	24	43	12	9		21
DMC	14	52	18	5		15
Undecided/no answer	27	37	13	9		28
All respondents	25	38	13	9		

NOTE: The survey question was "What is the most important problem facing the country [that] the government should be taking care of now?" Neither the columns nor the rows add to 100 percent, since only those problems and only those parties most often mentioned are reported here.

SOURCE: See Table 3–1.

38 percent of the March sample said the economy, 25 percent security, 13 percent the social gap, and 9 percent peace (see Table 3–6). Two weeks before the election, the figures were similar, although different from the April 1977 findings and the 1973 polls.

Internal problems and a very strong desire for change seemed to dominate the campaign in 1977. The Alignment voters most closely replicated the patterns of the past by assigning to security the number one place. For other groups, and especially for the DMC voters, internal issues predominated.

The secondary role of foreign policy as an issue and the de-

TABLE 3-7

Support for the Major Parties' Foreign Policy Positions, by Party Identification, March and June 1977

(in percentages)

| | Party Identification | | | | |
Survey Response	Likud	Align-ment	DMC	No answer	Total
March 1977					
Alignment's position	19	93	75	57	61
Likud's position	76	4	15	26	30
The left's position	0	1	5	3	2
No answer	5	2	5	14	7
All respondents	24	28	17	31	(N=1,217)
June 1977					
Alignment's position	8	84	60	41	38
Likud's position	91	9	29	42	53
The left's position	1	1	2	2	3
No answer	0	6	10	15	6
All respondents	39	23	16	22	(N=418)

NOTE: The survey question was: "Whose position are you closer to in foreign policy and defense matters?"
SOURCE: See Table 3-1.

ference shown by the population toward the leadership become clearer when Table 3-7 is examined. The March 1977 results are almost identical to the results obtained after the 1973 election.[6] The Alignment's position prevailed in foreign policy and defense matters. After the election results were known and the government had presented its program, the results flip-flopped. Support for the Likud's position jumped twenty-three points between March and June and the Alignment fell twenty-three points. Nothing substantial had happened in foreign affairs except for the changing of the guard. And yet the flow of public support was to the winning Likud's position. The erosion of the Alignment's dominance is evident in each voting group: even among Likud voters the Alignment enjoyed 19 percent support before the election, while afterwards only 8 percent of the Likud voters supported that position. In sum, the broad national consensus which had developed on foreign policy had a boomerang

[6] Arian, "Were the 1973 Elections in Israel Critical?" p. 163.

effect for the Alignment. When the Alignment was in power, that consensus was identified with the government and reinforced its power. But once the Alignment lost power, that same national consensus accrued to the benefit of the Likud, and many people identified with the new leadership much as they had identified with the old leadership in the past. The distinctions between the major parties on these issues were blurred, and this helped increase the legitimacy of the Likud both before and after the elections. The lack of perceived differences between the Likud and the Alignment was another factor which worked against the Alignment; the masses of voters were willing to give the Likud a chance. The pattern of deference of the population for its leadership transferred legitimacy to the Likud once it was in power and thus shattered completely the last vestiges of the Alignment's ideological dominance.

The Emergence of Class Politics?

The sharp turnabout in political fortunes which resulted from the 1977 elections is further illuminated by careful study of the social bases of electoral support in previous elections and by the pace and direction of demographic change within the electorate. For the Jewish population, comprising some 90 percent of the electorate, voting behavior before 1977 could best be understood in terms of Israel's dominant-party system. The 1973 elections (held two months after the traumatic Yom Kippur War) brought about an acceleration of those processes working within the society to erode the base of voting support of the Alignment. In 1977 the dominance of Labor was shattered, leaving in its wake a much more crystallized political system.

The dominant party—formerly Mapai, now Labor—had been identified with the epoch of independence and had remained in virtual control of the major decisions and key personnel appointments for half a century. No less important, the labor movement had been successful in imposing its values on the society as a whole. As party and movement values came to permeate the society, the distinction between party and state was often blurred. Achievements of state accrued to the benefit of the party.

The Labor party, the pivot of all government coalitions until 1977, became entrenched in office. Its socialist values notwithstanding, it became conservative in nature. It was anxious to preserve the gains it had won for the state, for the citizenry, and for its functionaries as well. Many of the revolutionary socialist ideals which were part of

Labor's legacy became empty maxims; pressures on public policy makers often led in another direction.

As a whole, support for the dominant party came from the more conservative elements in society. These included the elderly more than the young, women more than men, and the middle education and income categories. Labor was strongest in the category that contained the median respondent.

Israel's dominant party found support among all groups, but especially among those who identified with the period in which the party had risen to its peak, the period that culminated in independence. All the projects undertaken by the Jews in Palestine—immigration, working the land, security—were highlighted by the achieving of independence. After the founding of the state, these undertakings continued, sometimes within different organizational settings and institutional arrangements, but with much of the same symbolism and ideological justification. Anyone who had lived through the winning of independence in Israel was likely to identify with the dominant party. Jews who had immigrated to Israel before independence and immediately thereafter supported the Alignment heavily. The rate fell off for those who arrived after 1955 and for the Israeli-born.

Much of the program and appeal of the dominant Labor party in the independence phase must be seen in the light of the social and political realities which the Labor leadership had known in Eastern Europe in the first decades of the twentieth century. The farther one was from this reality, the more hazy the values of this period became. The precarious position of the Jew, the restrictions on his economic and political activity, the narrow range of occupations open to him, the spread of nationalist feeling, the undermining of traditional religious belief and behavior—all these led to the creation of the socialist-Zionist experiment. The Labor leadership, almost exclusively of East European origin, developed a party and an ideology that answered the needs of the nation as they saw them and experienced them. Likud, on the other hand, bringing to the problems of the country a different emphasis and a different ideological idiom, found its support for the most part among different groups. The Alignment was notably successful among the earlier immigrants and among those born in Europe and America. Likud appealed more to the native-born than to any of the immigrant groups, and more to those born in Asia and Africa than to the European and American-born. The symbols the Alignment used to evoke the epoch of independence and nation building were more effective among the old than the young, more effective among those who came before independence than among those who

TABLE 3-8

PARTY VOTE, BY EDUCATION AND PLACE OF BIRTH, 1969, 1973, AND 1977
(in percentages)

Level of Education	Place of Birth	N	Align-ment	Gahal	Reli-gious parties[a]	Other
1969						
Elementary or less	Asia-Africa	(179)	55	27	16	2
	Europe-America	(182)	69	10	18	3
	Israel	(63)	53	32	5	11
Through high school	Asia-Africa	(121)	56	27	7	10
	Europe-America	(364)	65	16	11	8
	Israel	(136)	46	28	14	13
More than high school	Asia-Africa	(12)	58	—	25	17
	Europe-America	(148)	58	17	8	18
	Israel	(80)	49	18	15	19
Total		(1,285)	59	20	12	9
1973						
Elementary or less	Asia-Africa	(56)	32	50	14	4
	Europe-America	(85)	55	24	18	3
	Israel	(51)	27	59	14	—
Through high school	Asia-Africa	(74)	38	32	4	26
	Europe-America	(153)	65	24	5	6
	Israel	(176)	43	42	4	11
More than high school	Asia-Africa	(7)	43	29	—	29
	Europe-America	(131)	44	31	10	15
	Israel	(126)	37	37	7	19
Total		(859)	45	35	9	11

TABLE 3–8 Continued

Level of Education	Place of Birth	N	Align-ment	Likud[b]	Reli-gious parties[a]	DMC	Other
1977							
Elemen-tary or less	Asia-Africa	(63)	38	49	5	6	2
	Europe-America	(82)	72	10	12	4	2
	Israel	(42)	21	72	7	—	—
Through high school	Asia-Africa	(104)	34	46	2	15	3
	Europe-America	(176)	43	24	9	22	2
	Israel	(178)	27	47	4	19	3
More than high school	Asia-Africa	(24)	13	33	21	33	—
	Europe-America	(148)	40	17	11	29	3
	Israel	(135)	19	22	13	42	4
Total		(952)	35	32	9	21	3

[a] Includes the National Religious party, Agudat Israel, and Poalei Agudat Israel.
[b] Includes Ariel Sharon's list.
SOURCE: See Table 3–1.

came after independence or were born in Israel, more effective among those born in Europe than among those born in Asia or Africa.

The opposition Likud, of which the right-wing nationalistic Herut (Freedom) movement and the bourgeois Liberal party were the major components, gave the appearance of being broadly based in its electoral support (as was the Alignment). But much of this spread was an effect of the difference between the Liberals and Herut. The Liberals are a bourgeois party that receives most of its support from middle and upper-middle-class merchants and businessmen. Herut, on the other hand, is a party that appeals disproportionately to lower and lower-middle-class workers and to Israelis born in Asia and Africa. And the followers of the Liberal party have higher levels of education than supporters of Herut. Thus, the spread evident for the Likud was the result of several differing tendencies, and it would be misleading to interpret the data from before 1977 as meaning that the Likud was beginning to generate the appeal characteristic of a dominant party.

The support of the Likud came heavily from the young, the Israeli-born, Israelis of Asian-African background, and those with lower education and income levels. Undeniably, many of these social and economic cleavages overlapped with differences in political opinion. To give but one example, the groups that tended to support the Likud also tended to have more hawkish opinions on foreign and defense policy. Those who were older, from European backgrounds, and better educated tended to hold more flexible views.

The religious parties, and especially the National Religious party, received about 10 percent of the vote. They had consistently been coalition partners of the Labor party. The supporters of the National Religious party represent many different types: traditional Jews from Asian-African backgrounds with low income and low educational levels; highly educated intellectuals of European origin; Israeli-born educated youth imbued with religious ideals through formal schooling in state-supported religious schools; a vigorous youth movement connected with the party and integrated with home life. But on the whole, the religious parties were more successful among those with lower levels of education. The picture is more complex when support for the religious parties is correlated with both education and place of origin, as Table 3–8 shows. European-American-born support for the religious parties tends to decrease with educational attainment. Among the Israeli-born, by contrast, support for religious parties increases with education. The pattern for the Asian-African born is harder to ascertain since so few of the respondents in this category had more than a high school education. What is clear, though, is that between the first two categories of educational achievement there is a very sharp decline in support for religious parties among the Asian and African-born as education increases.

The gathering strength of Likud is well documented in Table 3–9 which charts party vote by age over time. The direct relationship between age and Alignment support and the inverse relationship between age and Likud support are remarkably persistent over the three time periods. The oldest group changes its rate of support for the two parties very little, especially between 1973 and 1977. It is in the youngest voting group that the significant change comes about. The Likud, always strongest in this group, proceeds from 36 percent support in 1969 to 44 percent in 1973 and 51 percent by 1977. The

TABLE 3–9

PARTY VOTE BY AGE, 1969, 1973, AND 1977
(in percentages)

Age	N	Align-ment	Likud[a]	Reli-gious parties[b]	Other
1969					
24 and less	(210)	40	36	15	9
25–39	(414)	54	30	9	7
40–49	(272)	61	25	10	4
50 and above	(461)	62	21	14	3
Total	(1,357)	56	27	12	5
1973					
24 and less	(154)	39	44	6	11
25–39	(277)	37	44	7	12
40–49	(135)	48	35	7	10
50 and above	(310)	54	23	13	10
Total	(876)	45	35	9	11

	N	Align-ment	Likud[c]	Reli-gious parties	DMC	Other
1977						
24 and less	(144)	20	51	4	21	4
25–39	(336)	25	34	11	27	3
40–49	(156)	38	29	10	20	3
50 and above	(314)	53	23	8	15	1
Total	(950)	35	32	9	21	3

[a] Includes Gahal, the Free Center, and the State list. They formed the Likud in 1973.
[b] Includes the National Religious party, Agudat Israel, and Poalei Agudat Israel.
[c] Includes Ariel Sharon's list.
SOURCE: See Table 3–1.

Alignment loses more than half of its support in this youngest age group between 1973 and 1977, the same amount that the DMC attracts. The Alignment more clearly than ever can be seen to be the party of the older, more conservative voter; the Likud, the choice of the young; and—interestingly—the DMC, the party of the young adults.

TABLE 3–10

Party Vote by Ethnic Origin, 1969, 1973, and 1977
(in percentages)

Place of Birth	N	Align-ment	Likud[a]	Reli-gious parties[b]	Other
1969					
Asia–Africa	(341)	51	32	12	5
Europe–America	(733)	61	20	12	7
Israel					
Father, Asia–Africa	(73)	49	37	8	6
Father, Europe–America	(172)	48	26	12	14
Father, Israel	(64)	23	47	13	17
Total	(1,383)	55	26	12	7
1973					
Asia–Africa	(125)	39	43	9	9
Europe–America	(382)	53	26	10	11
Israel					
Father, Asia–Africa	(88)	40	47	8	8
Father, Europe–America	(194)	38	39	7	16
Father, Israel	(78)	40	44	8	8
Total	(867)	45	35	9	11

	N	Align-ment	Likud[c]	Reli-gious	Other	DMC
1977						
Asia–Africa	(191)	32	46	5	15	2
Europe–America	(406)	48	19	11	20	2
Israel						
Father, Asia–Africa	(111)	23	65	4	8	1
Father, Europe–America	(177)	23	23	11	39	5
Father, Israel	(68)	25	43	9	19	4
Total	(953)	35	32	9	21	3

[a] Includes Gahal, the Free Center, and the State list. They formed the Likud in 1973.
[b] Includes the National Religious party, Agudat Israel, and Poalei Agudat Israel.
[c] Includes Ariel Sharon's list.
Source: See Table 3–1.

If familiar voting patterns are generated by age and accentuated over time, the same is true for ethnicity (see Table 3–10). The Likud did not attain its relative success by drawing off votes from all social strata. It increased its share of the vote disproportionately in those strata in which it was already relatively successful. Conversely, Alignment strongholds (in demographic terms) were much less susceptible to Likud gains. Both the oldest age group and the European-American-born group continued to give about half of their votes to the Alignment in 1977.

The demographic composition of the electorate is an important key to the upsurge of the Likud and offers us an insight into trends likely in the future, assuming that patterns which held in the past will continue. At the time of independence, well over half the population was of European origin; thirty years later most Jews in the country were of Asian or African birth (including in this group those born in Israel; see Table 3–11). In the first generation of independence, many of these Asian-African immigrants supported the dominant Alignment as did their European neighbors. In the second generation, however, support patterns shifted. Native-born Israelis of Asian-African fathers were more likely to vote Likud than were their fathers. The Alignment managed to retain the support of the European-born but not that of their children, who were more likely to support the DMC in 1977. Age and ethnic origin reinforced each other to the benefit of the Likud and to the detriment of the Alignment.

Another clue to the unfolding trends of the future is evident

TABLE 3–11

JEWISH POPULATION OF ISRAEL, BY CONTINENT OF BIRTH, SELECTED YEARS, 1948–1976
(in percentages)

Place of Birth	1948	1954	1968	1976
Israel	35.4	31.4	44.0	50.9
Asia	8.1	19.0	12.8	10.4
Africa	1.7	7.9	14.4	11.7
Europe-America	54.8	41.7	28.8	27.0
Total population	716,678	1,526,009	2,434,832	2,959,400

SOURCE: *Statistical Abstract of Israel—1969* and *Abstract—1976*, Jerusalem, Central Bureau of Statistics, 1969, p. 44; and 1976, Table ii/18.

from the differences in birth rates among the various groups. Not only is the median age of the Asian-African groups lower (which in itself would indicate that more children are being born to this group than to others), but the birth rate in 1975 of Asian-African mothers was 1.83, as compared with 1.37 for European-American mothers and 1.49 for Israeli-born mothers. It should be noted that the birth rates for the three groups have declined since 1951 from 3.06, 1.54, and 1.73 respectively.[7]

The argument is, then, that above and beyond the special political circumstances of 1977, those groups that registered greatest support for the Likud in the election are steadily increasing and thereby accounting for a larger share of the electorate, while groups traditionally supportive of the Alignment are shrinking. The European-American-born population has traditionally been a bastion of Alignment support, and it is the group that is most quickly passing from the scene. It is clear that the ongoing support which this group, with its median age of 52.4, can provide for the Alignment is short term. In the postelection survey, this group reported giving 30 percent of its support to the Alignment, 24 percent to the Likud, and 13 percent to the DMC, with 24 percent refraining from divulging its vote. The population born in Asia (median age 42) and in Africa (median age 35) is younger than that born in Europe and America and tends to support the Likud much more heavily. This was true in previous elections and was strikingly evident in the 1977 elections as well. The Asian-African-born supported the Likud by a two-to-one margin in the June survey: 43 percent Likud, 21 percent Alignment, and 6 percent DMC, with 20 percent not reporting. The same two-to-one margin held for the youngest demographic group (Israeli born, median age 13.3), with the DMC showing an impressive 19 percent among the Israeli-born.

The implications of these differential support levels can be refined by using the large survey conducted in March 1977. A caveat is in order since the March sample showed the Alignment winning while the smaller June sample was closer to the actual voting results. But since we are interested in relative support rates we can turn to Table 3–12 which considers the correlation between continent of birth, period of immigration, and intended party vote. The largest, youngest population—the Israeli-born—supported the Alignment least heavily and the DMC most strongly. A huge part of this group has yet to enter the electorate, but if we project the rates of support of the

[7] *Statistical Abstract of Israel 1976*, Jerusalem, Central Bureau of Statistics, 1976, Table iii/21.

sample to the entire group it follows that the 1977 elections may be a harbinger of continued Likud success.

The group born in Asia and Africa has a median age between those of the other two country-of-origin groups and the highest rate of support for the Likud. The Alignment does best among those who immigrated earlier and the DMC among those whose immigration came later in the state's development. Among the European-American-born the Alignment does best. As indicated above, this group is the oldest and almost all of its members already vote.

Many of these patterns can be validated by considering the vote in the army. There the Likud did very well, winning 46 percent of the vote, compared with 22 percent for the Alignment and 16 percent for the DMC; in 1973 the figures for the Likud and the Alignment in the army were 41 and 40 percent, respectively. The Likud held its own in this predominantly young male group, the Alignment lost almost half of its strength.[8] The Likud's increase can be explained in terms of demographic change; the Alignment's loss must be seen as a political rout.

If present trends persist, the Likud may well be strengthened by the coming of age of individuals from groups which have historically been more supportive of the Likud. As more of the electorate is made up of Israeli-born voters whose fathers were born in Africa or Asia, the Likud's strength might well increase. But a countervailing force must also be noted. Increased education has been shown to moderate this tendency (see Table 3–8). The tendency of the Israeli-born of Asian-African background to support the Likud decreases as education increases. This same effect is in evidence for the Alignment supporters of European birth. Increased education tends to lessen support for both the Alignment and the Likud in their respective ethnic strongholds; increased education tended to be associated with voting for the small "other parties" in 1969 and 1973 and for the DMC in 1977, for which the support of highly educated Israeli-born voters was especially large.

A most important feature of the 1977 elections was the crystallizing of a tendency toward class politics in Israel. In the past, the dominance of the Labor party had precluded this possibility. The Labor party had won support from all strata, although its major strength was in the middle class. In previous elections much of the Likud's support came from a combination of lower-class and upper-middle-class voters, although most of these supported the Alignment.

---

[8] *Ha'aretz*, May 22, 1977, for the 1977 results and *Ma'ariv*, January 7, 1974, for 1973.

TABLE 3-12

Jewish Population of Israel, by Continent of Birth, Period of Immigration, Median Age, and Rate of Support for Three Major Parties

Place of Birth	Population, 1976 (in thousands)	Age, 1976 Median	% below 15	Sample[a] (N)	Likud	Alignment	DMC
Born in Israel							
Father born in Israel	305.5	8.5	68	(68)	38%	25%	19%
Father born in Asia	388.3	14.0	53 ⎫	(111)	62	21	8
Father born in Africa	330.0	10.0	70 ⎭				
Father born in Europe or America	482.5	20.1	37	(177)	22	22	39
Born in Asia or Africa, Immigrated							
1947 and before	141.0	Asia, 54.6 ⎫ Africa, 42.3 ⎭	0	(27)	48	37	7
1948–54	303.0	Asia, 42.1 ⎫ Africa, 35.0 ⎭	0	(101)	41	35	15
1955–64	134.4	Asia, 33.2 ⎫ Africa, 28.2 ⎭	6	(42)	43	29	17
1965 and after	86.0	Asia, 27.6 ⎫ Africa, 26.9 ⎭	17	(16)	56	13	19

Party Preference of Sample[a] comprises the Likud, Alignment, and DMC columns.

Born in Europe or America,
Immigrated

1947 and before	209.3	61.7	0	(69)	19	44	19
1948–54	240.4	52.9	0	(143)	14	50	22
1955–60	73.7	48.3	0	(26)	15	50	12
1961–64	70.5	47.6	3	(17)	12	47	41
1965 and after	186.5 {1965–71 37.7 1972 + 32.0}		18	(46)	24	39	20

[a] This is the March 1977 sample; 943 respondents indicated a party vote decision.

SOURCE: Population data are based on *Statistical Abstract of Israel 1976*, Jerusalem, Central Bureau of Statistics, 1976, Table ii/19. For source of survey data, see Table 3–1.

In the 1977 elections the Alignment's historical dominance was shattered and in its wake a major realignment of forces occurred. Many of the middle and upper-middle-class groups which had supported the Alignment abandoned their past voting behavior and revised the profile of the Israeli voter. The flow of middle-class voters and those of Asian and African background to the Likud was accelerated while many native Israelis of European parents and those with more than a high school education voted DMC. Age was directly related with Alignment support and youth with Likud voting, while the middle age groups supported the DMC more heavily than other age cohorts. Ethnicity was also related to' voting, with those of Asian and African background more likely to support the Likud, Europeans the Alignment, and the Israeli-born—especially those whose fathers were born in Europe—the DMC. Low income was related to Likud voting (although high income was also evident because of the presence of the Liberal party in the Likud), middle income to Alignment support, and high income to DMC preference. The data generated by level of education show high levels associated with the DMC, low levels predominantly with the Alignment, and middle levels with the Likud.

The Likud succeeded in adding substantial numbers of middle-class voters to its high-low class coalition in order to win the election. The DMC failed to penetrate deeply classes other than those represented by its Israeli-born elite leadership. The Alignment slipped on all fronts but held on most successfully to the older, European-born, less educated supporter. This situation raises fascinating social and political questions regarding Israel's future. Will the Likud be able to formulate policies that will satisfy its diverse supporters? Will the lower-class "outs" receive a larger share of the economic pie or will upper-middle-class demands forestall more comprehensive social welfare policies? Perhaps domestic policies will be relegated to second-class status as foreign policy matters dominate. If so, for how long? Will the DMC, whose members wish to play an active role in social and welfare policy, be able to expand their base of support to the classes they wish to serve? Will the Labor party be able to re-establish its hegemony over the working class now that it is in opposition in the Knesset and in control of the Histadrut? Will it be able to rejuvenate itself, attract the young and the Asian-African-born while retaining the allegiance of the old and the European-born? The answers to these questions will determine the direction of Israeli politics in the years to come.

More than governmental control passed to the Likud in May 1977. The atrophy of the Alignment's dominance changed the basic nature of political arrangements and assumptions. Political and ideo-logical dominance had skewed the political system to the point that many could not conceive of rule without the ruling party. In 1977 the very foundations of Israel's democratic structure were tested and found to be solid. Power bases, careers, and support patterns were all smashed on that fateful day in May. The future was strewn with question marks, but the past had been resolutely left behind.

4

The Likud

Benjamin Akzin

A Composite Party

Like most political groupings active on Israel's contemporary scene, the Likud (Hebrew for "gathering"), is the product of a complicated process of splits and amalgamations among diverse elements. In its present form, which crystallized late in 1976 and early in 1977, with a further change occurring immediately after the Knesset elections in May of the latter year, the Likud is a parliamentary bloc, a combination of several parties rather than a single party. The component parties are more than mere wings of opinion; they insist on preserving their several organizational structures and on emphasizing their distinct viewpoints and interests. This feature is obvious whenever it is necessary to formulate a common platform, make up joint lists of candidates for legislative and municipal elections, and decide on the Likud's representation in the cabinet, the committees of the legislature, municipal offices, and other positions of public importance. In this respect, Likud roughly resembles Maarach, the main political force in Israel prior to the elections of May 17, 1977, which is also a bloc of political parties that embraces varying shades of opinion.

Because of this composite character of the Likud, the surest way to understand it is to look into the origins and views of the bloc's individual components. These are, as of the time of writing and in the order of their size in the Knesset, Herut, the Liberals, La'am, and Achdut.

The Herut. The Herut (Hebrew for "freedom") movement is a political party that was formed at the time of Israel's emergence as an independent state in 1948 by the leaders of the Irgun Tsevaï Leumi (National Military Organization, also known by its Hebrew acronym,

Etzel), one of the three Zionist underground organizations that operated in Palestine during the years of British rule. Menachem Begin, head of the Irgun since 1942, became Herut's leader and has retained this position ever since, eventually becoming the country's prime minister in June 1977. The Irgun, formed in the 1930s by dissidents from the Hagana (Hebrew for "defense"), the original Jewish underground movement, was in its turn based on the political views of the Zionist-Revisionist wing of the Zionist movement. Most members of that movement, including its youth organization Betar, as well as most members of Irgun, joined Herut.[1]

---

[1] Initially the split between Irgun and Hagana centered on the manner of reacting to Arab attacks on the Jewish population. While Hagana held that activities ought to be limited to defending Jewish settlements and neighborhoods, Irgun demanded counterattacks as well. In 1938, when more of European Jewry felt themselves threatened by the expansion of the Third Reich and the British government sharpened its anti-Zionist stand, Irgun inaugurated a large-scale "illegal" movement of Jewish refugees into the country and began isolated acts of armed rebellion against the British. At the outbreak of World War II, Irgun suspended its anti-British activities and even cooperated with British authorities. On this issue a more radical group known as Lehi (acronym for Lohamei Herut Israel— Fighters for Israel's Freedom), under the leadership of Yaïr Stern, split with the Irgun. In 1945–1948, Irgun resumed its anti-British rebellion on a large scale, occasionally in cooperation with, but more often in opposition to, Hagana.

The Zionist-Revisionist movement, founded in 1923–1925 by Vladimir Jabotinsky, took the view that, as time passed, Arab and British opposition to Zionism would increase. To forestall that danger, it demanded a rapid Jewish mass immigration into Palestine and a more insistent stand in facing the British government. To secure Jewish settlers until such time as they became the majority of the country's population and the Jewish state could be founded, the Revisionists demanded that Jewish military and police units be formed, so that the settlers would not depend for their physical security on British manpower. To broaden the country's absorptive capacity for the immigrants, they asked for larger opportunities for private enterprise. To strengthen Jewish unity during the difficult interim period, they demanded that class differences be deemphasized. In all these respects they differed from the cautious World Zionist Executive led by Professor Haïm Weizmann, and from the labor wing within the Zionist movement, which preferred a slower pace of settlement as long as it promised to lead to a predominantly socialist society. After Hitler's accession to power in Germany and the consequent danger to European Jewry, the Revisionists became more insistent in their demands. While some groups in Zionism began to waver in the twenties and thirties on the goal of a Jewish state, the Revisionists stood firm at all times on that issue. Opposed in principle to the excision of Transjordan from the area of the Jewish National Home and the future Jewish state, they vigorously opposed all plans for a further partition of the country. Jabotinsky, the initiator of the Jewish Legion within the British army in World War I and subsequently an officer in one of the legion's batallions, served as the movement's charismatic leader until his death in 1940. To this day, Herut and related groups are often referred to as the Jabotinsky Movement. See J. B. Schechtman and Y. Benari, *History of the Revisionist Movement*, vol. 1 (Tel Aviv: Hadar, 1970); J. B. Schechtman, *Rebel and Statesman* (New York: Yoseloff, 1956); and J. B. Schechtman, *Fighter and Prophet* (New York: Yoseloff, 1961).

From the very beginning Herut's program emphasized the firm assertion of the claim of the Jewish state to the whole of historic Palestine, roughly corresponding to the area granted by the League of Nations to Great Britain as a mandated territory after the First World War. Even the first partition of the country undertaken by Great Britain in 1922, separating Transjordan from Western Palestine, Herut regarded as an injustice, and it assumed the same attitude toward the further partition of Western Palestine in 1948. Gradually the view emerged that, despite its moral claim to the rest of the country, Israel should not resort to war in order to acquire any territory beyond the 1948–1949 armistice lines. However, should it be possible to extend Israeli rule to any further part of historic Palestine through agreement or should Israel come to occupy any part of it in the course of a war forced upon it, Herut was in favor of asserting its claims.

Because of this emphasis, Herut early acquired the character of a party chiefly interested in foreign affairs, adopting on the whole a strongly activist policy. Ever since the Soviet Union developed an anti-Israel stand in 1951, Herut has advocated a pronouncedly pro-Western, mainly pro-American, orientation. When in the early 1950s the question of Israeli-German relations became acute, Herut, moved by a strong sense of national dignity, opposed first the conclusion of a reparation agreement with West Germany and subsequently the establishment of diplomatic relations. Thus, Herut came to be recognized as the foremost nationalist party in Israel. This did not affect Herut's stand in upholding the principle of individual equality and the cultural rights of Israel's Arab population. What Herut insisted on was that, as long as a state of war was maintained by the Arab countries against Israel, strict criteria be adopted in demanding loyalty from the country's Arab (and even more, from its Jewish) citizens and in combating disruptive influences as befits a country at war and in danger of extinction. Paradoxically, at all of the elections held since the establishment of the state, a small proportion of Arab (especially Druze) voters have supported Herut candidates.

Betar (also the name of the fortress at which Bar-Kochba and his followers took their last stand in their rebellion against Rome in 135 A.D.) is the Hebrew acronym for B'rit Trumpeldor, the Trumpeldor League, named after Joseph Trumpeldor, the founder of the Zionist pioneer movement Hechalutz and a co-founder with Jabotinsky of the Jewish Legion. The only Jew to attain officer's rank in Tsarist Russia, he was killed by Arabs in 1920 in defending Tel-Hai, one of the northernmost Jewish settlements in Palestine. Menachem Begin himself rose from the ranks of Betar and headed the Betar organization in Poland before World War II.

Without being a religious party in the strict sense, Herut on the whole maintained a positive attitude toward Jewish religious tradition, often supporting orthodox circles in their demands. Among other reasons for doing so, it viewed traditional Judaism as an additional and especially secure link attaching the individual to the Jewish community and as a help in maintaining the self-image of Israel as an essentially Jewish commonwealth. Herut also esteemed religion as a bond between the Jews of Israel and those of the Diaspora, since the latter largely perceived themselves as religious communities. Then there was the very pronounced assertion of the Jewish character and destiny of the Holy Land, characteristic of traditional Judaism. This gave the Jewish claim to the land a dimension of principle, transcending the merely pragmatic fact of a few million Jews' congregating in the country and establishing there a Jewish state. Facts could be questioned as to their moral legitimacy and finally overthrown; but the historical and national claim to the land, so fiercely upheld by religious tradition, vested the claim with a moral basis. Although it does not adhere to all of the demands of the strictly religious parties and despite the presence among the members and sympathizers of Herut of distinctly secular-minded elements, there is a strong empathy between Herut and Jewish orthodoxy. Herut is especially sympathetic to the fostering of religious education in the public schools, since such education intensifies the sense of Jewish self-identification and the perception of the innate justice of the Jewish claim to the Land of Israel.

On social and economic issues, Herut remained essentially faithful to the classical tenets of Revisionism. National solidarity was to be stressed rather than class antagonism; opportunities for private enterprise were to be broadened; and labor conflicts were to be submitted to compulsory arbitration, at least in the essential services and industries and as long as Israel was at war. Responding to the problems that arose in the state, Herut advocated vigorous measures against the proliferation of bureaucracy, red tape, and state-directed paternalism and sought to curtail preferential treatment of collective and Histadrut-owned enterprises in matters of taxation. But in time, the position of Herut shifted noticeably from free-enterprise liberalism toward a more pronounced social consciousness. With the increase of Herut's popularity among the working and socially disadvantaged groups in the population,[2] safeguarding the social and economic needs of these groups became an important part of Herut's program. A trade

[2] See pp. 110–111.

union under the name of National Workers' Organization, paralleling and competing with the Histadrut, had been established under the auspices of the Zionists-Revisionists as far back as 1934; but in 1963, a workers' faction affiliated with Herut, under the name of Tehelet-Lavan (Hebrew for "blue-white"), entered the Histadrut, garnering there a considerable and constantly growing proportion of votes.[3]

From the beginning, Herut's adherents and voters came from both middle-class and working-class elements within the population which were motivated by strong nationalist feelings. These were mainly of Eastern European or Sephardic origin. Gradually, the movement gained popularity among Jews newly arrived from Arab countries, especially among the second generation of these immigrants. Except in the elections to the Second Knesset in 1951, Herut gathered an ever-increasing proportion of the popular vote, and since the 1955 elections to the Third Knesset it has been the second-largest party. Never (except for the period 1967–1970) participating in the governing coalitions, Herut became the principal opposition party in Israel. It retained this position after merging with other parties into the parliamentary blocs of Gahal (in 1965)) and Likud (in 1973), in both of which it functioned as the strongest component, until the 1977 elections propelled Herut, together with its partners in the Likud bloc, into the role of the largest parliamentary faction and gave it control of the government.[4]

As in most Israeli parties, splits and defections took place in the Herut movement along with accretions from the outside; some public figures left Herut only to rejoin it later. But the central core of Herut faithful remained fairly solid, grouped around the party's leader, Menachem Begin.

The Liberals. Second in importance as a Likud component is the Liberal party. It is the heir to the oldest and once the leading group within the Zionist movement. Soon after the foundation of the World Zionist Organization in 1897, two wings of it, the strongly religious

---

[3] In the elections to the Histadrut, Tehelet-Lavan and other workers' groups which ultimately joined Likud achieved the following proportions of the vote: 1965—15.2 percent; 1969—17.3 percent; 1973—22.7 percent; 1977—28.8 percent.

[4] Running for the Knesset independently, Herut achieved the following results in the various elections: 1949—11.5 percent, fourteen seats; 1951—6.6 percent, eight seats; 1955—12.6 percent, fifteen seats; 1959—13.5 percent, seventeen seats; 1961—13.8 percent, seventeen seats. The bloc of Herut and the Liberals, under the name of Gahal, achieved in 1965 21.3 percent and twenty-six seats; in 1969, 21.7 percent and again twenty-six seats. After joining with other groups within the framework of Likud, Herut and its allies gathered in 1973 30.2 percent and thirty-nine seats, and finally in 1977 33.4 percent and forty-three seats.

Mizrachi (Hebrew for "Easterner") and the social-democratic Poalei-Zion (Hebrew for "workers of Zion"), set up their own organizational structures; other groups followed, forming Zionist parties or organizations of their own. But the core of the movement remained its principal force, refusing to emphasize points of difference and insisting on remaining united for the sake of the common purpose. After World War I, this central core became known as the General Zionist party. In the 1920s, the General Zionists, too, split into two factions. Faction A, led by Haïm Weizmann, then president of the World Zionist Organization, and with a strong following in Germany and Great Britain, adopted increasingly a pro-labor stand in economic matters and exhibited a readiness to compromise when dealing with the British administration of Palestine. Faction B, with adherents mainly in Palestine and Eastern Europe, defended more strongly the interests of the self-employed middle class and of private enterprise generally, at the same time favoring a more activist policy vis-à-vis the British government. American Zionists, at first divided, veered gradually toward Faction A.

Upon the establishment of the state, Faction A adherents in Israel, together with other smaller groups, formed a separate party known first as the Progressives and later as the Independent Liberals, while Faction B crystallized into the General Zionist party, later renamed the Liberal party. In Knesset elections, the Liberal party frequently came out as the third-largest party in the land, and once (in 1951) as the second-largest. In their attitude toward socioeconomic problems, the Liberals may be fairly described as the most determinedly private-enterprise-minded group in Israel. In foreign policy they, too, favor a pro-Western orientation and, though less insistent than Herut, affirm the justice of the claim of the Jewish people to the entire western part of historic Palestine. Though representing a none-too-observant and often outright secularist constituency, Liberals stand for respect for orthodox religious tradition, only qualifying it with the demand that nonorthodox viewpoints be equally respected. At times part of the governing coalition, at others in opposition, the General Zionists or Liberals always played an important part in Israeli politics under their successive leaders Israel Rokach, Joseph Sapir, Elimelech Rimalt, and Simcha Ehrlich. The party's following came largely from middle-class circles of European origin.

Gahal. Paralleling the efforts to consolidate the socialist parties, the 1960s witnessed similar efforts to bring about a coalescence of nonsocialist groups. Among the General Zionists two trends emerged: one favored amalgamation with the Progressives, the other a common front with Herut. In 1961, they united with the Progressives, forming the Liberal party. But further consolidation was thought necessary, and in 1965 the majority of the Liberals entered an electoral and parliamentary bloc with Herut under the name of Gahal (Hebrew acronym for Gush Herut Liberalim—"Herut-Liberal bloc"). Most former Progressives, unwilling to give up their moderate stand in foreign policy and their traditional alliance with social-democratic labor, thereupon withdrew and reorganized as Independent Liberals. Gahal became the precursor of Likud. Within it, the Liberals continued to pursue their policies, somewhat more pragmatic than those of Herut but generally agreeing with the latter. In the 1965 elections, Gahal gained twenty-six seats, and it retained the same number of seats in the 1969 elections even though, in the meantime, a few prominent Herut figures had left the party and contested the elections on their own. As a component of Gahal, the Liberals brought to the polls a smaller electoral following than did Herut, but it was a following that represented important economic segments and included experienced political personalities. From the union, the Liberals gained a more secure electoral basis guaranteeing that their parliamentary representation would not be reduced. Herut, on the other hand, gained a more moderate image and increased respectability.

On June 1, 1967, under the impact of growing Arab threats to destroy Israel, the announced closing of the Tiran straits to Israeli shipping, and the withdrawal of United Nations troops from the Israeli-Egyptian lines of demarcation, Gahal was invited to join the Labor-led cabinet. In the resulting government of national unity, Gahal was represented by six ministers, three from Herut (Menachem Begin, Haïm Landau, and Ezer Weizmann) and three Liberals (Joseph Sapir, Elimelech Rimalt, and Arieh Dultzin). A seventh addition to the national unity cabinet was Moshe Dayan, the former chief of staff of the Israel Defense Forces, representing the Rafi movement (Rafi being the initials of Reshimat Poalei Israel—List of Israel Workers), which had split off from the Labor party. Gahal remained in the cabinet until August 1970, at which time its ministers resigned at the insistence of Begin and most of the Herut leadership and rather against the inclination of the Liberal wing, following the cabinet majority's decision to enter negotiations under the auspices of United Nations-appointed Ambassador Jaring of Sweden on the basis of proposals which Gahal regarded as highly prejudicial to Israeli interests.

La'am. A further component of the Likud is the La'am faction (La'am meaning "toward the people"). The origin of this faction lies in the Rafi group which, under the leadership of Israel's first prime minister, David Ben-Gurion, had left Mapai, the country's largest labor party, in the 1960s and was characterized by a tendency to emphasize national rather than class interests. In 1969, most of the Rafi followers, led by Moshe Dayan and Shimon Peres, rejoined the Labor party, but some of them decided to continue an independent existence and presented themselves at the Knesset elections of that year under the name of Reshima Mamlachtit (National list or State list), which won only four seats. Finding themselves increasingly in accord with Gahal's (especially Herut's) foreign and domestic policy, this group, together with others that joined it, entered negotiations with Gahal toward the 1973 elections and, under the name of La'am, became one of the co-founders of the large parliamentary bloc, the Likud. With a following recruited variously from former Mapai adherents, members of cooperative agricultural settlements, individuals who at various times had followed Herut, and adherents of the Eretz Yisrael Hashlema movement (of which more anon), La'am's position approaches that of Herut on foreign and domestic affairs and differs but slightly from the Liberals' position on domestic issues. Among La'am's more prominent members one might name Yigal Hurvitz, a successful farmer and industrialist; Moshe Shamir, a writer and founder of Eretz Yisrael Hashlema, formerly active in the ranks of the socialist left; Eliezer Shostak, the founder of the National Trade Union movement within Herut; Zalman Shuval, a bank executive; and Amnon Lin, long prominent in Mapai.

Other Components and Associated Movements. The history of Likud would be incomplete if we omitted to mention another one of its original components, even though it no longer counts among its current constituents. This is the Free Center group (Merkaz hofshi) which was founded by Shmuel Tamir, one of the country's best-known trial lawyers, who had been active in the Irgun Tsevaï Leumi and later became one of Herut's most prominent figures. Leaving Herut in 1969, the dissidents obtained two seats in the Knesset elections. In time, two more Knesset members left Herut to join the Free Center. On the eve of the 1973 elections, the Free Center entered Likud as one of its constituents, receiving four seats within the ranks of Likud. Subsequently, the four Knesset members divided, and in the 1977 elections two of them were elected as members of the new party, the Democratic Movement for Change, while two others entered the Knesset as members of the La'am faction of the Likud.

The fourth present-day component of Likud, Achdut (Unity), is represented in the Knesset by a single member, Hillel Seidel, formerly a leading member of the Independent Liberal party and for a long time its chief representative in the Histadrut. Advocating a firmer foreign policy than most of the leaders of the Independent Liberals, he had no difficulty in entering Likud. On social policy he shared the views of the left wing within Herut and La'am.

Before passing to the precise standing of Likud in the two Knesset campaigns which it contested as a bloc under that name, we should mention two movements that affected the political scene very much to the Likud's advantage. These were the Tenua Le'maan Eretz Yisrael Hashlema (Movement for an Integral Land of Israel) and Gush Emunim (Bloc of the Faithful).

The Movement for an Integral Land of Israel was organized in the fall of 1967 by a number of public figures drawn from various circles and backgrounds, brought together by a common concern lest Israel be coerced or coaxed to give up any of the newly conquered parts of Western Palestine (Judea, Samaria, the Gaza strip, and the eastern part of Jerusalem). They insisted on the inclusion of all of these in the Jewish state on historical, emotional, and economic, as well as on security grounds. The movement's adherents also maintained that the Golan Heights and parts or all of the Sinai peninsula were necessary for Israel's security and welfare and that Israel had a fairly valid claim on these areas, but these held less of an emotional appeal to them and consequently were less emphasized in the movement's platform.

Of singular interest was the composition of the movement, unrivalled in Israel for the extreme variety of the political persuasions of its supporters. Side-by-side with old Etzel and Lehi[5] fighters and with active Herut members, there were figures like Haim Yachil, a former ambassador and at the time chairman of the Israel Broadcasting Authority; representatives of orthodoxy like Harel Fisch, rector of Bar-Ilan University; the country's leading poets, Uri Tzevi Greenberg and Nathan Alterman, the latter formerly the darling of the labor

---

[5] Lehi is the Hebrew acronym for Lohamei Herut Israel (Fighters for the Freedom of Israel). The group split from Etzel during World War II. Etzel took the view that as long as the war against Nazi Germany went on, rebellious activities against the British regime in Palestine should be stopped; it even cooperated with the British authorities in matters connected with the conduct of the war. Lehi, on the other hand, continued to fight the British regime throughout the war. Toward the end of the war, when Allied victory was already certain and Britain continued and strengthened its repressive policy in Palestine, Etzel, too, resumed active resistance against the British, and the two underground movements grew closer.

camp; one of the patriarchs of the labor and kibbutz movement, Yitzhak Tabenkin; Rachel Ben-Tzevi, the widow of Israel's second president and herself one of the great figures of the Zionist labor movement; and two of the former leaders of the strongly leftist Hashomer Hatzaïr (Young Watchman) organization, Moshe Shamir and Tzevi Shiloah.[6] The interparty character of this group gave expression to the wide popularity enjoyed by what, after all, was the Likud's principal plank—the demand that all of Western Palestine remain under Israel's control in one form or another. It also increased the Likud's prestige and respectability and undoubtedly contributed in no small measure to its success at the polls in 1973 and 1977.

The other movement, Gush Emunim, did not make its formal appearance till 1974, but its antecedents date back to the late sixties. Its followers set themselves the task of accomplishing what Herut and the Eretz Yisrael Hashlema had preached in theory, namely the settlement of Jews beyond the pre-1967 armistice lines. The beginnings of the movement can be traced to those men and women who resettled the Gush Etzion region west of Hebron, whose former Jewish settlements had been destroyed by Arab forces during the 1948 War of Independence; after trying to renew the ancient Jewish community in Hebron, they finally established a new Jewish suburb, Kiryat Arba,[7] on the city's outskirts. The group's basic idea was that, now that all of Western Palestine had come under Israeli control, Jews had a right to settle in every part of their ancient homeland and that volunteers ought to make use of this right. Before the reversal of governmental policy following the 1977 elections, the movement was opposed by the government, and this on two grounds. On the one hand, while opinion within the government and its supporters was divided on the question of principle, it was united in believing that such indiscriminate Jewish settlement beyond the pre-1967 lines would hinder progress toward a peaceful solution of the Israel-Arab conflict and therefore sought to restrict such settlement to those areas only which they believed essential to Israel's security and hoped to retain as the result of future negotiations: the immediate surroundings of Jerusalem, the Golan, the Jordan valley, a coastal strip south of Gaza and into northeastern Sinai, the southern tip of the Sinai peninsula, and a few points near the old armistice lines. On the other hand, devoted

---

[6] Most of the former Hashomer Hatzaïr membership is to be found at present in the ranks of the Mapam party, affiliated with the Labor party in the Maarach bloc. Some of them have moved leftward into the Shelli party or even into the ranks of communism.

[7] Kiryat Arba is mentioned in the Bible as another name for Hebron.

to a paternalistic conception of directing all significant developments from above and therefore distrustful of initiatives from other sources, especially where such initiatives were being taken by groups rightly suspected of sympathy with the opposition, the government was bound to resent the activities of the self-willed would-be-settlers. Only reluctantly and in very few cases did the government give its approval and a measure of support to the initiatives of the Gush Emunim and its predecessors. As a result, the settlements due to these initiatives remained few in number, far fewer than the sixty and more settlements established beyond the pre-1967 lines in accordance with governmental policy.

However, the popular impact of the movement was considerable from the very start and grew stronger with the formal creation of the Gush Emunim in 1974. The very opposition of the government to this movement seemed to stimulate its efforts and to increase the number of its supporters. The movement's following was largely recruited from younger orthodox Jews close to the National Religious party, and indeed, that party, long hesitating between an activist and a moderate stance, was swayed under the influence of its younger members into a position largely identical with that of Gush Emunim and of Herut. This resulted in the Likud's gaining the National Religious party as a prospective and, after the 1977 elections, actual partner. At the same time, quite a number of younger orthodox Jews, instead of voting, as before, for the National Religious party, went all the way and voted for Likud. It goes without saying that the nonorthodox circles inspired by the Gush Emunim movement became Likud supporters.

Likud's Growth. A factor that contributed to Likud's growing popularity throughout the years was the accumulating dissatisfaction with the deficiencies which crept up under the rule of Labor-led governments. The middle classes grew impatient with what they regarded as excessive and irksome interference of the government in their daily lives and pursuits as well as with the mounting wave of labor unrest. The disadvantaged strata, mainly Jewish immigrants from Moslem countries and their descendants, blamed the ruling party for their failure to advance more rapidly in Israeli society and for the fact that many of them remained on the lowest rungs of the socioeconomic and educational ladder, suffering real hardships. Constantly rising prices and housing shortages affected them more than almost any other group in the population and intensified their discontent. Some of them turned toward left-oriented Panther movements, but most of them, deeply patriotic, gave their support to Herut. Another accession of strength was provided by the newly arrived immigrants from the Soviet Union: thoroughly disappointed in socialism and moved by intense Jewish nationalism, most of them were attracted to Herut and, through it, to Likud.

None of this means that Likud was spared the splits and defections characteristic of Israeli party politics. Four active Herut members and Knesset deputies—Shmuel Tamir, Eliezer Shostak, Akiva Nof, and Ehud Olmert—left Herut in 1969 to form an independent group, joined Likud in 1973, and divided again in 1977, two of them remaining in the Likud and two outside. Benjamin Halevi, a Supreme Court judge who left the bench in 1969, was elected to the Knesset on the Herut list in the same year, afterwards declared himself an independent, and in 1977 joined the Democratic Movement for Change. General Ariel Sharon, one of Israel's war heroes, having left the army and joined the Liberals in 1973, was instrumental in cementing the Likud bloc, but then resigned his seat and party membership, only to return to Likud after the 1977 election, this time within the framework of Herut.

Nonetheless, Likud continued to grow. Repeated public opinion polls confirmed this fact and the steady decline of Maarach, the parliamentary bloc of the ruling Labor party and the more leftist Mapam. This trend, established in 1973, continued unabated. The important mayoralty of Tel Aviv, the country's largest city at the time,[8] was lost to the Maarach for the first time in thirteen years and fell into the hands of the Likud. In many other localities, Likud gained the mayoralty or became part of the ruling coalition. The weaknesses in Israel's military preparedness, made apparent at the start of the October 1973 campaign and for which the Labor-led government was largely blamed, had much to do with this development. But other factors contributed to it as well: rapid inflation, continued strife in labor relations, a rising wave of criminality, cases of corruption among individuals in the government hierarchy and in public enterprises, deteriorating foreign relations, internal squabbles in the leading circles of the Labor party, and, after Golda Meir's resignation, the new prime minister's indifferent public image. All of this created the impression of a cabinet and a ruling party rent by serious disagreements and incapable of dealing effectively with the problems of the day. To the adherents of a firm foreign policy they appeared too "dovish"; to the

---

[8] By the end of 1975, Jerusalem overtook Tel Aviv, with a population of 355,500 compared with 353,800. Tel Aviv, however, remained the municipality with the largest Jewish population, 346,600 to Jerusalem's 259,400.

proponents of territorial and other concessions they seemed too "hawkish"; they satisfied no one. Devoted socialists and trade unionists believed them to lean too much toward capitalism; the rest of the population regarded them as one-sided in defending the interests of the cooperative and collectivist sector. To conservatives they seemed too permissive; to others, too conservative. Religious circles regarded them as too secular in outlook; secularists, as too prone to give in to the orthodox. There was general dissatisfaction with the wage-and-price policy of the government, each interest group and stratum in the population wanting to restrain others but intent on raising its own real income. And so, there was a widespread demand for change.

Likud, as the principal opposition group, seemed in comparison more trustworthy than ever and profited most from this state of affairs. The only serious brake on this rise of sympathy for Likud was the movement in dissident Maarach and liberal circles and among hitherto nonparty intellectuals that crystallized around professors Amnon Rubinstein and Yigael Yadin and ultimately led to the formation of a "third force," the Democratic Movement for Change. In the meantime, the National Religious party, chastened by its poor performance in 1973 and under the influence of its activist wing, showed signs of veering from its traditional partnership with Labor toward Likud. It was in this atmosphere that, in the course of 1976, Likud and all other political forces in the country began to prepare for the elections to the Ninth Knesset, originally scheduled for the fall of 1977.

In an ill-conceived move, Prime Minister Yitzhak Rabin asked for the dismissal of the National Religious ministers from his cabinet in December 1976 and, faced with the imminent loss of his parliamentary majority, handed in his resignation. Under Israeli law, a prime minister's resignation is tantamount to the resignation of the entire cabinet. Since it was unlikely that an alternative coalition could be brought together and since, anyhow, all of the opposition parties were united in wishing for speedy elections, a law was rapidly passed, advancing the election date to May 17, 1977. According to Israeli practice, the existing cabinet continues to function until a new one is confirmed by the Knesset; but in the interval Rabin was found to have contravened some foreign exchange regulations, and Maarach replaced him with Shimon Peres, the minister of defense, as head of the list and its candidate for the prime ministership. This development weakened the Maarach even further and improved the chances of the opposition.

The Likud's Campaign

Faced with the prospect of early elections, Likud, like all the other parties and parliamentary blocs, took steps to prepare speedily for the coming contest. Four interconnected issues were involved: drafting the bloc's platform, organizing the campaign, negotiating with prospective partners, and putting up a list of candidates.

The Platform. Likud's platform left little room for discussion, since the main positions of the bloc were well defined. Still, formulations had to be found that would ,adequately balance the different nuances emphasized by the constituent parties in foreign and domestic policy and thus attract the largest possible number of voters. Another element, too, had to be considered: since this was the first time that Likud had had a chance of emerging as the main force in Parliament, its pronouncements had also to be carefully scrutinized from the viewpoint of their influence on foreign governments and world opinion. No single document was drafted to give expression to Likud's views; instead, a number of leaflets were published, each devoted to a specific issue. And these were supplemented by newspaper advertisements, the leading candidates' speeches, newspaper articles, and appearances on the radio and television.

As far as international policy was concerned, it was important to find a formulation that would satisfy both those who insisted on the retention of all the territories currently under Israeli control and the advocates of a somewhat more flexible approach. As a result, Likud's pronouncements stressed Israel's claim to Judea, Samaria, and the Gaza strip (all parts of Western Palestine), the demand that none of this territory pass under foreign rule, the right of Jews to reside in any part of it, the right of Arab residents to retain the citizenship of an Arab country, and the need for secure and defensible boundaries in Sinai and the Golan. On the aims and techniques of negotiations, there was complete unanimity as to the need to strive for comprehensive peace treaties with each of the enemy states rather than for partial or step-by-step arrangements, and on the importance of direct negotiations with each of them. Except for one dissenting voice very early in the process, there was no disagreement on the exclusion of the terrorist organizations grouped under the PLO as a possible partner in any Israeli-Arab negotiations. A further plank concerned Israel's interest in the condition of Jews in the Diaspora and in their freedom to emigrate to the Jewish state, with special application to the oppressive conditions under which Jews lived in the Soviet Union and in Syria.

Though Likud and its prospective voters represented a broad range of religious views, including strict orthodoxy, moderate traditionalism, religious innovation, and tolerant secularism, a reasonable formulation of the religious issue was easiest to achieve: it stressed respect for religious tradition and individual freedom of conscience. Nor did the plank on education and the broadcasting media present any difficulties. All components of the Likud were agreed on the need to combat the value-neutral or even alienated attitude that the educational network tended to assume toward Jewish and Zionist self-identification; this, the platform insisted, must be replaced by active education toward Jewish consciousness and Zionism, and the state-owned broadcasting media must be used to the same end. Stiffening labor morale, with compulsory arbitration as the main instrument, and nationalizing health services hitherto provided by semi-public, mainly Histadrut-controlled institutions, also commanded general approval.

Of greater delicacy was the fashioning of a socioeconomic plank. Hardest of all was reconciling those wings of Likud which regarded the encouragement of private initiative and freedom from governmental controls as the road leading to overall economic well-being, with the labor-minded groups in the movement that were anxious to preserve the largely cooperative and collectivist features characteristic of so much of the Jewish economy in Israel.[9] And then there was the overriding problem of raising the living standards of the economically and educationally disadvantaged sections of the population while not interfering with the interests of the wealthier and educationally advanced strata. A solution to this problem was sought that would cut across the organizational divisions between the Likud's components, but while the labor-minded groups representing the interests of the disadvantaged were to be found mainly in Herut, La'am, and Achdut, the interests of the more comfortable strata were represented principally in the ranks of the Liberals. The issue was further complicated by the fact that the disadvantaged sections of the population consisted largely of first and second-generation immigrants from Moslem countries, many of whom were Herut followers. Since the Histadrut—in the past the principal coordinating agency of Israeli labor and salaried strata and at the same time formally the controlling body of most cooperative and collective enterprises as well as of many large businesses—was not particularly popular among these strata, it

---

[9] This in contrast to Arab society in the country, which, for all its high percentage of Communist votes, clings to an exclusively individual or family-ownership type of economy.

was not difficult for Likud to seek to limit the Histadrut's role; but otherwise a fine balance had to be preserved in the Likud platform between the demands of a free-market economy and the pledge of special attention to the disadvantaged groups. As the election results were to show, this balance was achieved: support came to Likud from both sections of the population, though more from the poorer sections than from the more comfortable ones.

Campaign Organization. The campaign had to be organized in a hurry, since so little time was left till the election date. Somewhat to the chagrin of the older Herut and Liberal militants who doubted whether he would be equal to the task, the organization of the campaign was placed in the hands of Ezer Weizmann, the dashing former commander of the air force and a relative newcomer to Herut. Assisted by another retired general, Mordechai Zippori, and by Eliahu Ben-Elissar, a suave student of history and a close collaborator of Menachem Begin, Weizmann set about to organize the campaign. No sooner was it launched than Likud's unchallenged and by far most popular leader, Begin, suffered a heart attack that kept him hospitalized for most of the campaign's duration. This circumstance lent special importance to the work of the election staff.

Previous campaigns having shown the relative ineffectiveness of public meetings, posters, and campaign literature, less use was made of them this time. More attention was given to small gatherings in private homes and to speeches on the radio. The main role, however, was assigned to newspaper advertisements and to television appearances. Prime time was allotted on television to all lists participating in the campaign in proportion to their strength in the outgoing Knesset, and Likud, as the second-largest group, obtained large chunks of television time.

Weizmann, again to the dismay of the old party regulars, left the planning and designing of the television programs largely in the hands of a commercial public relations firm. Only a minor part of the time was given to speeches by the movement's representative politicians, and since Begin was unavailable, these were rather unimpressive. Most of each program was devoted to biting criticism of Maarach, Likud's principal antagonist; all other lists were left strictly alone. Likud itself was pictured again and again on each program as a rising sun on a bleak horizon, with the motto "Likud, force No. 1" inscribed in bold letters. Many thought this symbol monotonous, even crude. But it seems to have worked. Toward the end of the campaign, with Begin recovered, an hour-long live television debate was broadcast between him and Shimon Peres, Maarach's candidate for the prime ministership. A generally respected journalist who was on friendly terms with both men acted as moderator. Both debaters pulled their punches and were strictly polite, almost cordial, to one another. The debate worked to Begin's, and therefore the Likud's, benefit. His supporters were pleased with his performance. As for the doubters, they had been warned against a fanatical firebrand; the urbane and smiling debater, who seemed to be on familiar, first-name terms with the foremost leader of Maarach and whom Peres, despite gentle attempts at sarcasm, seemed to treat with a measure of respect, must have reassured many of them. It is indicative that some Maarach members criticized their leader's performance as too friendly toward Begin. And so the campaign wound up on a note of optimism and enthusiasm for Likud adherents. The optimists (except for the few observers who foresaw a definite victory for Likud) went so far as to hope for an equal number of seats, about thirty-nine or forty, for Likud and Maarach—this in the face of public opinion polls that, in the last days of the campaign, saw Likud trailing Maarach by some thirty-six to forty seats.

The Nomination Process. However change-minded the aspirations of Likud and of all its components, the mechanics of setting up a list of candidates had to follow more or less the established patterns of Israeli political life. Three cardinal principles had to be taken into account; the position of the movement's and of its constituent groups' acknowledged leaders had to be secured; each of these groups had to receive adequate representation, commensurate with its strength in the outgoing Knesset and with its estimated popularity; and within that representation, a balance had to be preserved between the claims of various subgroups and active party workers to obtain a maximum possible share of the "real" places on the list[10]—a balance that might tilt somewhat in one direction or another but that

---

[10] Since, under the proportional-representation system used in Israel, a candidate's chances to be elected vary with his or her place on the list, a preliminary estimate is made of the minimum and maximum number of seats which any given list is likely to win. The places within the minimum estimate are the only "real," or safe, ones in Israeli political parlance. Those between the minimum and maximum estimates are the "marginal" ones, affording their holders a chance, but not a certainty, of election. The next two to ten places (depending on the size of the party) on the list still carry some aleatory chance of entry into the Knesset, based on the possibility of some members' resignation or death. The rest of the places on the list (down to the maximum permitted, 120) offer no chances whatsoever. Hence the fierce competition for "real" places. Within this category, the order of placement is also fought over, but this only for its prestige value, denoting the relative importance of the candidate in the party hierarchy.

must not be completely upset lest this lead to disaffection and secession. In addition, the desirability of getting outside support by inserting in real places on the list well-known public figures had to be weighed against the dangers of giving up some of these real places, so highly cherished by the party workers, in favor of outsiders.

In the context of the 1977 campaign, the one uncontested leader of Herut and of the entire Likud was Menachem Begin, whose place at the top of the list was taken for granted by all. Not that from time to time voices were not raised within Likud or even Herut wondering whether a change in the leadership might not be contemplated. But so much greater was Begin's popularity among Herut members and potential supporters than that of any possible contestant that such voices were quickly silenced and the few would-be challengers were driven into untenable positions.

A similar consensus reigned among the Liberals concerning the position of Simcha Ehrlich, the party chairman and owner of a well-managed optical works, as their top candidate. And an almost equal unanimity existed in the ranks of La'am regarding Yigal Hurvitz, a successful farmer who had branched out first into agricultural and later into general industry (and, incidentally, Moshe Dayan's relative and friend). It was clear that these three would head the Likud list, and with them Ezer Weizmann (a nephew of the late Professor Haïm Weizmann who was for many years the head of the World Zionist Organization and the first president of the state of Israel). Below these leading four, the composition of the list, and especially of the first thirty to forty places regarded as fairly safe, was an arduous task indeed.

Though delicate, the negotiations regarding the proportion and order of the safe seats each of the three components was to receive were fairly brief. Of the forty-three mandates Likud finally won, twenty were assigned to Herut (numbered 1, 4, 6, 8, 11, 13, 14, 17, 19, 22, 24, 26, 27, 29, 32, 33, 35, 37, 39, and 42 on the list). The Liberals received fourteen places (numbered 2, 5, 7, 9, 12, 18, 20, 23, 25, 30, 34, 38, 41, 43). La'am obtained eight places (numbered 3, 10, 15, 21, 28, 31, 36, and 40). One seat, number 16, was given just before the deadline to a newcomer, as will be seen below.

During the preelection months the Likud held informal talks with outside public figures who shared some of the movement's views.

In the past, a high place on the list signified that the given candidate had a claim to eventual ministerial appointment; but lately the tendency has grown to elect the party's representatives in the cabinet by vote in a larger party forum, and this vote does not necessarily follow the order of placement on the list.

Some of these talks were undertaken on the Likud's initiative; others on the initiative of the outsiders interested in getting into the Knesset. Of particular significance were the contacts with Moshe Dayan, the famous former chief of staff and defense minister and, at the time, a Maarach Knesset member. In the end, Dayan refused to join, though remaining on the friendliest terms with Begin and separated from him only by fine points of policy on the occupied territories. General Ariel Sharon, another Israeli war hero, whose entry into politics had been stormy and whose influence had been decisive in originally cementing the Likud but who had later left it, also negotiated for inclusion in the Likud list. Almost up to the last, Sharon, who in the meantime had formed a small movement of his own, hesitated between running as the head of that movement and joining Likud. When, on the eve of the deadline for introducing the lists, he finally proposed to join Likud and asked for two safe places on the list, the Liberals vetoed his offer. Talks were also held with Mordechai Ben-Porat, a veteran member of the Labor party prominent among Jewish immigrants from Iraq, who held a seat in the outgoing Knesset and shortly before the elections resigned from his party; but these, too, came to naught. The only outsider who actually was given a safe seat on the list (number 16) was Hillel Seidel, a leading member of the Independent Liberal party, who joined Likud, forming its fourth component, the Achdut.

The main struggle took place within each of the Likud's original three constituent groups. Numerous individuals and subgroups put in their claims. The central offices and the districts, ethnic and occupational groups, old-timers and younger elements, all competed for places. Like Maarach and the National Religious party, Likud witnessed a particularly sharp attempt on the part of local districts and younger members to supplant members of the established party hierarchies. Instead of the former practice of handpicking the candidates and deciding on their order of precedence in the list by means of a nominations committee usually composed of the party heads or their trusted representatives, the hierachies had to agree to the more democratic mode of selection by one of the party's more representative institutions. There was an effective opposition to including individuals who already held responsible public offices but sought to obtain seats in the Knesset as well; similarly, the candidacy of members who had already sat for several terms was criticized. La'am, being a fairly new group composed of relatively young people, was hardly affected by this trend, and all of the public figures who had come together to form and to lead the party were selected and, indeed, elected. Considerable changes, however, occurred in the composition of the Liberals' list of candidates, with a few veteran Knesset members either voluntarily or involuntarily giving up their privileged places on the list to younger and less-known party members. The greatest change took place in the composition of the Herut contingent. Party stalwarts like Yohanan Bader, Haïm Landau, and Abraham Schechtermann were passed over in favor of comparative newcomers.

At the Polls

On election day, Likud's success exceeded the expectations of practically all observers. From 30.2 percent of the votes and thirty-nine seats it rose to 33.4 percent and forty-three seats, thus becoming for the first time the largest parliamentary force in the country. Immediately after the election, General Sharon's Shlomzion (Peace of Zion) group, which secured two mandates, joined the Herut component of Likud, thus raising the movement's parliamentary strength to a total of forty-five. Even greater was the defeat of Maarach, which fell from fifty-one mandates to thirty-two, and of its long-time allies, the Independent Liberals, who lost three of their four mandates. Profiting from the atmosphere of change even more than Likud, the newly founded Democratic Movement for Change gained fifteen seats, thus becoming the third-largest group in the Knesset. The National Religious party, now committed to an activist foreign policy very similar to Likud's, overcame its former weakness and entered the Knesset with twelve deputies. The stage was set for a government under Likud leadership, with the National Religious party as its obvious ally.

Of special interest in the composition of the Likud vote was its spectacular success in the development towns, where the disadvantaged strata were largely concentrated, in the poorer quarters of the cities, and in the centers of urban labor. Indeed, in most cases a far higher percentage of the electorate voted Likud in these areas than in the districts where the middle class and the well-to-do were housed; in the latter, most of the vote was given to Maarach and the new Democratic Movement for Change. In the country's kibbutzim only a few votes (though more than in any previous election) were garnered by Likud, but in the moshavim—Israel's cooperative agricultural settlements, hitherto a stronghold of the Labor party—Likud came out very strong. All this indicated that large parts of Israel's working strata, especially the low-income groups among them, were switching from Maarach to Likud. And since these groups were undoubtedly attracted to Herut and La'am more than to the Liberals, the outcome is indicative of the real electoral strength of the main components within Likud. An analysis of the election results makes it plain that Herut with its twenty Knesset members is certainly underrepresented while the Liberals with fourteen and probably La'am with eight members are overrepresented in the Knesset.

On June 21, a bare month after the Knesset election, elections were held to the congress of the Histadrut, the General Federation of Labor. This time, Maarach, shocked by its defeat in May, mobilized all its forces so as to retain its hold on that organization. This it accomplished, but once more Likud added to its strength even in the stronghold of the Labor party, gaining 28.8 percent of the vote and thus continuing a long-time trend.[11]

For the first time in Israel's history, a non-social-democratic party —the Likud, with the perennial opposition party, Herut, as its principal component—was called upon to form a cabinet.[12] Accustomed to social-democratic hegemony, the entire population had to adjust to what was a major shock. Many had expected that Maarach's strength would be reduced so that a coalition government possibly including Likud might result. But hardly anyone had foreseen so complete a change in the political landscape as a Likud victory large enough to enable it to form a government without help from either the Maarach or the Democratic Movement for Change.

Abroad, the shock was no less. Neither foreign governments nor the world's media nor even the Jewish communities abroad had considered the outcome at all likely. Labor governments in Europe were disturbed by the victory of the "right" in a country considered a safe patrimony of social-democratic rule. And everywhere there was concern over the expected intransigence of a Likud government at a time when many foreign observers were convinced that, for all its strongly expressed reservations, Israel would bend to pressure and concede practically all of the territory conquered in 1967 without getting any tangible peace prospects in return. Such an outcome would suit many of the parties concerned: the Arabs; most of the Third World governments, which were persuaded that they owed solidarity to the Arabs; the Communist countries; but also some very influential

---

[11] See above, note 3.

[12] It is true that in 1950, when David Ben-Gurion had some difficulty in forming a new cabinet, he suggested to the president to invite Pinchas Rosen, leader of the small Progressive (later Independent Liberal) party, to constitute a government, and this was done. But it was understood at the time that this was only a device to prepare the ground for Ben-Gurion. Indeed, after doing some spade-work for the Labor leader, Rosen turned down the offer, and Ben-Gurion was once more asked to form the cabinet.

elements in the West, which were moved by genuine sympathy for the Arab cause, or by their need for Arab oil and money, or by the hope of gaining the Arabs for the Western camp, or by a combination of all these considerations.

The Aftermath. Begin's success in rapidly constituting a workable cabinet and in taking his first steps allayed the fears to some extent and gave him and his government considerable prestige both at home and abroad. Immediately after the election, Begin issued a call for a cabinet of national unity, inviting all the parties except the Communists to join in. The call was rejected by Labor but contributed to internal unification. The invitation to General Dayan to enter the cabinet as foreign minister, though vehemently protested at first by Dayan's many personal opponents and by Maarach, on whose list he had been elected to the Knesset, was regarded in Israel and even more abroad as a master stroke; Dayan's reputation for astute pragmatism did much to reduce the fear that the new government would prove uncompromisingly dogmatic. When negotiations with the Democratic Movement for Change bogged down, Begin rapidly constituted a cabinet without them, leaving a few ministries vacant in case the DMC should reconsider. The task was accomplished with what was, for Israel, almost unprecedented speed. The election results were officially announced on May 26. After consulting with representatives of all Knesset factions, President Katzir asked Begin on June 6 to form a government. On June 19 the cabinet was formed, and on June 20, having received a vote of confidence in the Knesset, it was formally installed.

The parliamentary basis of the new government during the first four months of its existence was exceedingly narrow. Of the 120 Knesset members, only 62 joined the coalition: 45 from the Likud, 12 from the National Religious party, 4 from Agudat Israel (a strict orthodox party), and Dayan. In various votes in the Knesset, the cabinet was also supported by Shmuel Flatto-Sharon, elected as an independent. Finally, the cabinet could count in some measure on Rabbi Kalman Kahane,[13] who represented in the Knesset a small religious-labor group. The opposition, in addition to nine Knesset members utterly opposed to the cabinet and divided into four different factions,[14] comprised but two large groups, Maarach and the

[13] Not to be confused with Rabbi Meir Kahane, the founder of the Jewish Defense League in the United States, who also presented a slate of candidates with himself at the head but won few votes and was not elected.

[14] Five Communists, two representatives of Shelli, one member elected on an independent Arab list, and one on the list of the Civil Rights Movement.

Democratic Movement for Change, the former in deep disarray and sorely divided, the latter still undecided on its future course. Thus, the prospects that a Likud-led government under Menachem Begin would stay in power for the full four-year term of the present Knesset appeared quite good. As a matter of fact, public opinion polls conducted in August and September 1977 indicated that, should the cabinet encounter difficulties and be forced to call premature elections, Likud would win an even greater victory and might secure an absolute majority on its own.

At first, the new cabinet seemed to adopt efficient working methods, and the new prime minister certainly wielded greater authority than his predecessor. The government's firm public stand on Israel's territorial claims, which it held to be a matter of principle, and its desire to arrive speedily at peace treaties with the Arab countries, impressed the population and gave it a feeling that in any international settlement that might be reached, better conditions would be secured than under the previous leadership. There was also a fairly general expectation that economic and social issues would be managed more energetically and effectively. Thus, the morale in the country rose appreciably. However, by late summer the domestic program of the government seemed to stall, the international situation—as far as the public was aware—grew more acute, and the recurrent indisposition of the prime minister gave rise to uneasiness.[15] It was in these circumstances that on October 20, exactly four months after the cabinet's formation, the Democratic Movement for Change decided to join the coalition, and on October 24 four ministers belonging to the movement, with Yigael Yadin as deputy prime minister at their head, entered the government, giving it a solid parliamentary majority, 77 out of a total Knesset membership of 120. It seems that the DMC's decision was influenced by the knowledge of an impending breakthrough in Israeli-Egyptian relations. By joining the cabinet, the DMC hoped to render Israeli foreign policy more flexible and to contribute decisively to the achievement of much-needed internal reforms.

The government's popularity gained new heights with President Anwar Sadat's visit to Jerusalem in November 1977 and the public inauguration of direct negotiations with Egypt. Once the talks encountered snags, the atmosphere began to change. Differences arose within the coalition and, indeed, within the Likud as to the exact

---

[15] The prime minister's health is an important consideration: under Israeli law, as it stands at the time of writing, should the prime minister resign or die, the cabinet is deemed to have resigned. Since the personality of Begin dominates the present cabinet, any eventual reconstruction of the government under a different prime minister would raise complicated interparty and intraparty issues.

position to be taken, some coalition and Likud partners accusing the cabinet of excessive rigidity, others of readiness to concede too much. Most Likud followers continued to support the government line, but even among them doubts were expressed as to the correctness of certain specific moves.

Another source of difficulties lay in the handling of domestic problems. The expected streamlining of the public services failed to materialize, nor did their efficiency increase. No appreciable progress was made in meeting the needs of the underprivileged or in absorbing immigrants. The introduction of free secondary education was about the only reform that was generally applauded. After an initial period of quiet, labor unrest grew once more, and the new government was no more successful in coping with it than were its predecessors. In the economic domain, largely left to the discretion of Simcha Ehrlich (Liberal) and Yigal Hurvitz (La'am), ministers of finance and of industry and trade respectively, a series of measures was taken— reduction of subsidies on necessities, increase of the cost of public services, radical devaluation of currency, liberalization of foreign exchange regulations—which brought about a spiral of wage and price increases without improving the foreign trade balance or curbing inflation.

As a result of all these developments, the initial solidarity among the coalition partners began to wane. Even within the cabinet disagreements arose, and these became a matter of public knowledge. Divisions appeared within each of the coalition groups, including the component parties of the Likud. In the La'am group as well as in the DMC there was serious talk of possible splits. A year after the Likud government came into being, its future stability no longer seems as certain as in the beginning. Nonetheless it still enjoys a great deal of popular support, and Prime Minister Begin's personal popularity remains very high. A public opinion poll held in June 1978 among the adult Jewish population of the country reveals two significant findings. On the one hand, a very large proportion (36.6 percent) were undecided as to whom to support. On the other hand, among those who held definite opinions, more than half (33.1 percent as against 30.3 percent for all other parties) supported Likud. After adjusting the results to the total make-up of the population, taking into consideration the voting patterns of the non-Jewish minority, and on the assumption that the undecided group would divide the same way as the others, it seems that an election held at the time would have given the Likud fifty-one mandates, six more than it had received a year earlier.

5

The Decline of the Israeli Labor Party: Causes and Significance

Myron J. Aronoff

Undoubtedly the most dramatic and significant feature of the critical Israeli election of May 1977 was the loss by the Labor party of the position of dominance in the political system that it had held for approximately fifty years. It is clear that the election results reflected a vote of no confidence in the Labor party and its leadership by a significant sector of the electorate, and a vote for political change by a majority of the voters. This essay offers an explanation for the decline of the Labor party and an evaluation of the significance of this decline within the context of an analysis of the historical development of the political system. Its main hypothesis is that the Labor party lost power primarily because it, and its leadership, had lost legitimacy by becoming increasingly unresponsive to the demands created by a dynamically changing society. The explanation relates the decline in the responsiveness of the Labor party to three main variables: stages in the development of the political system; the nature of the mobilization and consolidation of political support and power (both within the party and in the country at large); and the changing role of ideology.

Labor and the Development of the Political System

The Formative Stage. The rough division of the development of the Israeli political system into three major historical stages is meant to emphasize the relevant aspects of the system characteristic of each period. This categorization identifies two main phases in the first major pre-state stage. The first phase (from approximately 1920 to the mid-1930s) was characterized by the mobilization of political support and power, and the second phase (from approximately 1935 to independence in 1948) was characterized by their consolidation. Together these two stages constituted the critical formative period.

One of the most important factors which contributed to Labor's successful dominance of the Israeli political system for almost fifty years was the fact that it played a major role in the creation and shaping of the major socioeconomic and political institutions of the pre-independence *yishuv* (the Jewish community in Palestine). Shapiro cogently analyzes the crystallization of the basic characteristics of the Israeli party-dominated political structure during this crucial formative period.[1] His work elaborates and documents in the case of Israel the conceptual scheme of Lipset and Rokkan, which postulates that the formative period of a political system, when all groups in the society are mobilized by the parties, is an essential key to understanding the system as it develops in later periods.[2] Coleman came to complementary conclusions in his reanalysis of a large number of community studies.[3] He demonstrated that the reaction of a community to disputes in its early formative stage "loads the dice" and determines the resolution of disputes for many years thereafter.

Although two major Labor parties, Poalei Zion and Hapoel Hatzair, were established in Palestine in 1906, they did not play a significant role in the World Zionist Organization prior to World War I. It was not until the creation of Achdut Ha'avoda in 1919 (through the merger of Poalei Zion with other labor groups) and the establishment of the General Federation of Labor (the Histadrut) by Achdut Ha'avoda and Hapoel Hatzair in 1920 that the major period of the mobilization of political support and power was begun through the efforts to organize and unite the labor movement in the *yishuv*. The merger of Achdut Ha'avoda and Hapoel Hatzair in 1930 to form Mapai created the political force that was to dominate the Israeli political system until May 1977. Shapiro emphasizes two major goals that motivated the drive for mobilization of the labor movement. First of all, the leaders of the labor movement needed support in their drive to obtain greater funds from the World Zionist Organization (wzo) and greater freedom in the use of these funds, particularly in order to gain recognition of the legitimacy of their demand that their achievements be measured by political rather than economic criteria. Second, the influx of new immigrants who needed jobs and housing

---

[1] Yonathan Shapiro, *The Formative Years of the Israeli Labour Party: the Organization of Power 1919–1930*, SAGE Studies in Twentieth Century History, vol. 4 (London and Beverly Hills: Sage Publications, 1976).

[2] Seymour Martin Lipset and Stein Rokkan, eds., *Party System and Voters Alignment: Cross National Perspectives* (New York: The Free Press, 1967).

[3] James S. Coleman, *Community Conflict* (New York: The Free Press for the Bureau of Applied Social Research, Columbia University, 1957).

not only in agricultural but also in urban areas required the expansion of the services the Histadrut provided in order to mobilize their support; and the funds required to provide these services could only be obtained through the wzo.

Gorni emphasizes ideological factors underlying the creation of these institutions and in general stresses a much greater role for ideology in the politics of this period than does Shapiro.[4] In fact most scholars have stressed the high saliency and importance of ideology for the leaders and activists of the labor movement during this stage and attribute the high degree of legitimacy of the leadership largely to their ability to articulate and implement the ideology of their followers. While the weight of the evidence seems to support these claims for the earlier period, Shapiro's stress on the pragmatism of some of the top leaders, particularly Ben-Gurion, and the importance they placed on the building of a strong centralized political organization provides invaluable balance to previous scholarly preoccupation with ideology. Shapiro's analysis of the central role of political organization provides insights that are essential for an understanding of later developments. Whether or not the concern of the leadership for the lack of ideological commitment and devotion to the goals of the labor movement on the part of the general membership reported by Shapiro was well founded, the nature of the economic and political dependence which they encouraged through the organizations they built was to have significant ramifications for the development of the political system.

By the mid-1930s Mapai was well on the way toward consolidating its dominance of the major agricultural movements (kibbutz and moshav) and of the Histadrut, with its comprehensive network of economic, social, educational, and cultural services through which Mapai recruited political support. It used the successful mobilization of the power derived from this support to consolidate its dominant position in the executive of the Jewish Agency. As a result Mapai gained control over the distribution of the enormous financial resources provided through the World Zionist Organization and over manpower—specifically, over the immigration certificates provided through the British Mandatory Government. These resources were distributed according to the "party key" system, with each party receiving a share proportionate to its size on the Jewish Agency executive. Mapai also recruited new manpower through the important

---

[4] Yosef Gorni, *Achdut Ha'avoda 1919–1930: Hayesodot Haraayonim Ve-Ha-Shita Hamedinit* [Achdut Ha'avoda 1919–1930: the ideological principles and the political system] (Ramat-Gan, Israel: Hakibbutz Hameuchad Publishing House, 1973).

role it played in illegal immigration (after the British imposed severe restrictions). During this period it also dominated the major military organizations, the Hagana and its elite adjunct, the Palmach. Mapai's success was aided by the weakness of the General Zionist movement, which lacked strong or charismatic leadership, organization, and a coherent ideology, and by the fact that the Revisionist movement (which got a later start) left the wzo (setting up its own New Zionist Organization) during this period, which prevented it from competing directly for the resources provided by the wzo. The fact that the unquestioned leader of the Revisionists, Jabotinsky, spent almost all of his time abroad and that there were no leaders even close to his stature in the Palestine branch of the movement at the time considerably undermined the Revisionists' ability to compete with Mapai. It was also during this stage that the leaders of Mapai succeeded in identifying themselves with broader Zionist and national goals and expanded their constituency by gaining legitimacy from wider segments of the community than were affiliated with their institutions.

During this formative period certain organizational patterns were established which were to persist with significant ramifications throughout all of the years in which Labor dominated the Israeli political system. The basic characteristics as they emerged in the period under discussion have been best described by Shapiro. Their development in the postindependence period in Mapai has been traced by Medding,[5] and in the Israel Labor party from 1968 to 1977 in my own publications.[6] There emerged a top group of national leaders, supported by a secondary echelon of leaders who controlled the party and Histadrut apparatus. The emergence of these two groups of political leaders ensured that political goals dominated economic affairs. A system of indirect elections to party and Histadrut institutions, and nominations by small central appointments committees, guaranteed elite control of these institutions. Dependence on the elite was reinforced by the predominance of functionaries of the party and the Histadrut among the "elected" members of these institutions. Certain categories and groups (particularly those most supportive of the top leadership) were overrepresented in these institutions while others were underrepresented. Recruitment and political mobility were based on personal loyalty through patron-client relationships. Democratic procedures and the party constitution were frequently

---

[5] Peter Y. Medding, *Mapai in Israel: Political Organization and Government in a New Society* (Cambridge: Cambridge University Press, 1972).

[6] Myron J. Aronoff, *Power and Ritual in the Israel Labor Party: A Study in Political Anthropology* (Amsterdam/Assen: Van Gorcum, 1977).

ignored or set aside in the name of allegedly higher values; frequently the leaders' wishes were equated with the national will or interests. Criticism of and opposition to the top leaders were considered illegitimate, and sanctions were placed on those who engaged in such activities.

The development of this strong and highly centralized political organization enabled the top leaders who dominated the party to gain access to the resources that were mobilized abroad and to control their distribution, thus enhancing their power. Although Shapiro documents cases of the misuse of public funds as early as 1927, they were suppressed or, in some instances, excused by claims that the guilty persons were good Zionists who had served the public and the "movement." According to Shapiro, such incidents discredited the party and weakened public confidence in the ability of the leaders. However, these incidents were few and minor in their scope and impact compared with the corruption scandals that rocked the party fifty years later.

The Second Stage: Institutionalization. The next stage, which I characterize as that of institutionalization, was the period during which many of the most important functions previously carried out by the quasi-governmental institutions, such as the Jewish Agency and the Histadrut, were transferred to the new national government and its ministries. This stage began in 1948 and extended into the mid-1960s. The paramilitary organizations of the various political movements, the Hagana, the Palmach, and the Irgun, were disbanded, and Zahal, the Israel Defense Forces, was created and subordinated to the minister of defense. Similarly the various politically affiliated educational "streams" were abolished with the creation of the state educational system, and the labor exchange was moved from the Histadrut to the Ministry of Labor. This process strengthened the power and authority of the new state, but at the expense of the Histadrut. As the dominant force in the new government, Mapai was in a stronger position than ever before: it directed these essential functions in the name of the state, and it had the coercive power of the state at its disposal.

In the immediate postindependence period Mapai and its leaders gained wider support and legitimacy as they became identified with the state and gained credit for having brought about the realization of the Zionist dream. Ben-Gurion articulated a policy of *mamlachtiyut,* or statism, which emphasized that the state and its various agencies, such as the army, should take over the pioneering role played previously by the various agencies of the labor movement, for example, the Histadrut. While the shift from a more specifically socialist ideology to a more general nationalist one broadened the potential and actual constituency of Mapai, it also sowed the seeds for internal conflict within Mapai which was partially based on a strong resistance to what was perceived to be an abandonment of traditional socialist principles.

With the consolidation and the expansion of the party's dominant position through its control of the machinery of the independent state, and with the rapid expansion of its constituency through the mass immigration of a socially and culturally heterogeneous population of new citizens—an increasing proportion of whom came from the Islamic countries of North Africa and the Middle East—Mapai attempted to incorporate these new groups into the party. In mobilizing their support, it relied ever more on material inducements without basically altering its ideology. Lissak observed: "The parties preferred the development of a gap between theory and practice to both ideological compromise with the new reality created as a result of the new immigration and, obviously, to forgoing from the start any attempt to enlist new immigrants, who were unacquainted with the ideological legacy of the various parties, into their ranks."[7]

Ideologies are inherently vulnerable, particularly when they must be applied in the governing of a nation. As Seliger states: "For when ideology is made to function in the here and now it becomes subject to strains and stresses that endanger its relative consistency. In fulfilling its function of guiding political action, each political belief system is faced with the challenge of change. All such systems must deal with change, attempting either to perpetuate or to prevent it. In the process they are confronted with the challenge of changing themselves."[8] As the labor movement moved from the pioneering vanguard of Zionism to the ruling party, its leaders increasingly were confronted with conflicts between ideology and political expediency, and more often than not they sacrificed the former in the name of the latter.

The reluctance of the leaders of Mapai to adapt their ideology to the rapidly changing realities of a dynamic society and their increasingly greater reliance on nonideological incentives to mobilize support

---

[7] Moshe Lissak, "The Political Absorption of Immigrants and the Preservation of Political Integration in Israel," a paper presented at the International Political Science Association Round Table on Political Integration in Jerusalem, Israel, September 9–13, 1974, p. 17.

[8] Martin Seliger, "Fundamental and Operative Ideology: The Two Principal Dimensions of Political Argumentation," *Policy Sciences*, vol. 1 (1970), p. 326.

among the electorate and within the party ranks accompanied the internal party processes of increasing deviation from constitutionalism and democratic procedures and the development of an informal oligarchic power structure. Political machines developed in Tel Aviv and Haifa, and the former became the base upon which a national party machine emerged and was consolidated. Through the distribution of housing, jobs, offices, favors, and other forms of patronage, the party was able to mobilize wide public support, and the machine politicians were able to consolidate their control of the party and the Histadrut apparatus and thereby guarantee the top national leaders unquestioned support for their policies.

During the early 1950s a group of leading members of the party's youth section, known as the Tzeirim, began actively criticizing Mapai's lack of internal democracy. This led them into an open confrontation with the dominant party machine, known as the Gush (Bloc). The first major public showdown occurred at the eighth Mapai party conference in 1956. When Moshe Dayan resigned as chief of staff of the army and entered active political life in 1958 he became the titular leader of the Tzeirim. The entry of Dayan and others, such as Shimon Peres, who was director general of the Ministry of Defense, into the arena elevated the stakes and intensified the conflict since their challenge threatened the old guard leadership, who saw them as serious competitors for succession to the leadership of the party and the nation.

There was a significant generational difference between the younger mostly native-born members of the Tzeirim and the older Eastern European–born men of the Gush and the old guard of the party. This generational difference reflected very different political socialization, style, outlook, and ideology. The members of the Tzeirim were technocrats with limited practical political experience and with no patience for what they considered to be the outdated and inefficient ideology of socialist pioneering through the Histadrut and other agencies of the labor movement. Their call to further curtail the powers of the Histadrut in order to strengthen the state and to increase efficiency brought them into confrontation with the leadership of the Histadrut and of the more ideologically oriented kibbutz movements. Strong personal antagonism had developed between Dayan, Peres, and Ben-Gurion on the one hand and Pinchas Lavon, the former minister of defense who became secretary-general of the Histadrut, on the other. This bitter conflict became known as the Lavon affair and led to very deep divisions within the party, which culminated in a split of Mapai and the formation of a new party, Rafi, led by Ben-Gurion, Dayan, and Peres in 1965.

In the elections of 1965, the Alignment of Mapai and Achdut Ha'avoda, led by Levi Eshkol, gained 36.7 percent of the vote, and Rafi, led by Ben-Gurion, received only 7.9 percent. Unquestionably the most significant of several factors which determined the outcome of the election was the fact that when former Prime Minister Ben-Gurion led his ardent supporters out of Mapai into Rafi, they left control of the vast party apparatus in the hands of the old guard, Prime Minister Eshkol, Golda Meir, and Pinchas Sapir. Many of Ben-Gurion's sympathizers did not leave Mapai to join Rafi because they were dependent upon the party or its related institutions for their livelihoods and/or they feared to jeopardize their political careers for what they viewed as a political gamble. Medding has aptly summarized the outcome of the election: "Organization triumphed over charisma and institutional power over prophetic morality."[9]

The Israeli political system has been characterized throughout its history by a process of fission and fusion, a splitting apart and a remerging of political parties. This can be seen as an important means through which an otherwise fairly rigid political system has adapted to stresses and pressures caused by rapid socioeconomic and political change. Whereas these splits and mergers have taken place with some degree of regularity at different phases in the development of the political system, 1965 stands out as a major threshold: in addition to the split of Rafi from Mapai and Mapai's joining with Achdut Ha'avoda to form the Alignment, there were major splits in the Communist party and in the Liberal party as well as an historically important alignment between Herut and the former General Zionist wing of the Liberal party to form Gahal (the base that would expand to become the Likud).

Whereas in the earlier splits in the Labor parties (for example in the split of Faction B from Mapai to form Achdut Ha'avoda in 1944) ideological differences had played an important role, in the 1965 split of Rafi from Mapai ideological factors were secondary to the struggle for leadership of the party. After the subsequent merger of Mapai, Rafi, and Achdut Ha'avoda, which produced the Israel Labor party in 1968, the factional politics that characterized internal party competition was almost exclusively a struggle over representation in party institutions and in the Knesset and cabinet and for leadership of the party. After the challenge to the legitimacy of the party's

---

[9] Medding, *Mapai in Israel*, p. 279.

veteran leadership that breached the unity of the leadership and divided the party in the mid-1960s, the role of ideology was in a steady decline both among the general public and among the different levels of party leadership. The decline in the role of ideology corresponded with a parallel rise in the importance of the party machine, which increasingly took over key political functions. In the long run this increased internal disunity, increased feelings of political inefficacy, and contributed to the party's growing lack of responsiveness to new demands and interests.

The Third Stage: Immobilism. This situation became even more serious and pronounced during the next stage, the period of immobilism between the wars of June 1967 and October 1973. During this period ideology all but disappeared except on ritual occasions. To maintain itself in power, the party relied almost exclusively on a combination of the resources of the institutions it dominated, the state and the Histadrut, inertia, the conservatism of the electorate, and the ineffectiveness of the opposition.

Several outstanding features characterized the Labor party and Israeli society during the period of immobilism, in particular (1) a widespread feeling of political inefficacy (powerlessness) and (2) a generally observed (and within the party, enforced) taboo on criticism of the top party leadership and their policy. In the course of extensive research on the Labor party during these years, I documented the general prevalence of expressed feelings of political inefficacy among all levels of party activists and leadership from the local branches through the members of the national party institutions up to, but not including, the top executive Leadership Bureau (which was the only national party institution the meetings of which I did not regularly attend).[10] The feeling of a lack of influence on the formation of any party policies of importance was so widespread and so freely expressed among the branch membership, activists, and leaders that I do not hesitate to call it universal. What was far more surprising was to find the same frustration among the functionaries of the party bureaucracy and the members of the Central Committee and Secretariat of the party. In fact, on rare occasions even ministers in the cabinet gave public vent to similar feelings. In a tense meeting of the Central Committee on March 5, 1974, for example, Shimon Peres (who was then minister of communications and transportation) complained, "I was not in the Government just to fix telephones. My romantic

---

[10] Aronoff, *Power and Ritual*, pp. 58–63.

inclinations go beyond that. . . . When I was asked why Rafi met as a faction, I asked why there was a meeting of Ministers from Mapai and Achdut Ha'avoda at a certain house? Why was I not invited? Why do I always have to ask what was decided at this or that (informal) meeting?" In this speech Peres alluded to his exclusion from the inner circle of the top leadership which met informally and decided most important policy issues and was referred to in both the media and among party activists as "Golda's kitchen cabinet." A similar informal forum under the leadership of Pinchas Sapir decided all important internal party issues. Thus, the almost universal sense of political powerlessness and the frustration that ensued from it were founded on an accurate understanding of the distribution of power and of the decision-making processes of the party, which I shall discuss shortly. Before doing so, I shall briefly discuss the second most significant aspect of political culture in the party during this period, the important taboos.

Outspoken criticism of the top national leadership, strong disagreement with the policies of the leadership, and even open expression of a wide range of conflicting views, loyalties, and interests were generally forbidden to most of the members of the two largest national party institutions (the Central Committee and the Secretariat) in the period preceding the war of October 1973. Strong normative and pragmatic sanctions assured the enforcement of the taboo except for specific members whose social roles gave them ritual license to break them. (Benny Marshak, a sort of court jester, was allowed to speak the truth because he was not taken seriously, and Shulamit Alloni, Labor's *enfant terrible*, was expected to act as an internal party critic until she exceeded the permitted limits and was dropped from a realistic position on the party's list of candidates for the Knesset.)[11]

The policy for which there was least tolerance of criticism was that which was (and is) the most important—security and foreign affairs. As early as 1970 isolated individuals and politically marginal public figures, such as university professors, began questioning the basic assumption upon which the government's security policy was based—that retention of the territories occupied in the war of June 1967 would guarantee the nation's security from another war for at least a decade. In a meeting of the Labor party Secretariat in May 1970 these criticisms of government policy were attacked as if they were tantamount to disloyalty to the country. The security situation was used to stifle criticism, terminate debate, and suppress con-

---

[11] Shulamit Alloni left the Labor party to head a new Citizen's Rights list and was elected to the Knesset in 1973 and in 1977.

troversial issues that the leadership preferred not to discuss. When a representative of the students' organization defended the critics saying, "We are a democratic society. It is healthy that people are thinking and concerned, and criticize," he was constantly interrupted by heckling. Alternative policies were prevented from being broached and seriously considered. The consequences of this situation proved to be disastrous in October 1973.

However, there were also special ritual occasions when selected members of the secondary echelon of leadership were allowed, within specified constraints, to violate these taboos and to engage in rebellious criticism of the leadership and its policies, to identify themselves as a special group differentiated from the elite and the grass-roots leadership, and to assert their own ideological position.

I shall focus my analysis on the relationship between certain institutional features, the dynamics of relationships of power, and the aforementioned characteristics of political culture in the Labor party during the period of immobilism to explain the lack of responsiveness of the Labor party to public demands, which, I argue, is the main reason for its defeat in the elections of May 1977. The discussion will consider the process through which candidates are nominated to party institutions and to the Knesset, the nature of representation on these bodies, the decision-making process which included the suppression of important issues, and what I consider ritual behavior in the party.

Candidate Selection. According to the late E. E. Schattschneider: "The nominating process . . . has become the crucial process of the party. The nature of the nominating procedure determines the nature of the party; *he who can make nominations is the owner of the party.* This is therefore one of the best points at which to observe the distribution of power within the party."[12] Nowhere is the validity of this maxim more vividly demonstrated than in an analysis of the nominations process in the Labor party (as well as in most other Israeli political parties prior to 1976, when some important changes took place).

Candidates for membership on party institutions and in the Knesset have traditionally been selected through a small committee known as the nominations or selection committee (*vaadat minuim*). This committee is appointed by the top party leadership, who generally choose their most trusted lieutenants from the secondary echelon of leaders to represent their views and interests on the committee. However, rather than entrusting this task to a surrogate,

---

[12] E. E. Schattschneider, *Party Government* (New York: Farrar and Rinehart, 1942), p. 64, emphasis added.

Finance Minister Pinchas Sapir had himself appointed chairman of the nominations committee charged with the selection of the party's candidates for the Knesset in the 1973 election. Evidently it was felt that at this critical juncture in the party's history the most powerful man in the party's informal hierarchy (the leader of the machine) needed to personally undertake this all-important task, since any person of lesser stature would probably have failed to enforce the extremely difficult decisions that had to be made.

In addition to balancing the demands for representation of the various internal party factions and interest groups, the nominations committee must ensure that those chosen are loyal to their patrons in the top leadership. Once the list is compiled by the nominations committee, it is submitted en bloc for approval by the appropriate party institution, which has the constitutional authority to make the nominations (in most cases, the Central Committee). I stress the ceremonial nature of this legitimating vote, since I could not find a single case in which the list proposed by the nominations committee was not accepted.

The Party Conference. The constitutional structure of authority in the Labor party resembles a pyramid in which the largest representative institution at the base, the party conference, is supposed to be supreme. However, in reality, there is an inverse relationship between constitutional authority and real power which is nowhere more obvious than in the party conference. The conferences of Mapai and the Labor party have traditionally been ceremonial shows of unity. They have generally given formal ratification and symbolic legitimization to decisions already made in smaller party forums.

The only two occasions when the delegates at Mapai conferences used their constitutional authority and made important decisions were in 1942 and 1965, when the top leadership was sharply divided on critical issues. The resolution of the power struggles at these conferences led each time to the minority faction's splitting away from Mapai and establishing an independent party (first Achdut Ha'avoda and then Rafi).

For the first Labor party conference in April 1971, the resolutions to be passed had been carefully prepared in advance and their ceremonial approval was a foregone conclusion. This was the result of the consolidation and control of the conference, through its Standing Committee, by the party machine organized and led by Pinchas Sapir. Known as the Preparation Committee prior to the conference, this committee traditionally prepared beforehand every aspect of the resolutions to be passed at the conference; once the conference was in session, it became the Standing Committee—and continued to dominate the proceedings.

The top party leadership carefully selected 63 percent of the 134-member Preparation/Standing Committee of the 1971 party conference through a series of nominating committees. The remaining 37 percent were elected from the kibbutz and moshav movements and the larger branches of the party. Older males from Eastern Europe were overrepresented on the committee, which was representative not of the party membership as a whole, but of the top and secondary level of party leadership and functionaries. In addition, 86 percent of the members of the committee were either elected party officials or functionaries of the party or of Histadrut-affiliated enterprises and institutions who were directly or indirectly dependent upon the party for their livelihoods. Regardless of their subdivisions into various interest groups and former party factions, the members of the Standing Committee had been selected for their dependence upon and loyalty to the top leadership. They were a distinct sociopolitical category—the secondary echelon of leaders and functionaries.

The Standing Committee originally decided that two-thirds of the members of the new Central Committee would be elected by the branch caucuses of the delegates to the party conference and one-third would be chosen by a central nominations committee. After a prolonged series of traditional manipulations, the proportion of the membership of the new Central Committee chosen by the central nominations committee was expanded to 45 percent and the membership of the Central Committee was expanded from 501 to over 600. Consequently the top leadership easily dominated the new Central Committee. The Central Committee was expanded in order to grant the demands of various groups for greater representation, but once enlarged it became so cumbersome that it was ineffective as a decision-making body.

The Standing Committee also formulated party policy on a wide range of issues and struck from the agenda of the conference controversial issues the outcomes of which the leadership feared would not support their positions. Two of the most important issues suppressed from the agenda of the conference—religion and the state, and issues related to the Histadrut (wage policy and labor relations) —were among the most salient issues for the delegates and for the general public. Significantly, Arian has shown that religious observance and affiliation to the Histadrut are the two most important factors in determining voting in Israel.[13] Given the reluctance of the party elites to allow free discussion and debate on these issues in the major party institutions and their tendency to suppress highly salient but controversial issues, one alternative was to allow symbolic debate of such issues in a controlled ritual forum.

The Standing Committee served admirably as such a forum because of the great dependence of the secondary echelon on the top party leadership; having successfully internalized party norms, they could be trusted to abide by the rules of the game. The rule that guaranteed the success of the ritual debates was that the outcomes were determined in advance. 'After the free expression of opinions in real debates, "consensual" formulations were reached (which, not coincidentally, coincided with the top leadership's policies) and were passed on to the conference delegates for their ceremonial approval. No minority reports from the Standing Committee were allowed on important issues. In this way particularly sensitive and controversial issues that could not be entirely suppressed were successfully defused. This was the fate, for example, of the highly salient and potentially explosive issue of ethnic relations in Israel.

In my previously published analysis of the successful control of the party conference through the suppression of issues and the ritualization of debate in the Standing Committee I particularly stressed the conservative effect and the temporary nature of the success of these procedures in maintaining the status quo and in keeping the party going. I warned that the appearance of unity and strength conveyed by the "successful" party conference was at best illusory, for the following reasons:

> There is widespread discontent among party activists who complain that they are not able to influence decisions on policy, particularly on issues which appear to the general public to be the most pressing domestic problems. These significantly were the very issues which were most carefully controlled, or even suppressed, in the conference. I stress that the "solutions" of consensual formulation within the context of carefully bracketed rituals and the suppression of issues through ritual procedures are *temporary*. Vital issues such as the relationships between ethnic groups, problems of poverty which are tied to the former issue and also to wage policies and labor relations, the question of what should be the proper role of religion in the state, and so

---

[13] Alan Arian, *The Choosing People* (Cleveland: Case Western Reserve University Press, 1973), p. 55.

forth, are questions which demand policies aimed at their solution in spite of the inherent difficulties involved.

The general public has increasingly stated its demands that solutions to these problems be found. The procedures which the top leaders have used successfully to postpone decisions on these issues have given them a temporary respite in which they have consolidated their control of the party. They have thus far refrained from proposing controversial policies which they feared might antagonize important sectors within the party and the public. But their successful use of these procedures of control was most effective with that supporting category closest to them and most dependent on the elite. The sanctions, both normative and otherwise, which enforced the loyalty of the members of the Standing Committee to the top leaders were becoming increasingly less effective as against the third level of local leadership, the general party membership, and the electorate.[14]

Representation within the Party. Before discussing the new threshold in the developing Israeli political system ushered in, or catalyzed by, the traumatic events of October 1973, I shall briefly summarize additional important characteristics of the Labor party during the period of immobilism. In addition to, and closely related to, the nominations process, the nature of the representation of various groups and interests on a party's governing bodies is an important means of evaluating the responsiveness of the party to various constituencies and to changes in the society. A comparative analysis of the representation of various groups and social categories on the main joint institutions formed by the three-party merger that created the Labor party in 1968 and those elected following the party conference in 1971 reveals an important pattern of continuity (with some interesting change) in the overrepresentation of certain groups and the underrepresentation of others. For purposes of analysis, each group's strength in the national party membership (expressed as a percentage) was divided into its representation on each governing body (also expressed as a percentage) to arrive at a mathematically "ideal" equitable distribution based solely on the relative size of party membership for each group.

Three of the most important factors which influence deviation from the ideal-type model of equitable distribution are: (1) the appointment of a significant proportion of the members of the

---

[14] Aronoff, *Power and Ritual*, pp. 94–95.

institutions through central nominations committees, which allows the top party leaders to give additional representation to those groups and individuals most closely supportive of them; (2) the organization of the three main cities, Tel Aviv, Jerusalem, and Haifa, and the two kibbutz federations and the moshav federation into separate districts; and (3) the granting of extra weight to kibbutz members in internal elections, which automatically guarantees their overrepresentation.

The comparative analysis revealed a striking continuity in the basic pattern of overrepresentation of Tel Aviv district and the kibbutz federations, which had increasingly greater overrepresentation on the smaller and more important institutions, reaching approximately three times the number their membership alone would merit in the top executive, the Leadership Bureau. The Tel Aviv district was the base of the national party machine from which successive national leaders drew much of their support in the major party institutions. There is a similar continuity in the pattern of overrepresentation of Eastern European-born politicians which correlated with the previously mentioned pattern since the representation of Eastern Europeans is most pronounced in the Tel Aviv and Haifa machines and in the kibbutz movement.

Most striking is the improved position of native-born Israelis, who have substantially increased their representation on all party bodies. This is obviously related to demographic changes; the aging veteran founders are gradually being replaced by an Israeli-born generation. The blatant underrepresentation (despite marginal improvement) of party members from the Islamic countries of the Middle East, the so-called Oriental Jews, is closely related to the underrepresentation of the development towns in northern and southern Israel, where Oriental Jews are a majority of the population. A final and most important finding was that a significantly large proportion of the members of the party institutions are dependent for their livelihoods on party and party-dominated institutions.

The dependence of such a large proportion of the members of the party's national institutions on the party for their livelihoods, particularly when combined with considerable political dependence on the top leadership who control the nominations, considerably limits the freedom of action of these individuals. This situation was a direct continuation of the pattern in the former Mapai. Medding draws the following conclusion from his analysis of Mapai:

> Its internal operations were flawed by insufficient attention
> to formal and universalistic criteria, particularly with re-
> gard to elections, which cast doubts upon the legitimacy

of its electoral processes, aroused internal dissent and made it possible for certain groups to impair the participation of others. On the other hand, these same processes were able to produce results that were highly representative in terms of the party's social diversity, even if there was a marked degree of control over the exact identity of personnel making up this representative group, which may not have been a true reflection of membership views.[15]

There are several important flaws in Medding's conclusions. In the first place, I have demonstrated that the party institutions were not representative, even in the most general usage of the term, of the party's social diversity with regard to ethnic, sex, and age composition, geographic distribution, or the division between agricultural and urban sectors. Second, Medding's use of the term "representative" ignores the key problem of accountability, that is, the responsiveness of the representative to his constituency. There are two major ideal-type representative-constituency relationships in the Labor party. There are those genuine representatives who are selected by well-organized and powerful interest groups, for example the kibbutz federations, who are then presented to the nominations committees as the choice of these groups. In such cases it is reasonable to assume that they are accountable to these groups. At the other extreme there are the so-called representatives whose so-called constituencies are largely fictional since they are not well organized and/or they do not choose their representatives.

The so-called representatives of ethnic, age, and sex categories are good examples of this. They are neither chosen by their constituencies nor accountable to them in any meaningful sense. They have been labeled "pseudo" and "symbolic" representatives, but I argue that the term "client" is more accurate in designating their dependence upon and accountability to the national party patrons who control their appointments.[16]

Most of the members of party institutions fall into an intermediate category; although they ostensibly represent a defined constituency, they are in no meaningful way held accountable to it. Almost all representatives of local branches on national institutions are local elites who are the clients of national patrons. They neither

---

[15] Medding, *Mapai in Israel*, p. 302.

[16] Moshe Czudnowski, "Legislative Recruitment under Proportional Representation in Israel: A Model and a Case-Study," *Midwest Journal of Political Science*, vol. 14 (1970), pp. 216–248; and Avraham Brichta, "Social and Political Characteristics of Members of the Seventh Knesset," in Alan Arian, ed., *The Elections in Israel—1969* (Jerusalem: Jerusalem Academic Press, 1972), pp. 109–131.

consult their branches before debates and votes in the national institutions (debates in branches rarely precede debates in the national institutions) nor do they usually report the results of debates, the positions they took, or the manner in which they voted. When asked to identify the constituency represented by a given member of the Central Committee, knowledgeable party functionaries invariably responded, "his mother!"; in other words, none. The fact that most members of the party's institutions have to account for their actions not to the constituencies for whom they ostensibly act, but to the top party leaders who chose them through the nominations committees, leads me to question the applicability of the term "representative" in an evaluation of their roles in these institutions.

The fact that the top party leaders have responded to the increasing demands of various groups for greater representation in these institutions, while giving the appearance of making these institutions more representative in their composition, has resulted in making them even less effective. Rather than limiting the representation of groups that were overrepresented in order to equalize the representation of groups that were underrepresented, the top leaders simply increased the size of the institutions to accommodate the additional members. This has resulted in inflating the institutions beyond the point where they can function efficiently. For example, the Central Committee now has over 800 members; the Secretariat was so obviously dysfunctional that it was abolished; and even the executive Leadership Bureau became so inflated that it ceased to be effective.

The major consequence of this process has been the bypassing of the constitutionally authorized (supposedly representative) bodies and the centralization of decision making and power in small informal groups of top leaders with euphemistic names such as Golda's kitchen cabinet and Sapir's new Gush. Under such circumstances the formal institutions became little more than rubber stamps used to give legitimation to decisions already reached. This was made painfully obvious to the members of these institutions on frequent occasions when they were called into session to debate issues that the media had reported as already settled by the top leadership. These factors contributed greatly to the erosion of responsiveness of the leadership to the party institutions and the growing gap between both and the general public. This process culminated after the trauma of the Yom Kippur War.

A Crisis of Confidence: Labor after 1973

I argue that this period represents a new threshold in the developing Israeli political system which was characterized in its initial phase by a major crisis of confidence in the credibility of the national party leadership and the Labor party as a whole. It led to a changing of the guard in the highest level of party leadership, the emergence of new internal party coalitions, and ultimately to the termination of the Labor party's fifty-year dominance of Israeli society. In evaluating the response of the party to the events of this period and the resultant changes it made, an appropriate subtitle would be "Too Little and Too Late."

Five years ago I wrote:

> The initial reactions of public shock at the unexpected outbreak of war began to be articulated from the grass roots to higher echelons of the party even while the fighting ensued. For example, in a meeting which the Secretary-General, Yadlin, called with local party leaders in which he reported on Government policy and developments of the war (October 17, 1973), many of the local leaders reported "deep shock among the people" and said that some people were "asking questions which reach the sources of trust"; and some claimed there was developing a "crisis of confidence in the Government." They listed as examples of the kinds of questions that were being asked: "Where was our intelligence?; Where were the reserves and why weren't they mobilized sooner?; and What did you tell us about the Bar Lev Line?" Yadlin, representing the views of the top leadership, replied, "The people will be wise. When the time comes for them to vote, they will vote correctly."[17]

As I have reflected on these events and on developments since I recorded this statement, it has come to symbolize for me more succinctly than any elaborate explanation the arrogance of power that had become characteristic of the leadership of the Labor party. They did not need to listen to what the public was saying, for they knew what was best for the people; and they were supremely confident that the people would realize that they, the leaders, indeed knew what was best for them. Only this mentality could explain the presumption that even in such a crisis the people would be "wise" and vote "correctly." While the local leaders who attended this meeting stressed the need for a special meeting of the Central Committee immediately after the termination of the war to raise important criticisms, Yadlin stressed the government's dilemma, which was, "what to *explain* to the people during the war."[18] One of the major charges leveled against the

---

[17] Aronoff, *Power and Ritual*, p. 145.

[18] Ibid., p. 145, emphasis added.

government from within and without the party was that the government had failed to resolve this dilemma with sufficient candor. Most important, the critics felt that the ministers most directly responsible for the "blunder" (a weak translation of the Hebrew *mechdal*) had failed to accept their responsibility for its tragic consequences.

The initial protests precipitated by the war were directed primarily against the key government ministers who were considered to bear the greatest responsibility for the *mechdal*, Minister of Defense Moshe Dayan and eventually Prime Minister Golda Meir as well. The initial demand was that they should resign. However, as the protest movement grew, a more comprehensive critique was made of the lack of responsiveness of the government to public concerns, which was largely attributed to the undemocratic procedures of the dominant Labor party. Eventually several important disclosures of corruption involving leading members of the Labor party created the widely accepted impression among the public that the Labor party bore a major share of the responsibility for the breakdown in public morals and for the general social malaise that was increasingly characterizing Israeli society.

The significance of subsequent events must be seen within the perspective of the parallel and complementary processes of internal criticism within the Labor party and an increasingly organized public protest movement. In each rare case in recent Israeli history when public opinion has had an effective impact on politics, it has been supported by groups within the dominant party and/or within the governing coalition cabinet. Thus, it was the combined effect of public opinion, coalition partners, and pressure within Mapai that forced Prime Minister Eshkol to relinquish the defense portfolio to Moshe Dayan in 1967 shortly before the Six-Day War. The failure to appreciate the importance of this reciprocal relationship between organized public opinion and pressure from within the Labor party in bringing about change has led the authors of a recent scholarly article on the response of the Israeli establishment to the war protest to underestimate and minimize the impact of the post-Yom Kippur War protest movement.[19]

It is also significant that the initial internal party criticisms preceded (by more than two months) the demonstrations of the demobilized veterans of the Yom Kippur War triggered by Moti Ashkenazi's successful one-man demonstration. (He was eventually

---

[19] Eva Etzioni-Halevy and Moshe Livne, "The Response of the Israeli Establishment to the Yom Kippur War Protest," *The Middle East Journal*, vol. 31, pp. 281–296.

joined by thousands.) Ironically, it was veterans of previous wars— former high-ranking officers affiliated with the Labor party group called Challenge (*etgar*)—who, according to my records, made the first critical evaluations of government policy after the war. In a meeting on November 26, 1973, the leader of the group, Joseph Nevo (the mayor of Herzlia and a military analyst for the news media) launched the debate with a critical analysis of government policy and a particularly critical assessment of the role of the minister of defense. He argued that the previous party (and government) policy known as the Galili statement needed serious revision "since the basic premise on which it was based—that there would be no war—was now irrelevant." Another member of the group seemed to express the views of a majority when he said, "Until the war I accepted what was said —that borders guaranteed peace. We were wrong and now [we] need to try a new path."[20]

Although the top leadership managed to prevent major criticism from being expressed at the first meeting of the Central Committee after the war on November 28, 1973, by carefully controlling the agenda, the next meeting on December 5, 1973, resulted in a volatile debate which lasted all day and into the early hours of the morning. In a series of closed meetings prior to this, the bosses of the dominant party machine led by Pinchas Sapir (who was then finance minister) had decided to continue to back Golda Meir as the party's candidate for prime minister in the forthcoming election (postponed because of the war), but to fight for major policy changes in the party platform.

The acrimonious debate at the December 5 meeting of the Central Committee focused primarily on criticism and defense of previous party policy and secondarily on criticism and defense of Moshe Dayan. Top party leaders associated with Pinchas Sapir attacked Dayan and claimed that the Galili statement of party policy was no longer operative. Golda Meir, Moshe Dayan, and their supporters refuted the charges and defended the Galili statement, insisting that it still expressed their policy. This led to a rare public confrontation between the two strongest leaders of the party, Meir and Sapir, in which Sapir narrowly averted a possible party split by preventing a vote on the issue and by proclaiming that each could follow his own interpretation of party policy. After the meeting Golda Meir castigated Sapir, telling him that his ploy had failed to resolve anything.

Golda Meir and Moshe Dayan had been anxious to gain approval of the Galili statement, especially its provisions sanctioning settlements in the territories occupied by Israel after the 1967 war. Sapir had been

---

[20] Aronoff, *Power and Ritual*, p. 146.

anxious to prevent this both because of his ideological opposition to the provisions for expanding these settlements and because he genuinely feared that a showdown between the prime minister and himself on this issue at this time would threaten party unity and might lead to a split. It is significant that previous direct confrontations between the top leaders of Mapai in 1944 and in 1965 had led to splits in the party. The events that followed shortly after this meeting indicated that the danger of a new party split was a real one.

Because an agreement between Labor and the major opposition alignment, the Likud, set the date for the 1973 election at the end of December, there was no possibility for new parties to submit slates for the election, and the existing ones chose not to change their lists which had been drawn up before the outbreak of the Yom Kippur War. This fact, in addition to the immediacy of the election after the war and the proximity of the impending Geneva Conference (which Labor exploited to its advantage), to a large extent prevented the full impact of the ramifications of the war from being registered in the 1973 election. In a real sense this impact was registered as a delayed reaction, along with the reaction to the events of the interim years, in May 1977.

Although Labor suffered a setback in the 1973 election, it retained its plurality and Golda Meir was charged by the president with the task of forming a new government. Because of difficulties with Labor's traditional coalition partner, the National Religious party, the prime minister designate proposed a minority government that would command the votes of only 58 Knesset members (out of 120), 54 members affiliated with the Labor Alignment (including Mapam) and 4 of the Independent Liberals.[21] However, the reluctance of Moshe Dayan and Shimon Peres to join the government, in protest against the heightened internal party criticisms of Dayan, brought into question the votes of the Labor Knesset members affiliated with the Rafi faction. The meetings of Labor's Central Committee on February 24 and March 5, 1974, were held against the ominous background of an impending party split.

The Changing of the Guard. On March 10 the Knesset voted its approval of the new government headed by Golda Meir, which included both the National Religious party and Dayan and Peres, who joined

---

[21] David Nachmias, "Coalition, Myth, and Reality," and Eliezer Don-Yehiya, "Religion and Coalition: The National Religious Party and Coalition Formation in Israel," pp. 255–284; in Alan Arian, ed., *The Elections in Israel—1973* (Jerusalem: Jerusalem Academic Press, 1975), pp. 301–305.

the cabinet in the "national interest" after a military incident on the Syrian border. However, the attacks on both Dayan and Golda Meir from within the party and from an increasingly organized public protest movement intensified. The combined pressure from both quarters resulted in the resignation of Golda Meir on April 11, 1974, which automatically brought down the government she had formed.

After Meir's resignation, the top leaders of the party made an unprecedented decision to allow a competitive secret election in the Central Committee to choose the party's new candidate for prime minister. The two candidates who competed for the post were Yitzhak Rabin and Shimon Peres. Had Pinchas Sapir, who was considered by most observers to be Golda's natural successor, accepted the plea of a delegation of party leaders to take the post there would not have been a competitive election. But Sapir declined the offer and threw his considerable support behind Rabin, which was sufficient to help Rabin win a narrow 298 to 254 vote victory over Peres. Sapir also refused a post in Rabin's new cabinet, choosing instead to take over the chairmanship of the Jewish Agency. Although he had built a dominant position in the party, at this critical juncture in the party's development Sapir made the very unusual decision to withdraw from direct involvement at the highest level of party government activity. He died approximately a year later. His last role in internal party maneuvers before his death was to support an effort initiated by Abba Eban to reconstitute Mapai as a formal faction in an unsuccessful attempt to regain its lost influence. Eban, who had strained relations with Rabin, had been excluded from the new Rabin cabinet.

This initiative was defeated by the new coalition that Rabin put together. He was backed by Sapir's successor as finance minister, Yehoshua Rabinowitz (an old ally of Sapir's) who was the boss of the Tel Aviv machine, his labor minister, Moshe Baram, who dominated the Jerusalem branch, and Joseph Almogi, who was at the time mayor of Haifa and boss of its machine. Almogi became chairman of the Jewish Agency after the death of Sapir. Peres, who emerged from his narrow defeat by Rabin as a leader of considerable stature, became minister of defense. Yigal Allon became minister of foreign affairs.

This coalition was initially strong enough to push through a controversial piece of legislation that was particularly unpopular among the public. The law, which authorized large government loans at low rates of interest to the political parties—at a time when the public was being subjected to new taxes and severe economic restrictions—was eventually invalidated by the Supreme Court. As the party bosses of the main city machines became more and more preoccupied with their ministerial duties they gradually lost their grip on their political bases. Rabin, who had no real political party experience prior to becoming prime minister, totally ignored the party institutions and thereby virtually eliminated the last semblance of the party's role in policy making. As the formal party institutions ceased to function with even the symbolic roles they had held under Golda Meir, desperate attempts were made to resuscitate the ravaged party. The "leading forum" (*haforum hamovil*), a group of top party leaders including Golda Meir and other veterans, was established to coordinate the policy of the government and the Histadrut through the party in a desperate attempt to reassert the role of the party in the governing of the nation. It was stillborn. In a heavy-handed attempt to streamline the cabinet, Rabin succeeded in antagonizing some of the very people who had put him in power and sowed further divisiveness within his own government. In addition, differences over policy coupled with their personal ambitions led to increasing strains between Rabin and Foreign Minister Allon, on the one hand, and Rabin and Defense Minister Peres on the other.

Change from Below. The political vacuum created by the abdication of leadership from above prompted the leaders of a dozen of the party's largest branches to call for a "revolution from below." While the changes the active group of local leaders initiated were far from revolutionary, some of them were significant. Unquestionably the single most important organizational change they succeeded in carrying out was the creation of eight new regional districts in the party. Although the decision to create these new geographic frameworks had been made at the previous conference, as long as the top leadership had exercised power they had prevented its implementation. They resisted the consolidation of relatively weak and divided branches into united districts, because this would give the branches more power and greater autonomy. However, as the national leadership was weakened through the major changes at the top, divisiveness, and lack of attention to internal party affairs, the combined efforts of the local leaders and key personnel in the party bureaucracy, particularly in the Organization Department, succeeded in establishing the new districts.[22]

As a result of a membership registration drive (prior to internal elections to the party conference) which was much more carefully supervised than in the past, some 50,000 applications were rejected

---

[22] This was part of a very significant process the development of which I have traced and analyzed from 1965. See Aronoff, *Power and Ritual*, pp. 119–144.

because of irregularities. This brought down party membership figures to under 250,000 (which is still an inflated figure). The most substantial reductions through the rejection of irregularities were in the two largest districts, Tel Aviv and Haifa, which were reduced from approximately 45,000 and 44,000 respectively to approximately 27,000 members each. This resulted in a substantial reduction in the number of delegates they were entitled to send to the party conference; indeed, it put them on a par with several of the newly created districts and reduced their dominance of party institutions. The tradition of granting overrepresentation to the agricultural movements was continued.

Consequently the overrepresentation of the older generation of Eastern Europeans, who dominated the two main city machines, was substantially reduced, and the representation of the younger continuing generation, the Israeli-born, and the Middle Eastern Jews was substantially increased in the party conference and the newly elected institutions. However, since the new Central Committee was inflated to 819 members, membership in this institution had become substantially devalued.

One of the most important fights waged by the new districts was over the composition of the key Preparation and Standing committees. Whereas previously their membership had been identical, for the second national party conference in 1977 this was not the case. The Preparation Committee was composed of 30 ranking leaders plus the secretary-general, and the Standing Committee comprised 201 members, two-thirds of them elected from the districts and one-third appointed by a central nominations committee. A substantial proportion (but not all) of the proposals of the Preparation Committee were authorized by the Steering Committee and sent to the conference unamended. In addition, the young Guard and Continuing Generation groups in the party formed an informal alternate preparation committee of their own in which they debated issues and passed resolutions, which they submitted to the Standing Committee. Some of these proposals were accepted and submitted to the conference as proposals of the Standing Committee, others were defeated in the Standing Committee and were presented as minority proposals to the conference. On rare occasions minority proposals were actually passed by the conference delegates. One important proposal, requiring rotation in elected offices and fixing a maximum limit on tenure of office, was an example of such a controversial proposal which was defeated in the Standing Committee but accepted in the conference.

Feeble Attempts at Reform. At the second party conference interest was riveted on the unprecedented election of the party's candidate for prime minister in this forum. Again Rabin won a narrow victory over Peres, but this time it was in the much larger forum of the conference rather than in the Central Committee. While the election indicated a healthy introduction of democratic competition in the largest and most representative party forum, the race came dangerously close to polarizing and splitting the party on a new factional basis. The new division was not clearly associated with the ideological policy differences between the two candidates, since the more "dovish" Rabin received the support of self-proclaimed "hawks," and the more "hawkish" Peres received the enthusiastic support of some of the party's leading "doves." Although a complex assortment of motives and factors accounted for the alignment and support of the two candidates, unquestionably the dominant factor was the power struggle. The contending factions fought over control of the party, and their competition did little to raise the level of the debate or to improve the party's morale or public image.

The proceedings leading up to and during the national party conference were unquestionably more open and democratic than in the past, yet the old manipulations and rituals prevailed. The conference did not even inspire most participants with the prospect of a substantially reformed and democratized party, and the election results soon proved that the party had failed to convince the majority of the electorate. A good example of the "too little and too late" character of Labor's reforms was the compromise system adopted for nominating its candidates for the Knesset. The new Central Committee approved the leadership's proposed seven-member nominations committee which would select 60 percent of the party's Knesset list, and the remaining 40 percent was elected by the party's fifteen districts. However, the final ordering of the list was also delegated to the nominations committee, which meant that the nominations committee could assign the "realistic" positions on the list and thus determine who would have a serious chance of being elected. This was a variation on a traditional theme. Only the most hopelessly politically naive person could have been deceived into believing that this gesture toward more democratic participation in the nominations process amounted to a substantive change of any real importance. This stood in dramatic contrast with the primary election of Knesset candidates by all of the members of the newly formed Democratic Movement for Change and the more democratized nominations procedures introduced by most of the other parties for the first time for the 1977 Knesset elections.

The Immediate Causes of Labor's Decline

Thus far I have dealt with the major variables which during the course of the development of the Israeli political system led the Labor party to become increasingly unresponsive to public concerns, which, I have argued, is the main underlying reason for its defeat in the 1977 election. In addition there were a number of interrelated specific factors which contributed to Labor's defeat. An historically shortsighted interpretation of the election results would undoubtedly place greater emphasis on the importance of these factors. However, since I have stressed the importance of a gradual, cumulative erosion of the party's responsiveness, I view these factors as the culmination of this process.

For example, the dominant pattern of upward mobility for leaders was based on an extreme form of patron-client relationships. The fastest and surest way to climb the political ladder for an ambitious, young politician was to become associated with, and to loyally serve, a strong patron among the top leaders. However, in most circumstances the primary obligation to loyally serve his patron did not allow the client to demonstrate or to develop independent initiative and leadership abilities. Therefore when the patrons were faced with the need to fill important leadership positions, they frequently overlooked their loyal clients (whom they considered "yes men") and chose political outsiders, often retired high-ranking army officers. A close confidant of Pinchas Sapir told me in reference to a disappointed ranking politician who had hoped that he would get Sapir's support as the party's candidate for prime minister, "If he had ever once said 'no' to Sapir, Sapir would have probably backed him for the premiership." Consequently at a most critical time, the party's and the nation's highest office was given to a man who completely lacked political party experience, Yitzhak Rabin.

Whereas Rabin cannot be faulted for the state of the party when he inherited the leadership (for he had never been involved in it), he bears a full share of responsibility for the further deterioration that the party underwent during his tenure of office. Rather than providing dynamic leadership and initiative in encouraging long overdue reforms, he basically ignored the party and reached most important decisions without even consulting it. To make matters worse, the party post of secretary-general was filled by one of the weakest politicians in party history. The term of Meir Zarmi (which coincided with Rabin's premiership), a kibbutznik without any personal political standing or power base, was characterized by his many resignations, all but the last of which were retracted. Rabin's choice for the head of the all-important party election team was a fellow former chief of staff of the Israel Defense Forces, Haim Bar-Lev. Bar-Lev, who began his political career only shortly before Rabin (as minister of commerce and industry in the cabinet of Golda Meir), completely lacked the political experience, skills, and savvy that were essential to success in the job. Although the two most experienced party experts on elections, Pinchas Sapir and his protégé Avraham Ofer, were no longer alive, there were many others more qualified for the position than was Bar-Lev.

However, even men with greater experience at their jobs turned in singularly unimpressive performances. Many commentators singled out Yossie Sarid (a particularly successful client of the late Sapir), who ran the party propaganda campaign in the media along authoritarian lines, for more than his share of the blame for the counterproductive effects of many of his efforts in the media. And throughout the entire campaign the efforts of many party workers were further hindered by the factional infighting that continued between the followers of Rabin and those of Peres.

Blunders and Scandals. Among the several strategic mistakes made by the Labor party leaders, two stand out for their particularly dire consequences for the party. Elections to the Histadrut had always preceded the Knesset elections until 1977. The Histadrut elections had always served not only to indicate electoral trends, but also to absorb a certain amount of voter protest against Labor (even though Labor has always done better in Histadrut elections than in Knesset elections). Given the results of both elections in 1977, it seems likely that had the Histadrut election come first it would have absorbed some of the punishment that the electorate wanted to give to Labor, and the drop in the Labor vote in the Knesset election would very likely have been less than it was. Many people who voted against Labor in the Knesset voted for it in the Histadrut.

The decision to separate the national election to the Knesset from the local elections to municipal councils, which had traditionally taken place on the same day, had particularly disastrous consequences for the Labor party. Probably the single greatest political advantage the Labor party had over other Israeli political parties was its reasonably well-organized party apparatus based on an extensive network of local party branches. It is no secret to those familiar with the workings of this apparatus that by and large local Labor politicians were more motivated to get out the vote for themselves and their local candidates than they were to drum up the vote for their national candidates. When they did both at the same time, the apparatus worked well. However, the decision to separate the two elections eliminated the motivation of local (self-) interest and accounted to a large extent for the relatively low turnout and performance of local Labor election workers. This had been anticipated by those who were familiar with the nature of the reciprocal relationships between the party center and local branches, but their warnings were ignored and the party paid the price for its leaders' poor judgment. There were many additional factors that influenced the general demoralization of the Labor party election workers, and most of them influenced the electorate as well.

The many public scandals arising from convictions of public figures on charges of corruption reached a peak in the so-called Yadlin affair, which became a major Israeli *cause célèbre* in the period preceding the election. Asher Yadlin, who directed the Histadrut's comprehensive Kupat Holim health services and was nominated as the party's candidate for governor of the Bank of Israel, was sentenced to five years in prison and fined IL250,000 for accepting bribes and making a false income tax declaration. During his trial Yadlin implicated several national Labor party leaders (including two cabinet ministers) in illegal fund raising for the party. Yadlin's conviction came six weeks after the suicide of his close personal friend, Minister of Housing Avraham Ofer, following the publication in the press of charges that Ofer had been involved in corruption. No formal charges had been brought against Ofer, and he swore his innocence in his suicide note, which claimed that he had been so hounded and badgered by the charges in the press that he could no longer cope with the situation. The shocking death of Ofer and the conviction of Yadlin one week before the Labor party conference, which raised suspicions of even wider corruption implicating several Labor leaders, were very serious blows to the party.

These events followed Prime Minister Rabin's ejection of the National Religious party from the government coalition for abstaining on a vote of no-confidence in the government (sponsored by the ultra-religious Agudat Israel party) over the scheduling of a special military ceremony on a Friday afternoon shortly before the advent of the sabbath. Rabin therefore presided over a minority caretaker government, which necessitated the setting of an election date earlier

143

than had been anticipated. In view of later developments, the timing could not have been more to Labor's disadvantage.

Following on the shockwaves of Ofer's suicide and Yadlin's conviction, the prime minister's wife was convicted of an infringement of the strict foreign currency restrictions which prohibited Israelis from maintaining foreign currency accounts abroad (except under special circumstances). Rabin tendered his resignation as prime minister. However, when the attorney general ruled that technically no minister (including the prime minister) could resign from a caretaker government, he appeared to vacillate, indicating he might change his mind, but finally chose to take an extended leave of absence and designated Defense Minister Shimon Peres "acting prime minister." This title apparently had no legal status. Rabin also stepped down from the top of the Labor party list, making way for Peres to head the party ticket as its candidate for prime minister—yet another serious blow to the Labor party. In addition, President Carter's statements about the need for a Palestinian homeland drove votes from Labor to the Likud among those who felt that the impending increase in pressure on Israel from the United States made it necessary for Israel to adopt a "hard line" if it were to resist making too many concessions.

These scandals and pressures arose at a time of serious economic hardship when Israeli citizens were being asked to tighten their belts in order to absorb heavy new taxes. Spiraling inflation, the devaluation of Israeli currency, and severe labor strife characterized by a multitude of strikes (particularly in the public sector) adversely affected all Israelis. Particularly hard hit were the poorest strata of the society, the occupants of the big city slums and the development towns, a disproportionately large number of whom came from the Islamic countries of the Middle East and North Africa. The election results indicate that this category was particularly disenchanted with the Labor party.

All of these forces produced a growing social malaise symbolized by decreasing immigration to, and growing emigration from, Israel. Objectively the Labor party was not solely responsible for all of these negative developments. Yet when one political party has played such a dominant role in the shaping of the society for so long, it is the obvious focus for the cumulative credit and blame which the citizens ascribe in response to their changing conditions. When, for the many reasons outlined in this essay, the dominant party was no longer responsive to the public's wants, sentiments, and interests, it lost its authority and right to rule.

Of course there must be an alternative or alternatives to which the voter can turn. The Likud succeeded in convincing an increasing number of Israelis that it was the only option for real political change. And for those who could no longer bring themselves to vote for Labor but could not support the Likud, the newly formed Democratic Movement for Change offered a viable alternative in the liberal center of the political spectrum. It is likely that the DMC won at least ten of its fifteen seats through the votes of former Labor supporters, particularly better-educated middle- and upper-middle-class Israelis from European backgrounds. In addition there were more long-range demographic trends (analyzed in Chapters 1 and 3 in this volume) that made their impact on the election results. However, they all boil down to the fact that the party that had dominated Israeli society for fifty years had lost its ideological or moral dominance by becoming arrogant in power and by ceasing to respond to the public, which then lost confidence in it and voted it out of power.

6

A Movement for Change
in a Stable System

Efraim Torgovnik

The Democratic Movement for Change (DMC) appeared on the Israeli political scene near the end of November 1976. Less than seven months later, the new party won 15 seats in the 120-member Knesset by capturing 11.6 percent of the vote in the election, making it the third largest party. And five months after the election, the DMC joined the government coalition. Four of its leaders obtained ministerial posts.

The DMC's goal had been to win enough seats so that no government could be formed without its participation—thereby putting the DMC in a position to implement its program for change. However, the Likud's modest electoral gain (3.2 percentage points over 1973) enabled it and the National Religious party to become the basis for a narrow coalition without the DMC.[1] Still, the DMC was partly responsible for ending the five-decade rule of Labor and giving respectability to the idea of change in an erstwhile stable political system. The DMC showed that a campaign in the beleaguered, security-conscious state of Israel could be based on domestic issues.

This discussion examines the conditions that accounted for the emergence of the DMC, its success in attracting visible public figures as its leaders, the basis of its organization, the voters and their concerns, the issues that the DMC raised during the campaign, and the DMC's postelection coalition negotiations. In part, this chapter is a response to Lipset and Rokkan's call for more research on the emergence of political groups. They argue that we know very little of the process through which political alternatives emerge.[2]

[1] Hanoch Smith, "Israel's Knesset Elections: An Analysis of the Upset," pamphlet distributed by the Foreign Affairs Department, American Jewish Committee, Jerusalem, 1977. Election data from Central Bureau of Statistics, *Election Results 1977* (Jerusalem, 1977).

[2] Seymour Martin Lipset and Stein Rokkan, *Party Systems and Voter Alignments* (New York: The Free Press, 1967).

Conditions for the Emergence of the DMC

Several factors in Israel's recent history and social system helped generate a political group such as the DMC. These include the Six-Day War, the social gap, concern about the state of the economy, and the emergence of new forms of political protest.

Prior to the Six-Day War, most Israeli Jews had accepted the existing partition of the former Palestine into separate areas for Jews and Arabs. But when Israel's spectacular military victory in 1967 resulted in the conquest of territory a number of times its size, attention shifted from qualitative nation building to the settlement of the newly acquired land. Many Israelis argued for retention of most of the territories—either for national security, or because of the Jews' historic right to the land. A few argued for extensive territorial compromise with the Arabs—if for no other reason than to retain the Jewish character of the state (which would be threatened by annexation of the West Bank with its million Arabs, for example).[3]

The economic prosperity that followed the Six-Day War was juxtaposed with poverty among certain social groups; one report pointed to the existence of about 250,000 children and adults in economic, social, or psychological distress.[4] This situation underscored the failure of salient Zionist ideas such as egalitarianism. It became a key issue for the DMC, which suggested structural reforms (such as the establishment of a coordinating social welfare ministry).

Although the public generally supported the ruling Labor Alignment's relatively moderate policies in foreign affairs,[5] hawkish political organizations were gaining momentum. Furthermore, surveys showed significant public dissatisfaction with the government's economic management; before the 1977 election, only 15 to 20 percent of the respondents said that the government was handling economic matters well.[6] Such conditions breed electoral change—and, indeed, the Labor Alignment's vote had shrunk progressively over several elections.

The DMC gave voters an alternative on domestic issues—com-

---

[3] Efraim Torgovnik, "The Election Campaign: Party Needs and Voter Concerns," in Asher Arian, ed., *The Elections in Israel—1973* (Jerusalem: Jerusalem Academic Press, 1975), pp. 59–94.

[4] *The Prime Minister's Report for Children and Youth in Distress*, Jerusalem, 1972.

[5] Louis Guttman, "Before and After the Election to the Ninth Knesset," *Bulletin*, no. 45 (Jerusalem: Israeli Institute of Applied Social Research, August 1977), pp. 7–12.

[6] Ibid., p. 9.

bined with a position not too distant from the Labor Alignment's on foreign policy and the territories. Switching to the Likud—which, like the DMC, emphasized domestic issues, but which had a hawkish foreign policy—was too drastic a move for most erstwhile Labor Alignment voters; the DMC was a more acceptable alternative. As it turned out, the DMC drew most of its support from former Alignment voters.

The impetus for new political organizations came after the 1973 war. The surprise attack by Egypt and Syria and the deaths of nearly 3,000 Israeli soldiers shattered the euphoria that had followed the Six-Day War. The sense of physical security—the very essence of Israel as a Jewish homeland—was threatened. There was a widespread feeling of depression and a sense of failure. Several protest movements emerged, demanding the resignation of Minister of Defense Moshe Dayan and Prime Minister Golda Meir because of Israel's unpreparedness for the war. The movements were largely responsible for the absence of Dayan and Meir from the Labor Alignment government elected in December 1973.

The removal of leaders of such stature proved that change could be achieved. It also portended the possible collapse of the party that had dominated Israel and the pre-state Jewish settlement since the 1920s. Thus, the instinct for self-preservation became another factor —in addition to dissatisfaction with Labor's policies or performance— which may have made key figures start thinking about abandoning the Labor Alignment and seeking their fortunes elsewhere. (In all fairness, such an interpretation of their motives is based on hindsight; at the time, few people seriously believed that Labor would actually be dropped from power.)

In its distress, the party apparatus of the Labor Alignment selected Yitzhak Rabin as its candidate for prime minister in 1973. His greatest assets were what he was not. He was not a politician, and he was not tarnished by the 1973 war (after finishing his assignment as Israel's ambassador to the United States, he had been literally sitting around waiting for Golda Meir to give him a new appointment at the time of the war). He still wore the laurels of victory he had won as chief of staff during the Six-Day War. The shadow over his selection was that it revealed the ugly hand of the party apparatus; this would become another key issue for the DMC in 1977.

Rabin relied on the old party apparatus—but it failed to maintain party discipline (and in 1977, it failed to deliver the vote). The struggle among the Labor Alignment's factions had an adverse effect on the government's work. The DMC would use this fact to point out the need for structural reform. The Labor Alignment mobilized ex-generals such as Aharon Yariv, former chief of army intelligence, and placed them in key government positions, but to no avail; their capacity for long-term loyalty to a political party was nil, and this simply gave further exposure to the machinations and the lack of internal party democracy. In the critical weeks before the 1977 election, Yariv left the Labor Alignment in an uproar and joined the DMC.

Amnon Rubinstein was quoted as having said in the early days of the Change movement: "Give me one general, and I'll turn the country over."[7] And, indeed, when Yariv and other ex-generals joined the DMC, they gave the movement great momentum. But the DMC, unlike the Labor Alignment, did not appoint ex-generals to top positions; they had to compete in the party's internal election.

Finally, there were several cases of corruption involving top Labor leaders, which the DMC skillfully related to the social system created by Labor.[8] While the scandals cannot be causally related to the DMC's success, they did reinforce the DMC's emphasis on the need for reform. Ironically, the fight against corruption was perhaps one of the few major achievements of the Rabin government. But then Rabin himself became implicated when his wife was charged with illegal possession of foreign currency; he resigned as head of the Labor Alignment's slate—right before the 1977 election—and the Alignment's lack of leadership became obvious and acute.

The Creation of the DMC

Since the early 1920s, political parties in Palestine and then in Israel have shown a passion for trying to hide a simple fact about themselves: that they are political parties. They prefer to be called movements and thereby benefit from the wider perspective (and possibly wider base) implied by this concept. A movement, according to Pizzarno, "produces a system of values which is in opposition to those current in the nation."[9]

The Democratic Movement for Change wanted to project itself as a widely based movement, with no class or ethnic label. It vehemently attacked the partisanship of the other parties and politicians. According to its first pamphlet, the DMC was "a movement of

---

[7] Reported by Shulamit Alloni in the Knesset, October 24, 1977.

[8] DMC, *What is the DMC?*, pamphlet, 1977.

[9] Alessandro Pizzarno, "An Introduction to the Theory of Political Participation," *Social Science Information*, vol. 9 (1970), p. 53.

Israelis of all strata of the nation and all parts of the land."[10] This approach was wise, for the founders knew that their visible leaders were, in fact, a rather elitist social group—composed largely of professors, lawyers, and businessmen—with a narrow geographical base. They were hardly a cross-section of the voting population.

In the aftermath of the 1973 war, a group of friends and neighbors (to use Duverger's phrase) gathered under the leadership of Professor Amnon Rubinstein, former dean of the Tel Aviv University Law School and columnist for the prestigious daily newspaper *Ha'aretz*. They understood that protest alone was not enough to change the system; to have any influence, they had to enter politics. So they formed a new political group which they called, appropriately, Change.

Nearly a year and a half later, another professor was showing an interest in politics. He was Yigael Yadin, the world-famous archeologist who had been chief of staff of the Israeli armed forces during the War of Independence. He had served on the commission that investigated the 1973 war and reportedly had been designated by David Ben-Gurion as his political heir.[11] In May 1976, less than a year before the 1977 election, Yadin finally declared himself to be a candidate. He stated that he stood for making the electoral system more democratic, changing the governmental structure, focusing on domestic issues, and being flexible on the territories. With his supporters, he formed a political group called the Democratic Movement.

Presumably, there were at least two reasons for Yadin's delay in entering politics. Among his potential activists, there were strong differences of opinion on the question of security;[12] Yadin had to bind them together with a consensus on domestic issues. He spent months roaming the country to measure the public's responsiveness to his views.[13]

The second possible reason is that he was waiting for Labor's impending disaster to become more apparent; only then would he feel that it was safe to move forward with his reform ideology. This emphasis on taking over after Labor's collapse was echoed by Meir Zorea: "All of the Labor leadership had to be replaced. . . . High-level Labor party activists suggested reform from within, but I believed

---

[10] DMC, *What is the DMC?*, pamphlet, 1977.

[11] See reference in *Yediot Achronot*, March 11, 1977; *Ha'aretz*, May 30, 1977; and Michael Bar Zohar, *Ben-Gurion* (Tel Aviv: Am Oved, 1977), pp. 1441–1442. Letter from Ben-Gurion to Yadin, March 9, 1964, Ben-Gurion Archives, Tel Aviv.

[12] *Ha'aretz*, November 24, 1976.

[13] Interview with Meir Zorea, MK from the DMC, November 1977.

that everything had to be built from new."[14] There were numerous men in key positions in the economy who saw things in the same light. "They were handpicked and were asked to recommend a number of friends as founder-organizers."[15]

Rubinstein's Change and Yadin's Democratic Movement publicized similar goals. But Change lacked a candidate with the stature of Yadin, and the Democratic Movement lacked the organizational apparatus of Rubinstein's party. So, seven months before the election, the two parties merged to form the Democratic Movement for Change.

The members of the two groups differed in age and status. Rubinstein's group consisted of younger professionals. Those in Yadin's belonged to the generation of nation builders who had reached adulthood before the War of Independence; they were part of the executive complex and included a number of ex-chiefs of staff and the president of a major semi-private bank.[16] When Yadin became the acknowledged head of the DMC, many of the people in his group retired to the background. He probably symbolized for them the stability, leadership, and coherence that Labor had provided in the past but lacked in the mid-1970s.

Before this key merger, Change had made other efforts to find suitable partners in order to grow. A group headed by Yonathan Shapiro and Asher Arian, both professors at Tel Aviv University, proposed that Change merge with the Civil Rights list headed by Shulamit Alloni, a vocal backbencher who had left the Labor Alignment. The executive council of Change rejected the proposal by a very narrow margin.[17] The opposition to the proposal was led by Rubinstein—who, it was claimed, feared the domineering personality of Alloni. However, a more credible explanation for Rubinstein's action is that he was being cautious about allying his party with anyone already involved in politics (and, therefore, possibly tarnished in the eyes of the public).

Duverger distinguishes between two types of parties on the basis of their organization: "Cadre parties correspond to the caucus parties, decentralized and weakly knit; mass parties . . . [are] based on branches, more centralized and more firmly knit."[18] Before the

---

[14] Ibid.

[15] Ibid.

[16] Ibid.

[17] According to Yonathan Shapiro, a member of the Change council, it was alleged that the eligibility of some council members to vote on this question had been tampered with.

[18] Maurice Duverger, *Political Parties* (London: Methuen Press, 1964).

election, the DMC organized itself as a mass party. After the election, it rapidly acquired some of the features of a cadre party—for example, it had difficulty in activating its branches. This rapid change from movement to cadre party suggests that the DMC was essentially a party with a mandate for a single, specific election.

The DMC was also what Neumann calls a party based on fundamental principles (as contrasted with parties based on patronage and expediency, such as the Labor Alignment).[19] One of its principles was democratic selection of the party's candidates. Except for the DMC, every party in Israel had an appointment committee for selecting its candidates; rank-and-file members had no role in the nominations. The DMC, however, chose to follow a more democratic procedure, similar to that in the United States, where the state primaries give party members a voice in the selection of candidates. The party held an internal election, in which all of the 38,000 registered members of the DMC were eligible to run and to vote. With a bona fide membership list of its own the DMC could call the public's attention to the fact that the membership lists of the Labor Alignment were fabricated.

However, its passion for a winning slate led the DMC to water down its principle of party democracy: the DMC executive committee forbade campaigning by the candidates in the internal election. This gave a clear advantage to those who were already well known, such as Rubinstein, Yadin, and the other ex-generals. In short, the DMC handicapped the unknowns in its internal election (much as the Labor Alignment handicapped new parties by sponsoring a law that limited their radio and television time). The unknowns who made it onto the DMC slate were those who had entered the party with sizable numbers of friends and allies. Whatever criticism can be leveled against the DMC for the lack of democracy indicated by the ban on internal campaigning, it must be admitted that this measure was effective in assuring that the DMC wound up with a strong list of candidates.

Activists and Leaders. Perhaps the greatest success of the DMC was its mobilization of visible activists and leaders, as well as large numbers of anonymous supporters. It brought together a variety of people who set aside their ideological differences on foreign affairs and the territories in favor of running together on the DMC's mainly domestic issues.

Some of them had been highly placed insiders with the Labor

---

[19] Sigmund Neumann, "Toward a Comparative Study of Political Parties," in Sigmund Neumann, ed., *Modern Political Parties* (Chicago: University of Chicago Press, 1956), p. 400.

Alignment—such as Meir Amit, head of the industrial conglomerate belonging to the Histadrut; Meir Zorea, head of the National Lands Authority (who had served with Yadin on the commission to investigate the 1973 war); and Shmuel Toledano, the prime minister's adviser on Arab affairs. These members of the elite would probably have been casualties of Labor's coming debacle. Others had belonged to the Free Center (a former party that had been a faction within the Likud for the 1973 elections, but joined the DMC in 1977); these included Knesset members Shmuel Tamir and Akiva Nof.

The identifiable groups that composed the DMC were the Rubinstein group (the former Change), the Yadin group (the former Democratic Movement), the Tamir group (the former Free Center party), the Amit group (former key people in the Labor Alignment), and the Oded group (a former pressure group of Eastern Jews who acted on behalf of the disadvantaged).

The DMC leaders tried to keep the party from taking on a factionalized structure. After Change and the Democratic Movement merged to form the DMC, the new party stipulated that, from then on, no group could join the party en bloc. Thus, the Free Center members joined the DMC individually. Another antifactional stipulation was that any Knesset member who joined the party had to give up his seat; Tamir and Nof of the Free Center did so.

The Oded group of Eastern Jews was extremely important to the DMC, whose public figures were mainly of Western origin and high socioeconomic status. The Oded group helped counterbalance the elitist features of the DMC, thus giving the party a potentially wider appeal.

The DMC vigorously criticized the Labor Alignment for being a collection of institutionalized factions—each of which demanded its pound of flesh in government spoils, thereby paralyzing the government and making it impossible to evolve coherent policies. While the DMC itself was a collection of groups with different policies, the groups were all bent on removing the Labor Alignment from power; thus, the DMC was a binding forum for hawks and doves alike during the election campaign. The general issue of reform was a common point of reference that helped overcome their differences in other areas—at least for the time being.

Why They Joined the DMC. Some of those who formed or joined the DMC had held key positions (or could easily have attained them) in the Labor Alignment's administration—yet they chose to cast their lot with the DMC. Yadin, for example, had been offered a ministerial post by Labor more than once, and Rubinstein had been offered a Knesset seat. Yariv had been a minister in the Labor government but had resigned.

Yariv explained his disenchantment with Labor on the grounds that the party suffered from a paralysis whose cure was prevented by uncompromising factions. Despite their access to high office, Yariv and others were not at the apex of power, and they saw little hope of achieving change from within Labor. The party was no longer being pulled forward by outstanding leaders such as David Ben-Gurion and Golda Meir; Rabin was simply one of many peers. It was obvious that change could not be undertaken by the Labor Alignment, since the comfortably entrenched components would not give up what they had. (The kibbutzim, for example, enjoyed a double vote in party forums, and each of the three major Labor factions had seven or eight of the forty safe places on the Alignment's list of candidates in the Knesset elections.) The factional structure of the party in turn made the government unwieldy: the cabinet had to include nineteen ministers in order to satisfy the competing claims of the factions.

The DMC, by contrast, offered an opportunity to reach the very top party leadership positions since all of the new party's posts were open. It also offered an opportunity to promise the voters that the party could do something new and dramatic for the country by holding out for reforms as its price for joining a government coalition. Furthermore, the party's leaders could expect that once the DMC took its place in the coalition, they would have continuing influence. Thus, a combination of campaign idealism and personal expediency motivated many of the politicians who joined the new party.

Then there were people like Shmuel Tamir of the Free Center, who had worn out his welcome in the Likud; his conflict with Menachem Begin had reached the point of no return. He had even softened his hawkish stand on the territories—a cardinal sin in the eyes of Begin, who saw a biblical justification for Israel's permanent retention of the West Bank. Tamir was an able and restless public figure who was hamstrung by the highly disciplined Likud; for him, as for others, the DMC offered a way out of a dilemma.

For more than 200,000 people—public figures and anonymous voters—the DMC was a channel for articulating a widely held feeling of despair over many aspects of the country's situation: inflation, governmental paralysis, machine politics, corruption in high places, poverty in the midst of prosperity, emigration, an unattractive life style. Once the DMC started moving, its call for political action was quickly answered by these disgruntled people, many of whom worked

TABLE 6–1

MAJOR-PARTY VOTERS, BY YEARS OF SCHOOLING, 1977 ELECTION
(in percentages)

	Years of Schooling		
Party	8 or less	9 to 12	13 and over
DMC (N = 50)	8.0	42.0	50.0
Labor Alignment (N = 96)	19.8	46.9	33.3
Likud (N = 104)	16.3	57.7	26.0

SOURCE: Data provided by Professor Asher Arian.

actively for the party without pay. The Labor Alignment, by contrast, loaded the government and Histadrut institutions with payrollers who worked for the party.

The DMC's Voters

Election studies in Israel have pointed to the relative stability of voting patterns since the establishment of the state in 1948. In recent elections, however, there has been a gradual loss of Knesset seats by the Labor Alignment. Still, few Israelis predicted the massive shift that occurred in 1977. After the election, Shimon Peres (who had become the Labor Alignment's candidate for the premiership after the resignation of Rabin) commented: "I expected the voters to give us a slap in the face—but not to cut our head off."[20]

Who were those who decided to shift their votes to the DMC in 1977? The new party had hoped to attract a broad range of voters from all walks of life. However, surveys showed that the DMC's base included much higher concentrations of some groups than of others.[21] In May, just before the election, a survey asked: "What party would you vote for if the elections were held today?" Table 6–1 shows that the DMC drew half of its support from those with some university education and another 42 percent from those with at least some high

[20] Related by Shimon Peres, leader of the Labor Alignment, May 1977.

[21] Data are based on public opinion surveys which were conducted by the Bureau of Applied Social Research, Jerusalem. Special thanks are due to my colleague, Professor Asher Arian, for making the data available.

TABLE 6–2

MAJOR-PARTY VOTERS, BY ETHNIC BACKGROUND, 1977 ELECTION
(in percentages)

| Party | Birthplace of Voter's Father | | | |
	Israel	Asia/Africa	Europe/America	Other
DMC (N = 50)	4.0	28.0	68.0	—
Labor Alignment (N = 96)	10.4	20.8	68.8	—
Likud (N = 104)	8.7	37.5	51.9	1.9

SOURCE: See Table 6–1.

school education. By comparison, only 26 percent of the Likud voters and 33.3 percent of the Labor Alignment voters had gone to college. The DMC voters, as expected, were mostly of European and American background, as were those of the Alignment (Table 6–2). And most of the DMC's voters were aged forty and over. High age and high income are likely to be positively correlated. Table 6–3 shows that 46 percent of the DMC voters earned IL5,000 per month or more, compared with 33.4 percent of the Alignment's voters and 29.8 percent of the Likud's.

TABLE 6–3

MAJOR-PARTY VOTERS BY INCOME LEVEL, 1977 ELECTION
(in percentages)

| Party | Monthly Income | | | |
	IL 2,999 and under	IL 3,000– 4,999	IL 5,000 and over	Not available
DMC (N = 50)	18.0	16.0	46.0	20.0
Labor Alignment (N = 96)	22.9	27.1	33.4	16.7
Likud (N = 104)	24.0	30.8	29.8	15.4

SOURCE: See Table 6–1.

TABLE 6–4

MAJOR-PARTY VOTERS, BY ECONOMIC AND ETHNIC DISTRICTS OF
TEL AVIV, HAIFA, AND JERUSALEM, 1977 ELECTION
(in percentages of valid vote)

	Tel Aviv	Haifa	Jerusalem
Rich European districts			
DMC	20	27	22
Labor	27	27	19
Likud	32	26	29
Middle-income ethnically mixed districts			
DMC	6	12	15
Labor	26	30	20
Likud	45	31	39
Poor Eastern districts			
DMC	3	2	7
Labor	17	19	16
Likud	53	41	52

SOURCE: Data provided by Hanoch Smith.

Since most DMC voters were of Western origin, the DMC pulled few votes in the development towns, which are populated mainly by Eastern Jews. The DMC's greatest support came from the large cities, where most of the people of European origin live. Hanoch Smith, an election analyst, reports that "the DMC gained 20 percent or more of the vote in the most opulent, overwhelmingly European-originated districts."[22] In the poor districts, the DMC's share was only 4 percent. A summary picture of the DMC's results in the three big cities, divided into income/ethnic districts, is seen in Table 6–4. It shows that the DMC's hopes for wide support from people in all walks of life did not materialize.

The Voters' Concerns. More than any other party, the DMC influenced—and was influenced by—the shift in election issue salience from foreign to domestic affairs. The literature reports that such changes in emphasis are rare. For example, the 1964 contest in the United States between Goldwater and Johnson saw a shift to domestic

---

[22] Smith, "Israel's Knesset Elections."

TABLE 6–5

MAJOR CONCERNS OF VOTERS, BY PARTY, 1977 ELECTION
(in percentages)

	Security	Peace	Economy	Social Gap	Other
DMC (N = 50)	26.0	14.0	36.0	14.0	10.0
Labor Alignment (N = 96)	25.0	12.5	30.2	13.5	18.8
Likud (N = 104)	31.7	10.6	30.8	9.6	17.3

NOTE: The survey question was: "In your opinion what is the major problem the government should deal with?" Respondents were given the following choice: security, economic problems, the social gap, peace, change in the electoral system, housing for young couples, inflation, education, and any others. In the March, April, and May surveys the issue of electoral change did not show salience among the voters. These figures are for March.
SOURCE: See Table 6–1.

concerns that has been attributed to the reemergence of New Deal type issues.[23] In Israel, the 1973 war changed the voters' concerns from domestic issues to foreign policy.[24] Before the war, the social gap had been the major concern of 18.7 percent of the Labor Alignment voters and 24.7 percent of the Likud voters; after the war (just before the 1973 election), these figures dropped to 3.2 percent and 8.6 percent, respectively. On the other hand, peace concerned only 9.3 percent of the Labor Alignment voters and 4.8 percent of the Likud voters before the war; after the war, with the Geneva Conference coming up, the figures were 49.5 percent and 20.7 percent.

In 1977, the shift to domestic concerns was highest among DMC voters (see Table 6–5); 50 percent of them saw the economy or the social gap as the major issue. This may be viewed as a reaction of the more comfortable classes to the inconveniences caused by economic and social unrest. Since the DMC started its campaign earlier than the other parties did, it may be credited with a leadership role in articulating the views of the electorate.

[23] Angus Campbell and Philip E. Converse, *Elections and Political Order* (New York: John Wiley and Sons, 1966); and David E. RePass, "Methodologies in Disarray: Some Alternative Interpretations of the 1972 Election," *The American Political Science Review*, vol. 70 (September 1976), pp. 814–832.
[24] Torgovnik, "The Election Campaign."

The interim agreement with Egypt, the presence of U.N. observers along the borders, and the American monitoring stations in the Sinai Desert went far toward alleviating the people's concern about security; for Eastern Jews, however, security remained a major concern. The media were concentrating on inflation and labor unrest; the general feeling was that the economy was out of control. Israelis are highly concerned about their standard of living and the future of their children; obviously, an economically adverse situation affects these deeply rooted factors.[25]

The state of the economy—in particular, the country's lack of self-sufficiency—was also linked to the nationwide concern for Israel's political independence and its ability to make its own decisions in peace negotiations with the Arabs. Yadin stated: "There is no greater danger to our spiritual future and our independence . . . than the aid we get from our brothers and friends."[26] Amit was more direct: "Two-thirds of our national deficit is covered by the Americans. We are becoming increasingly dependent on the United States, . . . exposing ourselves to strong political pressures which will be accompanied by painful economic sanctions."[27]

The key concern of the DMC's leadership—changing the election system to direct voting by districts—had no salience among the DMC's voters. Duverger has suggested that measurement of the disparity between the opinions of visible leaders and those of their constituencies indicates the degree of representation provided by the elites.[28] Disparity is not uncommon; McClosky, for example, showed that the views of rank-and-file Republicans were closer to those of the Democratic leaders than to the views of their own party's leaders in 1956.[29] Nevertheless, although the issue of electoral reform lacked salience among DMC voters, it did not elicit opposition; it fell under the general category of change, which the voters were for. The DMC's voters apparently took for granted that change would entail more democratic procedures.

---

[25] See *Current Surveys* (Jerusalem: Bureau of Applied Social Research).

[26] DMC, *New Line: Periodical of the Democratic Movement for Change*, no. 15 (April 1977), p. 4.

[27] *Yediot Achronot*, May 16, 1977.

[28] Duverger, *Political Parties*, p. 101.

[29] See, for example, Bernhard Hennessy, "On the Study of Party Organization," in William J. Crotty, *Approaches to the Study of Party Organization* (Boston: Allyn and Bacon, Inc., 1968), p. 9; Campbell and Converse, *Elections and Political Order*; and H. McClosky, P. J. Hoffmann, and R. O'Hara, "Issue, Conflict and Consensus Among Party Leaders and Followers," *The American Political Science Review*, vol. 54 (June 1960), pp. 406–427.

The DMC's Campaign Issues. According to Pizzarno, "A movement initiates an attempt at certain transformations, at a moment in which social conditions already contain the premises for such transformations, and so the ends of the movement seek to answer society's needs."[30] Yadin defined the DMC as a movement "founded in order to bring a radical change in the practices of government, society and the economy."[31]

The DMC's campaign advertising laid down the party's issue priorities: (1) emphasizing the early Zionist ideologies of hard work, productivity, and better labor-management relations; (2) changing the economic system to base it on the country's needs (rather than on party needs); (3) streamlining the government by eliminating some ministries and combining their functions; (4) changing the electoral system to make it more democratic; (5) closing the social gap; (6) closing the gap between word and deed (an allusion to the Labor Alignment's promise to reform the economy while it capitulated to the unions' demands); and (7) exploring all possible arrangements to assure the security of the state.[32] These goals became the substance of the DMC's appeal to the voters and of the debate with the other parties—especially with the ruling Labor Alignment, which the DMC held responsible for their negation or distortion.

At first, Yadin tried to play down the issue of security and a Palestinian state on the West Bank—arguing evasively (yet prudently) that it could be deferred until the Arabs showed signs of reduced intransigence. Finally, two months before the election, the DMC made public its stand: there could be no Palestinian state on the West Bank; the Palestinians should find national expression within the Kingdom of Jordan; the Palestine Liberation Organization (PLO) did not represent the Palestinians, and it could not be a partner in peace negotiations; the Jordan River would be the security border of Israel; the establishment of Israeli settlements on the West Bank would be guided by security considerations and would occur mainly in the Jordan valley; and, although the people of Israel had a historic right to all of the territories, the desire for peace mandated territorial concessions.[33]

This position was close to that of the Labor Alignment (and far from that of the Likud). Although the DMC tried to differentiate itself

---

[30] Pizzarno, "An Introduction to the Theory of Political Participation," p. 56.

[31] DMC, *What is the DMC?*; and *Yediot Achronot*, April 29, 1977.

[32] See for example *Yediot Achronot*, May 15, 1977; and DMC campaign pamphlets.

[33] DMC, *Platform*; *Yediot Achronot*, March 27, 1977; and *Ma'ariv*, September 18, 1977.

from Labor by emphasizing the issue of democratic change, its stand on the territories made it easy for Labor voters—the DMC's major targets—to defect to the DMC.[34] This is consistent with the literature: voters are likely to shift to parties that are ideologically close to their previous party.[35] On the other hand, the DMC's moderate stand on the territories was probably one reason why it failed to attract many Eastern Jews, who are generally more hawkish than those of Western origin.[36]

Many members of the DMC had expected the party to come out strongly against religion-oriented legislation that infringed on the rights of the secular population. However, this is a highly sensitive issue in Israel, so the DMC did not dwell on it—partly, we may assume, from fear of further alienating Easterners (who are generally more religiously observant than Westerners).

Issues Generated by the DMC's Opponents. The fact that the DMC's position on the territories was similar to that of the Labor Alignment resulted in accusations that the DMC, despite its call to throw out the ruling party, was actually seeking to form a post-election coalition with the Alignment. Yadin replied: "We have principles, and we shall fight for them. The issue for us is not who to go with, but *what* to go on. We shall cooperate with those who accept our minimum demands."[37]

On the one hand, this offered the DMC another opportunity to attack the Likud and the Labor Alignment for not being able to transcend their narrow party interests and think of the good of the country.[38] On the other hand, it eventually became a major burden to the DMC, imposing a constraint on party policy after the election. A similar process has been noted elsewhere: parties comprised of factions are forced to modify their stand during campaigns in a way that is reflected in their policy after the election.[39]

Another issue raised by its opponents was the alleged failure of

---

[34] See *Party Platform*, Labor Alignment, 1977.

[35] Asher Arian and Samuel H. Barnes, "The Dominant Party System: A Neglected Model of Democratic Stability," *The Journal of Politics*, vol. 36 (August 1974), pp. 592–614.

[36] See Asher Arian, *The Choosing People* (Cleveland: Case Western University Press, 1973).

[37] *Yediot Achronot*, August 17, 1977 and April 29, 1977.

[38] See DMC campaign advertisements.

[39] See Efraim Torgovnik, "Party Factions and Election Issues" in Asher Arian, ed., *The Elections in Israel–1969* (Jerusalem: Jerusalem Academic Press, 1972).

the DMC's highly vaunted internal party democracy. In terms of making its slate for the Knesset a representative cross-section of the party, the DMC's internal election backfired. At the time when the party was choosing its candidates, the surveys were predicting that the DMC would win twelve Knesset seats;[40] of the first thirteen people on the "democratically elected" slate, the only one of Eastern origin was Shmuel Toledano, the prime minister's former adviser on Arab affairs—hardly a direct representative of the disadvantaged. In fourteenth place—apparently too far down the list to stand a chance of winning—was Mordechai Algrabli, a leader of the Oded group, which was dedicated to the advancement of Easterners.

If the DMC had held its internal election under a regional system (of the kind that it prescribed for national elections), Easterners would probably have had a better chance of placing high in some of the districts. Perhaps this would have encouraged more Easterners to participate in the DMC contest and would have resulted in a number of Easterners' winning high slots on the DMC slate.

The Labor Alignment immediately accused the DMC of being a party of the whites and the rich; it pointed to its own list, on which a number of Eastern Jews had been given realistic places by the "undemocratic" appointments committee. Within the DMC itself, the Oded group talked of secession.

The DMC leaders kept the Oded people in the fold by convincing them that the party would make an earnest effort to deal with the social gap regardless of who was on its list. Finally, this group agreed to join the DMC campaign on the democracy issue—hammering on the claim that a qualified Westerner could work more effectively against the social gap than could an Easterner if he were only an appointed party hack. In a testimonial advertisement, a DMC member of Eastern origin said: "There are no Eastern Jews among the first six because I did not vote for them. We came to the movement to leave behind the . . . division according to ethnic origin. The problem of the social gap belongs to all of us; Yadin and Katz are fit to handle it, and I voted for them."[41] The DMC's antiparty campaign ad read: "To be an Eastern Jew is a question of birth, but to be a professional Eastern party hack is a mentality. I am happy to note that we have no professional Easterners in the movement."[42] But the Labor Alignment did not relent; it published numerous ads listing the addresses of

[40] *Yediot Achronot*, May 13, 1977; and *Ma'ariv*, April 29, 1977.

[41] *Ha'aretz*, May 8, 1977; and *Yediot Achronot*, May 13, 1977.

[42] *Yediot Achronot*, May 13, 1977.

DMC leaders who resided in expensive neighborhoods, and the DMC retaliated in kind.

The DMC was compelled to rely heavily on newspaper advertising and publicity because, under the law, the established parties received almost all of the free television and radio time; new parties received only a token. Nevertheless, the DMC propagandists used their limited amount of time dramatically: on both television and radio, they simply clicked a timer and said that they had no time to talk because the two big parties were conspiring against democratic elections.

Postelection Coalition Negotiations

When the coalition negotiations began, the DMC appeared to be what Neumann has called a party of principles; when the negotiations ended seven months later, it turned out to be a party of expediency.[43]

As the main payoff for the DMC's joining the government coalition led by the victorious Likud, Yadin demanded changes in the system; in line with the DMC's antiparty ideology, he considered ministerial posts to be of secondary importance. However, Menachem Begin skillfully avoided substantive discussions of policy, refusing to offer the DMC anything more than ministries. Consequently, the DMC initially chose to stay outside. Yadin counted on the cohesive force of his party's commitment to change to hold the DMC together. But cracks emerged. Meir Zorea, a member of the negotiating team, accused his colleagues of deliberately preventing the DMC from joining the Begin government.[44] The party's organization became slack and unresponsive.

Riker's minimum size principle states that when potential coalition partners have complete and predictable information about each other's future support, a coalition with the smallest possible legislative majority will be formed; when their behavior is less predictable, the coalition will have to be larger.[45] The perfect-information model is unsatisfactory because parties have varying degrees of control over their members, and there are likely to be ideological distances between the parties. It has been suggested that the size principle be supplemented with the ideological-distance model, which assumes that the dominant party will choose as partners the parties that are ideologically closest to it. The winning coalition will have the smallest number

---

[43] Neumann, "Toward a Comparative Study."

[44] *Yediot Achronot*, August 5, 1977; and *Ha'aretz*, August 7, 1977.

[45] William H. Riker, *The Theory of Political Coalitions* (New Haven: Yale University Press, 1962).

of such parties; any addition would increase the ideological distance between partners and require heavier payoffs.[46]

In Israel, coalitions have generally been much larger than the minimum needed. However, Nachmias contends that the Labor Alignment gave away little in terms of payoffs to the parties that supported it while gaining much in terms of cooperation and legitimization, which helped maintain its dominance for many years.[47] In 1977, Begin followed the same pattern in dealing with the DMC.

Before the election, Yadin had promised not to join any government that would not accept the DMC's principles. But this position had been based on the assumption that no government could be formed without the DMC (except one based on the unlikely combination of the Likud and the Labor Alignment). When the Likud won forty-three Knesset seats, it was able to add twelve from the National Religious party, two from Ariel Sharon's list, and five from small religious parties; with the support of the controversial Flatto-Sharon, it wound up with two more than the sixty-one needed to form a government.

In this situation, the DMC faced a classic choice: to get as much as possible politically and rationalize away its principles, or to stand by its principles and forgo a share of power (meager though it might be).

West Bank Policy. The Likud was in a comfortable position. Its agreement with its coalition partners involved relatively small payoffs—and these were ministerial, not ideological. The NRP had been taken over by a hawkish young faction, and its religious-nationalistic rationale for establishing settlements on the West Bank coincided with Begin's nationalistic-religious rationale for doing so. The scriptural definition of the historic Land of Israel was the basis for modern Israel's strong nationalistic claim to the territories. Begin had belonged to Betar, the militant youth movement associated with strong if not extreme Jewish nationalism. Thus, the coalition he formed with the religious parties gave him the opportunity to realize a cherished dream and reinforced his ideological and religious aspirations.

Could the DMC overcome such deeply rooted factors and compel Begin to plan the settlement of the West Bank only on the basis of security, not ideology? Could Begin persuade the DMC leaders, who had been reared on the idea of the partitionability of the Land of Israel, to support his extreme nationalism? Apparently the answer to both questions was no.

---

[46] See David Nachmias, "Coalition Politics in Israel," *Comparative Political Studies*, vol. 7 (October 1974), pp. 316–333, esp. p. 324.

[47] Ibid., p. 319.

Consequently, Begin concluded that the coalition negotiations with the DMC would have to avoid substantive ideological and policy questions and focus on ministerial payoffs. But the DMC repeatedly disclaimed any desire for positions per se; it wanted a share of the power only in order to change the system.

Begin refused to alter his hard line on the territories. Yadin reported, "We were told categorically that if we wanted to insert an item in the coalition agreement that this government, in preparation for peace talks, was willing for territorial compromise on the West Bank, then there was nothing to talk about."[48] Under pressure to join the coalition so that it could influence domestic policy, the DMC sought a formula that would even hint at security as a guiding factor in settlement policy; according to Yadin, this would blunt the ideological position of the future government. But it was rejected. Yadin's formula was: "The people of Israel have a historic right to the Land of Israel and to the areas of Israel which have security importance." The Likud agreed to modify its own formula only by the addition of a single word—and that, in parentheses: "The people of Israel have an eternal (historic) right to the Land of Israel that is unchallengeable."[49]

Even the hawks in the DMC suggested various formulas that implied a willingness to compromise on the territories. One proposal was to state awareness of the content of U.N. resolution 242, which calls for the return of the territories. Another suggested that there be no mention of the territories—just of a willingness to compromise. But the Likud rejected all of them. Thus, the issue of security emerged as a major obstacle to the inclusion of the DMC in the government. The slender hope the DMC had of moderating Begin's policy by controlling the foreign ministry was also shattered when this was given to Moshe Dayan. Contemplating the implications for Israel's foreign policy, one columnist asked: How, if Begin could not convince the compromising Yadin, could he expect to convince President Carter, let alone the Arabs?

Government Reform. In regard to the structure of the government, the most important issue for the DMC was the creation of a super ministry of welfare to narrow the social gap; this meant combining the welfare, labor, and health portfolios and national insurance (social security). However, the Ministry of Health had already been

---

[48] *Ha'aretz*, June 17, 1977.
[49] Ibid.

given to one of the Likud factions; this indicated to the DMC that the new government was already divided into estates according to factional needs. Ultimately, the Likud agreed to transfer the Ministry of Health to the umbrella Ministry of Welfare, but only after prolonged negotiations that Rubinstein called "a test of credibility and adherence to principles."[50] The transfer was to be made after a national health law was passed (with credit going to the Likud for its passage) or, at the latest, within one year.

The deadliest blow to the DMC's chances for joining the government came on the issue of electoral reform. The DMC wanted direct elections by districts to replace the nationwide system. Again, Begin manipulated the inexperienced DMC negotiators. First, the DMC agreed to leave one-third of the Knesset seats under the present system. Next, it expressed a willingness to divide the country into sixteen districts (instead of the twenty it had originally demanded); Begin agreed on "at least fifteen."[51] But the National Religious party was opposed to the plan, because its strength was demographic rather than geographic; it proposed that there be only six districts and that the voting be for parties rather than for people, in order to preserve its relative status. Begin suggested a compromise on ten districts.

The National Religious party rightly feared its demise under a district system; if Begin agreed to the DMC's demand for electoral reform, he would gain the DMC but lose the NRP. Begin would still have only a small majority—but he would have to make a heavy ideological payoff on the security and peace issues. There was little to be gained from replacing the NRP with the DMC—especially when Begin already had a government to his liking. However, his small majority required tight discipline in voting; there was no guarantee that in the future, over issues such as "Who is a Jew?" individuals or parties in the coalition would not break discipline. Consequently, Begin needed the DMC as an addition to the coalition to give him a cushion in Knesset votes. But he was unwilling to provide substantial payoffs simply for guarantees against such future contingencies.

Begin gave the religious parties a veto on the number of voting districts. As Rubinstein put it: "Eighty percent of the failure of the negotiations on the DMC's entrance into the government is over changing the election system. The Likud gave its religious partners a veto which it would not give the DMC on settlement of the territories."[52]

---

[50] *Ma'ariv*, August 5, 1977.

[51] Ibid., August 4, 1977.

[52] Ibid., August 5, 1977.

Hard Dealing. Begin the seasoned politician continued to make various offers to the DMC. He agreed in principle to electoral reform—but the "details" would be worked out by a committee, on which the coalition members could vote as they wished. Ostensibly, Begin was offering a democratic method for resolving the issue; actually, of course, the DMC would be outvoted on the committee and would not achieve its demands.

Time and again during the negotiations, Begin used this ploy to avoid committing himself to changing his position; instead, he would propose that key issues be decided by vote. He also agreed to free the DMC from coalition discipline during Knesset votes on electoral reform and religious matters. Settlement of the territories would be decided by the Knesset Foreign Affairs and Defense Committee. On political matters concerning the West Bank, the DMC would have freedom of expression and the right to abstain. Fully aware that the votes would be foregone conclusions and that it would have no influence, the DMC rejected this proposal.

Begin showed himself to be a superb but obstinate politician. He succeeded in appearing to want the DMC in the coalition, but even the DMC's hawks (who were closest to the Likud) admitted that the image was deceptive; Begin was simply creating a situation that would force the DMC to publicly refuse to join the government.

After four months of on-again, off-again negotiations, the talks broke down in September. It appeared that the Likud, unwilling to pay an ideological price, had lost a legislative cushion and that the DMC, unwilling to acknowledge the Likud's absolute ideological dominance, had lost ministerial posts, visibility, and cohesiveness.

In August, after a previous collapse in the negotiations, Rubinstein had said: "We need patience now. We must build the movement organizationally, and draw inspiration from Begin—who waited 29 years."[53] In fact, however, the DMC waited only until October—a few days before the portfolios reserved for the DMC were to be handed out to other parties. While the intellectual backgrounds of leaders like Rubinstein helped them withstand the temptations of the ministries that Begin dangled in front of them, veteran public figures like Tamir and Amit found little satisfaction in sitting on the back benches and doing routine legislative work. The old pros were in their sixties and saw the handwriting on the wall: it was now or never for them. So they opted to rationalize away the DMC's principles and to accept the offer the Likud had made a month before.

---

[53] Ibid.

Tamir and his allies succeeded in convincing Yadin that considerably less than what he had aspired to was better than being left out altogether—that the DMC could accomplish nothing by standing out in the cold with only its principles to keep it warm. With Yadin's go-ahead, it took only three days for the DMC's leaders and then the party council to formally approve the move. One council member, arguing for joining the Likud coalition, said: "To give birth, one must sometimes deviate from a certain principle. The DMC is very quickly becoming an old, unwanted spinster."[54]

Yadin became deputy prime minister, as well as acting prime minister in Begin's absence. While this did not give him meaningful executive powers and did not make him Begin's heir apparent, it did give him a favorable inside position for the eventual fight to succeed Begin. Yadin was given the power to coordinate the ministers dealing with social betterment and to control their budgetary allocations but not overall supervisory authority for them. He proved a major asset to Begin, tirelessly defending Begin's policies. Begin promised to change the electoral system to regional representation—but at the same time, he reassured the religious parties that their relative strength would be preserved. The number of regions was to be determined by a committee comprising the four coalition parties.

Publicly, Yadin claimed a state of emergency as an excuse for joining the government. The same ploy had been used in 1974 by Moshe Dayan; this time, however, the "emergency" was not the threat of a military confrontation with Syria, but the threat of a political confrontation with the United States.

Conclusion

In line with Duverger's statement that different views can find political expression in a proportional representation system, the DMC was indeed able to articulate the need for change. The situation contained the factors that Butler and Stokes suggest precede electoral change: the voters held strong attitudes on the issues, public opinion was divided, and the new party was clearly distinguishable from the others.[55] However, the DMC was unable to achieve any substantial reforms. In a two-party system, by comparison, even a fraction of the 11.6 percent of the vote won by the DMC might have been enough penetration for meaningful change.

---

[54] *Jerusalem Post*, October 21, 1977.

[55] David Butler and Donald Stokes, *Political Change in Britain* (London: Macmillan and Co., 1968).

Still, the new party was given a number of ministerial posts and a secondary role in policy. This will help assure the continued viability of the DMC—because a role in the government means rewards for its leaders, visibility for the party, and a base for recruitment and political participation. The DMC's contribution to the dumping of the traditionally dominant Labor Alignment presumably has given Israeli voters a greater sense of efficacy. The Likud's victory in the 1977 election, which was due in great measure to the DMC's siphoning off of voters from the Alignment, has demonstrated convincingly that the political scene in Israel today is neither static nor unresponsive—in distinct contrast to the past.

The evolution of the DMC as a third major party deviated from the pattern reported in Canada. There, the third party emerged after the formerly dominant party had been relegated to the opposition and its strength dissipated. But in Israel, the DMC's emergence preceded the Labor Alignment's loss of its dominant position and came before its ability to survive opposition status had been tested.[56].

The DMC had all of the features by which Schlesinger defines a party: it had a candidate (Yadin), it had a label (change), and it competed in an election.[57] It was successful in generating large-scale support. However, the principles that had attracted people to the party turned out to be an obstacle to the party's participation in the political system.

According to Pizzarno, a political struggle at the state level must involve negotiable ends—meaning that the DMC's goals would have to be subordinated to the government system dominated by the Likud. But the DMC was essentially a social movement—and Pizzarno notes that "the universalistic quality of a social movement is dependent on its ambition to substitute new values for values held by the dominant culture."[58] Thus, the DMC tried to subordinate the system to its principles, rather than vice versa.

Ironically, the DMC's ability to attract established public figures proved to be its undoing as a party of principles: the old pros could not live by idealism alone; they had to be where the power was. Once it became apparent that the DMC could not bring its principles into the government, Tamir and the other seasoned politicians led the

---

[56] Maurice Pinard, *The Rise of a Third Party* (Englewood Cliffs: Prentice-Hall, Inc., 1971).

[57] Joseph A. Schlesinger, "Political Party Organization," in James Gardner March, ed., *Handbook of Organizations* (Chicago: Rand McNally and Co., 1965), pp. 764–801.

[58] Pizzarno, "An Introduction to the Theory of Political Participation."

move to leave the principles outside; thus, the DMC became a party of expediency.

Had the DMC not joined the government, on the other hand, it might well have sacrificed itself for its principles. It would have had a difficult task in sticking together until the next election. Some of its leaders would probably have deserted the party in order to seek new links (or go back to old ones), and the DMC might not have had enough cohesion to survive. It would have shown itself to be a victory-dependent party, by its very nature lacking permanence—one of Duverger's "cadre" parties, "decentralized and weakly knit."[59]

Even in the government, the DMC will have to work hard at retaining the leaders and followers who were outraged by the party's abandonment of its principles. The DMC had introduced its principles in uncompromising terms reminiscent of those that militant social movements had used to present their ideologies in the past. It severely damaged its credibility by negating its well-publicized campaign pledge, "Our concern is not whom to join, but on what basis." Unforgivable to many people, this submission to political expediency was nevertheless understandable. In the final analysis, the DMC showed itself to be a party of personalities and not one with a clear course guided by a united leadership.

Although the DMC is now part of the coalition, it has no direct decision-making responsibility for the crucial issue of the territories. In 1970, when the Labor Alignment offered Begin's party a similar status in its coalition, he refused to accept such a minor role. In offering the same deal to the DMC, Begin may have been indicating his opinion of the new party. And the DMC, in accepting the deal, may have confirmed Begin's opinion.

Rubinstein, in sorrow and anger at the way things had turned out, refused to be considered for one of the DMC's four cabinet posts. On the contrary, he and other leaders of the original Change movement like Mordechai Virshuvsky began thinking of leaving the DMC and seeking greener pastures where their ideals could bloom. They boycotted the Knesset session at which the new DMC ministers were approved. If they had attended that session, they would have heard Shimon Peres, who opposed the vote of confidence in the newly enlarged coalition, admonish Begin: "I wish you would negotiate with the United States as well as you did with the DMC."[60]

---

[59] Duverger, *Political Parties.*
[60] Related by Shimon Peres.

7

The Lesser Parties in the Israeli Elections of 1977

Elyakim Rubinstein

Israel's multiplicity of political parties was emphatically reflected in the elections to the Ninth Knesset on May 17, 1977: twenty-two lists competed in the election; thirteen won seats in the Knesset. Out of these, four took 102 of the 120 Knesset seats (respectively, 43, 32, 15 and 12), while the remaining nine parties together won only 18 seats (see Table 7–1). Three out of the four major lists are described elsewhere in this volume. Our concern in this chapter is with the other ten lists. Only brief reference will be made to the nine lists that failed to win representation in the Knesset, polling less than the 1 percent of the popular vote legally required for representation.

The use of the word "list" rather than "party" points to a significant feature of Israeli elections, not only since the establishment of the state of Israel in 1948, but since the early internal elections in the Jewish settlement (*yishuv*) and throughout the British Mandatory period (1917–1948). The proportional-representation election system, which enabled even extremely small groups to achieve representation in the *yishuv*'s elected assembly and then in the Knesset, has encouraged small political factions to try their luck at the polls. From this point of view the 1977 elections were no exception.

Of course, many of the lists do represent parties, that is, political associations with platforms, regular membership, branches, and institutions. Six or seven of the ten lists that are the subject of our chapter are parties in this sense. Sometimes a list is an alignment or association of parties, as were the two major lists, the Likud and the Labor Alignment. At the opposite extreme are the one-man lists with a very specific and idiosyncratic character, like that of Shmuel Flatto-Sharon.

The lists discussed in this chapter and the number of seats they won in the Ninth Knesset are as follows:

1. National Religious party—12
2. Rakah (New Communist list)—5

TABLE 7-1

FINAL RESULTS, ELECTIONS TO THE EIGHTH AND NINTH KNESSETS

List	Popular Vote[a] 1977	Popular Vote[a] 1973	Popular Vote[a] Net Gain or Loss	Seats 1977	Seats 1973	Seats Net Gain or Loss
Eligible voters	2,236,293	2,037,478				
Votes cast (%)	1,771,726 (79.2)	1,601,098 (78.6)				
Invalid ballots (%)	23,906 (1.3)	34,243 (2.1)				
Quota for Knesset seat	14,173	12,451				
Likud	583,075 (33.4)	473,309 (30.2)	+3.2	43	39	+4
Alignment	430,023 (24.6)	621,183 (39.6)	−15	32	51	−19
Democratic Movement for Change	202,265 (11.6)			15		+15
National Religious party	160,787 (9.2)	130,349 (8.3)	+0.9	12	10	+2
Agudat Israel	58,652 (3.4)	60,012 (3.8)	+1.0	4	5	
Poalei Agudat Israel	23,956 (1.4)			1		
Democratic Front for Peace and Equality (Rakah Communists and Black Panthers)	79,733 (4.6)	53,353 (3.4)	+1.2	5	4	+1
Shelli (Moked in 1973)	27,281 (1.6)	22,147 (1.4)	+0.2	2	1	+1

Shlomzion (Ariel Sharon)	33,947 (1.9)			2		+2
Flatto-Sharon	35,049 (2.0)			1		+1
Independent Liberals	21,277 (1.2)	56,560 (3.6)	−2.4	1	4	−3
Citizens Rights	20,621 (1.2)	35,023 (2.2)	−1.0	1	3	−2
United Arab list (two Arab lists in 1973)	24,185 (1.4)	39,012 (2.5)	−1.1	1	3	−2
Hofesh (Black Panthers)	2,498 (0.14)	13,312 (0.9)	−0.8			
The New Generation	1,802 (0.1)					
Kach (Rabbi Kahane)	4,396 (0.25)	12,811 (0.8)	−0.55			
Women's party	5,674 (0.3)					
Arab Reform Movement	5,695 (0.3)					
Beit Yisrael (Yemenites)	9,505 (0.5)	3,195 (0.2)	+0.3			
Coexistence with Justice (Arab list)	1,085 (0.06)					
Zionist Panthers	1,798 (0.1)	5,945 (0.4)	−0.3			
Zionist and Socialist Renewal (Mordechai Ben-Porat)	14,516 (.8)					
Other lists in 1973	(7 lists)	40,624 (2.8)				

[a] For each year the popular vote is given, followed by the percentage of the total valid vote in parentheses. The net gain or loss figures for the popular vote are in percentage points.

SOURCE: Yosef Goell, "What the Voters Wrought," *Jerusalem Post*, May 27, 1977.

3. Agudat Israel—4
4. Shlomzion (General Ariel Sharon's list)—2
5. Shelli—2
6. Movement for Citizens' Rights—1
7. Poalei Agudat Israel—1
8. Independent Liberal party—1
9. Flatto-Sharon—1
10. Arab list (affiliated with the Alignment)—1

These lists represent a variety of political attitudes, ranging from the ultra-orthodox Agudat Israel to the anti-religious-establishment Movement for Citizens' Rights; from the rightist Shlomzion (which merged with Herut after the elections) to Rakah on the extreme left, articulating a clear anti-Zionist ideology. It comprises relatively large parties, like the National Religious party (included in this chapter mainly for reasons of convenience), and lists that were clearly set up for the purposes of the election only and have no ideological or political character of their own, like Flatto-Sharon's list.

The Religious Parties

Political scientists in Israel traditionally divided the Israeli political parties into three major groupings: the labor movement, usually comprising about sixty Knesset members (50 to 55 percent of the seats); the civil or center/rightist groupings, with about thirty M.K.'s (25–28 percent); and the religious groupings, with about seventeen M.K.s (12–15 percent); all the other groups generally held about 10 percent of the seats in the Knesset (including the Communists with about five M.K.s).

The balance of power between the two major groupings significantly changed in 1973 elections, held shortly after the Yom Kippur War, and they changed totally in the 1977 elections. The only grouping, in fact, that neither gained nor lost significantly in 1977 was the religious grouping.

Since the mid-fifties there have been three religious parties in Israel. The largest, the National Religious party (NRP; in Hebrew, Mafdal or Miflaga Datit Leumit) has usually had between ten and twelve M.K.s; the two smaller parties, Agudat Israel and Poalei Agudat Israel, are both more extreme in their religious views.[1]

---

[1] Some other parties sometimes have Knesset members who are orthodox. The Labor party (which encourages the separate existence of a small religious faction in the Histadrut, the Religious Worker) has a rabbi in its Knesset membership.

It should be noted that the religious parties represent only a part of the orthodox religious population in Israel. (The term religious in Israel *means* orthodox: there are few conservative and reform congregations, most of them small, and they are only reluctantly accepted by most of the orthodox establishment.) The orthodox population in Israel—to judge by the percentage of Israelis sending their children to orthodox schools—numbers about one-third of the population. Only 13–15 percent, however, generally vote for religious parties, a fact that causes some frustration to the religious parties.

The National Religious Party. The National Religious party has existed under this name since 1956. It was established then through the merger of two former parties: (1) Mizrachi, the first religious-national party in the Zionist movement, established in 1902, but which had become quite weak and small by 1956, losing in the Holocaust its main leader and many of its supporters; and (2) Hapoel Hamizrachi, a religious-social democratic party, established in 1922 as a faction in the Mizrachi and by 1956 the largest religious party in Israel.

Until the late sixties the NRP continued the political tradition of its two forerunners, what used to be called the "traditional partnership" between the NRP and the labor movement. Begun in the mid-thirties, this partnership was based on mutual understanding and shared interests. The largest party within the labor movement, Mapai, though the dominant party since the early thirties in the pre-state institutions and then in the state, was always in need of coalition partners. Its most devoted partners were Mizrachi and Hapoel Hamizrachi, later the NRP, which, beyond their share of government appointments in certain areas, limited their demands to religious legislation and public services.

Since its establishment the NRP has usually succeeded in electing eleven to twelve Knesset members and in winning 9 to 10 percent of the votes. In the elections of December 1973, however, the party won only ten seats. The main reason for this drop was the party's identification with Golda Meir's government, which was sharply criticized after the Yom Kippur War (although it was quite clear that the NRP ministers were *not* part of Meir's inner circle, which in fact made most decisions in foreign and security matters). At the same time, the NRP was being attacked by a part of the religious public for some of its leadership's failure to adhere to the party's basic principles. The

---

The Likud has a religious member from the Liberal party who is the son of a former Sephardic chief rabbi and himself became a minister without portfolio. *Zalman Segal* v. *The State of Israel et al.*

leaders, it was charged, were only concerned with obtaining cabinet positions.

In the years 1974–1977 the party again joined the Labor coalition, after a short time in the opposition in 1974. The NRP had traditionally supported the Labor-headed coalition government on all aspects of foreign, economic, and domestic policy. Since the Six-Day War in 1967, however, the younger generation of the party had gradually shifted the NRP's position on Judea, Samaria, and Gaza to one of opposition to any concessions in the lands of Eretz-Yisrael. This tendency became especially clear after the death of the leader of the party, Moshe Shapiro, in 1970. It led gradually to greater disagreement with the Labor leadership, but the awareness that the NRP would be much less effective and useful to its constituency in the opposition than in the coalition kept the party inside the traditional partnership. Between 1974 and 1977, differences between the party and Rabin's government grew. The younger leadership, which was very close to Gush Emunim, the radical group calling for Israeli sovereignty in Judea and Samaria, was particularly assertive, and the old guard reluctantly fell into line. The partnership became strained and inconvenient; NRP ministers sometimes served as an opposition inside the coalition. Matters came to a head in December 1976.

The confrontation began after a ceremony celebrating the delivery of new airplanes to the Israel Defense Forces was ended on Friday afternoon, very close to the beginning of the Sabbath. Usually no official ceremonies take place on or near the beginning of the Sabbath, but, because of special circumstances related to the Rabin-Peres rivalry, this rule was not observed. Poalei Agudat Israel introduced a no-confidence motion, and two of the NRP ministers abstained. The prime minister, acting upon advice from some of his party colleagues, "demonstrated leadership" and invoked a section of the Law of Transition 5709—1949 which states that a minister who abstains in a no-confidence vote is considered as having resigned from the government on the day the government states this fact to the Knesset.

Rabin so informed the Knesset on December 20, 1976. However, on the same day he announced his own resignation. According to a Basic Law this was considered the resignation of the whole government, requiring the selection of a transition government. At this juncture, a group of NRP members petitioned to the High Court of Justice claiming that since forty-eight hours had not elapsed after the announcement of the NRP ministers' resignation they should remain members of the transition government that would rule until new elections could be held. The High Court of Justice ruled against them.[2]

Ultimately, this was to the benefit of the NRP, which was now free to run its election campaign as an opposition party. The party leadership—especially the "youngsters," the faction led by Zevulun Hammer—were determined that the NRP should show a new face to the voters, one that would appeal to the younger generation of orthodox Israelis, many of whom had had doubts about supporting the NRP. One of the measures they took was the expulsion of Yitzhak Raphael, who had been a controversial figure in the party leadership for many years and until December 1976 minister for religious affairs. As a deputy minister of health in the early sixties, Raphael had been named in connection with criminal charges brought against an official of his department. The official was later sentenced to imprisonment for extorting contributions to a public enterprise during the building of a hospital. Raphael's name was involved in a judicial report on the affair, but later he was acquitted of complicity by the committee. Although this episode had slowed his promotion, Raphael was one of the central men in the party and headed a large faction. The success of the youngsters' maneuvers and their ability to turn some of Raphael's own supporters against him came as a great surprise.

After Raphael's departure, the campaign was focused on presenting the party as "The Beautiful NRP." The younger leadership managed to add to the NRP list, in a very prominent position, Rabbi Haim Druckman, a popular figure among the nationalist-orthodox younger generation close to Gush Emunim. This move, it was hoped, would draw Druckman's constituency into the party and satisfy Rabbi Zvi Y. Kook, the head of "Merkaz Harav" Yeshiva and the spiritual leader of Gush Emunim. Another campaign move was mobilizing the support of some nonorthodox circles, who helped improve the party's public image. The campaign stressed the party's positive achievements in the fields of education, religious services, and legislation. Throughout the campaign the party's leaders said that if their options after the election were coalition with the Alignment and coalition with the Likud they would choose the latter. This was partly a response to the insulting manner in which Rabin had removed the NRP from the coalition.

The results of the elections were positive from the NRP's point of view. The party won twelve Knesset seats instead of the ten it had taken in 1973. This was considered a great improvement, although in the past the NRP had held twelve seats in the Knesset more than once.

The NRP was the first party to announce its support for a coalition

---

[2] H.C. 621, 622, 624/76, 31(2)P.D. (1977) 8.

led by Menachem Begin. This decision was consistent both with the national trend revealed by the election results and with the policies adopted by the party in recent years. In the Likud government the NRP was granted the Ministry of the Interior (combined with Police, formerly a separate Ministry), the Ministry for Education and Culture (very important for the party because of its special stress on education) and the Ministry for Religious Affairs. Interior and Religious Affairs were "traditional" NRP ministries, while education was considered an important victory.

Agudat Israel and Poalei Agudat Israel. The smaller components of the religious group in the Knesset have always been Agudat Israel and Poalei Agudat Israel. These two parties are distinguished from the NRP by both their more extreme attitude in religious matters and by their traditional rejection of the secular ideological basis of Zionism. Their constituency has included the Hassidic and ultra-orthodox communities[3] and their political decisions (especially those of Agudat Israel) are subject to the consent of the Council of Torah Sages, namely the heads of the ultra-orthodox *yeshivot* (religious academies) and the most prominent Hassidic rabbis. As political parties that seek guidance in matters of political substance from a rabbinical body, they are unique. It should be noted, however, that since the early sixties the political authority of the sages has officially been recognized only by Agudat Israel and not by Poalei Agudat Israel. Both parties have rejected the secular character of Zionist ideology and have claimed that the Torah, as the basic constitution and ideological statement of the Jewish people, should be made the foundation of Jewish Israeli life. They also demand public observance of orthodox Halacha law and the elimination of the draft for girls and *yeshiva* students. The difference between Agudat Israel and Poalei Agudat Israel lies mainly in the sociological basis of their support, Poalei Agudat Israel being historically the party of highly orthodox working-class people. Both, but especially Agudat Israel, have a very steady core of supporters, ultra-orthodox Israelis concentrated mainly in Jerusalem, Bnei-Brak (an orthodox town near Tel Aviv), and a few other municipalities.

---

[3] Agudat Israel does not represent the *most* extreme of the ultra-orthodox groups. There are some relatively small groups in Jerusalem who oppose any participation in the political establishment of Israel and prohibit their members from taking part in elections. The largest extremist group is called Ha'eda Haharedit "the pious community"; part of it Neturei Karta ("guards of the city"), is located mainly in the district of Mea Shearim. The extreme orthodox community numbers approximately 8,000 people altogether.

Together, Agudat Israel and Poalei Agudat Israel have traditionally held five to six seats in the Knesset. In some campaigns they have
put up a common list, in others separate ones, and once, in 1949, they
joined forces with the two parties that later became the NRP. When
they have run separately, their seats have usually divided three-to-four
for Agudat Israel and two for Poalei Agudat Israel. In the elections of
1973 the two parties ran together and won five Knesset seats. They
did not join the coalition; indeed, the two parties together have not
entered a governing coalition since the early years of statehood,
though Poalei Agudat Israel did so on its own several times in the
sixties. Because of internal rivalries and especially the opposition of
extremist elements in Agudat Israel, the two parties again decided to
run separately in 1977.

Agudat Israel. Quite severe internal problems beset Agudat Israel in
the year preceding the elections. Most of these were connected with
strains and rivalries between different factions, based upon common
Hassidic or regional backgrounds in Europe. There are four main
groups in Agudat Israel, which presented themselves in the internal
elections held in the party in 1976 (the first in thirty-one years):

(1) The Central Faction, representing mainly the old-guard
Agudat Israel of pre-World War II Poland. Led by the circle of
the Hassidic Rabbi of Gur, this faction became central in Agudat
Israel in the forties, with the immigration to Israel of some of its
leaders.

(2) "The Faithful," a faction centered in the Old Settlement of
Jerusalem. It is composed of ultra-orthodox families who have
been in Israel for generations and who opposed the Zionist settlement's secular character, remaining in active opposition to it—for
many years (though not from the very beginning) in the framework of Agudat Israel.

(3) "Obeyance and Fulfillment," the supporters of Agudat Israel
in the extremist religious academies of Bnei-Brak. This faction is
known as the youngsters of Agudat Israel.

(4) The United Faction, consisting of Hungarian Hassidic and
yeshiva circles, also centered mainly in Bnei-Brak.

The last two groups are based sociologically on quite similar middle-
class circles and stick very much to the leadership of Hassidic rabbis
and *yeshiva* heads. The list of candidates was composed so as to
represent all these factions.

Agudat Israel's core support is very solid. (In fact it is slowly growing; the birth rate in the ultra-orthodox community is very high.) This fact (which allowed it to win four seats) and the general circumstances created by the 1977 elections gave Agudat Israel a key role in the creation of the coalition. Eager to complete his cabinet soon and avoid long and tiring negotiations, especially with the Democratic Movement for Change, the prime minister-designate wanted Agudat Israel as a partner in his coalition. After negotiations in which they won some important concessions in the religious field, both the party's leaders seemed to favor joining the coalition and the cabinet. By order of the Sages' Council, however, they joined the coalition without accepting a ministerial appointment. Their four Knesset members were compensated with the chairmanships of two important Knesset committees (finance, probably the most important committee, and welfare and labor), the vice-speakership of the Knesset, and a seat on the Foreign Affairs and Security Committee, none of which would otherwise have been allocated to them.

Poalei Agudat Israel. In 1977 the smaller faction of the ultra-orthodox camp in the Knesset, Poalei Agudat Israel, suffered a blow that reduced its representation from two seats (the number it had usually held since 1949) to one. Ironically, Poalei Agudat Israel's daily, *She'arim*, was the newspaper that had initiated the government crisis leading to the elections. Moreover, after Agudat Israel's extremists rejected a united list, Poalei Agudat Israel in turn refused to sign a "surplus vote agreement" with Agudat Israel—which, as it happened, might have given Poalei Agudat Israel a second Knesset seat.

This small party was formed by Agudat Israel followers in Germany and Poland in the twenties. They developed a social program that included the improvement of labor conditions for Jewish workers in factories and building and settlement in Eretz-Yisrael, in addition to the basic Torah program of Agudat Israel. In the forties, and especially after the establishment of the state of Israel, cooperation between this party and the Zionist groups developed, and at least until the late sixties the party took part in some governing coalitions. Its relationship with Agudat Israel was ambivalent; there were years in which the two parties cooperated and ran together for the Knesset, while in other years the relationship became tense and they ran separately. In order to appeal both to the ultra-orthodox population and to hawkish, younger orthodox voters, the party radicalized its attitudes in both the religious and political spheres. However, the party's problem has been its failure to become identified with the ultra-orthodox academic community in which Agudat Israel is deeply rooted. Despite its youth movement (Erza), it has not succeeded in developing young political cadres. On the one hand, its involvement in the establishment of kibbutzim and moshavim and its labor activities, in addition to its former partnership in the coalition, brought it closer to the Zionist camp and detached it somewhat from the extreme political groups in the ultra-orthodox world, including the younger generation of *yeshiva* students. On the other hand, some of the graduates of its youth movement grew closer to nationalist religious groups like Gush Emunim and preferred to vote for either the Likud or the NRP. The result was the blow the party suffered in 1977. Its only representative in the Ninth Knesset is the veteran Rabbi Kalman Kahane, who in 1948 was among the thirty-seven signers of the Declaration of Independence.

Poalei Agudat Israel did not join the government coalition. It has its own labor union, which bears its name, and its youth movement is alive, but it has to cope with the problems that stem from its position between the more orthodox Agudat Israel and the more nationalist NRP.

Shlomzion—General Ariel Sharon's List

Since the early years of Israeli statehood, General Ariel Sharon has been one of the most prominent figures in the Israel Defense Forces. He was the commander of most of the reprisal actions in 1954–1956 and commanded the parachuters who started the Sinai campaign of 1956; in the Six-Day War he headed a division; and he headed the Southern Command during a large part of the War of Attrition; in addition, he was responsible for the reestablishment of peace in the Gaza Strip, cleaning out most of the terrorist activities in the early seventies; finally, he was the initiator and commander of the Suez Canal crossing in the Yom Kippur War. He is generally recognized as a brilliant general, though he failed in his ambition to become chief of staff of the IDF.

Sharon's political career has been less successful. He retired from the army in the summer of 1973 and joined the Liberal party, with which he had reportedly had unofficial contacts for some years. Sharon became the most energetic advocate of the establishment of a large bloc that would be able to stand as an alternative to the Alignment, and he was largely responsible for bringing together the Herut-Liberal bloc, the Free Center (Shmuel Tamir's small party), and the

Reshima Mamlachtit (David Ben-Gurion's last small party) to form the Likud in September 1973.

But the honeymoon did not last. In the tense period after the Yom Kippur War, Sharon was at once a war hero commanding his troops on the western side of the Suez Canal—and a politician holding a prominent place in the Likud list. There was public criticism of this combination of roles, and Sharon left the army before the elections and was elected to the Knesset. But his heart was with the army, and he soon resigned his seat in order to keep his army emergency reserve appointment. Later he joined Rabin's office as an adviser to the prime minister despite fierce opposition from the new minister of defense, Shimon Peres, and the chief of staff, Mordechai Gur, who resented Sharon's appointment as an interference in the army's affairs. Sharon's departure from the Knesset in 1974 strained his relationship with his partners in the Liberal party, though he was still admired, especially by Begin and other members of Herut. Later Sharon resigned from his job as the prime minister's adviser, this time to return to his farm.

In 1977, however, Sharon renewed his intensive political activity. He first proposed returning to the Likud, but demanded that the leadership be determined by free competition, notably between Begin and himself. This was not possible. Moreover, he was regarded with great suspicion by his former partners in the Liberal party, mainly Simcha Ehrlich, the party's strong man. Finally Sharon formed his own party or movement, Shlomzion (Peace for Zion), which adopted a political line consistent with his former attitudes and very similar to that of the Likud. It seemed at first to attract significant support—as late as February there was talk of its winning five seats—but Sharon made mistakes that brought his popularity down. He first held unconventional negotiations with the dovish Independent Liberal party. Later on he had problems within his own movement, and a large number of his followers, many of them people who had held high academic or military positions, left Shlomzion, denouncing Sharon's undemocratic methods. At last he tried to reenter the Likud, but this time his way was blocked by his former party, the Liberals, whose leader, Simcha Ehrlich, fiercely opposed his return. Ehrlich claimed that Sharon, though a brilliant general, was unfit for politics. Even Begin, the Likud leader, who would have warmly welcomed Sharon, could not help. Sharon remained outside on the eve of the deadline for submitting lists—and ran on his own. In his campaign, Sharon did not differ from the Likud in his political attitudes; on the contrary, he named Begin as his partner and ally. His propaganda stressed his military talents and expertise and urged the voters to enable him to become the minister of defense.

In the elections Shlomzion won two Knesset seats. General Ezer Weizmann, number two on the Herut list, was the Likud's choice for minister of defense. Shortly after the elections, however, the two Shlomzion members united with Herut, under an agreement that gave them a certain representation in the party institutions. Sharon himself became minister of agriculture, as well as chairman of the Cabinet Committee for Settlement, a post that later placed him at the center of the public debate over settlements.

The Independent Liberal Party

The Independent Liberals were almost annihilated in the 1977 elections—a blow that was second in historic significance only to the defeat of the Alignment. In absolute numbers the Independent Liberal party dropped from four seats in the Eighth Knesset to only one in the Ninth.

The history of the Independent Liberal party goes back to the beginning of Israeli statehood. It emerged out of the General Zionists A in the pre-state *yishuv*, a moderate middle-class group associated with Haim Weizmann, the first president of the state of Israel and for many years president of the World Zionist Organization. This group was sympathetic toward the Histadrut and the labor movement, although it advocated a more liberal laissez faire economic system and took very moderate positions on foreign policy. It had its own youth movement, a small faction in the Histadrut, and a number of agricultural kibbutzim and moshavim. In 1948, shortly after the establishment of the state of Israel, the General Zionists A and associated groups united with Aliyah Hadasha, a small party of Jews of German and Austrian origin, who were outside the *yishuv* establishment. Their leaders were mainly Russian and Polish Jews. Together they formed the Progressive party, which in the Knesset elections between 1949 and 1959 always won four to six Knesset seats and usually joined the governing coalition, with its leader, Pinchas Rosen, as minister of justice.

In 1961 the Progressive party united with the other nonsocialist center party, the General Zionists (the General Zionists B of the mandatory period), a party of laissez faire identified with private industry, agriculture, and commerce. Together they assumed the name Liberal party and remained in opposition for four years (1961–1965).

In 1965, in the light of the internal split in Mapai, the rightist group in the Liberal party advocated forming a political bloc with Herut, in order to create an alternative power capable of challenging the government. The "leftist" or "center" element—the former Progressive party—was reluctant to form such a partnership because it regarded Herut's radical views in foreign policy as unacceptable as a basis for negotiation. Hence, the Liberal party split: the rightist element kept the name Liberal party and allied itself with Herut in the coalition known as Gahal, while the leftist elements became the Independent Liberal party. Most of its members were former members of the Progressive party.

The new-old party continued its tradition of joining the governmental coalition. After the Six-Day War in 1967 it adopted foreign policy positions very similar to those of the dovish elements of the Labor party, advocating territorial compromise in all the territories, including Judea and Samaria, in the framework of a full peace agreement.

After the split of the Liberal party, the Independent Liberals never again achieved the strength they had had in the framework of the partnership in the Liberal party. From 1965 on they held between four and five Knesset seats. They again became regular partners in the governmental coalition—and, in fact, enlarged their representation by taking advantage of the provision in the law which states that a cabinet minister does not have to be a Knesset member.[4] Thus, in the Eighth Knesset the Independent Liberals secured two ministerial seats in addition to their four Knesset seats. The party's traditional partner-

---

[4] Originally it was accepted that all cabinet ministers should be Knesset members, on the British model. In the early days of the state, however, David Ben-Gurion, the first prime minister, decided to leave open the legal possibility that ministers might not be Knesset members, mainly to allow for the appointment of professionals and specialists.

Gradually it became a pattern in Israeli politics, first in the small parties and then, to a certain extent, in the dominant party, that with the establishment of a new government some future ministers would resign their Knesset seats and other members of their party would take their seats in the Knesset. The ministers would retain all the rights and immunities of Knesset members except the right to vote in the house. Menachem Begin has claimed that by resigning their Knesset seats, such ministers show disrespect for the Knesset. Under an amendment to the law introduced by Begin, if a minister resigns his seat in the Knesset, he is automatically considered to have resigned from the cabinet too, and a new process of appointment to the cabinet is needed (now Section 21[B] of Basic Law: The Government). As a way around this, Knesset members who are to be appointed ministers and intend to resign submit their resignations just before being appointed. There has been some talk of adopting the Norwegian system, whereby Knesset members who resigned in order to enable others to take their seats while they themselves joined the cabinet, would reoccupy their Knesset seats if they lost their cabinet positions.

ship in the government was its main disadvantage in the elections of 1977.

In some respects, the party's ministers tried to act as an opposition inside Rabin's government. On the eve of the government's resignation, following the December crisis, the two Independent Liberal ministers wanted to submit their resignation. They were, however, "locked" into the government by the provision of Section 21(A) of the "Basic Law: The Government," according to which a minister's resignation comes into effect forty-eight hours after being submitted to the prime minister. The Independent Liberal ministers submitted their resignation on the afternoon of December 20, and the same evening Prime Minister Rabin submitted his own resignation to the president of the state, which according to the law constituted the resignation of the whole government. The Independent Liberal ministers claimed that they considered themselves out; the attorney-general, meanwhile, petitioned to the High Court of Justice for a decision stating that they were still members in spite of their resignation. The court (which had the opposite problem with the NRP ministers) decided that the Independent Liberal ministers were still inside the government, since their resignation had not been final when Rabin had submitted his resignation to the president.[5] On top of this, the party suffered internal crises during the campaign, including the departure of its veteran leader, Minister of Tourism Moshe Kol.

The shock that the party suffered in the 1977 elections seems to have been due partly to the fact that the party was too closely identified with the Alignment government, which was being punished by the public, and the High Court's decision forcing its ministers to remain within the government did not add prestige to either them or their party. More important, however, is the fact that traditionally the Independent Liberals' followers were people who wanted to support a center policy, between the positions of the Likud and the Alignment. In 1977 these people had a new option, a party with a good list of candidates that was not identified historically with the government establishment—the Democratic Movement for Change.

The Independent Liberals' sole representative in the Ninth Knesset was Gideon Hausner, former attorney general of Israel, the prosecutor in Adolph Eichmann's trial, and later a minister (without portfolio) in the 1974–1977 government. He did not join the Likud and advocated policies close to the Alignment's. The party itself

---

[5] The State of Israel v. Moshe Kol and Gideon Hausner, H.C. 623/76, 31(2)P.D. (1977) 3.

suffered mass defections, even of prominent members, before the elections, mainly to the DMC but also to the Likud. This drain continued after the elections, mainly to the Likud.

In the elections to the Histadrut held on June 21, 1977, the same pattern emerged: instead of the almost 6 percent the Independent Liberals had carried in 1973, they won only 1.4 percent of the vote—and this they achieved in partnership with Shulamit Alloni's Citizens' Rights Movement.

The Movement for Citizens' Rights

This movement was born in the summer of 1973 before the Yom Kippur War, while the lists for the Eighth Knesset were being drawn up. Shulamit Alloni, its founder, has been a well-known and quite controversial figure in Israeli politics since the early sixties. Born in 1929, she became a lawyer and a Mapai activist and succeeded in obtaining a Knesset seat in 1965 on the Mapai list. Her radio programs and press columns as well as her books defending civil rights had a wide audience. However, many of her activities were directed against the religious laws concerning marriage and divorce, and she became identified with anti-religious-establishment attitudes in Israeli politics. In 1969 she lost her place on the party's list, apparently because of her strained relationship with Golda Meir, then the prime minister and the party's leader. In the years 1969–1973 she continued her journalistic activities and published a book directed against what she called "the arrangement" (the coalition practices of Labor and the NRP in religious matters, mainly the "Who is a Jew?" dispute)[6] and sharply criticized the government's policy in this matter. In view of her inability to secure a Knesset seat on the Labor list (Golda Meir again opposed her) in the summer of 1973, Alloni decided to run on her own list and formed, in collaboration with a group of teachers and others, the Movement for Citizens' Rights. The list did far better than predicted in the elections held on December 31, 1973, in the aftermath of the Yom Kippur War, winning three Knesset seats. This success was attributed to Alloni's public record, which appealed to

---

[6] The question of how to define a Jew in Israeli law has been a source of contention between secular and religious forces for many years. Under Jewish religious law, a Jew is anyone born to a Jewish mother or properly converted; on the other hand, some argue that a Jew is anyone who so declares himself. In 1970 in Shalit v. Minister of the Interior (H.C. 58/68, 23[2] P.D. 477) the High Court ruled five to four that the latter definition was consistent with the law as it then stood. Immediately the government undertook to amend the law in favor of the religious definition.

certain groups, and to the large protest vote against the Meir government, much of which came from people who otherwise would have voted for the Labor party but who would not transfer their vote to the Likud.

In 1974, after Golda Meir's resignation, Alloni joined Rabin's new cabinet as a minister without portfolio. She soon left the government, however, when the NRP rejoined it, and served in the Knesset opposition. She faced a series of internal crises inside her own group. The gravest of these was a short-lived political association with Arieh (Lova) Eliav, a veteran labor figure (now a member of Shelli); when Eliav broke away, Alloni's third M.K., Marsha Friedman, an American-born academic from Haifa and a women's liberation activist, joined him.

As the 1977 elections neared, Alloni's position was threatened by the appearance of the DMC, and her campaign was directed against them. She did not—as did some other groups—join the DMC, rejecting the precondition that all DMC candidates resign from the Knesset before the elections. She criticized the DMC throughout the campaign, pointing to their lack of a clear program, especially in religious matters. In foreign and economic policy, she shared the views of the left wing of the Labor party and opposed the Likud on ideological grounds. Reportedly, she had some negotiations with other groups (in particular the Independent Liberals) but came to terms with them only in the Histadrut campaign.

The elections results were a disappointment for Alloni—she barely won a single Knesset seat—mainly because the protest vote of 1973 was transferred in 1977 to the DMC. Those who continued to vote for Alloni were interested in enabling her to continue her fight against the religious parties and establishment and also against the "rightist" tendencies in the government.

Shelli

Shelli, a small political alignment, offers an interesting illustration of the complexity of Israeli party politics. It was established to compete in the 1977 elections as a grouping of three main factions:

(1) Moked (Focus), which elected one M.K. in 1973. It comprised the former Israeli Communist party (Maki, the mainly Jewish Communist party) and Tchelet-Adom, a leftist group defining itself as Zionist-socialist and headed by Meir Pa'il, a former army colonel and history teacher at Tel Aviv University. Moked

was notable mainly for its leftist opposition to the government's policy in the Israeli-Arab conflict, but abandoned the Communist identification of some of its founders.

(2) Ha'olam-Hazeh, the faction headed by Uri Avneri, editor of the sensational weekly of the same name. Avneri served as an M.K. in 1965–1973 (the full name of his list was Ha'olam-Hazeh/Koach Hadash, "new power"). He failed to win reelection in 1973, and since there were many similarities between the policies he had been advocating and those of Moked in Arab-Israeli relations, the two groups negotiated a common list in 1977, something they had unsuccessfully attempted in the past. The list was called Shelli—an abbreviation of Shalom Lemaan Israel (Peace for Israel).

(3) Most important, the Black Panther faction, which had led protest demonstrations since the early 1970s. This group split repeatedly through the years. Some of its members ran separately, both in 1973 and 1977; some joined radical parties like Shelli and even Rakah.

The man who headed the Shelli list, Arieh Eliav, was a very interesting figure in Israeli public life. Formerly a deputy minister in two governmental posts and a secretary general of the Labor party, Eliav had been a prominent and devoted figure in many vital fields, including Jewish immigration to Israel and the development of new settlement areas, throughout the pre-state years and up through 1966. In the seventies he left the Labor party after an ideological dispute with Golda Meir's cabinet over the Arab-Israeli conflict and the territories. After splitting from the Alignment, Eliav briefly joined Shulamit Alloni's group and, after breaking with her, remained in the Knesset for a while in the framework of what he called the Independent Socialist list. Reportedly, he considered retiring from political life, but in 1977 he agreed to head the new Shelli list.

Shelli was supported by a certain number of intellectuals calling for Israeli-Palestinian entente. Its campaign was aimed at the former supporters of Moked and Avneri, as well as at leftist elements in the Alignment, mainly in Mapam but also in the Labor party. It called itself the Shelli *camp* to emphasize its identity as an alliance of various groups dedicated to peace.

Their hopes, however, were disappointed. Shelli won only two Knesset seats, no more than its component elements had held before the elections (Moked, one seat, and Eliav, one seat as an Independent).

They had another disappointment in the Histadrut elections, held on June 21, 1977: they lost more than half their power and secured only a little above 1 percent of the vote. The explanation for this rout was undoubtedly the general tendency of labor-oriented voters to strengthen the Alignment in order to help it retain its predominant status in the Histadrut. In the Knesset, Shelli became the most extremist left-wing element of the Zionist opposition.

The Communists: Rakah

Since the elections of 1973, only one Israeli party has borne the name Communist: the New Communist list, known by its Hebrew acronym, Rakah. In the years 1965–1973 there were two Communist parties, one predominantly Arab (Rakah), which was also the larger party, and one predominantly Jewish (Maki). The two parties were created after the split in the United Communist party, which existed between 1948 and 1965. Splits in the Communist camp in Israel, mainly between Jews and Arabs, had occurred frequently throughout the mandatory period, and the split in 1965 followed the old cleavage. Each of the parties tried to hide its national and electoral basis by sticking to the Communist slogans of class unity; but there was no doubt about their real character. Rakah, under tight instructions from Moscow, developed radical attitudes quite similar to those of the Palestinian movement, while Maki tended more and more, and especially after 1967, to strengthen its relationship with the Zionist camp, encouraged in this direction by its leader, the late Moshe Sneh, a leading figure in the Zionist movement in the pre-state period.

Eventually Maki (which won one Knesset seat in the elections of 1965 and 1969) united with Zionist radical leftist groups (including Tchelet-Adom), and Moked was established on the eve of the 1973 elections. Moked was a partner in the formation of the Shelli camp in 1977, together with Zionist elements.

Rakah was predominantly Arab, and although its official leadership included Jews and Arabs in equal numbers, it was common knowledge that it derived the major part of its votes from Arabs. Arab nationalism—more specifically, Palestinian nationalism—could express itself politically mainly through Rakah, since no list that denied the right of the state of Israel to exist could be submitted for the elections, according to the rule set by the High Court in 1965.[7]

In the seventies Rakah increased its activities in accordance with

---

[7] Yardor v. Chairman of the Central Elections Committee, Elections Appeal 1/65 19(3) P.D.365 (1965).

developments in the Palestinian movement, and, although it refrained from identifying itself with encouraging terrorist activities, it advocated the establishment of an independent Palestinian state and recognition of the PLO. It has been the only party to be thus completely detached from the Zionist camp and from the national consensus in Israel on vital political questions. The Party's parliamentary representation, which after the elections of 1965 (the first in which Rakah as such took part) and 1969 was three Knesset members, increased in 1973, after the Yom Kippur War, to four. Before the 1977 elections a much larger increase, even to seven or eight seats, was predicted; Israeli Arabs were becoming more radical, and the activities of Rakah had expanded in the Arab sector. The party was playing a delicate game, trying to stress its criticism of and hostility towards the government while avoiding any involvement in illegal activities that might endanger its position. It was clearly identified as the most extreme antigovernment political party.

As the 1977 elections approached, the party tried to demonstrate involvement in Jewish society too (though in fact its Jewish constituency has been extremely tiny). It made contact with one of the Black Panther groups and put one of its leaders in a safe place on the Rakah list, along with a non-Communist Christian Arab. The party also allied itself with extreme leftist Israeli groups and some former members of the other Communist party, Maki. The list ran under the name of Hadash (Hazit Democratit Le-Shalom U-le Shivyon, Democratic Front for Peace and Equality). The election results showed an increase in its power, mainly among Arabs (it took about 50 percent of the Arab vote), but not the great increase forecasted. In the Jewish sector it attracted very few votes . The only moderate increase in Rakah's total vote was due mainly to criticism from more extremist Arab groups and to the reluctance of middle-class Arabs to support a list that might draw an uneasy reaction from the government. It should be noted, however, that in the Arab cities and larger villages the percentage of the vote for Rakah was higher, in some places as high as 70–75 percent.

The results of the Histadrut elections were a disappointment to Rakah: they achieved only 2.57 percent, as compared with 2.41 percent in 1973—a very slight increase. Only 30 percent of the Arab voters in the Histadrut supported Rakah, as compared with 60 percent for the Alignment. Again, voters were reluctant to cause strained relationships in the Histadrut, which is both a large employer and a labor union and controls important public services including the largest health insurance organization in Israel.

The Arab Vote

In the elections of the First through the Sixth Knessets (1949–1965) the majority of Israeli Arabs steadily supported the dominant Jewish party or Arab lists affiliated with it.[8] Mapai and Mapum and their aligned Arab lists achieved 61.5 percent of the Arab vote in 1949, 72.1 percent in 1951, 69.7 percent in 1955, 64.5 percent in 1959, 61.8 percent in 1961, and 59.3 percent in 1965. In 1969 the percentage dropped to 54.7—and a drastic change occurred in 1973, after the Yom Kippur War, with the radicalization of the Palestinian movement: the figure went down to 39 percent. As the Alignment and its Arab satellite lists lost votes, the Communists gained. In 1961 the Communist party (then still united) achieved 22.7 percent of the Arab vote; in 1965, following the split in the party into a Jewish Communist party (which retained the old name) and a predominantly Arab Communist party (Rakah, the New Communist list), the Arab list got 22.6 percent of the Arab vote, as much as the united party had won in 1961. Since 1965, its power has been steadily rising: in 1969, about 34 percent; in 1973, about 37 percent; and in 1977, close to 50 percent. This, of course, reflects the change of mood in the Arab sector of the Israeli population: Arab nationalism and support for the Palestinians' attempts to win international acceptance have significantly grown. The Communist party, which is the only party that espouses Arab nationalist attitudes, has adapted itself in the last years to the Palestinian line; hence its success in drawing about 50 percent of the Arab vote in 1977, while only 27 percent went to the Alignment and its related list. Although the Communists won only five seats—as many as eight had been predicted—their support inside the Arab population had clearly risen.

The participation figures for the Arab sector, on the other hand, declined, from a peak of 92.1 percent in 1955 to 87.8 percent in 1965, about 84 percent in 1969, and only 72 percent in the 1977 elections. This decline is mainly explained by (1) the fact that Arab groups more extreme than Rakah (mainly the groups known as Bani el-Balad, Children of the Township) refrained from voting; (2) the fact that the 1977 elections did not coincide with municipal elections, which tend to mobilize Arab voters; and (3) the fact that people were confident that Rakah would do well.

---

[8] Jacob M. Landau, *The Arabs in Israel, a Political Study* (Oxford: Oxford University Press, 1969), Hebrew edition 1971, pp. 208, 256. Mapam itself has traditionally put an Arab in a safe place on its own list in most of the elections to the Knesset.

The Arab list affiliated with the Alignment—the United Arab list —suffered a serious blow in the 1977 elections. Traditionally there had been two Arab lists, headed by Arab notables who were nominated and helped out by the Alignment. In the elections previous to 1973 the Arab lists affiliated with the Alignment had generally won four Knesset seats. In 1973, owing to the rise of Rakah, they elected only three M.K.s, among them one Moslem, one Druze (who became a deputy minister), and one Bedouin (from the Negev, the southern part of Israel, the first Bedouin M.K. in the history of the state).

The consequent deterioration of the Alignment's strength among Arabs and the rise of Rakah resulted in 1977, for reasons connected with the trend toward Palestinian nationalism, in an additional loss of power for the Arab list affiliated with the Alignment: it achieved only 24,185 votes (1.4 percent) compared to 39,012 (2.5 percent) in 1973, and only one Knesset member, a veteran who had served in the Knesset off and on since 1949, Saif el-Din Zu'bi.

Most of the votes lost by the Arab lists went to Rakah. Some, however, went to a protest list initiated as a challenge to the tendency of the Alignment to stick to its traditional, veteran leadership, chosen on the basis of family (hamula) ties or regional affiliation, rather than to encourage young leadership that could answer the needs of a new generation of Arab intellectuals. The list was headed by Mahmud Abbasi, a former activist of the Israel Labor party, to whom Labor had allegedly promised a seat in the Knesset that had never materialized. Abbasi's list received only 5,695 votes, but had these votes gone to the Alignment-affiliated Arab list, they would have made it possible for that list to gain a second Knesset seat.

Surprisingly enough, in Knesset elections some Arab votes go also to the NRP. In previous elections the NRP had generally won one of its Knesset seats through Arab votes. This phenomenon is explained mainly by the fact that the NRP holds the Ministry of the Interior, which deals with the Arab municipalities, and the Ministry for Religious Affairs, which deals, inter alia, with the minorities' religious establishments. In 1977, 5 percent of the Arab vote still went to the NRP, although the number of votes was smaller than in the past. The Likud, the Independent Liberals, and Alloni's Movement for Citizens' Rights also took 1 percent each of the Arab vote.

The greatest disappointment in the Arab sector was Shelli's: this group, calling for Israeli recognition of moderate elements in the PLO, had made great efforts to attract support from Arabs, competing with Rakah on the grounds that it was also acceptable to the Jewish sector. Shelli, however, took only about 1 percent of the Arab electorate, some 2,000 votes.

Knesset Members Representing the Minorities. The minorities have traditionally been represented in the Knesset in three ways: through the satellite lists of the Labor party, through Mapam (the leftist part of the Alignment) which has usually included one Arab in its own list, and through the Communists. In most Knesset elections since the second, the minorities won six to eight Knesset seats (three to five from the Arab lists affiliated with Mapai-Labor, one from Mapam, and two from the Communists). In the 1977 elections the picture changed, for the reasons already discussed in relation to the Arab vote.

The Arab satellite list achieved only one Knesset member. In addition, the Alignment's defeat prevented Mapam's Arab candidate from entering the Knesset. The Communists (Rakah), meanwhile, increased their Arab representation from two to three. But the total number of minority Knesset members (Moslems, Christians, and Druzes) did not change since three Druzes were elected on other lists—two who managed to enter the DMC list through clever maneuvering before the internal elections in the DMC, and one on the Likud list. The total number, then, remained seven.

Flatto-Sharon

Shmuel Flatto-Sharon was the maverick of the 1977 elections, running on a one-man list.

Israeli political history has been, and still is, party dominated. Few Knesset members have been elected on a purely personal basis, and even fewer who were not well-known politicians formerly associated with parties. Shulamit Alloni, for example, was a former Labor M.K. who had fallen out with the party leadership and had been pushed off the party list. The Citizens' Rights Movement she launched as a result was built up on the basis of her liberal views in the civil rights sphere. Moreover, her list consisted of other names as well as her own and achieved three seats in its first campaign in the aftermath of the Yom Kippur War (in 1977 she won only one seat). When Uri Avneri ran in 1965 in the Ha'olam-Hazeh list, he was well known as the editor of the weekly bearing the same name. But, Flatto-Sharon was different. He was a wealthy Jew who had survived the Holocaust and who had come to Israel after the Yom Kippur War to avoid the charges he faced in France concerning his financial affairs. Once in

Israel, he remained under the constant threat of extradition—and so (some say) decided to run for the Knesset on a one-man list bearing the name "Flatto-Sharon—the lonely man to the Knesset." As a Knesset member he would enjoy immunity from extradition. His impressive campaign was concentrated partly in developing areas of the country, and he promised to initiate solutions for the problem of housing for young couples and the like. Despite an extremely poor knowledge of the Hebrew language (which he tried to improve after being elected) he won enough votes to grant him, had his list included another candidate, *two* Knesset seats. Flatto-Sharon's election came as a surprise, understandable only in the light of the general confusion and instability that prevailed on the eve of the election. After the election Flatto-Sharon supported the government, without formally entering the coalition. In his parliamentary work he used the services of an interpreter, but started delivering his speeches in Hebrew. This politically controversial figure won international publicity in 1978 for his activities concerning an exchange of political prisoners between East and West. Meanwhile, charges of irregularities in his campaign were being checked by the attorney general.

The Lists That Failed

Nine lists ran in the 1977 elections and were defeated. It is worth taking a look at them, because while a few were abortive lists that had had no chance whatsoever in the first place, others represented interesting trends in Israeli political life.

First, the ethnic dimension. Since the pre-state days, all the elections in the Jewish community in Israel have included lists that represented, or pretended to represent, the Jews of Oriental origin. In the pre-state years, the Ashkenazic Jews, mainly from Eastern and Central Europe, were the majority of the population and dominated the political elite. The Sephardic Jews, from Oriental and Middle Eastern countries, claimed that they were not adequately represented. In the mandatory period and in the early years of the state these groups achieved minor representation. But after some disturbances in Haifa in 1959 that dramatized the problem of ethnic discrimination in politics, the parties introduced Sephardic candidates into their lists, a practice they have continued ever since.

In addition, the early seventies saw the emergence of groups that called themselves Black Panthers (after the American movement bearing the same name). Many of their activists had lived in poor neighborhoods, and some of them had criminal records. Their chief claim was that the government had neglected the problems of the poor sectors of Israeli society. They ran (in two lists) for the Histadrut elections in September 1973 and seemed to have a chance of winning Knesset seats in the elections that were scheduled to take place in October; the period appeared quiet as far as foreign and security problems were concerned, and people seemed to be more interested in social problems. But after the Yom Kippur War and the postponement of the elections to December, security again became the dominant issue —and the Black Panthers were defeated in the elections.

As the 1977 elections approached there were splits among the Panthers; two groups ran on the Rakah and Shelli lists, and two others ran separately on their own lists. Only the Panther who ran with Rakah won a seat. Shelli's man was fourth on the list, not high enough to secure a seat, and both the independent Panthers were routed.

There were two other groups than ran on an ethnic basis in 1977 —a group of candidates of Yemenite origin, and a list headed by a former Alignment Knesset member, Mordechai Ben-Porat, who was of Iraqi origin but well known for his political activities beyond the ethnic sphere. Ben-Porat stressed these activities and his general political views in the campaign; his list was named Renewal. Both groups failed, although Ben-Porat's came close to achieving one seat, partly from a personal constituency.

One more list is worth noting: that of Rabbi Meir Kahane. Rabbi Kahane was the founder and leader of the Jewish Defense League in New York, which was active mainly in the early seventies in defending the interests of Jews in New York in various fields. After immigrating to Israel, Rabbi Kahane adopted an extreme rightist political ideology and even launched a program of assisting Arabs to emigrate. He ran first on his own list in 1973 and came close to achieving one Knesset seat. He ran again in 1977, but failed this time too, and his vote dropped drastically.

The two other lists that failed were a women's liberation movement and a group of uncertain character named the party of the New Generation. These, like most of the defeated lists, fell far short of the 1 percent of the total number of votes required for representation in the Knesset.

8

The Financing of Elections

Leon Boim

Although Israel is a party-state, it has no law of parties like those of the German Federal Republic and many other countries, and the parties have no legal-judicial status. Various laws and Knesset ordinances, however, recognize their existence and function. Justice Haim Cohen of the High Court of Justice has said, "Although the parties have no recognized status or legal authority in any of the matters which are within the jurisdiction of a local authority or the Government, no one would think of invalidating the action of one of these bodies, exclusively because it was done for party considerations, or with the knowledge of the parties."[1]

In 1969 Israel joined the growing "club" of democratic states that have introduced direct financing of parliamentary elections and of political parties from the national budget. The measure adopted in 1969 was regarded as an experiment, but since 1973 state financing of parties has become a permanent feature of political life in Israel.

Several studies have indicated that the per capita election expenses of the political parties in Israel have been among the highest in the world.[2] Since this phenomenon had negative implications for the entire Israeli economy, the problem of arranging and curtailing these expenses preoccupied the parties, political researchers, and the public as a whole.[3]

Until 1969 the parties were financed exclusively by membership

---

[1] High Court of Justice (in Hebrew—hereafter HCJ) 193/68, Josef Walker v. the Council of the Chief Rabbinate in Israel and others, vol. 22 (1968), p. 510.

[2] Arnold J. Heidenheimer, "Comparative Party Finance: Notes on Practices and Toward a Theory," *Journal of Politics*, vol. 25 (1963), p. 790; and Leon Boim, "Financing of the 1969 Elections," in *The Elections in Israel—1969*, Asher Arian, ed. (Jerusalem: Jerusalem Academic Press, 1972), p. 142.

[3] See Emanuel Gutman's contribution to the "Comparative Party Finance" symposium mentioned in note 2 and Dr. Z. Moses, "The Need to Limit Elections Expenses," *Ha'aretz*, May 28, 1965.

fees and contributions. The government's only contribution took the form of free radio time during campaigns, allotted to each party on the basis of its strength in the outgoing Knesset. In 1969 this was widened to include television time, allotted on the same basis, with a specified minimum provided for each party and for each new list.[4]

Under this arrangement, which is still in force, each party or list of candidates receives twenty-five minutes of radio air time and four additional minutes for each Knesset member, as well as ten minutes of television air time and four minutes for each representative in the Knesset.

The allocation of broadcast time on radio and television is determined by the chairman of the Central Elections Committee in consultation with the committee members and with the director general of the Broadcasting Authority. On the face of it, the allocation of equal amounts of "basic time" both to parties represented in the Knesset and to new lists fulfills the requirement of "equality of opportunities." Few would contest the right of parties represented in the Knesset to additional time, proportionate to their power therein. It seems to me, however, that new lists previously unknown to the public may need more time in which to introduce themselves.

The total broadcasting time allotted to one party under existing legislation may not exceed one hour on the radio and one hour on television. This provision makes the injustice in the distribution of broadcasting time between the parties represented in the Knesset and the new lists only slightly less conspicuous. This was especially noticeable during the electoral campaign to the Ninth Knesset when the two big parties, the Alignment and the Likud, took over most of the time on both media, while other parties could hardly make their presence felt.

But the provision of free air time during campaigns was no solution to the parties' problems of financing both their ongoing activities and their campaigns. Prior to the elections to the Histadrut of September 2, 1969, and the elections to the Knesset and to the local authorities of October 28, 1969, two laws were passed that attempted to ameliorate their plight: (1) The Law for the Protection of Remuneration (Amendment No. 5)—1968,[5] and (2) The Law for the Elections to the Knesset and Local Authorities in the Year 1969 (Financing, Limitation of Expenses and Auditing),[6] which, for the sake of brevity

---

[4] Elections Law (Ways of Propaganda)—1959, *Sefer Ha'hukim* [The book of laws—hereafter S-Ha] 284, 1959, pp. 138 and 567, 1969, p. 199.

[5] *S-Ha*, 543, 1968, p. 256.

[6] *S-Ha*, 550, 1969, p. 48.

will be referred to hereafter as the Election Financing Law. In addition, prior to the elections to the Eighth Knesset, the Knesset adopted the Law for Financing of Parties—1973.[7] Enacted on January 24, 1973, this law replaced that of 1969 and introduced regular financing of elections and political parties.

An earlier law—the Law for the Protection of Remuneration—Amendment No. 5[8] was passed by the Knesset on March 11, 1958. Its purpose was to ensure that every worker in Israel would receive full and prompt remuneration for work performed, which the law designated as an elementary right.[9] The law prohibited deductions from pay, other than in the cases enumerated in section 25a of the law. In particular, the deduction of regular payments to the workers' council in a plant was permitted unconditionally, but membership fees in workers' organizations like the Histadrut[10] could be deducted only if there were a collective agreement or a "work agreement" relating to such deductions or, in the absence of one of the two, if the worker had agreed to the deduction *in writing*. The imposition of such conditions was intended to preserve, to the extent possible, the entirety of the worker's pay.

In Israel it is not mandatory to be affiliated with a workers' organization, and many workers are not so affiliated although they continue to enjoy the protection afforded by workers' organizations and trade unions, particularly the Histadrut. For this reason, in 1965 an amendment to the Law for the Protection of Remuneration (Amendment No. 4)[11] was introduced, which permitted the employer to deduct the expenses of organizational and trade-union protection from the worker's pay even where the worker did not belong to any workers' organization, and the deduction was credited to the workers' organization.

Again in 1968, section 25 of the law was hastily amended: introduced on August 5, the amendment became law on August 14, 1968.[12] The new amendment, which is the one that concerns us here, allowed an additional deduction for party financing unless the worker

---

[7] *S-Ha*, 680, 1973, p. 52.

[8] *S-Ha*, 247, 1958, p. 86.

[9] *Divrei Haknesset* [The minutes of the Knesset—hereafter D-Ha], 1958, vol. 21 (1), p. 373.

[10] For a discussion of the organization and powers of the Histadrut, see Appendix A.

[11] *S-Ha*, 439, 1965, p. 14.

[12] Zamir, "Parties Financing Law," p. 449.

objected in writing to his employer. This deduction, or "party tax," took the form of an increment in the party membership fees already being deducted from the workers' pay. The intent of the amendment was to liberate the political parties from the headache of financing their own activities and from dependence on external economic factors. This legislation was an attempt to find a speedy solution to one of democracy's most difficult problems. Inevitably, it raised questions.

The minister of labor and other participants in the debate, for example, expressed doubt whether party taxes collected by employers and distributed by the Histradrut would be sufficient to cover the parties' expenses. Could the amendment alone ensure that the parties would no longer need to have recourse to independent methods of financing? Did the law ensure a socially just distribution of the burden of party financing? And did the operation of the law in its first year justify the hopes placed in it?

The answers were not encouraging. First, the amendment failed to produce the legal and institutional tools required to ensure the attainment of its goal. Second, from the social point of view, the amendment did not ensure a just democratic distribution of the burden of financing the parties. For one thing, the Law for the Protection of Remuneration was, by its very nature, directed only to part of the public—employees—and not even to the entire body of employees but only to those affiliated to the Histadrut. While it is true that the Histadrut represents the majority of workers in Israel, not all are affiliated with it, and even some of those who are eligible for membership like the self-employed or housewives, do not receive wages from an employer. Third, the financing of parties by way of an amendment to the Law for the Protection of Remuneration had been promoted by the Histadrut. The Executive Committee of the Histadrut decided on May 12, 1968, to collect the party tax at rates ranging from .1 percent on salaries of IL200–IL300 to .5 percent on salaries of IL600 and over provided that the tax did not exceed IL5.5 per month. Those earning less than IL200 were to be exempted from the party tax. It was clear that of the 590,000 workers who paid taxes to the Histadrut, 141,000 would be exempt from the party tax, as their monthly salaries were not high enough.[13]

As early as the end of 1968, the secretary general of the Histadrut announced that the total number of those liable for the party tax would be about 450,000 and that for the month of January 1969 the

---

[13] *Ba'histadrut* [In the Histadrut], No. 5, 1968, pp. 45–46.

income therefrom would reach IL400,000.[14] It was generally anticipated that the party tax would yield about 11 million Israeli pounds
per annum.[15] In fact, because many workers took advantage of the
right to withhold their consent, it brought in only IL3.8 million in
1969.[16] Spokesmen of the parties claimed that these sums would
suffice to cover their expenses for the internal campaign to the
Histadrut, but it was clear that no funds would remain to cover other
expenses or the costs of the electoral campaign for the elections to the
Seventh Knesset. The auditing team of the Labor Party Inspection
Institution reported that for the 1969 Histadrut elections alone the
Alignment's campaign costs reached IL8,565,626.[17]

Clearly, financing the parties through the Law for the Protection
of Remuneration was insufficient. However, as could be expected, the
political parties were not ready to give up this important—even if not
highly respectable—source of income. Although great numbers of
Histadrut members availed themselves of the right to refuse to pay
the political tax, income from it rose to as much as IL5.5 million in
1970. At the same time, the Histadrut objected that the collection of
the political tax had proved difficult. Consequently, on December 6,
1970, the Histadrut resolved to abolish the political tax and to increase
instead the ceiling on a "consolidated tax" collected from its members;
this would be raised from IL700 to IL1,000 per month. Of this
consolidated tax, 5.5 percent would be allocated "for the purposes
of the elections in the Histadrut and the Trade Unions and for the
needs of the parties represented in the Histadrut, proportionately to
their representation therein."[18]

The Histadrut has continued to collect the increased consolidated
tax and to allot 5.5 percent of that tax to the parties. The results have
been notable. In 1973, for example, the Histadrut transferred to the
election funds of the various parties the sum of IL12,923,280.[19]
According to *Ma'ariv* of February 19, 1975, the sum was IL17,084,000
for 1974 and it has been growing since.

---

[14] *Ha'aretz*, January 31, 1969.

[15] *Ba'histadrut*, No. 5, 1968, p. 46.

[16] *Ha'aretz*, August 17, 1968.

[17] *Ma'ariv*, March 22, 1970.

[18] *Piskei Din* (Judgments—hereafter PA-DI) 27 (1) 1973, The Histadrut v. Boaz
Moav and Twelve Others, p. 262, and "The Aaron Committee Report" in *Hahlatot
Ha'vaada Ha'merakezet* [Resolutions of the Executive Committee of the His-
tadrut], January 17, 1971, No. 3/71, p. 2.

[19] Abraham Bronstein, *Ha'hevra Ha-histadrutit Bein Ha'shanim 1969–1973* [The
Histadrut Society in the years 1969–1973], Tel Aviv, September 1974, p. 41.

The Election Financing Law

The Law for the Elections to the Knesset and Local Authorities in the Year 1969 was submitted to the Sixth Knesset as a private bill by six members of the Knesset representing rival parties. After a stormy debate and energetic objections from the parties that had not agreed to the formulation of the proposed law, it was finally passed on February 19, 1969, and published nine days later.

This law was enacted only for the purpose of the elections to the Knesset and to the local authorities that were to take place on October 28, 1969.[20] Its objectives were (1) to provide funds to finance the parties' campaigns, (2) to limit campaign expenses and (3) to provide for scrutiny by the state comptroller.

Election Financing. Section 2 of the law provided that the financing of the elections to the Knesset and to the local authorities in 1969 should be effected by the state treasury through its budget. This section also set down the total budget for this purpose—IL14,880,000—and the key for the allocation of those funds. The main problems were the determination of the budget ceiling and the criteria for allocating the funds.

The sum total of the elections expenses budgeted was determined on the basis of an expenditure of IL120,000 for each member of the Knesset. Over and above this sum each party was entitled to spend a further IL40,000 for each of its members of the Knesset, bringing the total permissible expenditure for each member of the Knesset to IL160,000—and the grand total for the elections to the Seventh Knesset to IL19,840,000.

Allocating the funds among the parties was the most difficult and complicated problem that arose both before and after the law was passed. The Knesset was faced with two possibilities:[21] either to distribute funds according to the relative balance of power of the parties in the outgoing Knesset, or to distribute them according to the relative balance of power in the incoming Knesset—that is, according to the results of the elections to the Seventh Knesset.

Following a challenge to the implementation of the law in the High Court of Justice, the court suggested to the Knesset a way of coming to grips with the problem. In an effort to assure equality of opportunity for all prospective candidates and to prevent the abuse

---

[20] Leon Boim, "Experimental Law," *Temurot*, no. 5, 1969, pp. 11–14 and *Intosai*, no. 16, April 1969, Vienna.

[21] *D-Ha*, 1968, vol. 9, p. 773.

of the system by small lists that were not serious contenders, the court ruled that any new party list should receive its allocation after it had met the electoral test and received at least one seat, on the condition that the list had consented in advance to inspection by the State Comptroller, in terms of the Law for the Elections to the Knesset and Local Authorities in the Year 1969 (Financing, Limitation of Expenses and Auditing), and had also complied with the provisions of the law.[22] The High Court of Justice further ruled that the Knesset must adopt one of two solutions: (1) to reenact the financing provisions of the Election Financing Law, *despite the inequality* contained therein if an absolute majority could be mustered in their favor, or (2) to amend the law as stated above so as to remove the inequality. On July 15, 1969, the Knesset adopted the second solution and amended the Election Financing Law in accordance with the recommendations of the court.[23]

Limiting Expenses. The Election Financing Law also was intended to limit campaign expenses. Election expenses constitute the best kept secret of political parties in many democratic countries. Moreover, political campaign expenses in Israel have been among the highest in the world.[24]

One of the aims of the Election Financing Law was to limit the campaign expenses of parties for the elections to the Seventh Knesset to a total of IL19,840,000 (plus an additional IL160,000 for any member elected from a new list, as stipulated in the amendment prompted by the High Court's ruling).[25] This was an ambitious goal: in 1961 campaign expenses had reached an estimated IL25,000,000, and in 1965 IL45–50,000,000 according to conservative estimates. Could the law achieve the reduction?

In the light of events, it would appear that on the whole it did. In this respect alone, and despite the criticism it received both from Knesset members and from the public the law was in principle effective. Campaign expenses in 1969 exceeded the amounts specified by the law, but not by enough to warrant action by the state comptroller.[26]

[22] HCJ, 98/1969, Aharon E. Bergman v. Minister of Finance.
[23] The Law for the Elections to the Knesset and to the Local Authorities in the Year 1969 (Financing, Limitation of Expenses and Auditing) (Amendment), section 2, S-Ha, 567, p. 201.
[24] Heidenheimer, "Comparative Finance," pp. 714, 799.
[25] D-Ha, 1968, vol. 18, p. 1664.
[26] The State Comptroller, *Inspection in Terms of the Law for the Elections to the Knesset and to the Local Authorities in the Year 1969 (Financing, Limitation of Expenses and Auditing)*, 1969, Jerusalem, February 8, 1970, pp. 6–7.

The Election Financing Law defined as election expenses all expenditures made by the parties for the *organization of activities connected with the electoral campaign* to the Knesset and to the local authorities and the costs of propaganda and promotion for those elections.[27] Under this definition, services rendered and contributions made in kind (advertising space donated by a sympathetic newspaper, the services of volunteers, free office space and transport services, and so on) were not regarded as expenses incurred in the general estimate of expenses of the parties for the elections. Thus, they were not subject to inspection by the state comptroller who did not refer to them in his report.[28] The election financing law referred to *electoral expenses only, not to the parties' income or to the sources of income* used for the parties' independent expenditures (the IL40,000 per M.K.) over and above the ceiling permitted under the law. The state comptroller's inspection therefore related to expenses for elections to the Knesset, not those for local elections, or for the Histadrut, which were to be calculated separately.

Under section 10(a) of the Election Financing Law, commencing on the day of publication of the law and up to the day of the elections inclusive, each party was entitled to request an opinion from the chairman of the Central Elections Committee as to whether a given expense should be considered an electoral expense or not. Thus, the Gahal list of candidates to the Knesset applied to the Central Elections Committee for an opinion as to how its expenses for the two elections should be divided.

On July 22, 1969, the chairman of the committee laid down criteria for the allocation of expenses, emphasizing the distinction between the expenses of the Histadrut Convention elections and the expenses of the elections to the Knesset and the local authorities. But these criteria left the parties some discretion in the allocation of expenses between the two electoral campaigns. The chairman's general rule was that the parties' expenses since September 2, 1969—the date of the elections to the Histadrut Convention—should be regarded as expenses for the Knesset elections, whereas expenses incurred before then should be regarded as pertaining to the Histadrut Convention elections. It was permitted to charge a part of the Histadrut election expenses to the Knesset elections, but expenses clearly relating to the Histadrut elections were not to be charged as expenses of the elections to the Knesset and to the local authorities.

---

[27] Sections 1, 3 of the Law.
[28] Section 1 of the Law.

The parties claimed that they expended only IL3,800,000 on the Histadrut elections, an amount which appeared unreasonably low. It was found out later that a number of parties including Labor spent almost as much on the elections to the Histadrut as on the elections to the Knesset and to the local authorities. The Histadrut elections cost the Alignment IL8,565,626; the Knesset elections IL9,763,934.[29]

The total expenditures for both the Knesset and the local authority elections were in fact much greater than those stipulated by the Election Financing Law. And to this total must be added another million pounds spent by the Central Elections Committee for transporting voters from one locality to another and back on election day so that they could cast their votes, as prescribed by section 4 of the law. In previous elections such transportation had been financed by the parties themselves (at nearly twice the cost, according to some researchers).[30]

Nevertheless, even if all of these sums are added together, it can be said that the Election Financing Law made an important contribution to the curtailment of party expenses in the elections to the Seventh Knesset. Whereas each vote in the 1961 elections had cost IL20 and in 1965 IL25,[31] in the elections to the Seventh Knesset each vote cost about IL12–15, which constituted a significant saving, conditions in Israel being what they were.

No doubt, the state of war in which the 1969 elections were conducted encouraged the parties to exercise self-restraint in the area of routine expenses. On the other hand, the introduction of television as an important factor in the campaign caused an increase in expenses; without the parties' self-restraint in other areas, induced by the Election Financing Law, this factor would have caused a much greater rise in campaign expenses.

The Election Financing Law did more than establish a ceiling for the 1969 elections expenses. To avoid the unethical use of money allocated to them from the state budget and to widen the scope of responsibility of the parties for the honest execution of the provisions of the law, principally with regard to respecting the ceiling on expenses, the law introduced a number of *institutional guarantees* for the attainment of its ends. Thus, for example, section 5 committed

---

[29] For the gap between the Histadrut and Knesset expenditures see *Ma'ariv*, March 23, 1970. The Alignment's expenditures are those mentioned by the state comptroller on page 2 of the *Report of the Results of Auditing of the Accounting System of the Alignment*.

[30] Gutman in "Comparative Party Finance," p. 714.

[31] Heidenheimer, "Comparative Party Finance," pp. 714, 799.

any party entitled to an allocation to inform the speaker of the Knesset through the intermediary of the representative of its faction, not later than August 1, 1969, of the number of its representatives who would be qualified to act in its name for the purposes of the law. The parties were obliged to append to such notification the written consent of such representatives to fulfill this function. Another, more important, institutional arrangement related to the inspection by the state comptroller of the accounts kept by the parties.

Scrutiny by the State Comptroller. The assurance of the state comptroller's inspection of the allocations to the parties was the *most convincing argument put to the general public* in favor of the Election Financing Law and to those Knesset members who opposed it. The status and prestige of the state comptroller and the general confidence in his complete independence, objectivity, and efficiency can be compared only with those of the judicial system in Israel. The assurance that the state comptroller would scrutinize the parties' implementation of the Election Financing Law reassured the public and persuaded those in doubt to agree to the state financing of election expenses, even in the difficult political, military, and financial situation of 1969.

All of the parties were united in their approval of the state comptroller's auditing of election expenditures. The general opinion within the parties and the press was that this guarantee had been effective and that, although the strict directives laid down by the state comptroller had sometimes made bookkeeping difficult, they had helped the central offices of the parties to withstand pressure from their branches for additional funds.[32]

Law for the Financing of Parties—1973[33]

After the Election Financing Law of 1969 had proved successful for most intents and purposes, it was quite obvious that the parties would seek to transform it into a permanent law. Indeed, on October 25, 1972, representatives of the parties originally supporting the financing bill in 1969 submitted to the Knesset for a preliminary debate a private bill designated Law for the Elections to the Knesset and Local Authorities (Financing, Limitation of Income and Expenses and Auditing) —1972.[34]

---

[32] Ma'ariv, March 30, 1970 and April 5, 1970.
[33] S-Ha, 680, 1973, p. 52.
[34] D-Ha, 1972, vol. 2, p. 143.

The bill was submitted for the first reading on January 1, 1973, and by a majority of eighty-seven to eight was transferred to the Finance Committee to be prepared for second and third readings.[35] Between the preliminary reading and the first reading the name of one bill was changed to Law for the Financing of Parties[36]—a name that made no mention of the purposes of the law. In fact, the bill provided for financial aid to political parties, restriction of income and expenditures of the parties, and the state comptroller's supervision over such income and expenditures.

Following a lengthy debate, the Law for the Financing of Parties —1973 was adopted by a majority of seventy-eight to seven.[37] Since this law provided for current budgetary allocations to the parties, which were keen to receive such allocations for the month of January 1973, the law was made retroactive to January 1, 1973.

This law has remained in force with minor adjustments. The state comptroller has been making annual audits of parties' income and expenditures and has been issuing annual reports on party funds; in the election years 1973 and 1977, the state comptroller issued two separate reports concerning current expenditures and elections expenses.

Financing. Aside from the fact that it was made permanent, the main novelty of the law was the provision of direct budgetary allocations to parties not only for the financing of electoral campaigns but also *for the financing of current activities* between elections, to the extent of 5 percent of election expenditures, on the basis of the relative balance of power in the incoming Knesset.

Before analyzing the law in detail and in order to be able to understand its implementation, certain basic concepts need clarification. The law defines, among others, three important terms:

(1) A *faction* is defined as
- a party submitting a list of candidates while being a faction in the outgoing Knesset, and which is represented by at least one member in the new Knesset; or
- a party whose representative or representatives are recognized by the Knesset Committee as a faction; or
- a combination of two or more parties maintaining a joint faction in the Knesset.

---

[35] *D-Ha*, 1972–73, vol. 12, p. 1076.

[36] *D-Ha*, 1972–73, vol. 12, p. 1062, and Appendix B, p. 1394.

[37] *D-Ha*, 1972–73, Appendix B, p. 1362.

This definition reflected the situation in the Seventh Knesset, where mergers and splits were frequent.[38]

(2) *Expenses* are defined as the expenses of a faction incurred for the organization of its activities, propaganda and public relations, and the maintenance of organizational and ideological liaison with the public, including commitments relating to such expenses.

While the 1969 law had defined only election expenses, the 1973 law defined expenses in general. In addition, however, it distinguished between "election expenses" (expenses incurred by a faction in connection with electoral campaign) and "current expenses" (all expenses of a faction other than election expenses).

Unlike the 1969 law and unlike the original bill submitted for preliminary debate to the Seventh Knesset, the present law does not provide for the financing of elections to local authorities, an omission that is likely to put some strain on the parties during the scheduled 1978 local elections.

(3) A *financing unit* is defined as an amount determined by the Finance Committee of the Knesset for the purposes of this law, and announced in *Reshumot* [Official gazette].

Unlike the 1969 law, which had determined both the amount allocable for each seat in the Knesset and the entire budgetary allocation to the parties, the law of 1973 did not determine the total allocation or even fix the financing unit at a specified amount; Knesset Member Israel Kargman told the Knesset in the preliminary debate: "As this Law is of a permanent nature, it cannot specify amounts of money which change from one Knesset to another."[39] Instead, the law authorized the Finance Committee of the Knesset to fix the financing unit whenever needed. The total amount of political financing resulting from the committee's resolution concerning the financing unit appears as a separate item in the national budget. The national

---

[38] The Eighth Knesset witnessed many fusions and splinterings. For example, Knesset Member Benjamin Halevi left the Likud and established a separate single-member faction; Knesset Member Arieh Eliav left the Alignment and merged with the Ratz faction, creating a new faction, Ya'ad, which subsequently split into two, the Independent Socialists (two members) and Ratz (two members); the Free Center, a component of the Likud, split into two, the Free Center (two members) and the Independent Center (two members); subsequently but not immediately the new Free Center split off from the Likud; and three small factions in the Likud, the State list, the Independent Center, and the Land of Israel Movement, merged toward the end of the term of the Eighth Knesset into La'am without leaving the Likud faction.

[39] *D-Ha*, 1972, vol. 2, p. 144.

budget is approved by the Knesset; thus, in the final analysis it is the plenary session of the Knesset, not the committee, that approves the annual expenditure resulting from the Law for the Financing of Parties.

The rapid inflation in Israel has made necessary frequent successive increases in the financing unit, culminating in a 1975 decision to tie it permanently to the consumer price index. On January 25, 1973, the day after the enactment of the law, the Finance Committee of the Knesset fixed the financing unit at IL180,000 per seat. It also fixed the dates for the disbursement of the allocations for the financing of current activities.[40] Compared with IL120,000 allocated for each seat in 1969 (since when the consumer price index had risen by fifty percentage points) the initial financing unit might be regarded as modest. However, on July 22, 1973, the Finance Committee raised the financing unit to IL195,000.[41] Only two days after the publication of this decision, on August 16, 1973, the financing unit was raised again, this time to IL292,000 per seat.[42]

The Yom Kippur War broke out in October 1973, and the elections scheduled for October 30 were postponed until December 31. The new financing unit remained in force. However, election broadcasts had already started before war interrupted the campaign. When it was decided to hold the elections in spite of the war, the Knesset held that those broadcasts would not be taken into consideration in the allocation of new broadcast time.[43]

During 1975 the consumer price index rose precipitously and the rate of inflation became unpredictable. As a result, on October 29, 1975, the Finance Committee resolved to increase the financing unit to IL420,000.[44] At this point, the committee tied the financing unit to the consumer price index, retroactive to October 1, 1975.[45] In the budget proposed for fiscal 1977 the treasury set the figure for the financing of the election due that year at IL72,000,000 and the figure for current party expenses at IL44,000,000 on the basis of a financing unit of IL600,000.[46]

---

[40] *Kovetz Takanot* (Collected regulations—hereafter K-T), February 14, 1973, no. 2970, p. 786.

[41] *K-T*, August 14, 1973, no. 3046, p. 1790.

[42] *K-T*, September 1, 1974, p. 1894.

[43] *S-Ha*, 718, 1973, p. 10.

[44] *K-T*, November 15, 1975, no. 3424, p. 362.

[45] "Index"—consumer price index as published from time to time by the Central Bureau of Statistics.

[46] The bill of the National Budget for fiscal 1977, the chapter on the Ministry of the Interior, section 14, p. 16.

211

The government of Prime Minister Rabin was forced to resign for political reasons in February 1977. Consequently, parliamentary elections were held on May 17 instead of at the end of October 1977 as anticipated. As a result, the ruling Labor Alignment was ousted from power and superseded by the Likud for the first time in twenty-nine years. The Rabin government lost its parliamentary majority when the ten National Religious party representatives joined the opposition. After their defection the minister of finance failed to obtain the Knesset's approval for the proposed budget. Finally a consensus was reached on a transition budget for the period April–July 1977, which had been prepared by a special committee comprising representatives of both the coalition and the opposition. The committee effected severe cuts in most spheres of government activity, but not in the allocations for the financing of parties and elections.[47]

The Finance Committee's decision to increase the financing unit by 44 percent and to tie it to the consumer price index caused considerable public wrath. Indeed, it became final only after having been challenged in court. It has been in force ever since.

Section 2 of the Law for the Financing of Parties—1973 entitles each faction to receive state financing: (1) in the election period for the financing of the campaign and (2) for the financing of current activities, every month commencing on the date of publication of the results of the elections to the Knesset until the month of publication of the results of the elections to the next Knesset. Thus, a party that has failed to place any representatives in the new Knesset is still entitled to a payment for the financing of its current activities during one month.[48]

The treasury discharges its obligations under the Law for the Financing of Parties through the speaker of the Knesset, who transfers the appropriate amount to the bank account of each faction under the terms prescribed by the law. While the amounts payable for election expenses are calculated on the basis of one financing unit for each seat in the Knesset obtained by the faction concerned, those for current monthly financing are computed on the basis of 5 percent of the financing unit per seat.

The 1973 law introduced a change in one disbursement of election funds as compared with the 1969 law. Each faction submits

[47] *Reshumot,* "Hukei Taktsiv" (Budgetary Laws), 70, March 31, 1977, p. 2.

[48] This happened to the list of former Knesset Member Ben-Porat. Although his campaign was not successful and he failed to be reelected, he received the payment for the financing of current activities for another month, which eased the burden of debts taken for the purpose of his electoral campaign.

to the speaker a confirmation from the chairman of the Central Elections Committee stating that it has handed in a list of candidates to the next Knesset. It is then entitled to an advance payment amounting to 60 percent of the financing unit for each listed member of the Knesset. Thus, any member who leaves a faction, whether in order to establish a new faction or in order to join another, reduces the allocation due to his original faction.

After the elections, a faction that has obtained at least one seat in the new Knesset is entitled to receive the amount due for the financing of elections as follows: 85 percent of the total immediately following publication of the results of the elections, according to the number of seats obtained; and the remaining 15 percent after the state comptroller has submitted a positive report to the speaker of the Knesset, as prescribed in the law—all, of course, net of the amount of the advance payment. However, if a faction obtains fewer seats in the new Knesset than in the outgoing Knesset, it is likely to encounter severe financial difficulties. Under section 4(c) of the law, the excess of the advances paid to such a faction is deducted from the first payment due to it subsequent to the elections and if necessary from later payments for the financing of its current activities.

When this rule was introduced, the drafters of the law did not expect that it would work against the big parties. In the elections to the Ninth Knesset, however, the Alignment lost nineteen of its fifty-one seats. Consequently the advance payment it had received— 60 percent of fifty-one times the financing unit—exceeded the total to which it was entitled by its performance in the election. In absolute figures, the Labor party alone (that is, apart from Mapam, its partner in the Alignment) was left with a debt of more than IL7,000,000. To this an accumulated debt of IL30 million should be added, making a total of IL37 million.

The Independent Liberal party found itself in a similar position, though its debt was smaller, having succeeded in winning only one seat as compared with its three in the previous Knesset. It had received advances exceeding IL1,000,000 and had expended some IL2,400,000. As a result it had to reimburse more than IL400,000 to the treasury. As of 1977 this party had a deficit (including loans for campaign purposes) of roughly IL1,200,000. The resignation of the Rabin government and the resulting early scheduling of the elections caught all the parties completely unprepared—and in need of an immediate source of funds. Therefore, by general consent, on February 8, 1977, the Knesset passed an Amendment to the Law for the Financing of

Parties (Temporary Provision)—1977,[49] which empowered the treasury to pay an advance of 36 percent of the financing unit for each seat in the Knesset thirty-five days before the date fixed by the original law for the payment of advances. This in itself was not remarkable. However, the Temporary Provision was enacted after the trial of Asher Yadlin, which had involved corruption in the political parties, and public sensitivity concerning the financial affairs of the parties was acute. For this reason the early advance was restricted by two conditions: (1) any faction requesting an early advance had to file a written commitment, signed by a majority of its members, that it would submit a list of candidates to the Ninth Knesset on the date specified by the law; and (2) the special advance was to bear interest at the rate of 0.5 percent for each week or part thereof between the date of disbursement and the regular date of payment of the advance prescribed by the original law.

The Law for Financing of Parties—1973 provides also for the financing of new lists, in line with the amendment to the Law of 1969. And it provides for the financing of Knesset members who have left their factions and have refrained from forming new factions, but who nevertheless wish to run on separate tickets. Such members are entitled to receive public funds on the same terms as one-member factions, provided that they run as the head of the new list.

The conditions for receipt of funds for the financing of elections and of current activities have remained unchanged. They are contained in section 6(a) of the Law for the Financing of Parties—1973, as follows:

(1) The faction must submit to the Speaker of the Knesset a list of two to eight persons who will be authorized to act on its behalf in all matters connected with this Law. At least one such person must be a Member of the Knesset, and at least one must declare himself to be, and must be declared by the faction to be, familiar with its financial affairs;

(2) The faction must submit to the Speaker of the Knesset a statement signed by its representatives for the purpose of this Law, as above, to the effect that the faction has made all the necessary arrangements in order to ensure proper maintenance of its accounts in accordance with the guidelines issued by the State Comptroller;

(3) The faction must inform the Speaker of the Knesset of the number (or numbers) of its bank account (or accounts).

[49] S-Ha, 844, 1977, p. 82.

The factions can replace their representatives for the purposes of the Law for the Financing of Parties, provided that they comply with the above conditions.

Limiting the Parties' Expenses and Income. Although the name of the Law for the Financing of Parties—1973, unlike that of the 1969 law, does not reveal that limiting the expenditures of the parties is among its objectives, it contains specific provisions for that purpose. In addition, there is a much more basic difference between the two: the 1973 law for the first time regulated, at least prima facie, not only expenditures but also income and placed this matter, too, under the scrutiny of the state comptroller.

The law sets a ceiling for direct election expenditures by the parties, whether in cash or pledges. This ceiling is composed of one financing unit multiplied by the number of members of the faction elected to the new Knesset plus the amounts raised by the faction from other sources, provided that such amounts do not exceed one-third of the former amount. Because the financing unit increases automatically with every increase in the consumer price index, the treasury's outlays for campaign financing have grown very considerably since 1973. It should also be borne in mind that this ceiling applies to the treasury's campaign contributions alone; in order to arrive at a grand total for campaign expenditures, one would have to add the political allocations of the Histadrut and of the Jewish Agency.

There is a difference between the way funds are allocated for the financing of elections and for the financing of current expenses. Whether a faction comprises one party or several, it receives its election allocation as one faction. It is not so with regard to current party expenses. Each of the parties combining with others in a parliamentary faction or electoral bloc, is regarded as a separate party, has separate central organs and branches, and conducts independent party activities;[50] the section of the law governing current financing allocations treats them as separate factions.

Limiting Income. The 1973 law introduced an original and ingenious scheme for limiting the parties' income. It does not prohibit contributions by individuals, nor does it limit the amount of such contributions. Neither does the law prohibit or limit contributions from individuals, groups or corporations abroad. It does, however, state that parties "will not receive," directly or indirectly, contributions

---

[50] *D-Ha*, 1973, vol. 12, p. 1351.

from any local corporation or registered partnerships. This, too, is under the scrutiny of the state comptroller, who must expressly state in his report whether a faction has or has not received contributions from a corporation as defined in section 8. If the state comptroller reports that a faction *has* received a contribution from a domestic corporation, or has expended for current activities amounts greater than those allowed, the law provides for monetary sanctions: the speaker will refrain from remitting to the delinquent faction three consecutive installments for current activities and will refund those installments to the treasury.

Scrutiny by the State Comptroller. The 1973 law provides for the state comptroller's inspections of electoral and current expenses of parties and, to a limited extent, of their income. Since the law was made retroactive to January 1, 1973, the state comptroller inspected both the expenses for the elections of December 31, 1973, and the current expenses of the parties for all of 1973.

On February 22, 1973, the state comptroller issued new guidelines for the maintenance of the parties' accounts. They specified that the factions were to keep their books up to date and to follow generally accepted accounting principles, reflecting all income and expenses, including expenses obligated and income not yet received for which express commitments existed.[51]

On February 18, 1975, the Knesset adopted the Law for the Financing of Parties (Amendment)—1975. This amendment provided that if a faction divided into two and each of the two new factions comprised one-half of the members of the original faction, the new factions would enjoy equal rights to all benefits under the law following their recognition by the Knesset Committee.[52] In order to provide for more flexibility in the deadlines for the submission of faction reports to the state comptroller and of his reports to the Knesset the amendment also empowered the Finance Committee of the Knesset to prolong—in consultation with the state comptroller—all deadlines prescribed by section 10 of the law; new deadlines would be published in *Reshumot*.[53]

The first report of the state comptroller under the Law for Financing of Parties—1973 was submitted to the speaker of the

---

[51] *K-T*, February 22, 1973, no. 2974, p. 845.
[52] *S-Ha*, 762, 1975, p. 84.
[53] Ibid.

Knesset and published on April 4, 1974.[54] It comprised ten separate reports on the audit of party accounts relating to election expenses and eleven reports on the audit of current expenses accounts. In his summary report the state comptroller states that most factions had maintained proper accounts, thus making the auditors' task easier. Although some deviations from the guidelines had come to light they were not serious enough to "significantly impair" the completeness and reliability of the accounts or to require one of the financial penalties prescribed by the law.

One important question treated in the state comptroller's report was that of contributions from Israeli corporations. The intention of the law was to release political parties from dependence on wealthy corporations operating in Israel that might press them to adopt stands in the Knesset favorable to the corporations' self-interest. As pointed out again and again in the state comptroller's reports, various types of legal incorporation are very common in Israel; notably, many entities owned by parties or by organizations affiliated to parties are incorporated, although many of these are engaged only in rendering services to the party, such as maintenance of buildings where party activities are conducted. Such entities receive income which covers their expenses.

Uncertainty also exists concerning another type of legal entity affiliated to parties—the kibbutzim. These cooperative agricultural settlements are also business enterprises, often wide in scope, and there seems to be no reason why the prohibition on contributions to parties from Israeli corporations should not apply to them.

Since the legislature had not clearly defined "receipt of contributions from corporations in Israel," the state comptroller did not consider that "it was necessary and just to assert that receipt of such services or contributions [from party-related corporations and agricultural cooperatives] constituted receipt of contributions from corporations in Israel contrary to the law." At the same time, the comptroller deemed it desirable that the legislators should make explicit the regulations that would apply in this area.[55]

In his report the state comptroller dwelt on another feature of the 1973 campaign—the placing of advertisements in the press on behalf of factions by groups of supporters or even by unidentified advertisers. He was of the opinion that some of these advertisements might have been paid for by corporations; if this had been done with

---

[54] The State Comptroller, *Inspection in Terms of the Law for the Financing of Parties—1973*, Jerusalem, April 4, 1974, p. 8.

[55] Ibid., p. 8.

the knowledge of the faction concerned, he pointed out it might constitute receipt of a forbidden contribution from a domestic corporation.

Finally, the comptroller stated that the law and the audit performed under its provisions had been successful in imposing some regularity on campaign financing and in restricting the expenditures of the parties. He also suggested several amendments to the law and expressed his hope that they "would contribute to more regularity and economizing of expenses, which were the goals of the state comptroller's audit of those matters."[56]

The second report of the state comptroller was submitted to the Speaker of the Knesset on July 4, 1975,[57] and included ten separate reports on the current expenses of ten factions; reports on the expenditures of six other factions, most of them small, had been submitted a month earlier. This time, two parties failed to observe the new deadline for presentation of their accounts; however, the law imposed no sanctions and the comptroller accepted the accounts. In all of his separate reports the comptroller gave positive opinions, pointing out deficiencies in bookkeeping.

Perhaps the most interesting finding was that expenditures of most parties for the 1973 elections and for current activities in the years 1973–1974 were far below the amounts permitted by the law. (See Tables 8–1 and 8–2.)

The rise of the consumer price index resulted in a great increase both in current expenses and in the 1977 campaign expenses. Even so, in both categories most of the parties spent much less than they were allowed to under the law. The grand total for all of the parties' current expenses in 1977 was the enormous sum of IL52,747,740 of which IL32,877,240 was provided by the state. However, "according to their books" (as the state comptroller put it) they spent only IL44,874,749. The total allowed for electoral expenses was IL108,322,620 (a high sum not only in relation to the economic situation of the country but also in comparison with electoral expenses elsewhere) of which IL69,636,000 was financed by the treasury. In practice—again, "according to their records submitted for audit"—the total electoral expenditures of all parties came to IL97,092,381.

The state comptroller noted that every year since the passage of the Law for the Financing of Parties—1973, on the occasion of submitting his reports, he had commented on the difficulties en-

---

[56] Ibid., p. 9.

[57] The State Comptroller, *Inspection in Terms of the Law for the Financing of Parties—1973*, Jerusalem, July 4, 1975.

TABLE 8–1

CURRENT EXPENDITURES OF THE FACTIONS, 1973
(in Israeli pounds)

Faction	Actual Expenditures	Ceiling
Mapam	1,143,499	1,165,500
Herut	1,895,085	2,497,500
Liberal party	998,269	1,831,500
State list	383,756	594,000
National Religious party	1,946,494	1,998,000
Agudat Israel	557,512	666,000
Poalei Agudat Israel	284,263	499,500
Independent Liberal party	615,099	666,000
Rakah	446,354	499,500
Progress and Development	175,709	499,500
Moked	115,253	499,500
Free Center	196,906	499,500

SOURCE: State Comptroller's Report, *Inspection in Terms of the Law for the Financing of Parties—1973*, Jerusalem, April 4, 1974.

TABLE 8–2

CAMPAIGN EXPENDITURES FOR THE 1973 ELECTIONS, BY FACTION
(in Israeli pounds)

Faction	Actual Expenditures	Ceiling
Alignment	14,555,337	14,820,000
Likud	7,759,492	8,060,000
National Religious party	2,855,615	2,860,000
Agudat Israel—Poalei Agudat Israel bloc	1,420,959	1,560,000
Independent Liberal party	1,046,614	1,040,000
Rakah	579,012	780,000
Ratz	189,890	780,000
Progress and Development	524,287	780,000
Moked	325,000	780,000
Arab list	280,000	780,000

SOURCE: State Comptroller's Report, *Inspection in Terms of the Law for the Financing of Parties—1973*, Jerusalem, April 4, 1974.

countered in the course of his audit and had recommended amendments to the law. These had been discussed several times by the Finance Committee of the Eighth Knesset and by a subcommittee formed for that purpose, but the proposed modifications in the law had not occurred. Thus, in his 1977 report the comptroller again summarized his findings and repeated his request for discussion of the following points.[58]

(1) Clarification of the meaning of the term "party," which appears in the definition of the term "faction" in the law, and of the link between the activities of parties and those of other bodies that are affiliated or identified with parties in various ways, and which in practice foster party goals.

(2) Extension of the prohibition on contributions from corporations—applicable at present to domestic corporations alone—to corporations abroad.

(3) Definition of "election expenses" so as to make clear that these are expenses made for the purpose—and during the period —of elections to the Knesset. Section 7(a) of the law speaks of the ceiling on election expenses "during the elections period"; election expenses not incurred during the electoral campaign are not included in calculation of such expenses but neither are they included among current expenses.

In his letter to the speaker the state comptroller also questioned what he considered the excessively rigid sanctions applicable to a faction with whose accounts the state comptroller found fault. The comptroller recommended that the subject be reconsidered. Such a faction might be denied regular payment of its allocated funds even if the infraction were relatively small, the amount of the penalty being rigidly proportional to the number of members of the faction concerned.[59]

He also urged consideration of the possibility that the requirement of inspection of accounts be extended to groups that had ceased to be factions after having received funds from the treasury.

The recommendation to amend section 17(a) of the law was

---

[58] In 1977, the state comptroller did not publish his reports, as was his habit prior to 1976, but submitted them to the Speaker of the Knesset only, each on one mimeographed page, accompanied by a letter to the speaker. Although not published, the contents of those reports were mentioned by the mass media. The author received copies of the above-mentioned reports and letter from the state comptroller's office.

[59] Ibid., p. 4.

perhaps the most important. Under this section a faction that has notified the speaker of the Knesset in writing that it does not wish to receive financing from the treasury is exempted from the provisions of the Law for the Financing of Parties—1973. The state comptroller recommended that the law state explicitly "that such faction, too, should not be allowed to receive contributions from a corporation, as the significance of this restriction for good government is of a general nature."[60] The state comptroller also recommended that the law require the factions to specify the identity of contributors to their current expenses or election funds. At present the factions reveal only the total amount of contributions received.

The state comptroller's letter to the speaker of the Ninth Knesset closed with an explicit recommendation that the Ninth Knesset promptly undertake a comprehensive revision of the Law for the Financing of Parties. "The Law in its present form," he said, "allows only for a very limited audit, this making way for phenomena which this Law and the very introduction of State financing of party activities had intended to avoid."[61]

Conclusion

The 1977 election ended the twenty-nine year rule of the Labor party and placed Menachem Begin and his Likud party in power. This radical political change was caused partly by the unfortunate accumulation of evidence of corruption in the ruling party. The Israeli pollster Mona Zemah, who almost accurately forecast the results of the 1977 elections, has stated that, when asked their reasons for changing their votes, the great majority of respondents mentioned corruption in the elite of the Labor party. When asked to specify, most respondents "mentioned the case of the former Chairman of the Kupat Haholim Haklalit (General Sick Fund of the Histadrut), Asher Yadlin, who was the candidate for the post of Governor of the Bank of Israel."[62] The Yadlin affair merits greater attention.

In his bribery trial before the Tel Aviv District Court, which found him guilty, Asher Yadlin claimed that he had transferred the entire sum of the bribe (IL80,000) to the Labor party. He also claimed that since 1969 (the year in which the first law on state financing of political parties was enacted) and through the 1973 elections (when the permanent Law for the Financing of Parties was already in force)

---

[60] Ibid.

[61] Ibid., p. 5.

[62] Aryeh Avneri, Hamapolet [The landslide] (Tel Aviv: Revivim, 1977), p. 16.

he had been engaged in raising funds for the Labor party at the instigation of those in charge of the financial affairs of that party. He even mentioned the names of important Labor leaders at whose suggestion he had raised and transferred to the party millions of Israeli pounds for its elections expenses in various years including 1973. He took this occasion to tell the court that he had been told by his predecessors that they, too, had been transferring to Mapai funds raised in dubious ways.

This was a grave accusation, and opposition representatives from the Likud—both in the Knesset and in the Histadrut—were quick to propose motions on the subject. However, the Tel Aviv District Court, which condemned Asher Yadlin to five years in prison, rejected the above allegations.

The Yadlin trial was held in February 1977, a short time before the elections, and it was clear that the opposition would make use of it in its campaign against the Alignment. Following a stormy debate in the Knesset, the matter which fell under the Law for the Financing of Parties—1973, was turned over to the state comptroller, with a request to return it to the legal advisor of the government only if a suspicion of a criminal offense arose.[63] At this writing it cannot be determined when the comptroller will complete his investigation or in what form his findings will be made public.

Although Asher Yadlin's revelations concerned the Labor party, there could be no doubt that, at least prior to the introduction of party financing from public funds, the parties in Israel had from time to time obtained funds in roundabout ways. This occurred even prior to the establishment of the state. Knesset member Arieh (Lova) Eliav stated with his usual candor: "the price of democracy, paid by the Zionist democracy for about four generations—was the financing of parties . . . all parties."[64] In the pre-state years, Eliav said, funds for the financing of parties were appropriated, under a "gentleman's agreement," from the total contributions received for the development of the country. "*All* parties behaved that way, such behavior resulting from the belief in the personal integrity of leaders in charge of public funds." The system was agreeable to all, "in particular since the people in charge of the deposit were spotless and pure." In Eliav's opinion there was no justification for branding as immoral an accepted system of party financing that had survived for four generations.[65]

---

[63] *Ha'aretz*, March 11, 1977.
[64] *Ma'ariv*, January 21, 1977, February 16, 1977.
[65] Ibid.

This is by no means the only testimony concerning the methods of financing of *all* parties in Israel before and since the establishment of the state. Additional evidence has been given by Yaakov Halfon, the former head of the Control Institute of Mapai, who revealed how all the parties—each in its own way—financed their activities.[66] Halfon's experience with Mapai and the Labor party was extensive, and he had very close relations with Pinchas Sapir, Yitzhak Rabin, and Ariel Sharon; he had also served as the adviser and campaign manager to Knesset Member Shmuel Flatto-Sharon.

Halfon told students at the Bar Ilan University that "since 1949 the parties have received 'under the table' between three-four hundred million Israeli pounds for the financing of their electoral campaigns" and that "the invisible financing was not restricted to one party only."[67]

Moreover, judicial action against leaders of parties other than Mapai for collection abroad of money for the financing of their election campaigns is not new in Israel. In 1954 two important leaders of the National Religious party (Rabbi Nurok and Rabbi Rosenberg— later Ben-Meir) were brought to trial for receiving foreign currency for the electoral campaign of Mizrachi without offering it to the treasury as prescribed by the law. Both were acquitted, but their trial revealed that more than one party had received funds from foreign sources.[68]

The trial of the lawyer Yehuda Spiegel, in connection with the construction of the Tel-Giborim hospital in 1964 was also associated with party financing. Spiegel—then deputy director general of the Ministry of Health—was found guilty of receipt of a bribe from the company entrusted with the designing of the hospital.[69] One witness stated that at least a part of the bribe was intended for the financing of the internal elections of the National Religious party. The defendant, who chose to remain silent, was pronounced guilty on February 19, 1964, and sentenced by the Magistrate's Court to twenty months of imprisonment, of which eight were suspended. The High Court reaffirmed Spiegel's sentence.[70] Justice Moshe Landau stated that in the trial "a most distressing phenomenon known as 'the spoils system' has been revealed in all its ugliness, that is—that a party in

---

[66] Ibid., February 16, 1977.

[67] Ibid., January 11, 1977.

[68] Ibid., February 25, 1977.

[69] Penal Case No. 1715/63, the Tel Aviv Magistrate's Court.

[70] *Pa-Di* 18, 1964, vol. 4, p. 7, I.P. 316/64.

power regards itself as entitled to bestow public posts and other benefits on its followers, disregarding State and practical reasons."[71]

Suffice it to say the corrupt practices pertaining to party financing were not unique to 1977—or, indeed, to Israel. The problem is world-wide and has infected democratic societies since the emergence of political parties.

In 1976 the International Political Science Association established a Study Group on Political Finance and Political Corruption for research into a permanent and reasonable solution of the problem of financing elections throughout the democratic world. This group is affiliated with Herbert E. Alexander's Citizens' Research Foundation, which has long been engaged in the study of political financing in democracies, in particular in the United States. The studies and publications of this foundation clearly show that this is a general problem, not confined to any one country.[72] Manifestations of corruption in the field of election financing in the United States and elsewhere indicate that the scope of this problem in Israel is hardly unprecedented although local publications could lead one to believe otherwise.

In any event, the number of countries that have chosen to introduce state financing of parties in one form or another is steadily growing. At this writing, it has been introduced in Puerto Rico (1957), Austria (1961), West Germany (1966), Denmark (1969), Norway and Sweden (1970), Italy, Canada (Quebec led the way in 1973), the United States (1974) and—last but not least—Israel.

Hence, the question in Israel should not be whether it was right to introduce state financing of elections (the matter of current party expenses should be considered separately) but how to amend the Law for the Financing of Parties in order to make fraud and corruption more difficult. It is clear to me that the recommendations of the state comptroller should be implemented. Other possible measures could be devised from the recently revealed convictions. Decisive steps in this direction are likely to improve the parties' ethical standards in the field of financing and to assure the Israeli taxpayer that the funds remitted to the parties will be expended in full conformity with the

---

[71] Ibid., p. 9.

[72] Citizens' Research Foundation, Princeton, N.J. (a series of studies); Herbert E. Alexander, *Financing Politics, Money, Elections and Political Reform* (Washington, D.C.: Congressional Quarterly Press, 1976); Herbert E. Alexander, *Campaign Money, Reform and Reality in the States* (New York: The Free Press, 1976).

provisions of the law and the requirements of proper administration. Widening the scope of the state comptroller's inspection of party accounts, making it similar to that accepted in other fields, also would have a positive effect. The sooner and more thoroughly these reforms are achieved, the better for the state of Israel and its citizens.

9

The Media in the Israeli Elections of 1977

Judith Elizur and Elihu Katz

A strong case can be made that the media played an important role in the Israeli elections of 1977. It should be said at the outset, however, that this role bears only little resemblance to the one envisaged for the broadcast media by those who believe, naively perhaps, that election campaigns ought to be better designed to serve the needs of a rational electorate.[1] As far as enlightenment is concerned, the rules of the game in Israel essentially prohibit the broadcast media from addressing the issues; radio and television are mere platforms for party political broadcasts, and these—as we shall show—are not especially enlightening. Among the three major media, only the press is free to report the campaign as it sees it.

The influence of the Israeli media in 1977 is discernible only partially in their direct contribution to the calculus of the concerned voter. They were not particularly effective as rhetorical agents either: there were a few emotional outbursts in party advertising on television, but altogether, campaigning was distinguished by ritual rather than by passion—and in the newspapers, by reporting rather than by editorializing.

The influence of the media is to be found elsewhere. It is to be discerned, first of all, in the process that is now widely called agenda

Research for this paper was supported by grants in aid from the Levi Eshkol Institute and the Faculty Research Fund of the Kaplan School of Economics and Social Sciences at the Hebrew University. We wish to thank Esther Sagi for research assistance. Nakdimon Rogel and Nathan Cohen of the Israel Broadcasting Authority gave us wise counsel. We acknowledge with thanks the data made available to us by staff members of the Israel Institute of Applied Social Research, especially Dr. Ze'ev Ben-Sira and Hanna Levinsohn, and by Dr. Mina Zemach, research director of Modi'in Ezrahi.

[1] Jay G. Blumler, Michael Gurevitch, and Julian Ives, *The Challenge of Election Broadcasting* (Leeds: Leeds University Press, 1978); Elihu Katz, "Platforms and Windows: Reflections on the Role of Broadcasting in Election Campaigns," *Journalism Quarterly*, vol. 49 (1974), pp. 304–314.

setting.[2] This process began months before the campaign as a consequence of the role of the press in exposing corruption in the establishment, which led—during the campaign itself—to the withdrawal of the prime minister from the leadership of the Labor party. It continued in the tacit agreement among the major parties as well as the media that domestic, rather than foreign, policy was to be the focus of the campaign. Thus, investigative reporting and agenda setting, we shall argue, were the major loci of media influence in 1977.

The influence of the media is also to be seen in their contribution to the process of democratic succession. If it were not for the independence of the media from government and the democratic tradition in which such independence is embedded, the transition might have gone badly, as indeed it has in most new nations where the government of the day controls the media.[3] The cool performance of the media, particularly television, during the dramatic night on which Labor was unseated for the first time in the twenty-nine-year history of Israel undoubtedly smoothed the transition. We cannot prove this, of course, but we believe it.

In what follows, we shall consider the role of the media with respect to each of three kinds of effect: (1) the direct contribution to the decision making of the voter, by persuasion or by provision of needed orientation, taking account of the first-ever debate between the two leading candidates; (2) the agenda-setting function of the media, including the influence of investigative journalism on the agenda; and (3) the role of the media, particularly television, in smoothing the succession. First, however, we shall sketch out the political and legal rules which constrain the media during Israeli elections and consider some of their consequences. In conclusion, we shall consider the case for revising the rules.

The Political and Legal Context

Restricted Broadcasting. Broadcasting in Israel is operated under the aegis of a BBC-like Broadcasting Authority, largely independent of government and financed by a license fee levied on set owners. There is no commercial advertising on television. Broadcast journalists strive

---

[2] Maxwell McCombs and Donald Shaw, "The Agenda Setting Function of Mass Media," *Public Opinion Quarterly*, vol. 36 (1972), pp. 176–187, and more recently, Maxwell McCombs, "The Agenda-Setting Function of the Press," Communication Research Center, Newhouse School of Public Communication, Syracuse University (mimeo.).

[3] Elihu Katz and George Wedell with Michael Pilsworth and Dov Shinar, *Broadcasting in the Third World: Promise and Performance* (Cambridge, Mass.: Harvard University Press, 1978).

for political balance and neutrality and succeed in this on the whole, despite complaints from all sides. Ironically, these services are denied to the public during election time as a result of the Election Law (Propaganda), adopted in 1959 and amended in 1969, which clearly betrays the political parties' fear that the visual media might have excessive influence on the voters. The law altogether forbids candidates to appear on television (or in the cinema) during a 30-day period prior to Knesset elections. Moreover, during the 150-day period prior to an announced election, broadcasters are required to scrutinize their schedules to see whether any program gives undue advantage to a particular party. The effect of all this is to constrain broadcasters to remove political programs and to avoid serious involvement in the campaign. Given the multiplicity of parties in Israel, these restrictions make life a lot easier for the broadcasters and for the parties, but more difficult for the citizen just at a time when he is most in need of help.

News events related to the campaign may be reported—Mrs. Rabin's bank account, for example, or Mr. Begin's health—provided the candidate is not portrayed, but it is clear even to those who advocate a minimal role for television during the campaign that the thirty-day ban denies information to the public and inevitably distorts news coverage. Thus, in the 1973 elections, Israeli viewers were not shown film of Golda Meir's visit to Washington, and in 1977 coverage of the Independence Day celebrations—which fell within the thirty-day preelection period—studiously avoided portrayal of the political elite of the country. The request of the Broadcasting Authority to lift the ban for that one day was denied by the Central Elections Committee, headed by a justice of the Supreme Court, which oversees the law. On the other hand, Meir's interview on "This Is Your Life" and the extended news coverage of Peres's assumption of the leadership of the Labor party when Rabin stepped down were ruled admissible in 1977, despite opposition protest.

By default, the primary political role remaining to broadcasting during campaigns is to provide a platform on which the parties can display themselves. It is during these party political broadcasts—on radio and on Israel's single nationwide television channel—that voters can get a close view of the candidates (though not usually the leading ones) and watch the documentary features and mini-entertainments that the parties themselves produce and deliver to the radio and television studios for transmission.[4]

---

[4] In fact, entertainment is explicitly illegal under the law (par. 8) but a political ballad or satire has been deemed acceptable.

Under the terms of the law, the allocation of air time among the parties is based on the number of members belonging to each party in the outgoing Knesset. Thus, during the twenty-one days of the 1977 campaign, Labor and the Likud had about three-and-one-half and three hours respectively at their disposal, whereas a new grouping —with no representation in the previous Parliament—received only the minimum allocation, ten minutes on television and twenty-five minutes on radio. This was the amount of time allocated to the newly established Democratic Movement for Change (DMC), although the DMC would emerge as the third largest parliamentary bloc. Thus, the law not only prevents independent coverage of the election campaign by the broadcast media; it also imposes upon viewers about thirty minutes per night of political broadcasting in prime time, subdivided among the parties in direct proportion to the status quo ante.

The Central Elections Committee is required to preview all material prepared for broadcasting, but sometimes only a few hours remain between submission of the tape by the parties and the scheduled hour for transmission. This time constraint allows for little more than removal of the most flagrant violations and results in the escalation of vituperative programming whenever one of the larger parties feels that it has been wronged.

In general, these regulations constrain the larger parties to seek creative (and expensive) solutions to the problem of filling up their allotted time. The Likud, for example, experimented with short bursts, appearing several times an evening, almost American-style, with spot items often accompanied by song. An equally radical solution in the opposite direction was the pooling of party time to produce a Labor-Likud debate, the first ever in Israel.

The initiative for the confrontation came not from the Broadcasting Authority, but from Begin at the very outset of the campaign when he offered to debate the Labor Alignment candidate, then presumed to be Rabin. Labor turned down the suggestion, reputedly because it was unwilling to give Likud equal status with itself in the public eye, inasmuch as it had run behind the Alignment in the past. However, later in the campaign, when Peres replaced Rabin, the party was anxious to give its new candidate maximum exposure in order to build his leadership image. Likud was likewise concerned to have Begin appear before the voters in order to demonstrate his fitness for office after a serious heart attack.

Both rivals refused to allow candidates of additional parties to join the debate. Apart from the fact that most of them had expended their allotted broadcast time, the other contenders were simply ruled out by the big two, who were anxious to create the impression that a vote for any other party would be a wasted one. As a matter of fact, Yosef Burg, the leader of the National Religious party, suggested a radio, rather than television, debate with Labor and Likud. This offer was swiftly refused.

Once the approval of the Central Elections Committee was given, the Begin-Peres debate was scheduled and broadcast on the final evening of the campaign. A half-hour in length, it took the form of both contenders answering questions put to them by a neutral interlocutor, a professional journalist. At no point during the pre-debate arrangements did the Broadcasting Authority step beyond its role of mere conduit enabling the parties to reach the public; it did nothing to initiate the program or enlarge its framework or to represent the public interest in any other way. Its role throughout the political broadcasting period was strictly technical, and thus consistent with the philosophy of nonentanglement in the affairs of the parties.

The major effect of depriving the public of the professional services of radio and television during the campaign is to enhance the importance of the daily press.

The Role of the Press. Coverage of the 1977 election campaign in the press was extensive, from straight reporting of breaking news on page one to special sections, at first several times a week and then daily, covering party meetings, speeches, internal problems, finances, and gossip about candidates. There were letters to the editor, features, columns, and editorial comment in abundance. The press supplied the voters with coverage in detail, interpretation, and much speculation—all of which were absent in the electronic media.

The importance of breaking stories in the 1977 campaign was unusually great. In earlier campaigns, once the candidates heading the main tickets had been selected, the races were cut and dry for the most part. This year, however, there were sensations and upheavals from start to finish. A major story for most of the year preceding the elections was Yigael Yadin's entry into politics and his efforts to form a new party, which culminated in the emergence of the DMC. Another major story, whose implications were ignored almost as assiduously as the DMC's emergence was explored, was Begin's health. His heart attack in March, at first described as a digestive upset, removed him from active participation on his party's behalf until the very end of the campaign. Yet Likud publicity built up his leadership image as though nothing had happened, and most political feature articles took his dominant role for granted.

231

The third breaking story that constantly supplied fresh material for the front page was the internal struggle in Ma'arach, the Labor Alignment. The first phase of this story focused on the Rabin-Peres rivalry and the choice of party leader; the second, postconvention, phase focused on the Rabin bank account scandal, followed by charges (subsequently dropped) concerning Abba Eban's foreign earnings. These stories found their way easily into the sequence of exposés of financial corruption in all branches of the establishment and notably among prominent Labor leaders. The third phase was dominated by the unprecedented dumping of the party candidate for prime minister in favor of the defeated challenger.

The details of the Rabin bank account were uncovered by the Washington correspondent of *Ha'aretz*, the independent morning daily, and published on March 15, 1977. The torrent of columns, editorial comment, and letters to the editor, in addition to breaking developments in the investigation of the case, shook public opinion. Television could only highlight the issue: it was the press that provided details, comment, and speculation on this all-absorbing subject, culminating in Rabin's withdrawal from the race and his replacement by his archrival, Peres.

Certainly, the full reporting and discussion of these events, which occurred in the latter phase of the campaign, were very damaging for the Alignment. Coverage of lesser stories, even those having no direct connection with the campaign, also had political implications: for example, the tragic helicopter crash in which fifty-four soldiers were killed brought national life to a standstill on May 11, 1977. By implication, the party in power was responsible; indeed, the Likud virtually said so.

Some of this investigative reporting made its way into the news bulletins of television and radio, and often it received extensive treatment as current affairs. But the analysis of these and other matters as election *issues* could be treated professionally only by the press. It is this agenda-setting role of the media on which we shall elaborate below.

Political Advertising in the Press. If the role of the press is magnified as a result of the emasculation of broadcasting during election campaigns, it is even further enhanced by the rule that allocates time for party political broadcasts according to the proportional formula. One can speculate that if all parties had had equal access or if a more equitable formula had been used to allocate time, not only would the debate among the parties have had a better airing but the need for newspaper advertising would have been less.

The law's effect on the campaign strategy of a new grouping such as the DMC, therefore, was to cause it to make the press its main channel for reaching the voters. Thus, the DMC began its newspaper campaign very early, even before its party convention determined the list of candidates, in order to make itself known to the public. The DMC campaign was so extensive that the Labor party attacked it for extravagant spending and queried the legitimacy of its sources of funds. (This gave the DMC an opportunity to stress its broad support from voluntary contributors, who had given IL4 million, and helped create the impression of an anti-Labor groundswell.)

The fact that the DMC placed its message in the press so conspicuously constrained the other parties to do the same. Attacks and counterattacks in advertising texts were a frequent feature of the major parties' campaigns, with both Labor and Likud hitting the DMC and the DMC replying in kind. The same battle was waged by Labor and Likud against the DMC on television, but here the DMC's very limited time allocation prevented it from fighting back. This may have helped create sympathy for the DMC as the underdog, while at the same time keeping before the public the anachronistic rules of time allocation. Whereas Labor and Likud appeared every night for three weeks on television, the DMC made a total of three brief appearances, one in each week of the campaign.[5] Other small parties and new groupings were at a similar disadvantage on television.

Party advertising in the newspapers, as distinct from news and editorial coverage, began as early as January 1977, well in advance of the party conventions, the formulation of platforms, or even the choice of candidates. Both the Likud and the DMC spent heavily and conspicuously from the start, forcing the Labor party to follow suit. From the outset, Likud ran an aggressive, abrasive campaign designed to convince the public that it could win this time; the DMC first had to make its existence as a new political entity known and then convince voters to back it; Labor had to defend its record against universal attack while its candidates fought each other as much as they fought other parties. The religious parties ran their advertising campaign almost entirely without reference to the issues raised by the other contenders for public support; the other small groupings strove either to hold on to or to carve out their place in the sun.

The law governing campaign expenditures provides IL580,000

---

[5] Broadcasting Authority data. The DMC divided its ten minutes into three broadcasts of three, four, and three minutes, respectively.

from the public treasury for each candidate elected to the Knesset. This money goes to his party for the purpose of covering campaign expenses: 60 percent is provided as an advance. Therefore, each party makes an estimate of how many seats it expects to win and sets its ceiling on campaign expenditure on the basis of these "safe" places. For example, the Labor party based its outlay on the assumption that it would win the same number of seats it held in the outgoing Knesset, namely, forty-four. In fact, it won only twenty-eight.[6] The DMC based its allocations on the assumption it would win nine seats.[7] This method of allocating public funds, while creating a good measure of public control over party expenses, is again a status quo device, favoring large and established political groupings over small parties and new-comers. The allocation per member has also been criticized for being too generous.

Actual expenditures on newspaper advertising as tabulated by the Israel Advertisers' Association were about 20 percent of the total campaign outlay of the parties (see Table 9–1). The figures confirm that the small groupings had no chance of matching the kind of expensive advertising campaign launched in the early stages of the campaign by the big parties. Several of these small parties literally ran out of money as the race heated up and the big spenders kept up their high level of outlay.

The parties' division of advertising expenditures among the papers was similar to that of commercial advertisers, with the lion's share going to the mass circulation afternoon dailies. *Ma'ariv* received approximately one-third of the total, *Yediot* about 25 percent, *Ha'aretz* 15 percent, and all other papers together the remaining one-third.[8]

The Effect of the Media in the 1977 Election

Having considered the rules of the game as far as communication is concerned and having speculated upon some of their institutional

---

[6] Although this entitled it to IL19 million in public funds, the party spent IL26 million on the campaign, leaving it with a massive deficit. See newspaper reports such as that in *Ma'ariv* of May 29, 1977, after the campaign, which describes the financial plight of the Labor party.

[7] In fact, the DMC won fifteen seats and took the unprecedented step of return-ing an unused IL1 million to the public treasury, since its expenditures were less than the mandatory allocation. (*Ha'aretz*, October 11, 1977.)

[8] *Otot* (a monthly publication of the Israel Advertisers' Association), no. 12 (May 1977), p. 14. It is interesting to note that, even with political advertising, total advertising volume in the daily press in the first three months of 1977 was no higher than in 1976. Party advertisements accounted for 15 percent of total inches published.

TABLE 9–1

PARTY EXPENDITURES ON NEWSPAPER ADVERTISING, JANUARY–MAY 1977
(in Israeli pounds)

Party	Expenditures
Labor Alignment	
Labor party	IL3,705,918
Kibbutz youth	62,687
Total, Labor Alignment	3,768,605
Likud	4,183,199
Shlomzion (Ariel Sharon)	390,387
Democratic Movement for Change[a]	3,533,358
National Religious party	1,244,398
Rakah (Communist)	52,637
Independent Liberals	815,046
Citizens' Rights (Shulamit Alloni)	385,614
Shelli	427,446
Flatto-Sharon	875,988
Women's party	77,025
Kach (Rabbi Kahane)	246,598
Gush Emunim[b]	427,167

[a] Including January outlays for Shinui, a post-1973 protest movement that merged with others to form the DMC.
[b] Did not run an independent list but campaigned for others.
NOTE: In June 1977 one U.S. dollar was worth approximately IL .10.
SOURCE: Data supplied by the Research Department of the Israel Advertisers' Association in June 1977.

consequences, we turn now to the question of the media's effect on the campaign. As suggested at the outset, we shall consider the role of the media under three headings: orientation and persuasion, agenda setting, and the problem of succession.

The Media and Decision Making: Orientation and Persuasion. The one thing that all the polls are agreed upon—however different their predictions of the final outcome—is that an unusually high proportion of the electorate made their decisions during the course of the campaign.[9] Fifty-five percent of respondents in the postelection wave of the Continuing Survey reported having made up their minds in the

[9] Election studies of the 1950s and 1960s in the United States, England, and elsewhere indicate that about 20 percent make up their minds during the campaign itself. But with the weakening of party affiliation in recent years, this proportion has increased. Even so, the Israeli figure is remarkably high.

month or so preceding the election, compared with 35 percent—also a high figure—who answered similarly following the elections of 1973.[10] The trend toward weak party loyalty and the concomitant rise in late decision making has been noted both in Britain and in the United States.[11]

The high proportion of late deciders in Israel, however, probably reflected more than a weakening of party loyalty. The elections of May 1977 were preceded by the traumatic war of 1973, the protest movements that came in its wake, disappointment with the Rabin government, and finally the political scandals that marked its last days. It is widely assumed, but unproven, that seething disapproval of the Alignment was already widespread but was not given expression in the elections of 1973 for reasons of national solidarity. Referring to data from the Continuing Survey, Louis Guttman dates the point at which opinion turned away from Labor and toward Likud in early March 1977,[12] some two months before the election and before Prime Minister and Mrs. Rabin went to Washington on their ill-fated visit.[13] Be this as it may, the fact remains that the votes of a large proportion of the electorate were still subjectively "available" during the three weeks of the campaign.

---

[10] The Continuing Survey is a joint project of the Israel Institute of Applied Social Research (IIASR) and the Communications Institute of the Hebrew University. Founded in June 1967, in the difficult days prior to the Six-Day War, the survey has increased from three-to-four times a year to biweekly. Thus, continuing data on a series of indicators are available for the ten-year period beginning in 1967. Both the 1974 and 1977 postelection surveys of the Continuing Survey found that about 25 percent of respondents made their decisions during the final week. This figure is corroborated by Modi'in Ezrahi, in its postelection poll, though its overall figure for decisions during the campaign is lower than the IIASR figure (35 percent versus 55 percent), perhaps because of differences in question wording. The Research Branch of Modi'in Ezrahi is a private polling organization directed by Dr. Mina Zemach.

[11] See Blumler, Gurevitch, and Ives, Challenge. For the United States, see Samuel Kirkpatrick, ed., American Electoral Behavior: Change and Stability, Sage Contemporary Social Science Issues, no. 24 (Beverly Hills: Sage, 1976). The weakening of party loyalty is accompanied by the increasing importance of candidate images, on the one hand, and of issues—particularly domestic issues—on the other.

[12] See the interview with Louis Guttman in the Jerusalem Post for May 19, 1977, "Labor Lost long before Tuesday." A longer-term analysis by Professor Guttman appears in the Post for August 26, 1977 and is reprinted in Louis Guttman, "The Israeli Public, Peace and Territory: The Impact of the Sadat Initiative," Jerusalem Institute for Federal Studies, January 1978 (mimeo.). We shall refer at several points to Guttman's analysis.

[13] Rabin and the new American President apparently were not personally compatible, while Mrs. Rabin was discovered to be in illegal possession of an American bank account.

Moreover, people attributed greater influence to the campaign in 1977 than in 1973. Asked by the Continuing Survey to appraise the campaign in retrospect, 44 percent answered affirmatively that "the campaign helped [me] to learn which party is closer to [my] views." The comparable proportion for the 1973 campaign was 19 percent. This increment in enlightenment was attributed in some measure to television. To the question why they watched election broadcasts, respondents most frequently answered "to understand the political programs of the parties," and the percentage giving this reply was somewhat higher in 1977 (23 percent), than in 1974 (17 percent). But the group answering "to help me make up my mind whom to vote for" remained as small as it was in the previous election (about 10 percent).[14] In other words, the motivation for viewing political broadcasts —even though they were party-sponsored—apparently had more to do with seeking general orientation than with seeking specific guidance. This interpretation gains support, we think, in the high percentage that reported viewing political broadcasts for the excitement of following the race. This percentage both is higher than in 1974 (16 percent compared to 9 percent) and stands higher in rank order than in several other European elections of the mid 1970s where similar questions were asked.[15]

A survey conducted by the Research Branch of the Modi'in Ezrahi asked those who had made up their minds during the campaign to indicate which media had helped them with their decisions.[16] Summarizing across first, second, and third choices, personal influence was by far the most important medium (50 percent said they had been influenced by conversations with friends), followed by newspaper articles (33 percent) and television broadcasts (29 percent). Party platforms and leaders' proclamations were mentioned with high

---

[14] The 1973 election was held on December 31; thus the postelection survey was taken in 1974. This battery of questions is based on Jay G. Blumler and Denis McQuail, *Television in Politics: Its Uses and Influence* (London: Faber, 1968). A Hebrew version of the battery was prepared and analyzed by Michael Gurevitch for the Israeli elections of 1969 and appears in Asher Arian, ed., *The Elections in Israel—1969* (Jerusalem: Jerusalem Academic Press, 1972). The present data are not immediately comparable, however, since respondents were asked to choose the most important reason in the battery of motives rather than to assess the importance of each item separately. Only rank-order comparisons are possible.

[15] Employing rank orderings, these comparisons are with three 1974 elections in Belgium, France, and Britain, and the 1976 election in Germany. Only the Belgians ranked excitement very high. See Alison J. Ewbank and Claude Geerts, "Voters' Attitudes to Election Campaign Communication: Some Results from Four European Countries Compared," in *Proceedings of the Meeting on TV and Elections* (Turin: Edizioni RAI Radiotelevisione Italiana, 1977).

[16] See footnote 10 above.

frequency, but these are not sorted out according to the media which delivered them. The debate between Peres and Begin, newspaper advertising, party broadcasts on radio, and informal meetings in homes are each mentioned with some frequency (8–16 percent). Probing further, analysts of this survey found that only half the voters claimed to be reading the political parties' newspaper ads, and 70 percent of those who did said they did not believe them. Our impression from the Continuing Survey—although impossible to compare statistically with these data on newspaper advertising—is that the party political broadcasts on television, which are also advertisements, were attended to, and believed, by many more people. It may not be irrelevant to note that Israelis have no experience of advertising on television and thus may not have the well-developed sense of "discount" which is common among adult viewers of commercial television elsewhere.

Summarizing to this point, we suggest (1) that voters deliberated over this campaign more seriously than they had in previous recent elections, (2) that attention to the media was therefore particularly high and was issue-oriented, and (3) that newspaper articles and the televised party broadcasts were the major sources of influence, more in the sense of orientation than persuasion.

Given the rules of political campaigning in Israel and the active search for orientation, it is easy to understand the importance attributed to newspaper articles. It is less easy to understand why party political broadcasts should rank almost as high as newspapers. But it certainly suggests that had the broadcast media been permitted a more active role in providing orientation, broadcasting—television in particular—would have played the leading role.

The single important innovation of the campaign as far as the role of televison is concerned was surely the Begin-Peres debate. Presented on the final evening of campaigning, it came too late to be effective in any major way—although as many as 10 percent say that they did not decide until the final day. The debate itself was noteworthy more for its agenda-setting function—as we shall note in the section following—than for its influence on voting decisions. Proving that such a debate could be held at all, and without amending the existing rules of the game, was probably its most important effect.

Eighty percent of the population watched the debate, and of these only 10 percent saw less than the whole of it.[17] About 30 percent of the viewers found the debate useful for understanding the issues, the

---

[17] From the Continuing Survey of May 1977, several days after the election.

TABLE 9–2

ANALYSIS OF PRESS ADS, BY PARTY, 1977 CAMPAIGN
(in percentages)

Contents of Appeal	Labor	Likud	DMC
Prestige, authority, famous names	28	26	29
Fears: war, blow to democracy, unemployment, uncertainty	15	19	18
Frustrations: social gap, discrimination, women	7	5	3
Unity: consensus, national pride	5	33	11
Initiative, action	4	12	9
N (times mentioned by respondents)	(134)	(482)	(441)

SOURCE: Content analysis of election advertisements in daily press, February-May 1977. Note that columns do not add to 100 percent, although most of the Likud's appeals fall into the five major categories reported in this table.

parties' positions, and the personalities of the candidates. Twenty percent said the debate helped them decide, of whom 15 percent claimed that the debate reinforced them in their decision, 4 percent said it moved them out of the camp of the still-undecided, and 1 percent said it changed their mind. In the Israeli system of proportional representation (and putting aside questions of sampling and other errors), there are no grounds for arguing that the debate was influential in the making of voting decisions.

Even if direct appeals to voters cannot be said to have been the decisive factor in the election, the appeals of the parties—in their newspaper ads and television broadcasts—are revealing.[18] They may well have contributed—wittingly and unwittingly—to the image of the parties and the climate of the campaign.

A striking difference among the three parties is evident in the contents of their appeals: the Likud in one out of every three ads appealed to the electorate in terms of national cohesiveness and pride; this was six times more often than Labor. The DMC did so twice as frequently as Labor. Appeals to feelings of frustration were highest in Labor ads, in an attempt to gain the support of dissatisfied ethnics, women, and the poor, although one might have expected this line to

---

[18] The following discussion is based on a content analysis of appeals in newspaper advertisements and party political broadcasts. It is a very rough measure of differences, conducted by our research assistant. Unlike the data in the following section on "agenda setting," these were not checked for reliability. The data should be treated as impressionistic and descriptive.

be more characteristic of those who attacked the status quo than of its defenders. Another switch, this time of left-right positions, is revealed in the fear appeal: Likud, hitting Labor's record, placed more stress on uncertainties than did its rival. Finally, all three parties made extensive reference to prestigious figures who had endorsed them, urging the voters to emulate their choices.

Party slogans also reflected differences in the immediacy of appeals, their directness, degree of activism, and aggressiveness. The demand for change came from right, center, and far left. Likud's opening shot, a full-page ad in all the papers proclaiming itself the number one power in Israeli, politics, set the tone for its entire campaign. Its logo bore the motto "No. 1 Power," and the slogan at the bottom of every ad was, "There is but one power in the country with the strength to change the government," or, in abbreviated form, the even more emphatic "Change the government."

The DMC, which grew out of one of the post-1973 protest movements called Change, incorporated in its name and slogan the demand, "There must be a change." In most of its ads it also added a direct appeal: "With your help we will bring about a change." Smaller parties claimed to be the truest among the champions of change (Citizens' Rights, Shelli, the Communists). Even the National Religious party, by calling itself "the party of values," implied that a change in that direction was necessary.

In response, the slogans of the Labor Alignment were, "Now more than ever, Labor" (a pale equivalent of Franklin Roosevelt's "Don't Change Horses in Mid-Stream") and an unfortunate "We are the address for renewal and change," abbreviated to "We are the address." Labor's opponents easily turned around this last slogan to its disadvantage: "They are the address for all the failures of the past."

Comparison of the images presented in the newspaper advertising of the three largest parties reveals predictable differences, given their challenger-challenged roles. All tried to give themselves admirable characteristics in almost equal measure (see Table 9–3). Labor put great stress on the image of its leader and top team as reinforcing past allegiances and voting decisions. The DMC, as the newcomer in the race, presented its team almost as frequently but for the opposite reason, in order to make its leaders known. The Likud down-played this aspect of the campaign considerably, perhaps because it did not feel that its team was its strongest card.

Instead, Likud worked hard at convincing the public that, after twenty-nine years of trying, this time it would succeed in doing what it never had done in the past, namely, win. It adopted a tone bordering

TABLE 9–3

IMAGE BUILDING IN NEWSPAPER ADS, BY PARTY, 1977 CAMPAIGN

(in percentages of ads including appeals of the stated type)

Appeal	Labor	Likud	DMC
Past record of achievement or party traits	21	23	22
Building leader's or top echelon's image	38	14	32
Attack on rival(s), past failures, poor leadership	40	37	42
Defense of record, apologia or self-criticism	10	—	—
Interparty dialogue	3	2	4
Exaggerated self-confidence, "We'll be in the government . . ."	—	30	1
Witchhunting, punishing others	—	14	6
Continuity	4	44	—
Change	1	8	44

SOURCE: See Table 9–2.

on braggadocio from the very outset and maintained this high decibel level uninterruptedly to the end of the campaign. This was coupled with an extremely aggressive attitude to all comers, including the DMC, and indeed a vituperative one towards the Labor Alignment for military and economic failures past and present. (After the port strike in March and again after the tragic army helicopter crash in May, Likud called on the voters to "punish" the Alignment.)

An ironic reversal can be found in the continuity/change dimension: Labor was so anxious to escape blame for its past deeds that it refrained from taking credit for its accomplishments, which a government of long standing might have been expected to do. Likud, by contrast, tried to associate itself with everything good in the national past (much of which, of course, had been accomplished under Labor) in order to make itself liked. As might have been anticipated, the DMC argued most strongly for change, but even in response to this open challenge Labor did not make a clear statement with respect to the need for change, again in order not to remind the voters of its failures.

Perhaps Likud's greatest accomplishment in its image building, beyond its ability to convince the voters that it was a winner, was the right-left switch it achieved. We have noted the ingredients: posing as the most Zionist of Zionist parties, the most concerned for work-ers' welfare, the most concerned to act effectively to cure the country's economic ills. Above all, it addressed those to whom the old Herut nucleus in Likud had been anathema for a generation, insisting that they had nothing to fear. Part of Likud's image-building strategy was to keep Begin invisible until late in the campaign (oddly enough, his physical incapacity aided in the achievement of this goal); meanwhile the party built up confidence among its potential supporters that it could be trusted with the reins of state. And when Begin was men-tioned in party advertisements, pains were taken to present a "new" Begin, the family man, approachable, warm, concerned, devoted. No flinty fanatic here! The task of winning this apprehensive public's trust was aided, no doubt, by the corruption of Labor's leaders that was revealed during the campaign. Likud was able to present itself as the true heir to the ideals those venal Laborites had betrayed: in-deed, David Ben-Gurion's picture adorned Likud's final ad on election day!

The DMC shared with Likud a response to public demands for change, energetic leadership, and idealism in the image it projected. It was able to make an impressive first showing on Israel's political map despite being practically shut out of television. The DMC drew its con-stituency from a far more limited segment of the population than either of its two major rivals, and its leaders were members of the political elite of the old establishment who had become disaffected from both right and left. Its success in garnering 13 percent of the popular vote may prove to be unrepeatable if it ceases to answer pub-lic needs as well as it did in 1977.

While party broadcasts on television followed along the same lines, there were fewer important differences among the parties in the content of appeals, degree of vituperation, and number of issues ad-dressed than there were in the newspaper ads. The Alignment and Likud displayed equal numbers of candidates in their broadcasts, they hardly differed in the extent to which they dwelt on issues, and they mounted about an equal number of attacks on each other—numerous attacks and counterattacks in both cases.

Thus, the charges of corruption that had exercised the public during the year preceding the election campaign found their echo in the television messages of the parties. One night the Labor Alignment presented a man who claimed to have given his savings to the Likud to help pay off party debts but said he had never been repaid. The next night Likud presented the same man, this time claiming that the previous night's tape had been doctored by Labor to make it seem as though he was accusing the Likud of wrongdoing, whereas he had had no such intent. The viewing public was not able to determine where the truth lay. The limited time available for approval by the chairman of the Central Elections Committee may have been a factor in these tapes' being passed for broadcasting in the first place.

Another case involved an Alignment portrayal of imaginary events that might take place if Likud were to win the elections. In an attempt to dramatize potential conflict between workers and a rightist regime, the Alignment filmstrip which appeared the very first night that election publicity was broadcast showed a fabricated scene in which the army was called out by the Likud government to put down a demonstration of rioting workers. The filmstrip aroused immediate protest from the Likud and was the subject of much press comment as well.

Where the parties differed most, however, in their use of television was in style. The Likud divided its time into smaller segments so that it would appear several different times—almost American-style—during the election broadcast period. It used ballad singing and other folksy audio-visual techniques. Labor was more traditional and more paternalistic: its chief spokesman, Ephraim Katzir, was one of the senior statesmen of the party, known also, however, for his deep knowledge of traditional lore. (Some months later, he was chosen president of the state.) Its programs were ten to fifteen minutes in length. On several occasions, the Alignment showed snapshot glimpses of its leader, Shimon Peres, with particular visual effectiveness. In television terms, the National Religious party—which used its air time to emphasize its wholesome, constructive activity in behalf of the collectivity—probably deserves the prize for best use of the medium. But these are subjective judgments, of course.

Agenda Setting. In countries such as England, where the media are active participants in campaign exegesis, there is tension between parties and the media over the "right" of the media to set their own agenda of issues. The parties argue that they, not the media, are charged with putting issues forward for public discussion, and they actively resent and protest competition from the media. Whom do the media "represent," they ask. Ostensibly, this sounds like a strong argument. In fact, however, it is not difficult to show that political parties often avoid issues they find uncomfortable and that issues often remain unjoined because the parties refuse to argue with each other. Thus, the media reply that they, more than the parties, "represent" the conscientious citizen's right to know.

That the *salience* of an issue (rather than the parties' stand on the issue) may decide an election has often been remarked.[19] Thus, if one party is widely considered competent in foreign affairs and another in domestic policy, the decisive contest may be over which set of issues receives more attention from the public. While often remarked, the media's role in agenda setting has only recently attracted systematic empirical research.[20] The question is whether the media are more effective in telling people what to think *about* than in telling them what to think. Or, to put the matter more subtly, one can say that three perceptions of reality are involved in an election campaign: that of the public, as the result of its direct and indirect experience of various aspects of reality; that of the media, interpreting reality to the public, creating sensitivity to and awareness of issues as well as simply informing—in a word, setting the agenda of priorities and saliences; and that of the parties, presenting themselves in such a way as to answer the implied demands of the public and media agendas.

In this section, we compare media, public, and party agendas. While we cannot "prove" that the media in themselves, or the parties (acting through the media) dictated the public agenda, there is an interesting story to be told of how "what to think about" may have determined the outcome of the Israeli elections of 1977.

On the eve of the election, a number of serious domestic issues were vying with the ever-demanding issue of security/territories/peace. A year or so before the election, it became apparent that the stormy protest movements organized in the wake of government unpreparedness for the 1973 war had all but disappeared from the political scene. Moreover, since 1976 was an election year in the United States, events in the strife-torn Middle East did not require major policy decisions by Israeli leaders, who like their Arab counterparts were waiting to see who would take over the White House. As long as the Lebanese conflict was successfully contained, major issues such as the status of the West Bank, Israel's borders, and peace negotiations could be and were held in abeyance. Meanwhile, domestic issues rose in importance on the public agenda. Galloping inflation, labor unrest, and a government that did not impress the public with its ability to

---

[19] A good discussion can be found in Bernard Berelson, Paul F. Lazarsfeld, and William N. McPhee, *Voting: A Study of Opinion Formation in a Presidential Campaign* (Chicago: University of Chicago Press, 1954).

[20] See, for example, McCombs, "The Agenda-Setting Function of the Press." Also see Lee B. Becker, Maxwell E. McCombs, and Jack M. McLeod, "The Development of Political Cognitions," in Steven H. Chaffee, ed., *Political Communication*, Sage Annual Review of Communication Research, vol. 4, (Beverly Hills: Sage, 1975).

TABLE 9–4

The Public Agenda: The Issues Most Salient for the Voters, March and May 1977

March 1977		May 1977	
Issue and rank order	Percentage of respondents citing issue	Issue and rank order	Percentage of respondents citing issue
1. Inflation	34	1. Inflation	46
2. Peace negotiations	30	2. Corruption	35
3. Standard of living	26	3. Peace negotiations	33
4. Corruption	25	4. Strikes	23
5. Tax burden	22	5. Political leadership	20
6. Political leadership	21	6. Standard of living	18

NOTE: The survey question was "What in your opinion are the three issues which will influence the results of the elections?" (Thus, the columns do not add to 100 percent.)
SOURCE: Ma'ariv, March 28, May 15, 1977.

cope with these economic issues competed for headlines with a succession of financial scandals involving public figures, most of them belonging to the ruling Labor establishment. A growing conviction that the entire political structure was due for overhaul lay behind stories of protest movements and internal factionalism in existing parties.

In a poll taken by Herbert Smith for Ma'ariv, the mass circulation independent evening paper, in March 1977, a representative sample of Israelis was asked, "What in your opinion are the three issues which will influence the results of the elections?"[21] Their replies can be taken as constituting the public agenda at the outset of the political campaign. Smith polled again shortly before the elections in May, asking the same question, and received a different list of issues. Table 9–4 gives the results of his surveys.

Analysis of the March list shows three of the top six issues to be economic concerns, with inflation a hotter question even than the issue of peace negotiations. In the May list, there are also three economic issues, but strikes have replaced the tax burden as one of them. The outstanding shift, however, is the rise to second place of

[21] Smith is a private pollster who was commissioned to conduct election surveys by Ma'ariv.

another internal issue, that of corruption, which was formerly fourth in order of importance. In jumping to second place, it displaced peace negotiations, which moved down to third place. On both lists, inflation ranks first. The higher percentages characterizing the top issues in the May list reflect a somewhat higher degree of public consensus than in March as to the most important issues of the hour. The two leading issues, inflation and corruption, were perceived as failures of the party in power and challenged it to develop a powerful answer in order to meet the criticism of the opposition.

There is no doubt that the public was dissatisfied with government over these issues. Smith asked in late March, "In your opinion is the government successful or unsuccessful in its handling of economic affairs?" Thirty percent replied "not so successful" and 43 percent said "not successful at all," compared to 40 and 7 percent respectively in 1973. The Continuing Survey shows essentially the same results on economic policy, and corruption (especially the case of the governor-elect of the Bank of Israel in February) is named as the single most important vote-influencing factor in another survey.[22] While it is true that the electorate was almost equally divided in its support for the two major parties—Likud and Labor—on both economic and foreign policy, it is evident that with respect to domestic issues, Labor could only be defensive, while with respect to international issues—and despite the security failure in the 1973 war—there has never been a loss of confidence in Israel's ability to cope. Moreover, the expertise and relative success in diplomacy associated with the long years of Labor experience were generally acknowledged.[23] Obviously, this is the issue on which the Labor party might have taken the initiative. Surprisingly, as we shall see, it did not.

Here, then, is the public agenda. We want now to ask two questions: (1) Does the public agenda—and particularly the relative decline of the foreign/security issue in favor of domestic issues—reflect the agenda of events in the media? and (2) How do the public and media agendas compare with the agendas proposed by the parties themselves?

To answer the first question, we must look to the press. Radio and television, for the reasons enumerated already, were essentially outside the campaign, and the news programs largely followed the newspapers' lead. Table 9–5 illustrates the news agenda as presented to the readership by the leading morning and afternoon independents,

---

[22] Modi'in Ezrahi.

[23] Consensus on matters of foreign policy has always been strong, and in line with the (Labor) government's positions. See Louis Guttman, *The Israeli Public.*

TABLE 9–5

THE MEDIA AGENDA: LEADING STORIES IN TWO DAILY NEWSPAPERS, MARCH–MAY 1977
(in number of stories)

	Ma'ariv		Ha'aretz	
Month	Foreign	Domestic	Foreign	Domestic
March	16	10	21	6
April	9	14	12	11
May	8	6	12	2

NOTE: Both newspapers appear six times a week. Holidays in April reduced the number of days of publication; May is given only until election day, May 17, 1977.

SOURCE: Content analysis of headlines, Ma'ariv and Ha'aretz, March 1–May 17, 1977.

Ha'aretz and Ma'ariv, between March 1 and May 17, 1977. Both papers carried far more foreign affairs than domestic stories as their leads in March, but in April, because of the Rabin withdrawal and labor unrest, the situation reversed itself. May again saw greater prominence given to foreign affairs. However, the breakdown within these categories is significant for any comparison with the public agendas of March and May presented in Table 9–4.

If we accept that there is something of a time lag between the appearance of specific issues high on the media agenda and their appearance on the public agenda, Table 9–5 is at least partially explanatory of the shift in the public agenda between the March and May soundings of public opinion.[24] The events of April brought to the fore two domestic issues in particular: labor unrest widespread throughout the Israeli economy (in particular, among doctors, port workers, bank tellers, seamen, and air traffic controllers) and corruption involving the highest echelons of the political establishment. These are the two issues that shifted the balance in the media agenda from foreign issues to domestic problems. And these are the two issues that show up most strikingly in the May public agenda: strikes, which were not among the six top issues in the March list, now are issue number four in order of importance, and corruption, which

[24] We stress that the media agenda is only a partial explanation since many members of the public had direct experience of the reality of labor unrest—when they did not receive the services they expected in banks, for example.

jumped ten percentage points, becomes issue number two, even displacing peace negotiations for the second spot.

Having examined the agenda of press and public during the two-and-a-half-month period from March to mid May, we now turn to the issues put forward by the parties themselves. Specifically, we must ask whether the messages placed by the parties in their political advertising in newspapers and in the party-originated television broadcasts sought to direct the attention of public or press similarly to or differently from what we have seen so far.

Table 9–6 gives a rough content analysis of political advertising in newspapers and on television for the campaign as a whole. It is clear from Table 9–6 that the Likud emphasized domestic matters more than the Labor Alignment; 75–80 percent of Likud messages compared with 60–70 percent of Labor messages gave primary emphasis to internal affairs. Moreover, the proportions in the two media are remarkably similar. While this difference is in the expected direction, it seems far more important that *both* major parties placed most of their emphasis on domestic matters. Thus, only about one-third of Labor messages were devoted to foreign affairs. Rather than seek to thwart the increasing attention of media and public to the domestic matters on which it was so vulnerable, Labor, on the whole, chose to acquiesce. It did play up its foreign policy record—that is clear

TABLE 9–6

THE PARTIES' AGENDA: ADVERTISING IN NEWSPAPERS AND ON TELEVISION, 1977 CAMPAIGN

(in percentages)

Party	Issues Mentioned in Newspaper Ads			Issues Mentioned in Television Ads		
	Foreign	Domestic	Total	Foreign	Domestic	Total
Likud	25	75	100	20	80	100
Labor	40	60	100	33	67	100
DMC	13	87	100			

NOTE: The table reflects a content analysis of party advertisements between February and May 1977—189 ads for Labor, 270 for Likud, and 325 for the DMC. Since some ads dealt with more than one issue and others did not deal with issues at all but were organizational announcements, the percentage breakdown is based on 134 issue mentions for Labor, 182 for Likud, and 441 for the DMC. SOURCE: See Table 9–2.

from the proportions in the table—but overall it appears to have accepted the agenda dictated by press and opposition.

Why it did so is not so hard to guess. First of all, perhaps, it had little choice. Judging by the public agenda of May, which we feel reflects the media agenda of the previous month, the electorate was demanding answers to a complex of specific issues against a background that was increasingly anti-establishment. The public wanted to know what each party would do about inflation, corruption, and peace negotiations. It wanted a solution for the labor situation. It was looking for effective political leadership. Last among the top six issues was the omnipresent concern over the standard of living. Five domestic testing points, one foreign—and an overwhelming desire for some sort of new start, for change.

If Labor had been able to develop answers to the internal questions, alongside its foreign policy record, it might have done better on election day. But its political house was in disarray, its economic leadership appeared ineffectual, unable to control the labor unrest or rampant inflation, and its leadership was tainted with corruption. It allowed its opponents to sound more energetic, and it did not blow its own horn sufficiently to remind the voters of its massive accomplishments in building up agriculture, industry, housing, and education during its twenty-nine years in office.

A further breakdown of the treatment of internal issues reveals that Labor stressed social and cultural issues rather than economic ones; Likud hammered on the economic concerns of the public (the right stealing the left's thunder); and the DMC, the child of protest, stressed political reform and social issues. Labor did not provide an answer to the perception of its past failures in the economic realm or to the high level of concern about these questions revealed by an examination of the public agenda. Thus, it appears that Labor was drawn into the domestic arena by the challengers, but its response was only halfhearted.

Second, Labor not only countered the domestic challenge weakly, it also underplayed its strength on foreign issues. It did so, perhaps, because differences of opinion *within* the Labor Alignment made an innovative statement on foreign policy almost impossible. It could talk with pride about the warmth of its many previous contacts with American and European leaders, but substantively, on the question of how to reach out for peace, it had nothing new to say.

Thus, the electorate voted in a frame of mind that all but ignored international issues. The agenda of issues that preoccupied the voters as they went to the polls was one on which the media and the parties were in essential agreement—and domestic matters were by far the more salient.

Nevertheless, two nights before the election—on the last day of official campaigning—the voters got an important reminder that their agenda priorities might be wrong. Presiding over the debate between Peres and Begin was the distinguished journalist Yeshayahu Ben-Porat, the agreed choice of both parties to put questions to their candidates.[25] Looking at the issues facing Israel, Ben-Porat began by asking the candidates squarely what each would say about relations in the Middle East to the President of the United States.

If this, indeed, was the major issue facing the society in May 1977, it deserved to be the leading question in the election campaign just as it was in the debate. That it was not the leading issue on the parties' agenda goes to show, once again, that the parties cannot be counted on to pose issues that have no political payoff. Even the press moved from foreign to domestic issues in April, as we have seen, but foreign affairs predominated again in May. The active intervention of electronic journalism, however, charged as it is with political neutrality, can constrain candidates to face issues they might otherwise seek to avoid. At the same time, it is worth noting that Begin's hawkish reply to Ben-Porat's opening question gave no intimation either of the centrality that the issues of peace making would assume under his aegis or of the surprising ways in which he would respond to them. Probably he did not know himself. These are the lessons of the first-ever television debate between the two party heads.

Smoothing the Succession. The British tried to introduce their great innovation—public-service broadcasting, supported by a license fee but independent of government—to the Empire, but little is left of what was begun in most of the former colonies. In almost every one of the new nations that emerged from British sovereignty, broadcasting is directly controlled by government, even if there was some initial effort to try out the BBC model.[26] The French did much better in exporting their model, because the ORTF was itself a branch of government.

---

[25] Studies of presidential debates in the United States include Sidney Kraus, ed., *The Great Debate* (Indianapolis: Indiana University Press, 1962), and most recently Jack M. McLeod, "The 1976 American Presidential Debates: Audience Effects and Implications for Political Communication Formats," in *Proceedings of the Meeting on TV and Elections*, pp. 265–285. Later this year the American Enterprise Institute will publish the proceedings of its Conference on the Future of Presidential Debates, held in Washington, D.C., October 19–20, 1977.

[26] Katz and Wedell, *Broadcasting in the Third World*.

Democratic sentiment aside, the dysfunction of state-controlled broadcasting systems is that they do not readily accommodate political change. So long as a one-party government remains unchallenged, the system seems to work. But broadcasting stations seem invariably to be the first targets of revolution. The old guard is murdered and new leaders replace them on the television screens. Democracy, on the other hand, tends to leave the former leadership physically intact and gives the opposition a chance at the microphone.

Among new nations, Israel is a major exception in this respect. Broadcasting was a branch of the Prime Minister's Office from 1948 to 1965. Despite this hiatus, the British influence reasserted itself— as it has done in so many other Israeli institutions—and a BBC-like Broadcasting Authority was established by law in 1965. Television joined radio under the aegis of the new authority when it was introduced in 1968. Since then (and even before, to a considerable extent), the balance between government and opposition has been studiously reflected in the media, even though the Labor party reigned supreme from 1948 to 1977.

In 1977, as in the previous eight elections since the establishment of the state, voters and media alike expected Labor to win. Indeed, virtually all political observers—and even the polls, with one exception —foresaw a victory, albeit a narrow one, for the seemingly perennial first party.[27] It was television that first announced the probable upset. In a representative sample of polling places, Israel Television asked voters to recast their ballots in a television-sponsored voting booth, and within a few hours after the polls closed the election-night computer was showing the Likud ahead by a substantial margin. Rather than express disbelief as the rest of us did, Herbert Smith, the analyst-in-charge, and the television professionals chose to take the preliminary results seriously. Far more important than the fact that their choice proved right is the fact that they made election night into a media event. On the American model, an Israeli election is covered as a race, and the best men—that is, the best party—are declared the winners. At the same time, there is no question about the "legitimacy of opposition": the losers are familiar and acceptable faces.

The professionalism of the public-service broadcasters was a major factor in smoothing the transition. Switching back and forth

---

[27] Elisabeth Noelle-Neumann has argued that measures of perceptions of who will win are more sensitive to change in the climate of opinion than are measures of actual vote intentions. These data appear to contradict her thesis. See Elisabeth Noelle-Neumann, "Turbulences in the Climate of Opinion: Methodological Applications of the Spiral of Silence Theory," *Public Opinion Quarterly*, vol. 41 (1977), pp. 143–158.

from one party headquarters to the next, the cameras finally came to rest on Begin and his (unbelieving) acceptance of victory, then on Peres and his concession of defeat. The display of professional cool that accompanied the end of the seemingly eternal rule of Labor made the event appear altogether natural. This surely will be difficult to grasp for readers familiar with political rotation, nor can we "prove" that broadcasting actually served the function we are attributing to it; but so it seems to us. And if we are right, television made a contribution to the first real test of the process of democratic succession in Israel.

We have reviewed the role of the mass media (1) as agents of influence and information, (2) as agenda setters, and (3) as heralds of legitimate political change. The media's influence on voting decisions is surely the least of their effects. Yet there may well have been more media influence this time than in previous Israeli elections, or indeed in typical elections elsewhere. It is true that the media best reach those who are actively seeking to be influenced—and these usually are the people who are most interested in politics and most likely to have interpersonal sources of information and opinion. But in the present instance, a large proportion of the population apparently sought to be influenced: there was great uncertainty until the last moment, and many persons said, when asked, that the media—especially newspapers and party political broadcasts on television—had contributed to their decisions even though they did not acknowledge that seeking guidance had motivated their exposure to broadcasting.

Moreover, as we have repeatedly underlined, the kind of investigative reporting that led to or abetted the exposure of failure and corruption began long before the campaign and continued right through it. The beginning of the erosion of support for Labor can be dated even earlier, however. Analyzing data from the Continuing Survey, Louis Guttman points (1) to the continuing disappointment over Labor's economic policies dating even to the period before the Yom Kippur War and (2) to the growing proportion of voters between the 1973 and 1977 elections who declared themselves uncertain, or unwilling to say, for whom they would vote "if the elections were being held today." By the end of 1976, the proportion of uncertain respondents had reached 60 percent, and, discounting certain fluctuations following key exposures (Mrs. Rabin's bank account, Mr. Rabin's resignation), it remained almost as high until very close to election day. In effect, Guttman here discounts even the influence of recent investigative reporting, arguing instead for a cumulative abandoning of Labor over a period of years. "Influence goes on between election campaigns" is the appropriate dictum.

But even if we accept the vote-guidance role of the media, it is clear—at least for this election—that agenda setting is a more interesting focus. As Guttman himself says,

> the uncertainty stemmed from the dilemma created by supporting the foreign policy of the [Labor] Alignment government, yet severely criticizing its treatment of internal affairs. On questions about foreign affairs, the distribution of answers of those who had not yet decided was almost identical with that of those who had already made up their mind in favor of the Alignment. Conversely, for questions on the handling of internal affairs, the distribution of answers of those vacillating was almost identical with that of those who had already decided for the Likud. Apparently, when uncertainty declined, the undecided respondents were giving more weight to internal matters than to foreign affairs.[28]

We arrived at this conclusion rather differently. Comparing the agendas of press, parties, and public, we found the press moving from foreign to domestic issues as the campaign progressed; we also found evidence that the public had moved in the same direction. Looking at the attention given by the parties to domestic as compared with foreign policy, it was no surprise that the Likud and the DMC gave their primary emphasis to domestic matters; far more surprising was the extent to which the Labor Alignment followed suit.

Among the three news media, only the press is free to set an agenda of its own choosing. Radio and television are mere platforms for party rhetoric, as used to be the case in England. The confrontation between the two leading candidates around issues that were raised "in behalf" of the voter may be a harbinger of the kind of change that has taken place in British broadcasting in recent years. Being exceedingly careful to give balanced coverage to all sides, broadcasting in England—and elsewhere in Europe—has taken the lead in identifying the issues, explicating them, and forcing the parties to take a stand on each.[29] This reform is badly needed in Israel, particularly for those groups in the population for whom television is the primary vehicle for engagement with the society. The politicians do not trust the broadcaster to do this job fairly or well, and they are

---

[28] Guttman, The Israeli Public.
[29] Blumler, Gurevitch, and Ives, Challenge of Election Broadcasting.

not likely to let him try any time soon. But the British experience is, as always, an important precedent for Israeli democracy.

That does not mean that the ideal format for campaign broadcasting is the debate. In fact, some observers are having second thoughts about whether the debate—at least in its American form—is a very useful way of explicating issues. It is surely an interesting way; and it has the advantage of overcoming the kind of selectivity that makes voters tend to listen only to their own side. In these days where people seem to be taking sides less vociferously, it would be wise to consider other broadcasting formats as well. But confrontation —of the candidates with each other, and of the candidates with the issues—is certainly the key to both interest and understanding.[30]

Party political broadcasts deserve to be continued, because the parties must have unmediated access to the voters. Care must be taken that they not deteriorate into American-style advertising spots. Several serious questions about "truth in advertising" arose this time, one flagrant example of which was the tailoring and speeding up of documentary film footage of police dispersing a political demonstration to illustrate Labor's warning that the Likud might use the army to break strikes. The review procedure provided for in the election law may be inadequate to cope with new media techniques of bending truth.

Finally it should not be forgotten that most change in the politicial system occurs between—not during—election campaigns. The slow erosion of support for Labor and the rise of the "don't know" group since the 1973 war, perhaps even before, is a telling example.

---

[30] Michael Gurevitch, in *Proceedings of the Meeting on TV and Elections*, pp. 368–369; and Guttman, *The Israeli Public.*

10

Israel's Foreign Policy
and the 1977 Parliamentary Elections

Bernard Reich

Foreign policy was not a decisive issue in the election that brought the Likud bloc and Prime Minister Menachem Begin to power in Israel in 1977. This is not to say that it was not important, for it was, but rather that it was not contentious. Identifying the main questions and appropriate responses to them, at least in broad terms, was not a subject for substantial debate. Foreign policy and security have been central to the Israeli system since its establishment, and the primary objectives—ensuring the nation's existence and security in the face of Arab hostility—have remained essentially constant. Israel's continuing (though changing) dispute and periodic warfare with the Arab states is its preeminent problem and affects all of its domestic and international policies. The pursuit of peace and the assurance of security in a hostile region continue to dominate Israel's political life and especially its foreign and security policy, although the policies designed to achieve those goals have been modified over time.

Israel's independence in May 1948 was greeted by an attack of Arab armies acting in loose coordination under the auspices of the Arab League. Although that first war was halted by Armistice Agreements (signed in 1949 between Israel and each of the four contiguous Arab nations—Egypt, Jordan, Syria, and Lebanon) and the stage was set for peace negotiations, none of the ensuing efforts to achieve peace yielded any substantial positive result at least in the period up to the June War of 1967. Instead, major wars in 1956, 1967, and 1973 (as well as the Egypt-Israel War of Attrition of 1969–1970) and continuing small-scale conflict have established a negative pattern of relations that has dominated the environment in which Israel's foreign and security policy is formulated and executed. Israel has continued to recognize that peace and cooperation with the neighboring Arab states are vital for the survival and development of the Jewish state over an extended period, and this has remained a cornerstone of its policy since independence.[1] Successive governments have included these goals in their official programs and have sought to attain them.

Israel's general approach to foreign policy began to take shape once it became clear that peace would not follow the armistice accords. Israel looked beyond the circle of neighboring Arab states and the Middle Eastern region to the broader international community. The effort to establish friendly relations with the states of the developing world and Europe, as well as with the superpowers, was conceived as having a positive impact on the Arab-Israeli conflict, in addition to its strictly bilateral political and economic advantages. The bilateral relationships were also viewed as mechanisms to ensure Israel's deterrent strength through national armed power and through increased international support for its position. Israel has seen Europe and the developing world (especially Africa and Latin America) as important components of its overall policy. It has sought to maintain positive relations with Europe based on the commonality of the Judeo-Christian heritage and the memories of the Holocaust and with the developing world based on Israel's ability to provide technical assistance in the development process. Despite substantial effort in these sectors, the centrality of the Arab-Israeli conflict has enlarged the role of the superpowers.

Israel's leaders early recognized the crucial role the great powers would play in ensuring the country's defense and integrity. In the euphoric days following independence, it was assumed that neutrality in the cold war was possible and that Israel could establish and maintain friendly relations with both East and West (that is, the Soviet Union and the United States). This was in accord with its perception of its national interest and seemed to be a realistic assessment in light of the policies and activities of both powers in the period immediately following World War II. Increasingly, Israel's position became Western (and especially United States) oriented. The West provided Israel with the political and moral support and the arms and economic assistance essential for its survival and defense, while the Soviet Union increasingly identified itself with the Arab cause. The relationship with the United States became the most significant because, in addition to providing various forms of aid and moral support, the United States assumed a central position in the effort to achieve an

---

[1] Israel's Declaration of Independence (May 1948) proclaimed: "We extend our hand to all neighbouring states and their peoples in an offer of peace and good neighbourliness. . . ."

Arab-Israeli peace.[2] The American Jewish community also helped to create a special link between Israel and the United States.

The June War of 1967 modified substantially the content of the issues central to the dispute between Israel and the Arabs and the focal points of Israeli policy. Israel occupied the Sinai Peninsula, the Gaza Strip, the West Bank of the Jordan River, the eastern sector of the city of Jerusalem, and the Golan Heights and adopted the position that it would not withdraw from those territories until there were negotiations with the Arab states leading to peace agreements that would recognize Israel's right to exist and accept Israel's permanent position and borders.[3] Throughout the period between the June War (1967) and the October War (1973) the central focus of attention in the Middle East was the effort to achieve a settlement of the Arab-Israeli conflict and secure a just and lasting peace. In this effort (based to a substantial degree on United Nations Security Council Resolution 242 of November 22, 1967), the regional states, the superpowers (and lesser powers), and the main instrumentalities of the international system were engaged. Israel focused its attention on peace and security objectives and developed positions concerning the occupied territories, the Palestinians, and related questions that provided the basis for its policy after the October War. Although some of the interwar efforts were promising, peace was not achieved, and little movement in that direction resulted. Instead, the October War erupted and created a new environment for the quest for peace and for the development of Israeli foreign policy.

The October War and After

In the wake of the October War, the modifications in Israel's policy were primarily matters of tactics and nuance rather than objectives. The primary goals remained the achievement of an Arab-Israeli settlement and the assurance of security in the interim. This continuity resulted in part from Israel's collective conception of its fundamental international position—and the limited policy options which flow therefrom—which was not substantially altered. Israel's view of Jewish history as one of persecution and anti-Semitism generating an

---

[2] For a detailed examination of this relationship, see Bernard Reich, *Quest for Peace: United States–Israel Relations and the Arab-Israeli Conflict* (New Brunswick, N.J.: Transaction Books, 1977).

[3] The Arab states argued that negotiations were impossible (and recognition of and peace with Israel could not occur) until Israel withdrew from the occupied territories. The "three no's" of the Khartoum Arab summit meeting of 1967 became the central Arab position—diametrically opposed to that of Israel.

emphasis on self-preservation and self-reliance, its view of itself as geographically isolated and without dependable allies, its geographical vulnerability, and its need to acquire and produce arms for self-defense—all of which influence its security policy—were reaffirmed by the October War. Israel believed it had won a military victory (which could have been greater had the cease-fire not intervened) and that its strategic concepts had been vindicated.[4]

Israel recognized the dangers inherent in its increased isolation in the international community and its dependence on the United States, and in the wake of the war it attempted to reaffirm and reestablish the ties that had been disrupted as a result of the conflict and the attendant use of the Arab oil weapon. An intensive effort was launched to restore Israel's traditionally close relations with the states of Europe, although, with Israel's increased economic and military needs and diplomatic isolation, the relationship with the United States became more central. After the October War, as before, the United States remained critical to Israel's security, to the search for peace in the Arab-Israeli zone of the Middle East, and to the continued prosperity of the Jewish state. But there was an ambivalence and an uneasiness in Israel's postwar policy, which sought to solidify the support and aid of the United States while reducing Israel's dependence.

Within this general framework, Israel continued to focus on one central issue: the Arab-Israeli conflict and its impact on Israel's quest for peace and security. As Prime Minister Rabin put it, "Israel's position is we want peace, a real one. We want boundaries of peace that will make Israel capable of defending itself by itself. We do not want a peace agreement that ends up as peace on a piece of paper. We want peace based on the realities of relations between the peoples of all the countries involved in the area."[5] Israel's conception was of a "real peace, a true peace," a "peace of reconciliation" that would include an end to hostilities and open borders across which goods and people

---

[4] General Chaim Herzog, subsequently Israel's ambassador to the United Nations, summarized the Israeli view of "the incredible military victory gained on the field of battle in the Yom Kippur War" in these terms: "Caught surprised and unaware, and despite the initial reverses and heavy losses, the Israeli people, military command and, above all, fighting men rallied, turned the tide and brought on a victory that saved the nation. Many of the great events in a 4,000-year-old history pale into insignificance beside what was achieved on the battle-field in the Yom Kippur War. Israel has every right to draw courage and faith for the future from its performance in what the Israelis may well remember as their war of atonement." Chaim Herzog, *The War of Atonement* (Jerusalem: Steimatsky's Agency, 1975), p. 291.

[5] Rabin Interview, *U.S. News & World Report*, June 23, 1975, p. 30.

could move freely.[6] Israel continued to focus on the dilemma posed by the hostility of the region in which it is located and the realization that peace was not a realistic possibility in the short term. Security and the policy essential to its attainment thus were central to Israeli thinking.[7] Israel's view of the need for secure and defensible borders and an assured supply of modern and sophisticated military equipment was reinforced by the conflict. It was the type of attack that took place in October 1973 that convinced Israel that secure and recognized borders (as noted in United Nations Security Council Resolution 242) were not achievable on the pre–June War lines.[8] The war reaffirmed for Israel the strategic value of the occupied territories, since the fighting took place not within the frontiers of pre-1967 Israel but rather in the occupied areas far from Israel's main population centers. And it demonstrated the importance of the Israel Defense Forces (IDF). Israel saw the need for creating a stronger IDF and for maintaining the regional military balance and allocated resources to achieve those ends.

The eventual disposition of the occupied territories related directly to the quest for peace and security,[9] and prior to the 1973 war it was widely discussed. The official position was not to have a precise policy, although there was broad, informal consensus on several points: the River Jordan would be Israel's security border; the actual Jordan-Israel border would be negotiated; Israel would remain on the Golan Heights; the Gaza Strip would not be under foreign control; Sharm el-Sheikh would remain under Israel's control and would be linked to Israel by a continuous strip of land whose borders would be

---

[6] In an address to the Knesset on June 3, 1974, on the presentation of the new government, Rabin defined Israel's goal in these terms: "True peace is not merely a peace between diplomatic representatives, but peace between the peoples, a peace which finds expression daily, in open borders, across which contact can be established in all spheres of life." See also his press conference in Washington on March 8, 1977, in New York Times, March 9, 1977.

[7] On the centrality of security considerations in Israeli thinking, see Bernard Reich, "Israel's Quest for Security," Current History, vol. 62 (January 1972), pp. 1–5, 48, and 52.

[8] Abba Eban in the United Nations General Assembly on October 8, 1973, noted that if Israel "had gone back to the previous armistice lines . . . then the attacks of 6 October . . . would have done such destruction to our vital security that perhaps Israel and all its people . . . might now all be lost, swept away in a fearful massacre." See also the statement by Golda Meir to the Knesset on October 16, 1973, and her press conference on October 13, 1973.

[9] For a more detailed discussion of Israel's position on the occupied territories, see Bernard Reich, "Israel and the Occupied Territories" (Department of State, 1974), mimeo.

negotiated.[10] Similar views were involved in the Allon plan of then Deputy Prime Minister (and later foreign minister) Yigal Allon, who developed a complex scheme to deal with the problem of the West Bank.[11]

After the October War, Israel's view continued to be that the final determination of lines (in other words, the extent of Israel's withdrawal from the occupied territories and the permanent borders of the state) would depend, in part, on the negotiating situation. Clearly, the extent of territory to be relinquished would vary with the extent of concessions made by the Arab negotiators and with the situation at the bargaining table. In the final analysis, the territories were viewed as bargaining counters to be traded for progress toward peace or at least regional coexistence.[12] Israel continued to stress the need for defensible borders which would allow it to defend itself by itself without the need for external guarantees and assistance.[13] The final lines, however, would have to be agreed to and recognized by Israel's neighbors and would have to be secure. Therefore, Israel would not return to the insecure and unrecognized armistice lines that had existed on June 4, 1967, and which could not be defended.[14] On "Issues and Answers" on March 13, 1977, Prime Minister Rabin noted, "The answer is, without any qualifications, Israel will not return to the lines that existed before the 1967 war." Israel would not retain or return *all* of the occupied territories. Partly indicative of Israeli intentions and thinking was the establishment of some 100 settlements in the areas occupied in the June War. Although settlement did not necessarily determine the final Israeli posture, it provided a beginning point for negotiations.

In Israel's view, the status of Jerusalem was not linked to the problem of the occupied territories. For Israel, "Jerusalem is the capital . . . and it is going to remain so"; it would never again be

---

[10] Golda Meir in a speech to the Labor party convention, April 4, 1971. This general thinking was often reflected in popular opinion, as numerous public opinion polls show.

[11] For further details on the Allon plan, see Yeroham Cohen, *Tochnit Allon* [The Allon plan] (Israel: Hakibbutz Hameuchad, 1972).

[12] On "Issues and Answers," March 13, 1977, Prime Minister Rabin said: "For a real peace, Israel is ready for territorial compromises. Not to go back to the lines that existed before the Six Day War, because they are not defendable. But we are more than ready for compromises."

[13] See, for example, Rabin's press conference on March 8, 1977, in *New York Times*, March 9, 1977. For further elaboration of this perspective, see Yigal Allon, "Israel: The Case for Defensible Borders," *Foreign Affairs*, vol. 55 (October 1976), pp. 38–53.

[14] See Rabin interview, "Issues and Answers," July 14, 1974.

divided, and "internationalization" was "totally unacceptable."[15] The issue involved was thus limited to respecting the religious sensibilities of other faiths and providing for the religious administration of the holy places; it was not a question of the political future of the city.

The Palestinian Arab issue became more intense and more widely discussed after the October War. Israel's position, which continued to reflect prewar thinking, had three operative components: terrorism, refugees, and the political future of the Palestinians.

Palestinian terrorism remained a clear issue. It posed a threat to Israeli security and thus was a matter to be dealt with by security forces—whether it occurred within Israel or in the occupied territories. Terrorism was not seen as an act of national liberation: it was something to be dealt with quickly, forcefully, and with great effectiveness.

The second question was that of the Palestinians as refugees. Their ultimate disposition was regarded as a humanitarian problem, revolving around the implementation of United Nations resolutions that called for repatriation or resettlement with compensation and for "justice for the refugees." Israel consistently argued that there were limits on the extent to which repatriation could take place, although the basic point was that those who wished to return to Israel and live in peace would be allowed to do so.[16] The assumption was that most would be resettled somewhere other than in Israel.

The third element was the political future of the Palestinians. After the June War, Israel's reaction to this question was expressed by Golda Meir, who, when asked what ought to be done about the Palestinians, essentially responded that there was no separate Palestinian people and that the Palestinians not only were included in the West Bank population then under Israeli control but also constituted a substantial portion of the population of Jordan on the East Bank of the river. She believed that the distinction between Palestinian Arabs on the West Bank and Jordanian Arabs on the East Bank was artificial. Subsequently, there was a more specific and precise formulation of the Israeli position. Israel regarded the PLO's quest for "legitimate

---

[15] Rabin interview, "Issues and Answers," July 14, 1974. Rabin went on to elaborate in these terms: "I don't believe that Jerusalem is going to be divided again. . . . I don't believe that the Holy City should be divided again. On the other hand, I believe there must be solutions to allow free access to the other two religions, to the Christians, to Muslims, and there should be a solution that will give the administration of the holy places to the two religions. . . ."

[16] As part of the Israeli argument, it has been pointed out that there has been an exchange of refugee problems and this must ultimately be accounted for in the solution. Thus, the 600,000 or 700,000 Jews who fled from Arab countries in the late 1940s and early 1950s and came to Israel must be included in the determination of repatriation, resettlement, and compensation.

261

national rights" as little more than a euphemism for the destruction of Israel as a Jewish state in the Middle East. Israel recognized that "in the settlement the Palestinian problem has to be solved because without its solution, there will be no durable peace in the Middle East," yet it insisted that a settlement must be between Israel and the Arab states, since the "key to peace, as well as to war, lies in the relations between the Arab countries and Israel. . . . The only solution . . . is to make peace between the Arab countries and Israel."[17] Israel continued to believe that the creation of a third state in the area between the Mediterranean and Iraq was unnecessary for Palestinian self-identity and would, in any event, not be viable.[18] In a formal cabinet decision of July 21, 1974, it was noted that Israel would continue to work for a peace agreement negotiated with Jordan[19] based on the existence of only two independent states: Israel and a Jordanian-Palestinian state east of Israel.[20] Israel and Jordan would

---

[17] Rabin, "Issues and Answers," July 14, 1974.

[18] Professor Shlomo Avineri, then director general of the Israeli Foreign Ministry, argued against the establishment of a separate and independent Palestinian state on the West Bank in these terms: "Such a state would add elements of instability and dissension, it would leave the refugees in the camps, and it would create power vacuums. It will have only one rationale—to become a springboard for the further destruction of Israel proper. If the rationale is stability, if the rationale is a solution of the Palestinian refugee problem, a West Bank state cannot fulfill those goals." Shlomo Avineri, "How to Solve the Palestinian Problem," *Near East Report*, May 4, 1977, p. 71. A very similar presentation may be found in Shlomo Avineri, "To Solve the Palestinian Problem," *New York Times*, May 15, 1977.

[19] The decision read in part: "Israel will continue to strive for peace agreements with the Arab States on the basis of defensible boundaries secured in negotiations held without prior conditions. The Government will work for negotiations for a peace agreement with Jordan. That agreement will be based on the existence of only two independent States—Israel with unified Jerusalem as its capital, and an Arab Jordanian-Palestinian State east of Israel within boundaries to be fixed by negotiation between Israel and Jordan. In that State the self-identity of the Jordanians and Palestinians will find expression in peace and good-neighbourliness with Israel."

[20] In June 1975, Rabin said: "Israel believes that in the context of an overall settlement, the Palestinian issue should be solved. We believe that the solution of it is that within the original Palestine of 1918 there should be two states— Israel, the Jewish state, and east of it a Jordanian-Palestinian state. Where the boundaries will be is a matter of negotiations. We don't see any room for a third state between Israel and Jordan. I would say that more than that, we would not negotiate with the so-called Palestine Liberation Organization because what they present, by the philosophy, is the goal of the elimination of Israel. . . . A Jordanian-Palestinian state—we believe this is the solution to peace between Israel and Jordan, and the solution of the Palestinian issue." Rabin interview in *U.S. News & World Report*, June 23, 1975, p. 30.

In an address to the Knesset on January 19, 1977, Foreign Minister Yigal Allon stated that Israel "will continue to oppose vigorously the sterile idea of the establishment of a third state between Israel and Jordan."

determine the future of the area since Jordan is the government of most of the Palestinians. This "Jordanian option" was Israel's preferred position. Israel made clear its continued opposition to negotiations with the Palestine Liberation Organization and other terrorist organizations whose declared purpose was the destruction of Israel[21] but appeared prepared to negotiate with Palestinian representatives committed to peaceful coexistence with a Jewish state of Israel.[22] It viewed the PLO's formula—a democratic, secular state of Palestine—as fatal to the state of Israel.[23] Israeli spokesmen continually pointed out that no PLO spokesman had ever accepted Israel's existence.

The views and policies of the post–October War governments of Prime Ministers Golda Meir and Yitzhak Rabin, described above, provided the basic positions for the 1977 campaign and the post-election Likud government.

The Campaign

In 1977, as in some past elections, foreign and security policy issues were not in the forefront of the campaign.[24] The major parties were

---

[21] Israel's position was restated on numerous occasions. See, for example, Rabin's speech of the Prime Minister's International Conference of the United Israel Appeal, Jerusalem, January 23, 1975; his interview on Israel Television, February 14, 1975; Interview on "Galei Zahal" (IDF broadcasting station), April 1, 1975; his press conference in Washington, June 12, 1975; an interview published in *Time Magazine*, July 21, 1975, p. 25; and his interview on "Issues and Answers," September 7, 1975. In a speech to the United Nations General Assembly on September 30, 1975, Yigal Allon noted that Israel was "categorically negative about the absurd pretensions of the so-called Palestine Liberation Organization" to speak in the name of the Palestinians. He characterized the PLO as a "congeries of feuding terrorist gangs whose principal victims are the Arabs of Palestine themselves, and whose primary aim is the annihilation of the State of Israel and the genocide of its people." *New York Times*, October 1, 1975.

[22] On "Issues and Answers," on March 12, 1977, Prime Minister Rabin summarized Israel's position in these terms: ". . . peace eastward of Israel would be negotiated between Israel and Jordan. And within this peace agreement the Palestinian issue can and has to be solved. I believe that it will be advisable to the Jordanians to include in their delegation representatives of the people who live in the West Bank, leaders of the cities. . . . When it comes to the PLO I believe that we have nothing to do with it, because the essence of their existence is their commitment to the destruction of Israel."

[23] The civil war in Lebanon, which began in the spring of 1975, confirmed for Israelis their perception of what the PLO meant by a democratic, secular state since Arafat had often cited Lebanon as the model for his dreamed-of state in Palestine. Israelis drew the lesson that a Jewish minority would be subject to a fate similar to that suffered by Lebanon's Christians at the hands of the Palestinians and Lebanese Muslims in the civil war.

[24] In an assessment of foreign policy issues in the 1969 election, Ernest Stock wrote: "Paradoxically, the great issue of foreign policy facing the country at the

in broad agreement on the central foreign policy issues, and their platforms and pronouncements, which remained vague and general, were not too dissimilar.

The 1977 campaign was longer than usual and focused on concerns primarily of a domestic nature (economic problems, political scandals, and the need for change and reform) rather than on foreign policy and security. No central, overriding issue emerged. Much of the voters' attention seemed to be drawn to the jockeying for position within the parties (the Rabin-Peres efforts to control the Labor Alignment, for example)[25] and to the emergence of new political forces (such as Yigael Yadin's Democratic Movement for Change).[26] Each party's efforts seemed to be centered on portraying itself as the group to reinvigorate the system and meet potential challenges at home (especially) and abroad. The diverse and relatively minor issues that developed in the foreign policy arena were met with responses of a general nature, imprecise on specifics.

Although the campaign lacked a foreign policy and security focus, the major parties developed positions that presented the electorate with some choice. These were articulated in a series of statements and advertisements, as well as in the official platforms.[27]

The Labor-Mapam Alignment, as the mainstay of the outgoing government and the target of the campaigns of the other parties, sought to stress its accomplishments and the importance of policy continuity. Its basic foreign policy positions, which were well known to the voter, underwent no substantial change for the campaign. They were summarized in the "Election Special" tabloid in these terms:

> The Government's firm but flexible foreign policy has pro-
> tected Israel's vital security interests while pursuing every
> prospect of peace and preserving the sympathy and under-
> standing of our friends—especially the United States, whose
> support is essential for the maintenance of our armed

---

time of the 1969 election campaign—whether peace or security was to be accorded a higher priority in the composition and conduct of the next government—did not become a subject of major debate or even of controversy among the principal participants." Ernest Stock, "Foreign Policy Issues," in Alan Arian, ed., *The Elections in Israel—1969* (Jerusalem: Jerusalem Academic Press, 1972), p. 41.

[25] Despite their reputations as dove (Rabin) and hawk (Peres), their conflict did not reflect major ideological differences on foreign or domestic policy issues—it was primarily a personality clash.

[26] This major new political party was founded to respond to domestic problems and reform more than to foreign policy issues. See Chapter 6.

[27] The focus here is on the central themes of each party's position. More details on the views of Labor, Likud, and the DMC are considered elsewhere in this chapter.

strength. For the first time in Israel's history . . . we have had a year of almost perfect quiet on the borders. By reject-ing both extremes—the Likud's "not-an-inch" policy and the Rakah-Shelli "give-it-all-back" policy—strengthening the borders by planned settlement, insisting that any agreement must provide for secure, defensible frontiers, and calling for a solution of the Palestinian Arab problem in the framework of peace with Jordon—the Alignment Gov-ernment has kept open the road that may, one day, lead to peace.

The platform adopted by the Labor party convention on February 25, 1977, stressed peace with the Arab states within defensible borders achieved through territorial compromise. It rejected the policies of return to the pre–June War borders and of refusal to give back any of the territories. But the quest for peace and security required defense preparedness, and since there was a danger of war, "security needs must remain at the center of the needs of the state" and the strength and ability of the IDF must be reinforced. Friendly relations with the United States had to be fortified. To achieve peace, Labor supported a Geneva Conference with its 1973 participants and rejected "the invitation of representatives of PLO and terrorist organizations." It rejected "the establishment of an additional separate Palestinian Arab state to the west of the Jordan River."[28]

The DMC's position was that Israel would agree to return some of the occupied territories for peace, although in the West Bank security was the overriding consideration and the Jordan River had to serve as Israel's security border. It sought a solution to the Palestinian problem in the West Bank linked to Jordan—no independent Palestinian state could be created in that territory.[29]

The Likud's platform focused on "positive initiatives for peace," the "continued strengthening of the IDF," and cooperation with the United States. Its noteworthy difference from the positions of Labor and DMC was in the stress on "Israeli sovereignty between the Mediterranean and the Jordan; Eretz-Yisreal for the Jewish people."[30]

---

[28] *Jerusalem Post*, February 27, 1977.

[29] In an election ad published in the *Jerusalem Post* on May 5, 1977, the DMC said its program was one of: "Insisting that Jerusalem remain Israel's capital and the Jordan River her security border, and that Israel retain control of such territory west of the Jordan as is necessary to hold that border," and "Agreeing to only one Arab State between Israel and Jordan's eastern border, with its name, regime and character to be determined by its residents. The Palestinian national entity will find its expression in that state."

[30] The Likud platform's foreign policy and defense section contained, *inter alia*, the following planks: "B. Positive initiatives for peace—direct negotiations with

At the left end of the political spectrum were the Communists and the "doves" who built their campaigns around the need to end the Arab-Israeli conflict and to attain peace. Shelli, a new party formed by an alliance of the Independent Socialists, Moked, and Ha'olam Hazeh and including a faction of the Black Panthers and other small groups, presented as its leading candidates some of the most prominent doves in Israel (including Arieh "Lova" Eliav, Meir Pa'il, Uri Avneri, and Matityahu Peled). Its positions were distinctly different from those of the government and its mainstream opponents and followed the views of the Israeli Council for Israeli-Palestinian Peace. Shelli recognized "the national aspirations of the Palestinian Arab people" and noted that "Israel will negotiate a peace settlement with the neighboring Arab states, and with the recognized authoritative representatives of the Palestinian Arab people including the PLO, if necessary." Its view of the territories was: "Israel will . . . withdraw from the territories captured in the Six-Day War (with minor adjustments to be negotiated)."[31]

The Democratic Front for Peace and Equality included Rakah (New Communist party) and other left and Arab organizations and individuals. It was headed by Meir Wilner and Toufik Toubi of Rakah and Charlie Biton of the Black Panthers. It adopted a "peace platform" that advocated withdrawal from all the territories occupied in the 1967 war and the creation of an independent Palestinian state alongside Israel. It called for the immediate reconvening of the Geneva Peace Conference with the participation of all parties to the conflict including the PLO.[32]

The religious parties were further to the right. Agudat Israel, an

---

the Arab states without preconditions and without foreign directives. C. The continued strengthening of the IDF with weapons systems and training, together with the reduction and prevention of waste and inflated budgets. D. Establishing the relationship between Israel and the United States on the basis of cooperation while developing the awareness of the strategic importance of a strong Israel for the United States and the West." Likud platform, published in the *Jerusalem Post*, May 13, 1977.

The *Jerusalem Post*, March 2, 1977, reported the Likud position as "Judea and Samaria will not be yielded to foreign rule. Between the Mediterranean and the River Jordan there will be Israel sovereignty only." Eretz-Yisrael is Hebrew for Land of Israel. It is the usual Hebrew name for Palestine within its Mandatory boundaries.

[31] *Jerusalem Post Magazine*, May 13, 1977.

[32] Rakah (the Communist party of Israel), in an election statement, noted that "peace is possible" and proposed "a just and realistic peace plan; a solution to the Israeli-Arab conflict, and to the Palestinian question." The basis of its position was that Israel would withdraw to the lines of June 4, 1967. *Jerusalem Post*, February 3, 1977.

orthodox faction that emphasized religious issues, opposed withdrawal from the West Bank but indicated a willingness to accept withdrawal from the Sinai and the Golan Heights in exchange for peace. The National Religious party, which included Gush Emunim elements, opposed withdrawal from the West Bank.

Shlomzion, the party headed by Ariel Sharon, advocated an "annexationist" position (not too dissimilar to that of Likud) and called for the linkage of parties advocating similar views regarding the territories. The more peripheral parties whose focus was on other issues (such as civil rights) tended to adopt foreign policy positions compatible with those of the mainstream parties.

Although security and foreign policy were not central *issues* in the election, clearly they weighed on the minds of the electorate and affected the voting. It seemed generally agreed that the Labor government had not performed as well as expected and required since the October War. The post-1973 war malaise of the Israeli system and its full implications became clear only after the 1973 elections and damaged the image of the Labor party. Specific events just prior to the elections also had an impact. A report of the state comptroller issued at the end of April, in which he questioned the state of maintenance of equipment in the army and criticized waste and theft, raised doubts about IDF preparedness and about Labor's correction of the factors that had contributed to the problems of 1973. The matter was debated in the Knesset.[33] When an army helicopter crashed causing substantial loss of life, the episode seemed to be linked in the minds of voters to the comptroller's findings and to faults in Labor's management of the system.

Although not major issues, the questions of relations with and dependence on the United States and Israel's ability to withstand anticipated pressure from the United States figured from time to time in election speeches and advertisements. Carter's pronouncements concerning the Palestinian and territorial elements of an Arab-Israeli settlement raised some doubts about the direction and the content of American policy and its potential inimical impact on Israel. By early May, Israeli concerns about the U.S. role in an Arab-Israeli settlement and about arms supply by the United States to Israel were apparent, despite reassurances.[34]

---

[33] *New York Times, Washington Post*, May 3, 1977.

[34] In an article in the *New York Times*, June 17, 1977, former Foreign Minister Abba Eban attributed part of the blame for Labor's poor showing to Carter's policies.

267

The New Government

On May 17, 1977, Israel's electorate gave Likud the largest proportion of the vote (33.4 percent) and the largest number of seats in Parliament (forty-three). The Labor Alignment was reduced to 24.6 percent and thirty-two seats while the DMC secured 11.6 percent of the vote and fifteen seats. The National Religious party achieved twelve seats and 9.2 percent of the vote, and the other religious parties, Agudat Israel and Poalei Agudat Israel, won five seats with a combined 4.8 percent of the vote. Ariel Sharon's Shlomzion attained 1.9 percent of the vote and two seats. At the left end of the spectrum, the Democratic Front for Peace and Equality won 4.6 percent of the vote and five seats while Shelli won two seats and 1.6 percent of the vote. The remaining seats were secured by Flatto-Sharon (one), the Independent Liberals (one), Citizens' Rights (one), and the United Arab list (one).

Israel thus chose a new regime, of which the Likud bloc led by Menachem Begin emerged as the leading political force. Foreign and security policy must be given but a small share in explaining the reduction in support for Labor and the increase in Likud's position.[35] Despite this, the victory of Likud and Begin foreshadowed substantial change in the system, some of which would affect foreign and security policy. First, a new group, formerly confined to the opposition, would now be in control.[36] Likud was assigned the task of forming the government, defining its programs, and establishing the machinery to implement policy. Likud was not ready for this task, and there is evidence that it had not expected to incur the obligation.[37] Its personnel, with relatively few exceptions, lacked the experience of high-level government service which would have prepared them for effective leadership of the administrative bureaucracy. In part, this led to the practice of retaining in various government positions those who had served under the previous Labor governments.

---

[35] Begin would disagree. In an interview in *Newsweek*, May 30, 1977, p. 36, when asked which aspect of his program appealed most to the voters, he responded: "Our security policy, which has the support of the majority of our people. We said we cannot give up Judea and Samaria. If we gave it up, it would destroy our security, and all the cities of Israel would be within the range of enemy artillery."

[36] Although generally in opposition to the government, the parties constituting Likud had joined the government at the time of the 1967 war for a three-year period to form the "wall-to-wall" government of national unity which effectively excluded only the Communist parties. It withdrew from that coalition in a dispute over Israel's acceptance of United States Secretary of State Rogers's cease-fire initiative in June 1970.

[37] See Begin interview, *Newsweek*, May 30, 1977, p. 36.

Some modifications in foreign policy appeared likely. Begin had earned a reputation as a hard-liner, and his leading role in the Irgun in the 1940s, which the media played up following the election, associated him with terrorism. But the nature and extent of change remained uncertain. Begin was also seen as honest and decisive, an articulate advocate of his strongly held views. Strong leadership and decisive actions, especially in the field of foreign policy, seemed likely to characterize the Begin government. Outside Israel, his victory generated a wave of pessimism concerning the prospects for a settlement since Begin was viewed as a hawk, unyielding and rigid and somewhat doctrinaire.

Clearly, the government would have to formulate and execute its policy within the framework of popular opinion and in concert with the views of the newly elected Knesset. Israelis maintained a deep mistrust of Arab intentions, and many held the belief that the Arab states were committed to Israel's destruction. The PLO's reaffirmation of its Covenant earlier in the year reinforced Israeli fears. The overall Israeli perspective appeared to be one of great caution, and any government would be expected to yield as little as possible in exchange for as much as possible from the Arabs. Begin and Likud fit the bill very well.[38] Reflecting those views, the new Knesset appeared to hold a harder foreign policy line than its predecessor. The dovish Shelli party and the Communist Front had attained only seven seats. The remaining Knesset seats had gone to members who held views similar to Likud's on many of the central foreign policy and security issues.

Among the crucial postelection decisions of the new prime minister was his choice of a foreign minister. For this position, Begin chose former Defense Minister Moshe Dayan who was then a Labor party member of Parliament. Among the factors involved in the decision was that Dayan was well known abroad (and could provide an image abroad for the otherwise essentially unknown government) and held views similar (though not identical) to Begin's concerning the West Bank.[39] The nomination did, however, create quite a furor in Israel, and numerous objections to the appointment were raised. Israelis were concerned about Dayan's association with the difficulties

---

[38] Some suggested that Begin's hawkish stand might also facilitate relinquishing territories when necessary since, with his hard-line credentials, he could not be accused of weakness by the general population.

[39] Some observers suggested additional elements in the decision among which the more prominent were that Dayan was a "hero" to many American Jews, that American politicians thought well of him, that he knew how to talk to the Arabs, and that he would provide some flexibility in the government's West Bank positions.

encountered at the time of the October War and his role in the now defeated Labor Alignment. Members of the Labor party voiced resentment and concern, and the DMC's coalition talks with Likud were stalled as a result of the nomination. Despite the controversy, Begin held firm and Dayan became the foreign minister.[40]

Toward a New Policy

It was inevitable that foreign and security policy would become an early and prominent concern of the new government (no matter what the election results) given the centrality of the Arab-Israeli conflict in Israeli life and given the Carter administration's effort to achieve a settlement and to reconvene the Geneva Conference in 1977. Movement toward a settlement had begun before the election and its conclusion reopened the diplomatic effort. The pressures on the new government to adopt and articulate its positions on the central foreign policy issues were great, and over the initial months of the new government's tenure that position began to emerge. The issues which had been central to the election platforms of the major parties and which had figured in the Carter pronouncements on the Middle East also appeared as the main concerns of the Begin administration. These included the three major elements of the Arab-Israeli conflict (the definition of peace, territory and borders, and the Palestinians) and the nature of the relationship with the United States.

The Begin government—like the outgoing government, and indeed all Israeli governments before it—focused on the need to establish peace between itself and its neighbors. In presenting the government and its policies to the Knesset on June 21, 1977, Prime Minister Begin noted: "Our prime concern is prevention of a new war in the Middle East. I call upon King Hussein, President Sadat and President Assad to meet with me—whether in our capitals or on neutral soil, in public or away from the spotlights of publicity—in order to discuss the establishment of true peace between their countries and Israel."[41] This reiterated a position held by previous governments and placed the primary focus of the government on the need to achieve a true peace.[42] The definition of peace continued to include the end of war,

---

[40] On Dayan's willingness to leave the Labor party and join the Begin government see his interview in *New York Times*, June 5, 1977.

[41] In his first postelection statement, on May 18, Begin made a similar pronouncement concerning possible meetings with Hussein, Sadat, and Assad.

[42] In its presentation of the basic outline of government policies to the Knesset on June 21, 1977, the Begin government noted: "With the approach of the Geneva Conference and direct negotiations, the Government declares Israel's readiness

full reconciliation, and an open border across which people and goods could cross without hindrance. The government also indicated it was prepared to participate in the Geneva Conference if it reconvened.[43]

The question of borders was more complex. Its several components included the problem of Jerusalem, the extent of territory to be returned to Arab control, and the shape of Israel's final borders. In Israel's view, Jerusalem was not occupied territory. In a press conference on July 20, 1977, in Washington, Begin described his position in these terms: "We have a national consensus. In other words, all parties, except one, the Communist Party, which is completely subservient to Moscow, agree that Jerusalem should stay undivided and should be the capital city of the State of Israel."

On the broader question of occupied territories and withdrawals, the new government could rely on a general consensus opposing a return to the armistice lines of 1949 (which had existed until June 4, 1967, the outbreak of the Six-Day War). Total withdrawal from the occupied territories was thus ruled out. In an interview on "Issues and Answers" on May 22, 1977, Begin noted: "I would like to point out we have on this a national consensus"; only minor modification of the armistice lines, Israel would "reject unconditionally." Begin's assessment of the national consensus appears accurate. Although there was disagreement concerning the final lines to be established and the extent of compromise on territorial retention, none but the small dovish parties (Shelli and the Democratic Front for Peace and Equality) argued for full return of the territories occupied in the 1967 conflict.[44]

The focus of territorial disagreement was the West Bank (referred to by Israelis as Judea and Samaria). It was on this issue that there was a substantial difference between the Begin-Likud view,[45] which

to conduct the said negotiations in order to achieve a genuine, contractual, and workable peace which will bring about normalization of life in the region."

[43] See the government's outline of policy presented to the Knesset on June 21, 1977, and Dayan's press conference, August 9, 1977.

[44] Thus, for example, in an article in the New York Times, June 17, 1977, former Israeli foreign minister Abba Eban, while critical of the Israeli parliamentary majority which opposed territorial compromise in the West Bank, noted the basis of the Israeli consensus on territory and security in these terms: ". . . no vision of a secure Israeli society can be realized within the perilous straitjacket of the pre-1967 lines. Demilitarization, security agreements, a balance of deterrent strength and international support can reduce the need for changes in the previous lines under a peace settlement, but cannot eliminate that need totally. If American policy espouses the June 4, 1967 lines, it loses contact with the most moderate possible consensus in the Israeli political system."

[45] It should be noted that Likud is actually a bloc of parties which do not hold totally identical views on all issues. Some elements of Likud (especially those

opposed relinquishing territory, and the compromise views articulated by Labor and the DMC.[46] Begin's position was rather specific:

> I believe that Judea and Samaria are an integral part of our sovereignty. It's our land. It was occupied by Abdullah [King of Jordan] against international law, against our inherent right. It was liberated during the 6-day war when we used our right of national self-defense, and so it should be. . . . You annex foreign land. You don't annex your own country. It is our land. You don't annex it.[47]

In its presentation of the basic outline of the government's policy to the Knesset on June 21, 1977, the new administration described its view in these terms: "The Jewish people has an eternal historic right to the Land of Israel. The inalienable legacy of our Forefathers. The Government shall plan, create and encourage urban and rural settlements on the soil of the homeland."[48] In an impromptu news conference immediately after his election victory, Begin, while noting that he would negotiate Israeli withdrawal in Sinai and the Golan Heights for peace, was adamant about the West Bank and the Gaza Strip: "What occupied territories? If you mean Judea, Samaria and the Gaza Strip, these are liberated territories and an integral part of the land of Israel."[49] But Begin has also reiterated and increasingly focused

---

from the former Liberal party) hold views on the territories which are closer to those of Labor and the DMC than to those of the Herut wing of Likud. In the following discussion, the view identified as Likud is that articulated by Begin and the government after the election.

[46] The nonidentity of DMC and Likud-Begin views concerning the West Bank was clearly indicated in the terms governing the DMC's entry into the government coalition in October 1977: "The DMC will retain freedom of expression and freedom to abstain in the Knesset on political matters relating to Judea and Samaria. . . . The Knesset Foreign Affairs and Defense Committee will have the final say on settlement, if a DMC cabinet member demands a debate there." *Jerusalem Post International Edition*, October 25, 1977, p. 3. For further elaboration of the DMC position and the coalition negotiations, see Naomi Shepherd, "Yadin's DMC— A New Force," *Present Tense*, vol. 5 (Autumn 1977), pp. 31–37.

[47] Begin on "Issues and Answers," May 22, 1977.

[48] An important and special feature of the government's policy outline was the following provision: "The Knesset has legally empowered the Government to extend by decree the State's law, jurisdiction, and administration over the entire area of the Land of Israel as shall be specified in the decree. This legal and parliamentary authority is at the Government's discretion. It shall not be implemented so long as negotiations over peace agreements are being conducted between Israel and its neighbors. It shall involve the selection of a suitable time, the Government's political consideration, a special debate in the Knesset and approval by the Knesset."

[49] *Washington Star*, May 18, 1977.

on the more conventional and central, and more generally accepted, security argument: that the West Bank is a strategic area from which enemy forces could place all of Israel's major cities within the range of their artillery[50] and which has great military importance for Israel. Any adjustments in borders would have to reflect this factor, in the view of Israel's parliamentary majority.

Closely related is the establishment of Israeli settlements in the occupied territories and their future status. The Labor governments, between 1967 and 1977, generally tried to limit settlements to those that could serve a security function and sought to avoid conflict between the settlements and the local Arab populations (thus, settlements were generally established in areas with relatively small Arab populations). There were, however, exceptions to this approach, and some settlements, such as Kiryat Arba at Hebron, were established for a combination of ideological, religious, traditional, and historical reasons.

The Begin government has deviated from this policy in that settlements in Judea and Samaria have not been restricted to those that are primarily security oriented. Likud doctrine considers Judea and Samaria integral parts of Eretz-Yisrael and views settlement as a natural and inalienable Jewish right in all of Eretz-Yisrael. Thus, settlements could be established irrespective of their usefulness for security.[51] Elsewhere (for example in the Sinai and the Golan Heights —areas not historically part of Eretz-Yisrael) settlements are established primarily for defense and security reasons. In the first instance, apart from their security aspect, settlements reaffirm a claim to Jewish sovereignty in Eretz-Yisrael, while in the latter they help establish a claim to defensible borders. It was in support of this principle that on July 26, 1977, the Begin government recognized three previously illegal Israeli settlements on the West Bank (Kadum, Ofra, and Maale Adumim) as permanent legal entities. This decision was criticized by President Carter and Secretary of State Vance, who viewed the settlements as obstacles to peace and contrary to interna-

---

[50] "Then there is a question of our national security. If we should withdraw from Judea and Samaria, please understand, everybody should have a look, a glimpse at the map. All our cities and towns would be in the range of the conventional artillery provided by the Soviet Union to the Palestinian State and the range of that artillery now is 43 kilometers, 900 meters. Not only Jerusalem would be in crossfire, even Tel Aviv, Rehovot, Beersheba. All our civilian towns, all the civilian population. It is just inconceivable that we should agree to such a mortal danger to our mothers and sisters and women and children." Begin on "Issues and Answers," May 22, 1977.

[51] See Moshe Dayan's statement to the Knesset on September 1, 1977.

tional law.[52] Begin defended the decision and rejected U.S. criticism: "We left no doubt in our talks [in Washington] about our position. Jews have the right to live anywhere in Judea and Samaria and the Gaza Strip."[53]

The Palestinian question was another subject on which substantial consensus had long existed in Israel. Palestinian terrorism was viewed as a threat to be dealt with by Israel's security and defense forces. There was no significant division of opinion in Israel's political mainstream on this question. There was also general and continuing agreement that the refugee issue was a humanitarian problem that must be resolved. Views on this question had not significantly changed; Foreign Minister Dayan expressed the basic position in these terms: "We wish we could achieve a real peace treaty with all the Arab countries around us and the solution for the refugees, the Arab refugees and compensation to the Jewish refugees."[54] He suggested that the solution to the Arab refugee problem was to be found in their being "settled in the Arab countries where they are" and not in the founding of a separate Palestinian state.

The broadest and most articulate consensus in the Israeli system continued to revolve around the question of a Palestinian state and the PLO: Israel would not participate in discussions with the PLO and would not agree to the establishment of an independent Palestinian state on the West Bank and in the Gaza Strip. Israel's refusal to deal with the PLO was based on its perception of the nature and purpose of that organization, which it saw as committed to the destruction of Israel. The Palestinian National Covenant, its ideological charter, states that the creation of Israel is "null and void" and expresses implacable hostility to the existence of Israel, even in its pre-1967 borders. Dayan summarized the government's position in a statement to the Knesset on September 1, 1977, in these terms:

> The stand of the Government of Israel vis-à-vis the PLO is clear and explicit. We oppose both U.S. dialogue with the PLO and that organization's participation in the peace conference for two reasons: first, the PLO's murderous essence and nature and its rejection of Israel's very existence; second, the Geneva Conference is one conducted between

---

[52] See Vance's statement quoted in the *Washington Post*, July 27, 1977, and Carter's press conference on July 28, 1977. There is debate about the legality of Israel's settlements in the occupied territories.

[53] *Washington Star*, July 27, 1977.

[54] Dayan on "Issues and Answers," October 9, 1977.

States and its objective is to bring about the signing of peace treaties between States, and not with any organization which is not a State.[55]

Rather than deal with the PLO, Israel preferred the participation of Palestinian Arabs who were not members of the PLO, within the Jordanian delegation at a reconvened Geneva Peace Conference.[56] Israel viewed the establishment of a PLO-dominated state on the West Bank as but a prelude to an eventual and inevitable effort to destroy Israel.[57] Such a state was seen as not viable, a spawning ground for radicalism. Thus, in Israel's view, it would not solve the Palestinian problem but would pose a danger to Israel. Foreign Minister Moshe Dayan summed up the Israeli position on "Issues and Answers" on October 9, 1977, by saying, "We shall not discuss a Palestinian state, in whatever manner it will be presented. We shall just not go in negotiating about it and we shall not sit down with the representatives of the PLO." Israel's views concerning a Palestinian state are very deeply held and generate a position on which Israel is apparently prepared to confront even the United States. Dayan has articulated this quite clearly:

If the U.S. insists on a Palestinian state, I think that any Israeli Government would reject it. And if we have to make the choice tomorrow of what to do—have a breach with the U.S. . . . . or accept a Palestinian state—we would rather have these problems with the U.S. than agree to a Palestinian state, which we seriously think would eventually bring the destruction of Israel.[58]

Dayan's reference to the United States and the possibility of a United States–Israel "problem" concerning the PLO also suggests the importance of the United States–Israel relationship.

---

[55] In an interview on "Issues and Answers," May 22, 1977, Begin was asked whether there were any conditions under which the PLO could participate in Geneva and responded: "Not at all. They cannot participate in the negotiations. They have a so-called Palestinian charter in which they say in Article 19 that the formation of the State of Israel is null and void from its inception. What are we going to negotiate with them? The destruction of the State of Israel? That is absolutely absurd. So they are not partners to our problems." See also Begin's press conference in Washington on July 20, 1977.

[56] See Begin's press conference on July 20, 1977, in Washington and Dayan's press conference of August 9, 1977.

[57] In an interview in *Newsweek*, October 17, 1977, p. 33, Dayan said that the PLO's "aim and target is to destroy Israel" and a Palestinian state on the West Bank "would be just his [Yasir Arafat's] base for an attack against Israel."

[58] *Newsweek*, October 17, 1977, p. 33.

The relationship with the United States continued to be seen as crucial after the elections. In his speech to the Knesset presenting the new government and the outlines of its policy on June 21, 1977, Begin noted: "We shall endeavour to deepen the friendship between ourselves and the United States of America." But that task was complicated by the Carter administration's dismay at Begin's victory, which in its view appeared to slow the timetable for movement toward Geneva and a settlement.

The Carter administration began its Arab-Israeli initiative in January 1977 on the assumption that the time was propitious for such an effort. Over the succeeding months, the specifics of the U.S. conception of a settlement became more clear, and these seemed to conflict with Israeli perceptions and policies. The process was well underway by the time of the Israeli elections—Secretary of State Vance had visited the Middle East and regional leaders had met with Carter. Elements of the President's concept of a settlement—involving the definition and assurance of permanent peace, territory and borders, and the Palestinian issue—had already been made public. The Carter approach had been based, in part, on the assumption that the Labor party would win the election, and the ascendancy of Likud seemed to put this approach in jeopardy. The response was cautious —a "wait and see" attitude was adopted and a hiatus in U.S. diplomacy was assured. But the administration sought to put the best face on the victory and spoke in somewhat optimistic terms about the results. President Carter said he hoped "that the election of Mr. Begin will not be a step backward toward the achievement of peace."[59] Begin's initial statements following the election suggested areas of possible contention, as various Likud positions contrasted sharply with those of the United States. Begin visited the United States in mid July. The purposes of the visit were manifold, but the crucial items on the agenda included the establishment of personal rapport between the new prime minister and President Carter and substantive discussion of the elements of the settlement. Their meetings occasioned no substantive changes in the policies of either power, but they appeared to have laid a foundation for mutual confidence. Carter and Begin appeared optimistic as a result of their meetings.[60]

---

[59] *Washington Post*, May 22, 1977.

[60] In his press conference in Washington on July 20, Begin noted: "I think I can say that we established a personal rapport . . . I can assure and reassure all the friends of Israel and of America there isn't any confrontation between our two countries. To the contrary, during the last few days, friendship between the United States and Israel has been deepened. And that personal rapport between the President and myself will be helpful in the future."

Nevertheless, conflict soon followed on the issues of settlements in occupied territories and Palestinian representation at Geneva.

In September, the United States sought to attain agreement on a method for Palestinian representation at Geneva, and the concept of a unified Arab delegation including Egypt, Syria, Jordan, Lebanon, and the Palestinians, to participate opposite an Israeli delegation, was put forward. Toward the end of September, the Israeli cabinet agreed to this suggestion, but Dayan made it clear that this did not alter Israel's view of the PLO. Israel insisted that Palestinians could participate in the unified Arab delegation provided that they were not members of the PLO and were part of a Jordanian delegation. No negotiations would take place with the Arab delegation as such. After the opening ceremonial session, the Arab group would split up into delegations representing the various Arab states for negotiations. There would also be no change in United Nations Security Council Resolution 242 (1967).

In October, Israel and the United States clashed again. The subject was the joint United States–Soviet Union statement of October 1, 1977, which Israel strongly opposed because of the increased involvement of the Soviet Union and the reference in the document to the "legitimate rights of the Palestinian people," which seemed to imply a PLO role in the negotiating process and the establishment of a separate Palestinian state. To address these issues, a United States-Israeli "working paper" which dealt with reconvening the Geneva Conference was devised by Carter, Vance, and Dayan during a meeting in New York in early October. The working paper did not signal any major changes in Israel's position on the substantive issues.[61] Israel and the United States were not in agreement on the precise role of the Palestinians (especially the PLO) in the settlement process, the concept of a Palestinian homeland, the extent of Israeli withdrawal from the occupied territories, and the shape of Israel's final borders. But, the working paper and various statements by President Carter and other senior U.S. officials over the ensuing weeks tended to reassure the Israelis and seemed to reduce the tension in the relationship which had developed following Begin's visit to Washington in July.[62]

---

[61] Text available in *New York Times*, October 14, 1977.

[62] The working paper was sent to the Arabs for their consideration as a means of attaining the proposed Geneva Conference. The agreement seemed to be that a reconvened Geneva Conference was appropriate but the procedural aspects of the conference and the agenda, as well as the details of the substantive positions, remained uncertain and disputed.

Prospects

The election of 1977 brought Menachem Begin to the post of prime minister for the first time and in so doing terminated, at least temporarily, the rule of the Labor party in Israeli politics. This presaged changes and shifts in the foreign and security policies of Israel, which slowly took shape in the first months after the election. Begin emerged as a decisive and popular leader with strongly held and firmly implemented views—in sharp contrast to his immediate predecessor, Yitzhak Rabin. Israeli foreign policy acquired a new style. At the same time, the substance of policy had some new elements, especially with regard to the West Bank and the Gaza Strip and the linkage of the Jews of Israel (and their foreign policy) with the historic Eretz-Yisrael. Although some areas of policy were not carefully delineated, the foreign policy position of the new government was quite clear. Despite some discord on specifics, there developed a wide-ranging consensus on the central issues that seemed to permeate the overwhelming majority of the Knesset and of popular opinion: no return to the lines of June 4, 1967, no negotiations with the PLO, and no independent Palestinian state on the West Bank. The various strands seemed to coalesce by the fall of 1977 and to provide a more precise basis for the future policies of the new government. Given the existing situation, it appeared that these positions could serve over an extended period. Then in November—after the efforts to reconvene the Geneva Conference seemed to have reached an impasse with the Arabs' refusal to accept the United States–Israel working paper— Egyptian President Anwar Sadat made his historic visit to Israel.

Sadat's trip set in motion a series of events that gave new momentum to the effort to achieve an Arab-Israeli settlement. In so doing, it raised questions and unleashed substantial debate concerning the future foreign and security policies of the Israeli government and its main parliamentary opponents. It also seemed likely to generate some change. Israel's positions had not been tested previously in direct negotiations with the Arabs, so the extent and nature of change in such a situation was uncertain. Israeli policy would be modified to accommodate the new situation, and the existing government policies provided the consensus from which new positions might develop, the starting point for Israel's negotiators in any effort to reach a settlement. Their modification would depend on the nature of the circumstances under which they would be tested, and until such negotiations took place the maximal positions seemed likely to remain essentially constant.

In the wake of the Sadat visit, there developed an awareness in Israel that some action concerning policy on the Arab-Israeli conflict and related issues was needed. The past luxury of avoiding detailed and specific policy positions because of the refusal of the Arab states to negotiate directly with Israel was altered by the Sadat visit and the ensuing effort to maintain a dialogue. Clearly, the new situation required extensive discussions within the government (as well as in Parliament and in the public arena) to determine the specifics of the position Israel should adopt. Israel had to be ready to enter the negotiating process and thus it had to determine what its final positions would be and whether or not to accept Arab negotiating positions and offers. Dayan urged Israel to reevaluate its positions in the light of the Sadat overture so that a dialogue could be maintained and peace pursued.[63] He suggested that Israel would soon have to decide on its final positions concerning the various elements of the conflict so that it could enter the bargaining process. The opposition generally agreed with the government that a time of decision had begun. As Abba Eban, then an opposition member of Parliament, put it, "A discussion that has been rhetorical, semantic, procedural—a ten-year exercise in prenegotiation—will soon be focused not on words and gestures, but on concrete things."[64]

In response to Sadat's visit and his speech to the Knesset, Israel's political leaders generally rearticulated the main elements of the national consensus concerning the concept of peace, the problems of defensible borders, withdrawal from the occupied territories, the rejection of a Palestinian state, and the role of the PLO. At the same time, there was an increased expression of the need for peace and the willingness to negotiate and to make hard decisions and agree to compromise in order to achieve peace. While the foreign policy posture devised in the wake of the 1977 election identified Israel's negotiating position and its basic concerns and demands, the eventual policy would be a variant determined in the negotiating process. Clearly, Israel was prepared to bargain, as Begin noted in his response to Sadat's Knesset speech: "I suggest, and this is in the name of a majority in this Parliament, that we shall discuss and negotiate about every point. . . . Everything must be negotiated and can be negotiated. No side will say the contrary. No side will present preliminary conditions."

---

[63] This was the main theme of a Dayan press conference broadcast on Israel Television's "Moked" program, November 23, 1977, and widely reported throughout the world.

[64] Abba Eban, "Israel's Hour of Decision," *New York Times*, November 22, 1977.

To initiate the negotiating process Israel proposed plans for the Sinai Peninsula and for the West Bank and Gaza Strip that reflected its existing position and its continued deep mistrust of Arab intentions while making modifications in response to the changed environment generated by the Sadat initiative.[65]

In Sinai there would be demilitarization, from the Gidi and Mitla passes to the old international frontier. Between the Suez Canal and the passes there would be limited Egyptian forces. Israeli settlements in Sinai would remain and would be defended by an Israeli force. During a transition period of a few years Israel would maintain a defense line in Sinai, including air bases and an early warning mechanism. This defense line would remain until the withdrawal of forces to the international frontier. Freedom of navigation in the Tiran Straits, which was a cause of war in 1967, and the ability of Israel to reach the port of Eilat at the head of the Gulf of Aqaba must be assured either by joint Israeli-Egyptian forces or by a United Nations force whose removal would be impossible without the agreement of both sides and a unanimous United Nations Security Council decision.

For Judea and Samaria (the West Bank) and the Gaza district, Israel proposed the end of the military government and the establishment of administrative autonomy by and for the residents. The residents would elect an administrative council (by general, direct, personal, equal, and secret ballot), which would administer all activities (such as education, religious affairs, transportation, agriculture, health, labor, and social welfare) relating to those territories except for security and public order. All residents would be able to choose to become citizens of Jordan or of Israel. In various matters Jordan and Israel would cooperate in such areas as legislative activity. Israeli residents would be allowed to settle and to acquire land in the territories. Freedom of movement and freedom of economic activity for residents of Israel and of the territories would be assured. Israel argued that although it had a claim of sovereignty in Judea, Samaria, and Gaza, it realized that other claims exist, and thus suggested that the matter of sovereignty be left open for the sake of agreement and peace. Access to the holy places in Jerusalem would be guaranteed in

---

[65] For the English texts of the Israeli plans for the West Bank and the Gaza Strip, as read by Prime Minister Begin to the Israeli Parliament on December 28, 1977, and the outline of Israel's views concerning Sinai, see *New York Times* and *Washington Post*, December 29, 1977.

a special proposal to be drawn up. Israel also proposed that this be reviewed after five years.[66]

Israel saw its plans as departures from its previous posture, as positive responses to the Sadat initiative, and as a basis for further negotiations. But negotiations did not continue. Sadat withdrew his representatives from the political discussions in Jerusalem and the military talks ceased. The process seemed to come to a halt in the spring of 1978, although it was resumed under United States auspices in England in July. Then in September, the United States succeeded in convening a meeting of President Carter, President Sadat, and Prime Minister Begin at Camp David.

The Sadat visit and the talks that followed, the Carter approach and U.S. efforts to achieve a settlement, the Begin election and the policies of the new government combined to generate, in 1978, some malaise within the Israeli system concerning its direction, leadership, and policy. Although a national consensus existed on Israel's policy on the central issues of the conflict, there was clearly disagreement on specifics and on the tactics to be employed. These generated public concern and debates within the government and in Parliament. There was a feeling that perhaps this opportunity might be lost or that Israel's position, and its relationship with the United States, might deteriorate further. The critical attitude of Israel's doves concerning Begin's approach found some support in the Labor opposition and in the views of some members of the government. Public concern was manifest in demonstrations and rallies which took place in an effort to influence government policy. In this context, the Camp David summit gave Begin an opportunity to reaffirm the basic lines of Israeli policy and to develop new approaches.

The 1977 elections brought to power a government with different personalities, new viewpoints and policies, and a decisive leadership. This would have presaged change even if Sadat had not launched his initiative and if Carter had not focused U.S. policy on resolving the Arab-Israeli conflict. It was the new negotiating situation, however, that eventually provided the occasion for a modification in Israel's

---

[66] In response to questions posed by the United States concerning the decisions to be taken following the five-year period, Israel's cabinet decided on June 18, 1978, in part: "The Government of Israel agrees that five years after the application of the administrative autonomy in Judea, Samaria and the Gaza District, which will come into force upon the establishment of peace, the nature of the future relations between the parties will be considered and agreed upon at the suggestion of any of the parties." Embassy of Israel, Washington, D.C., "Policy Background: Israel's Reply to Questions Posed by the U.S. Concerning Israel's Peace Plan," June 20, 1978, p. 1.

foreign policy beyond that anticipated at the time of the elections. Egypt significantly altered its position, and the United States, playing its indispensable diplomatic/political role, brought about the Camp David summit. In response to these developments (more than in response to domestic circumstances or the election results), Israel modified its position concerning Sinai and, to a lesser extent, the West Bank and the Gaza Strip. Clearly, between May 1977 and September 1978, Israeli foreign policy entered a new phase. From a broader perspective, however, the novelty of this phase was less profound than its continuity. The Arab-Israeli conflict and the United States-Israel relationship remained the focal points of Israeli policy, and on these points the national consensus reaffirmed in 1977 was still intact.

11
Conclusion

Asher Arian

How would the Knesset elections of 1977 be viewed if we could analyze them with the perspective of years rather than months? Which changes would appear significant and which ephemeral?

Social science is sometimes accused of having a conservative bias because many writers describe the present as the inexorable result of the past. If philosophers tell us what a better world would be like, social scientists seem to explain why it cannot be attained. One reason for this is that—with the possible exception of that brought by revolutions and wars—social change is incremental rather than abrupt.

The major result of the 1977 elections was the replacing of the Labor Alignment by the Likud as the governing party after twenty-nine years of Labor hegemony. But beyond that simple fact based on the election results a whole range of questions arises regarding the Israeli political system. What caused the shift and what resulted from it? Did the shift change the nature of Israel's political system? Did it become less ideological, less hierarchical? Was the 1977 election a deviation from the norm of Labor superiority or does it presage the rise of a new dominant party, a system of rotation, or perhaps an era of less stable coalitions? In what sense will the second generation of Israeli politics differ from the first?

A Realigning Electoral Era

It is impossible to point to any one factor as the cause of Labor's loss in 1977. The important thing is the process of decline rather than the moment of defeat, and to this many factors contributed, each of them gaining strength over time. It is inappropriate to speak of a critical election. In a dominant-party system such as Israel's until 1977, many forces had to work in coordination to bring about change.

Over the years, the parties had been partially successful in ensuring the perpetuation of their power in spite of electoral change. The basic fact remains, however, that parties in democratic systems are vulnerable to shifts in electoral behavior, and while Israeli politics gave the appearance of being stable, the relative strength of the parties actually shifted greatly. Mapai was always first, the National Religious party always strong enough to add its Knesset seats to the governing coalition. But voting behavior was much less stable, and the fate of any given candidate was determined by his place on the party list.

What proved to be much more stable than the fate of any given party was the performance of a given party grouping. That is, until the 1970s the variation in the vote for the labor camp or the nonlabor camp or the religious parties was very small indeed.[1] Parties of the left (including the Communists) never won fewer than 64 or more than 69 seats in the 120-seat Knesset. The center and right parties ranged between 27 and 34 and the religious parties between 15 and 18. For the 1949–1969 period, the average deviation for the labor grouping (excluding the Communists) was one percentage point. The average deviation for the center-and-right and religious groupings was even lower: 0.8 and 0.6, respectively. The disparity between the stability of the grouping and the variable strength of individual parties within the grouping was great.

Campbell has classified presidential elections in the United States as maintaining elections, deviating elections, and realigning elections.[2] Using a notion of a "normal" division of the vote and an extended time perspective, he concludes that most presidential elections in the last hundred years have maintained the pattern of partisan attachment prevailing in the preceding period. In a deviating election, short-term forces bring about the defeat of the majority party, but the basic division of party loyalties is not seriously disturbed. In a realigning election (or a critical election, in Key's phrase), a new party balance is created. The election of Roosevelt in 1932 in the depths of the Great Depression is a dramatic example of a critical election; the realignment of party forces that it revealed has allowed the Democratic party to maintain a majority position in the United States for more than forty years.

---

[1] See H. Smith, "Analysis of Voting," in Asher Arian, ed., *The Elections in Israel—1969* (Jerusalem: Jerusalem Academic Press, 1972), pp. 63–80.

[2] Angus Campbell, "A Classification of the Presidential Elections," in Angus Campbell, Philip Converse, Warren Miller, and Donald Stokes, *Elections and the Political Order* (New York: Wiley, 1966), pp. 63–77.

Key characterized an election as critical when "more or less profound readjustments occur in the relations of power within the community, and in which new and durable election groupings are formed."[3] Many thought that the 1973 war could be seen as a turning point in Israeli politics since it shattered so many myths and previously held conceptions. The publication of the 1973 election results soon after the war provided a rare opportunity to compare the voting behavior of large segments of the population. Since much of the population was serving in the army on election day, the results were especially informative, for the army is rather homogeneous in its composition—predominantly young and male (although women and the not-so-young are also represented).

If the experience of the 1973 war was to have had far-reaching effects in the future, it would have been best to search for signs of these effects in those groups that were most directly involved in the war and those whose political beliefs and partisan attachments were still relatively flexible. If the army went Likud by a large majority, we might interpret the war as a shared experience of the generation then reaching maturity which would have an impact on the politics of the future. The new tendency would be different from the dominant one in the previous generation; the younger generation, which comprised a larger share of the electorate and was raising its children in a new climate of opinion, would eventually come to prevail.[4]

The election results did not indicate that the voters behaved very differently on election day from the way they had behaved before. The army results gave the Likud 41.28 percent of the vote, as opposed to 39.54 percent for the Alignment.[5] In the general population, the division was 30.2 percent and 39.6 percent, respectively. It is true that the Likud outpaced the Alignment in the army returns. But even before the war it was well known that the Likud was strong among younger voters. The Alignment won from the army voters the same share as it did from the general population. Using this indicator, it was inappropriate to conclude that the 1973 elections were critical; at most, tendencies already in process were accelerated as a result of the war.

If critical elections "are likely to increase the political polariza-

---

[3] V. O. Key, Jr., "A Theory of Critical Elections," *Journal of Politics*, vol. 17, 1955, p. 4.

[4] David O. Sears, "Political Behavior," in Gardner Lindzey and Elliot Aronson, eds., *The Handbook of Social Psychology*, vol. 5 (Reading, Mass.: Addison-Wesley, 1969), esp. pp. 370–399.

[5] *Ma'ariv*, January 7, 1974.

tion of important segments of the electorate,"[6] then the 1973 elections were not critical. There was no clear large-scale shift of group allegiances from one party to another. Previous patterns were accelerated; no new polarization was obvious.

In a dominant party system, it may be more useful to discuss a "realigning electoral era"[7] than a critical election. During such an era, the dominant party's electoral support slips from its grasp. Duverger pointed out that each period tends to have a doctrine that is dominant.[8] A dominant party identifies itself with the doctrines, ideas, methods, and style of the epoch. As time passes, as the "dominant doctrines" shift, the power base of the dominant party might well be eroded. No one act, or failure, is enough to explain this decline. If the dominant party fails to be attentive to changes in the dominant doctrine of the period, or is unable to adjust to such changes, its position may be weakened. Structural rigidity, vested interests, or the inability of the leadership to perceive change may hamper its response. If the dominant party does not keep in tune with the dominant mood, it can only decline.

Labor's epoch was clearly the independence era, which culminated in 1948 with the establishment of the state. The fact that Labor had difficulty in attracting the votes of the young—the generation that had grown up since independence—indicated a partial short-circuiting of the party's claim to dominance. This decline was evident in the voting results.

The 1977 elections ended the realigning era by deposing the dominant party. As we would expect in a dominant-party system, the opposition itself did little to depose the ruling party. The Likud's strength increased steadily; demographic and ideological forces were harnessed behind it. The Alignment's greatest loss was to the Democratic Movement for Change. Alignment votes that went to the DMC determined the fall of the Alignment and the rise of the Likud. It may be that in future elections the Alignment will win again, but it will not automatically regain its position of dominance. Dominance is a set of power relations, and a state of mind. Dominance is difficult to deny to the party that has it, and extremely hard to rewin for the party that has lost it.

The four years between the 1973 war and the 1977 elections served as a period of incubation for many of the problems of the

---

[6] Campbell, "Classification," pp. 75–76.

[7] Ibid., p. 75.

[8] Maurice Duverger, *Political Parties* (New York: Wiley, 1963), p. 307.

Labor party. By 1977, the cancer was fully developed and it took its fatal toll. The processes that accompanied this growth were complex; some of them deserve further exploration.

The Political Party

Since well before the founding of the state the political party has been the major force in Israeli political life. It was the political party that led, educated, housed, and defended the immigrants who came before and immediately after the founding of the state. The labor movement was preeminent in these activities—and especially Mapai—but other parties also developed programs to fill basic needs unattainable through the mandatory power or from the infant state bureaucracy. Concomitantly, organizational structures developed which would facilitate these operations and help determine the central role to be played by the parties and their functionaries in the political battles of the years to come.

By the 1960s the party system began to change. One problem faced was generational: the sons of the founders—Moshe Dayan being the clearest example—were pushing for positions of leadership at the same time that the older generation, exemplified by David Ben-Gurion, was becoming weary. The tensions involved in this conflict surfaced eventually with the breaking away of Rafi from Mapai in 1965. The Lavon affair—the failure of a security mission in 1954 and the controversy over the investigations stemming from it—again became a live issue, but problems of political succession were also evident. After a dozen years of independence, charisma had given way to routine and the party activists who had spent so many years in the background suddenly found themselves competing for the starring roles.

The Israeli method of electing the Knesset—a proportional-representation system with fixed lists presented by political parties or other political groupings—was a carry-over from pre-state days. The voter could indicate the party of his choice, but he was unlikely to have any influence in determining that party's list of candidates. This situation led to a strengthening of party discipline since the candidate had to please the party bosses in order to retain his position. But it also made the candidate's political future very insecure; a drop in public support might cost him his job even if he was thoroughly liked (or disliked, or unknown, as the case may be) by the voters of his party.

The Israeli political system developed a unique way of adapting to these difficult circumstances. Multiparty blocs appeared which fit the situation perfectly. These blocs (or alignments) reduced intra-bloc competition and made the political future of the leadership more secure. Not only that, the creation of these blocs allowed for a loosening of the tight ideological rhetoric that had characterized Israeli politics for so long. In order to achieve ideological consensus, vaguer formulations were necessary. Yet the ideological nature of Israeli politics could be retained in the more intimate statements of the parties to their membership. An additional layer of political affiliation was added to the fabric of Israeli politics: this allowed the parties to retain rigid ideological forms of communication while at the same time developing more pliable ones; it reinforced the symbol of immediate party identification for the members while widening the appeal of the party beyond the committed; and it secured the future of the ruling elite by largely removing the uncertainty inherent in the democratic process.

A good case in point is the history of the Liberal party, formerly known as the General Zionists. This centrist, bourgeois party had had its ups and downs. In the first elections in 1949 it won seven seats and in the next elections in 1951 it jumped up to twenty. It fell to thirteen in 1955 and back to eight in 1959. In 1961 the General Zionists merged with the Progressives, and together as the Liberal party they won seventeen seats. Before the 1965 elections that merger broke down, the former Progressives emerging as the Independent Liberals (independent of the Liberal party) with the former General Zionists retaining the name of the Liberal party. It was at this point that the post-split Liberals formed a bloc with the Herut movement, Gahal, which competed in both 1965 and 1969. In both elections Gahal won twenty-six seats. By 1973 the bloc was enlarged to include other groups (especially former members of the Labor camp) and it won thirty-nine seats. In 1977 the Likud was formed as a slightly enlarged bloc retaining the same basic partners. It emerged the victor, winning forty-three seats.

What is important for our purposes is to note that the last time the Liberals stood for election on their own was in 1961. How well they would do today standing on their own is a moot question, but it should be noted that analyses of the Likud electorate indicate that it includes far more Herut-type voters (Israelis of Asian or African origin, for instance) and far fewer of the Liberal type (upper-middle class). The question is also politically irrelevant since as a result of the 1977 vote the Liberal party was successful in placing fourteen of its members in the Knesset. Estimates are that were they to run alone they would place fewer. Proportional representation in this case means reflecting the bargaining positions of the parties comprising the bloc rather than their relative weight in the electorate as a whole.

This process of alignment is not the monopoly of the nonsocialist camp. Mapam, for instance, has done very well using this method. Aligned with the Labor party since 1969, Mapam has regularly won eight seats since it last stood for elections alone in 1965. In the three elections before, it had won nine seats (1955, 1959, 1961) following a split with the Achdut Ha'avoda faction in the early 1950s. Mapam did not do well in 1977, but this reflected the general decline of the Labor Alignment. It seems doubtful whether it would have fared better running alone.

The primacy of the party is especially evident in its contacts with its members. There the party can be adamant, ideological, principled. Between parties, arrangements of mutual satisfaction are worked out. Ideological pronouncements must be adjusted so as to emphasize agreement and minimize conflict. Formulae for the distribution of seats, patronage, and power must also be devised. To give but one example: the Likud agreement for Tel Aviv stipulates that the Liberal party will nominate the Likud candidate for mayor but allows Herut the right to veto the candidate. Obviously the bargaining process in a case like this encompasses more than just the qualifications of the Liberal party's candidate for the post of mayor.

Nationalization of Services

Another factor that greatly weakened the Labor party over the years was the progressive nationalization of social services which began immediately after the founding of the state.[9] From the beginning of the British mandate in 1919 until independence in 1948 almost all services were provided by particularistic groups, the political parties, or the federation of labor unions (the Histadrut). Even national organizations such as the Jewish Agency of the World Zionist Organization were under the effective control of the labor parties, and especially Mapai. No state apparatus existed to solve the problems of an immigrant society being formed in an indifferent and sometimes hostile environment.

The party benefited from this situation. First, it provided a ready outlet for the ideological energy that many brought to the country. Settlement, agriculture, absorbing immigrants, providing jobs, schooling, housing, and medical care all advanced the goal of building a

[9] See Amitai Etzioni, "The Decline of Neo-Feudalism: The Case of Israel," *Comparative Public Administration.*

Jewish homeland. Second, these activities justified the political organization and the recruitment of members in the eyes of the activists and their supporters. A system of indirect membership was developed whereby membership in the party automatically afforded membership in the Histadrut. The fact that the same set of leaders controlled both organizations furthered the flexibility and control of these leaders. The pattern of interlocking directorships ensured power, the high rates of membership assured income to the party and support on the part of the membership.

Ben-Gurion was the personification of the system of interlocking directorships. He headed Mapai and was secretary general of the Histadrut almost uninterruptedly from its founding until 1935, when he became head of the Jewish Agency which has been characterized as a government in the making. His conception of the proper role of each organization was largely determined by the organization he headed at the time when he expressed his views. With the founding of the state in 1948 and his ascension to the office of prime minister, Ben-Gurion became a champion of statism, transferring many of the functions filled by particularistic organizations such as the parties and the Histadrut to the state bureaucracy. Because of Ben-Gurion's charisma and his role as undisputed leader he was successful in convincing many that the time had come to make the switch. A sovereign nation state must provide services and equal rights to all. While this may sound very reasonable today, it must be understood in light of the conditions that prevailed in the pre-state period.

Bickering among the various political parties was very intense. Some even fostered the underground militias which opposed the policies of the national leadership toward the British on the one hand and toward the Arabs on the other. Menachem Begin's Irgun group was one of them. The Palmach, an elite commando strike force, was identified with the leadership of the Kibbutz Meuchad federation. The Hagana was the largest military group and was dominated by Mapai. While certain policing activities were legal, for the most part these groups operated underground, procured their arms as best they could, and had to function under the constraints placed on them by the British mandatory power, the local Arab units, and the competing Jewish militias.

Upon becoming prime minister, Ben-Gurion was determined to put an end to this situation and set up the Israel Defense Forces in 1948. The party functionaries had always delegated Ben-Gurion complete authority on defense matters and little objection was recorded. Furious debates took place, however, with Begin's right-wing and the Palmach's left-wing units. The showdown came when Ben-Gurion gave the order to sink the *Altelana*, a boat loaded with ammunition for the Irgun, in Tel Aviv harbor—this in a period when the Jewish community was not suffering from a surplus of arms.

Ben-Gurion was less successful when he called for the nationalization of the school systems. These too had been largely party dominated. The Histadrut ran a socialist "track" school system, and there was a parallel religious "track" as well as a general "track" largely unaffiliated with political groups. Many of the party activists, and especially those involved in the socialist track, objected to merging the two for the goals of national unity and uniform education. Ben-Gurion's position was that particularist education was inappropriate in light of the need for absorbing immigrants from many lands and forging them into a single nation. Interestingly, Ben-Gurion was able to overcome the opposition of his own party's functionaries but was less successful with the religious parties. They argued for the continuation of their autonomous school system, and the law of 1953 that set up the public school system provided for two tracks, a religious one and a general one. Ben-Gurion was forced to accept this partial victory because of his dependence on the National Religious party for the continued stability of the government coalition. The law also allowed the ultra-orthodox Agudat Israel and the kibbutz movements to operate their own school systems.

Paradoxically, one of the arguments used in Mapai circles for abandoning the track system was that the socialist track was the larger. Therefore, the argument went, labor could afford the nationalization of the service since most parents preferred to see the labor parties dominate the system and its curriculum. The truth of the matter was that many parents (especially new immigrants) sent their children to the schools of the dominant party without any clear ideological commitment to the movement. With the decline of the labor movement, especially among the young, and the parallel decline of party-affiliated youth groups, some argued that the abolition of the track system in the public schools would prevent the party from providing the second generation with the value system needed for continued support of the socialist revolution.

A crucial function that became heavily dependent on party was the distribution of jobs. In order to be employed, the job seeker would apply to a labor exchange. These were controlled by the various parties, but the most important one was operated by the Histadrut. In an era of immigration, the Histadrut was obviously in a very good position to provide jobs since many of its projects (building housing, manufacturing, manning the bureaucracies needed to run its many undertakings, and so on) demanded relatively large-scale manpower and could provide concealed underemployment at full pay. Full employment was always an important principle of Israel's labor parties; efficiency and productivity were always relegated to second place. Obviously, a public or semi-public undertaking could afford this while a private enterprise could not. It is not surprising then that the labor exchanges of the Histadrut were powerful influences in the lives of the immigrants flowing into the country.

A "key system" was developed whereby each party could provide jobs in proportion to its political strength. This again gave the labor parties, and especially Mapai, an important advantage. Cooperation developed between the various exchanges, but the key system ensured the importance of patronage in the political system and provided the political machine the wherewithal to meet the demands of the immigrants. Many immigrants developed feelings of deep gratitude to the party and apprehension if the party seemed to be losing strength or if the machine bosses suspected that the recipient was no longer faithful. While the material dependence of the immigrant on his party decreased objectively over the years, the psychological dependence persisted. By 1959 when the labor exchanges were nationalized, immigration rates were down and the unemployment level in the economy was low. The passing of the law transferred a once-important function to the state.

Two other functions for which nationalization has been proposed are health insurance and pension funds. Both of these are extremely important in explaining the Labor party's ability to perpetuate its dominance. The opposition of the machine politicians prevented the transfer as long as Labor was in power, although it was proposed early in the history of the state. Now that the Likud is gaining power this may well change. Not only is there an ideological reason (statism) to make the transfer, there is also the belief that transferring these services will further weaken the power base of the labor movement.

The Histadrut's Sick Fund (Kupat Holim) is by far the largest provider of health services, covering some three-quarters of the population. Its facilities are the most comprehensive and widespread. To avail oneself of these services, one has to be a member of the Histadrut. Were this not the case, Histadrut membership would probably tumble, which in turn would bring the attendant problems of budget and program shrinkage. The Histadrut's pension plans are a prime source of capital for Histadrut industry, services, and activities. Nationalizing these would seriously hinder the leadership's flexibility and power base.

As the party weakened with the generational change and the new career options which were presented to the machine leadership, the party bureaucracy increasingly objected to the processes of statism that had been so prevalant under Ben-Gurion. The party bureaucracy of the 1960s and 1970s succeeded in preventing further nationalization of the services that underpinned their power.

Why did the party divest itself of many of its bases of power? The clearest answer is Ben-Gurion. His belief in statism and his ability to carry the party with him reinforced the ideological appeal of setting up a national bureaucracy to provide egalitarian services as is appropriate in a modern sovereign state. Why was the tide turned? After all, statism had been one of Ben-Gurion's and Rafi's rallying cries. The answer is that with Ben-Gurion's withdrawal from Mapai and Rafi's reunification with the party in 1968 as the Labor party (without Ben-Gurion), the Rafi leadership was co-opted by the old-time Mapai leadership. While they continued to articulate their ideological demands, they soon practiced many of the forms of pragmatic politics they had castigated when they had been in the opposition. The former leaders of the political machine were now in power (Levi Eshkol, Golda Meir, Pinchas Sapir) and they were not inclined to further weaken the bases of the party's power. After the 1973 war, the second generation leadership found itself preoccupied with other, more pressing issues; the transfer of services to the national bureaucracy was held in abeyance. It is likely to be renewed by the Likud government and to continue to alter power relations in Israeli politics.

The Crisis of Succession

Another explanation for the decline of the dominant Labor party based on a broader historical perspective than the months immediately preceding the 1977 elections is suggested by Yonathan Shapiro.[10] What he emphasizes is the fact that the party underwent a crisis of succession of political leadership. With the passing of time and the exit from the political scene of many of the key political actors, the older arrangements that had existed could no longer be perpetuated and the party entered a phase of disintegration. Since Shapiro's ex-

---

[10] Yonathan Shapiro, "The End of a Dominant Party Regime," in Asher Arian, ed., *The Elections in Israel—1977* (Jerusalem: Jerusalem Academic Press, forthcoming).

planation contains rich analytic insight, it is well worth examining at some length.

The ruling elite of Mapai (the largest party of the dominant labor movement and the party of most of Israel's national leaders) was composed of two major groups: those born in the period 1885–1890 and those born at the turn of the century. These groups represented two distinct generational units in Israeli politics. The first group immigrated as part of the second *aliya* (wave of immigration) between the years 1905 and 1912 and were instrumental in setting up the major political organizations of their day, the Achdut Ha'avoda party in 1919 and the Histadrut in 1920. These organizations were to dominate much of the political and economic activity of the Jewish community in mandated Palestine. Ultimately, the leader of this group, David Ben-Gurion, became Israel's first prime minister, which he remained, with brief interruptions, until 1963.

The younger group arrived in the third *aliya* (1919–1923) and were greatly influenced by the Russian Revolution of 1917. Both groups came from Poland and Russia, both were highly motivated ideologically and politically, and each constituted a small fraction of the Jews who immigrated to Palestine. But because these groups came first and set up important organizations in a political void, because they were young, energetic, and self-sacrificing, their successful efforts meant that they would be the leaders of the state of Israel when it was founded in 1948.

An implicit symbiosis developed between these two groups. The older group were the statesmen, making the grand decisions and setting policy. The younger group controlled the party machine, faithful to the leadership, dependent on it, working for it—and in return exacting their own perpetuation in power, since in the last analysis the leadership was also dependent on the party machine. Alongside the formal relations of officeholders, activists, and voters there came into existence an informal system in which the hierarchy was clearly understood and in which the interdependence of each group with the other was evident.

Shapiro argues that the crisis came in the 1950s when the older group began to leave political life. With the acknowledged leadership fading from the scene, a crisis of succession loomed. The informal relations which had been such an important part of the division of labor within the generational units of the party could not be easily transferred. The long years of shared experience and the generational solidarity which this produced prevented the flow of young, new leadership into the ranks.

A fascinating case in point is the political career of Moshe Dayan. After Dayan left the army as chief of staff in 1957, Ben-Gurion wanted to make him a government minister. The major objections, as one might expect in a hierarchical system in which the political apprenticeship is very long, came from the second stratum of the ruling elite. It was Golda Meir and Zalman Aranne who pointed out that Dayan should be trained as a politician in more humble surroundings than the cabinet.[11] By trying to bypass the third *aliya* group of Mapai leaders, Ben-Gurion infuriated the party machine.

Ben-Gurion had no choice but to relinquish power to the third *aliya* group. But upon leaving office, he became a bitter critic of this group and ultimately split with the party he had founded. In 1965 Ben-Gurion set up Rafi with support from some of the bright young men he had fostered in the defense establishment, such as Dayan and Peres. The new party appealed to many young Israeli-born supporters who resented the fact that the party machine, as they saw it, deprived the party of adaptability and blocked access to positions of power. Ben-Gurion's move caused a dramatic split in the party faithful and even within the machine itself. Many were torn between two long-time allegiances: between the former leader of the party, Ben-Gurion, and the traditional leaders of the party machine.

The party machine was revitalized quickly by Pinchas Sapir, then minister of the treasury, before the 1965 elections. Sapir was younger than many of the leaders of the machine group, having immigrated from Eastern Europe in 1930. But as treasury minister, Sapir was able to hold the machine together by setting policies that favored groups and individuals supportive of the party and its clients. The autonomy of the organization and the effectiveness of the party's machine were hindered by this developing dependence of the party machine on the organs of government. Shapiro's point is an important one. As long as the structure of the party machine was hierarchically autonomous, career aspirations centered on the apex of the machine power pyramid. These activists cherished their independence and the independence of their organization. They could be honest brokers between their party's political leadership and the organizations and individuals whose support the party needed on election day. With Ben-Gurion's resignation and Sapir's taking over control of the party machine while serving simultaneously as minister of the treasury, the key positions of the party machine were less attractive for ambitious politicians than were key posts in the national government. Their ambition now was to sit

---

[11] See Shabbtai Tevet, *Moshe Dayan* (Boston: Houghton Mifflin, 1973), ch. 20.

in the Knesset or the cabinet. The symmetrical relationship between the machine and the top leadership was broken. The machine leaders were suddenly dependent on the top leadership for career advancement, just as the lower levels of the machine hierarchy were dependent on the machine leadership. The machine operated best when it was autonomous and when the machine's own internal structure was characterized by hierarchy and dependence. But in the 1960s the machine leadership lost its independence. It could no longer trade off its support and activity for influence on ministers and policy. The spheres had merged and the party machine lost its status since its leadership was now in competition for major party and national posts. They were also less effective 'as brokers between the leadership and the followers. With the ascension of the third *aliya* group to power, the party organization suffered and it was eventually to be felt in the voting results.

The leadership attempted two methods of solving the crisis of succession. One was to ally themselves with other parties, thereby gaining depth of leadership. Before the 1965 elections they formed a joint list with Achdut Ha'avoda whose leaders had split from Mapai in 1944. Before the Six-Day War in 1967 Mapai exhibited a lack of leadership in foreign and security policies. These were, after all, the areas in which Ben-Gurion had predominated. After some hesitation, Dayan was made defense minister and Rafi was included in the National Unity government. In 1968, the Mapai leadership consolidated this process by forming, along with Rafi and Achdut Ha'avoda, the Israel Labor party.

The second method was by introducing new elements into the party leadership. Before the 1973 elections (and war) Sapir and his party decided to appoint former army heroes to positions of importance in the government as members of the Labor party. If we recall that Mosca argued that the ruling class has perfected some highly valued characteristics, it makes sense to expect army generals to play a prominent role in Israeli politics. Mosca called such characteristics "social forces." "As civilization grows, the number of the moral and material influences which are capable of becoming social forces increases. For example, property in money, as the fruit of industry and commerce, comes into being alongside of real property. Education progresses. Occupations based on scientific knowledge gain in importance."[12]

---

[12] Gaetano Mosca, *The Ruling Class* (New York: McGraw Hill, 1939), pp. 144–145.

It became natural for those endowed with success in this "social force" to play an active role in politics. But their backgrounds did not prepare them for party politics, let alone the intricacies of running a party machine. Yitzhak Rabin and Haim Bar-Lev could not match the political performance of Pinchas Sapir and Avraham Ofer. But it would be unfair to expect them to. Sapir and Ofer would probably not have been successful in conducting war. The difference was, of course, that Rabin and Bar-Lev (and others) were called upon to run a disintegrating party at a most difficult moment. It is little wonder that they failed. They were the victims, not the causes, of the passing of dominance from the Labor party.

The Next Generation

According to Mosca, the social forces in a given society indicate the reservoir of potential talent to be tapped for the ruling elite. The young pioneers who set up the dominant political organizations in the 1920s were at the peak of their careers in the 1940s when their children came of age and began seeking their own way. Most of these children did not find politics an attractive career since the best jobs were filled by relatively young people. Moreover, a clear "social force" had emerged: defense. The army, the security establishment, the problem of procuring arms for the Jewish community, service with the British armed forces in the Second World War, all these attracted the bright young men and women of the 1940s. By the 1960s two processes overlapped: the aging and retirement of the traditional political leadership and the retirement in their mid-forties of a generation of defense and army leaders as a result of the early retirement policy of the Israel Defense Forces. The apex of the political pyramid was vacated just as the apex of the military pyramid was being rejuvenated. It was only natural, Mosca would tell us, for these experienced army officers who had succeeded in a field that was clearly a "social force" to assume positions of responsibility and authority in politics.

This horizontal movement from the apex of one elite pyramid to the apex of another is called in Hebrew "parachuting." Instead of climbing to the top of the political hierarchy the way a foot soldier would, a general is parachuted in, bypassing the customary apprenticeship of years in the ward, the branch, and the lower levels of the national party hierarchy. It is not surprising that the objections to this bypassing of traditional channels of advancement came from those who had been serving as second-stratum leaders, waiting their turn to assume the role of the top leaders.

The problem is one of leadership succession. The Israeli parties are prone to crises of succession since the terms of office of party leaders are not limited and the incumbent usually becomes entrenched. In the case of a Ben-Gurion or a Begin, this affords the respective party years of sure leadership. When the crisis starts, however, it is usually intense.

Both the Alignment and the Likud have experienced an influx of political leaders with army backgrounds who have vied for the top spot. In Herut, both Ezer Weizmann and Ariel Sharon have tried unsuccessfully to unseat Begin or at least to share power with him. Both of these men had very impressive army careers before entering politics. Both figured prominently in the Likud's creation and victory in 1977, but Begin's role as top leader remained unchanged.

The aftermath of the 1973 war accelerated the process of leadership turnover in the Labor-Mapam Alignment. Rabin, Peres, and Allon replaced Meir, Dayan, and Abba Eban in 1974 as prime minister, defense minister, and foreign minister, respectively. Although Dayan's appointment in 1967 had presaged the shift, the later development clearly indicated the emergence of a younger leadership with strong roots in the defense establishment and the eclipse of the old-time party leadership. This became even clearer in the ensuing years of the Rabin government where an uneasy bifurcation existed in the ranks of the Labor members of the cabinet between those with a military past and those with a party machine past. The second generation with military backgrounds took over the government, while the second-generation party leaders took over the party, but their power in the government was diminished. A strong, unified leadership failed to emerge.

The crisis of succession plagued both the Likud and the Alignment in the 1977 elections. Begin suffered a heart attack before the election and was inactive for much of the campaign. Rabin and Peres battled for the first place on the Alignment list, and while Rabin finally won by a slim margin, the fissures that were created as a result of the contest were not easily healed. Ultimately, Rabin vacated the position because of the exposure of his wife's illegal foreign-currency bank account, and Peres campaigned in the 1977 elections in the number one spot.

The one party that had successfully passed political leadership to the second generation was the National Religious party. The average age of the twelve NRP Knesset members elected in 1977 was considerably lower than those of the other major parties. In addition, one of its three government ministers was in his thirties, another in his early forties. Political leadership had clearly passed to the Youth Faction headed by Zevulun Hammer and Yehuda Ben-Meir. While they retained Yosef Burg, an older man, at the head of their list, it was clear that power had been transferred to the young. This development was all the more impressive in that it had been accomplished through the outmaneuvering of a veteran political activist, Yitzhak Raphael, who had run the National Religious party machine for years. By careful coalition building and adroit use of parliamentary procedure, the youth faction was able to prevent Raphael's inclusion on the party list for the 1977 elections. In another important political move, the party placed Rabbi Haim Druckman in the second place on the list. Druckman is widely identified with the Gush Emunim movement, and his inclusion was probably decisive in winning over many young religious voters. While they were not yet at the head of the list, it was clear that the youth faction was at the head of the party.

In a sense, the emergence of the Democratic Movement for Change reflected the crisis of political leadership succession discussed above. The DMC provided an alternative channel of upward mobility for leaders (political, military, economic, and academic) who disdained the opportunity of competing for positions of leadership in the discredited Alignment. Yigael Yadin, a university professor, had long been considered a promising young leader. Amnon Rubinstein, another professor, personified the upper-middle-class desire to bring about change in the handling of the country's affairs. Shmuel Tamir had once challenged Begin's leadership of Herut and had run successfully as the head of his own list (Free Center) in the 1969 elections. Meir Amit was the head of the Histadrut's industrial conglomerate (Koor) when he joined the DMC. Aharon Yariv was a minister in Rabin's cabinet and a member of the Labor party. These men could have attained roles of political leadership in many of the existing parties. But they sought to set up a new party. This move was certainly in tune with the public mood of the moment. But it also reflected the disarray of the party system in 1977; both party leadership and electoral support were in flux, it was felt. A bold move might create a party that would have a pivotal position in coalition calculations. While the DMC did not succeed in winning a pivotal role (the Likud and the religious parties could rule without them), their fifteen seats were an impressive achievement in Israeli political terms.

In an important sense, Begin represented continuity with the Alignment leadership, for he was the last of the older generation still active in politics. While younger than the founding fathers of the labor movement, he had held top leadership positions since the pre-state period. After thirty years of statehood, all of the others were relative newcomers to the leadership scene. The authority associated with the formative years was enjoyed only by Begin.

This was one of the reasons for the appearance of strong tendencies toward the democratization of the nomination process in 1977.[13] The competition was intense and the deference paid the founding fathers was generally gone. Also, the corruption alleged in many of the parties was directly associated with the lack of turnover and the hierarchical nature of the patronage system. Signs of democratization were obvious in most of the big parties. Ironically, the DMC, with the most democratic nomination procedure, had the least representative list. On the other hand, the nominating committee that the Labor party continued to use generated a balanced and representative list.

The most extreme example of democracy in the 1977 elections was the DMC's poll of its members to determine the composition of its list. Eighty percent of the 35,000 members participated in this unprecedented primary. Herut used a tiered system that allowed its 640-member party Center to select its list. After the first place on the list (Begin) was voted for on a separate ballot, thirty-five names were chosen by vote, and these were clustered in groups of seven on yet another ballot. Then votes were held for places two through eight, places nine through fifteen, and so on. After the Herut list was assembled, it was merged with the other component parties' lists to form the Likud list.

The Liberals, La'am (of the Likud), and the National Religious party all used secret balloting in central party institutions to prepare their lists. While the Labor party used the nominations committee, the classic means of undemocratically choosing candidates in Israeli politics, two important changes were made in 1977. For the first time, the principle of rotation was adopted. A candidate who had served eight years as a Knesset member would have to win the support of 60 percent of the party's Center in order to be placed on the list by the nominating committee. In fact, seven—including three well-known leaders, among them the speaker of the Knesset—failed to pass the Center's vote. Ten others passed, although the strength of their vote in the Center was not correlated with the place on the list they were eventually assigned. For many other parties, candidate selection remained a matter of negotiations among party leaders.

---

[13] Giora Goldberg, "Democratization and Representativeness in Israeli Political Parties," in Arian, ed., *The Elections in Israel—1977*, forthcoming.

The Aftermath

The 1977 elections produced the first Israeli government led by the right Likud and not led by the left Alignment. The Likud continued the growth it had shown in recent elections and the Alignment continued its downward trend. The emergence of the DMC cost the Alignment heavily and allowed the Likud to win more seats than the Alignment. The National Religious party retained its pivotal position as coalition ally, this time joining the Likud.

As a result of this historic shift, it might appear that the country had turned to the right. In fact, ideology was not an important explanation for the final results of the election. The differences between the two major parties as perceived by the electorate had diminished, and as a whole the country had moved to the right in its response to the questions of foreign and defense policies. It was the lack of differentiation of the two major parties' ideological positions that increased the Likud's chances. If their policies had been considered irresponsible, the voters would have been repelled by them. But once the ideological gap diminished, the Likud's ideological legitimacy increased, and with the Labor party in disrepute for nonideological reasons, the Likud became a prospective winner.

The bifurcation of the ideological spectrum in Israel was really reintroduced after Sadat's visit to Jerusalem at the end of 1977. Before then, talk of territorial compromise was academic since, it was pointed out, there was no one to talk with. Both Golda Meir's and Rabin's governments took a tough line regarding the territories, and the general impression was that no territorial concessions could enhance the likelihood of peace and security. Before Sadat's visit and during the period of the 1977 elections the question was not whether Rabin/Peres would be too soft, but rather whether Begin would be too tough.

The 1977 elections were obviously an important watershed of Israeli political history, but not everything changed overnight. The political party remained the preeminent feature of political life, communication continued to be permeated with ideology though pragmatic political considerations were rarely lost sight of, and the basic conservative nature of the Israeli political system reasserted itself.

The elections were refreshing in that for the first time the Israelis had put their democracy to the ultimate test. Leadership was changed peacefully accordingly to rules set by law. They also put a heavy strain on the consensus that had developed through the twenty-nine years of Alignment rule. In the Likud's first year in office, major changes were undertaken, yet on closer inspection some of these seemed to be continuations of past policies. The question of drafting women for army service, for example, again stirred public controversy. The question ultimately was how strict could one be in determining the nature of a female draftee's religious belief and observance. While the Likud liberalized the rules for conscientious objectors under pressure from its religious coalition partners, it could point to continuity of policy from the days of the Alignment.

The Likud also introduced a sweeping liberalization of the economy by suspending control of foreign currency transactions. It also pressed to remove subsidies on food, while approving loans to troubled corporations that might have been forced to close in a more capitalist environment. The Likud was unsuccessful during its first year in office in curtailing government or public expenditures or in seriously fighting the 40-plus percent inflation. This record was similar to that of the Alignment. The debate over foreign policy was the loudest, but it was not completely clear what the difference between the two major parties were. Moreover, within each of the parties a whole range of political opinion could be found. In Begin's own Herut party, he could be considered a moderate, even though he was widely perceived as an extremist. Peres's position became much softer after be became leader of the opposition. Were he to return to power, his position might again harden.

The Likud's victory meant its rehabilitation. Long stigmatized by many for its role in the pre-state period, the Likud finally won complete legitimacy. Its organizational apparatus in the 1977 elections proved far superior to the Alignment's and its electoral base seemed to be expanding. It was most closely associated with the majority segment of the population from Asian and African backgrounds and had won important support in the new middle class. While the future would present many challenges, the government seemed to have organizational and leadership qualities that would allow it to continue to rule. Finally, the Likud's winning of power underscored the place of ideology in Israeli politics: both the medium and the message were cast in ideological terms.

APPENDIX A

The Histadrut

The Histadrut, or General Federation of Labor, is the largest workers' organization in Israel. It is also the largest employer of labor and a major industrial power. It rivals the state as a provider of social services (some say its membership would drop by half but for the fact that it offers the cheapest and most comprehensive health insurance in the country) and its internal elections are closely watched national political events. The great institution of the labor movement created by the founding generation, the Histadrut has become, by any standard, the establishment.

Foundation. The Histadrut was founded in 1920 as the central organization of the Zionist workers in Palestine, of whom there were then some 5,000. In accordance with their socialist ideals, they banded together to work out cooperative solutions to the special problems they faced in their mission of building a Jewish homeland. Most were immigrants from middle-class, Eastern European, urban environments, new not only to the Middle East but also to the work they had come to do, as farmers and laborers and engineers, in transforming the land. The task was not merely to organize a labor force but to create one. Through the Histadrut, they sought to make the best use of their human and material resources and to absorb future waves of immigration, fitting newcomers into the development effort and into communities. Ultimately the Histadrut became a quasi-government for the Jewish pioneers in Mandate Palestine, acting as a labor exchange and organizer of trade unions, a major employer in its own right, and the

---

This description of the Histadrut is based on two information booklets put out by branches of the Histadrut—*Histadrut, the General Federation of Labour in Israel* (Tel Aviv: Histadrut, International Department, Information Division, 1976) and Dan Giladi and Sarah Morris, *Histadrut: A Profile*, rev. ed. (New York: American Histadrut Cultural Exchange Institute, 1975)—and on conversations with Dr. Daniel Elazar.

303

leading provider of welfare services for its members. When Israel's independence was declared in 1948 it was the first secretary general of the Histadrut, David Ben-Gurion, who became the nation's first prime minister.

Economic Functions. Some forty national trade unions are affiliated with the Histadrut, and 90 percent of all wage earners in Israel belong to them. Overall, the Histadrut represents almost 50 percent of Israel's population, including some 1,350,000 Jews and 130,000 Arabs. Membership is open to all men and women over the age of eighteen who earn their livelihood by their own labor. Housewives without outside occupations may become full members, and young workers between the ages of fifteen and seventeen may join the Histadrut's Working Youth Organization.

The affiliated unions (and occasionally the central bodies of the Histadrut itself) perform all the normal functions of trade unions, at the national, local, and plant levels, negotiating collective bargaining agreements with employers, settling disputes, and in general representing the interests of labor. On the other hand, trade union policies in Israel have reflected the special history of the Histadrut, taking into account not only the needs of the workers but also the economic possibilities of the country and the development priorities imposed by the external threat. The Histadrut has considered itself not an adversary but a partner of government and management, albeit the partner whose special charge it is to see that the minimal demands of wage earners are met. Part of its mandate has been to take a national view. This partnership was reinforced over the years by the fact that both government and Histadrut were dominated by Mapai, then the Labor party.

The distinction between labor and management and between labor and government in Israel is further blurred by the fact that the Histadrut owns and operates industrial and commercial enterprises accounting for as much as 20 percent of Israel's GNP in 1975. This peculiarity too has its roots in the socialist ideals of the pioneering days. What could be more fitting than that the workers collectively should take on some of the jobs that needed doing? Today every member of the Histadrut is a shareholder in Hevrat Ovdim, the Workers' Society, the holding company embracing all of the Histadrut's business and commercial ventures. These include some of the major enterprises in Israel, ranging from heavy industries to travel agencies, banks, and department stores. In addition, the great majority of cooperatives (agricultural cooperatives, but also industrial and services cooperatives) are affiliated with Hevrat Ovdim.

In 1958 the Histadrut Convention adopted the principle of worker participation in the managing bodies of Histadrut enterprises, and a few years later profit sharing was endorsed. In practice, however, "industrial democracy" spread slowly; the ideological fervor of the leadership has not always been echoed by the rank and file, and Histadrut enterprises have faced their share of labor unrest. In recent years the distance has grown between Histadrut functionaries and the workers. Union locals have gone out on wildcat strikes, oblivious to the protests of the central bodies of the Histadrut that are theoretically responsible for keeping the labor peace. With a nonlabor coalition now in power nationally, the Histadrut leaders may find themselves freer than in the past to pursue policies independent of the government or even in opposition to it.

Social Services and Cultural Activities. Kupat Holim, the Workers' Sick Fund, provides comprehensive health insurance to 75 percent of the Israeli population. (Some organizations have been allowed to join the Sick Fund without joining the Histadrut. Virtually all Israelis not covered by the Sick Fund carry some other form of health insurance, but none is provided by the state.) Just over half of Histadrut dues are automatically allocated to the Sick Fund. It employs more than half the practicing doctors in Israel and dispenses free care of all kinds in some 1,100 local clinics and 16 major hospitals. It also provides medical attention to all immigrants on arrival. The Histadrut's various pension plans benefit about 80 percent of salaried workers, and its social welfare fund owns and manages twenty-two old age homes for members and their parents, offers aid to the unemployed in the form of interest-free loans, and helps the underprivileged generally.

The Histadrut runs twenty-eight vocational training schools, awards a large number of educational scholarships and grants, and offers a wide range of adult classes, notably in the Hebrew language. It also runs libraries and sponsors such recreational endeavors as drama and folk dancing groups, choirs, orchestras, and sports teams. The Histadrut publishes two daily newspapers and many journals and operates one of the largest book publishing houses in Israel.

Organization and Elections. The Histadrut is a highly centralized organization with elected institutions at every level. Membership is personal—it is not enough to be a member of an affiliated union or political party, an individual must also join himself. Dues, which amount to almost 5 percent of the worker's wage, are paid directly by his employer into a central fund, from which are financed the Histadrut's various activities.

Each local Histadrut branch is governed by a Local Workers' Council elected by all Histadrut members in the district, and each union is governed by a council elected by the union membership. The supreme institution of the Histadrut is the General Convention, elected every four years by the entire Histadrut membership. The General Convention decides basic policy, has the power to amend the constitution of the organization, and elects the Council, which meets at least twice yearly. The Council appoints an Executive Committee, which elects the secretary general and the Executive Bureau, the real day-to-day executive of the Histadrut.

Up until 1977, elections to the General Convention of the Histadrut were held roughly two months before Knesset elections and were barometers of the Knesset outcomes; in 1977, because the parliamentary elections were called early, the Histadrut elections fell about a month after the Knesset elections. The two campaigns more or less merge, though the broadcast media distinguish between them in allocating free air time to the parties and, theoretically at least, they are separately financed. Like Knesset elections, Histadrut elections are run on the basis of proportional representation and the party-list ballot. Essentially the same parties participate in both.

Since 1968 the parties in the Histadrut have been financed partly through deductions from workers' pay; in 1970 the Histadrut instituted a "consolidated tax" on members, of which 5.5 percent was earmarked "for the purposes of the elections in the Histadrut and the Trade Unions and for the needs of the parties represented in the Histadrut, proportional to their representation therein."

The Histadrut and the Nonlabor Parties. The nonlabor parties long remained outside the Histadrut. Herut even tried to compete, setting up parallel unions and health programs. But in the end practical considerations outweighed ideological ones: Herut's health plan could not hope to offer the comprehensive coverage and dense network of hospitals and clinics that made the Sick Fund so attractive, and the party had to face the fact that its members were joining the Histadrut. In 1963 it made the decision to create a faction within the Histadrut and participate in General Convention elections. As the strength of the nonlabor parties has grown, and particularly since the Likud's victory in the Knesset election of 1977, there has been speculation about what would happen if the Likud were to win control of the Histadrut. At the last Histadrut election Labor still came out well ahead, but it suffered losses while Likud gained. The paradoxical possibility of the Labor Federation's falling into nonlabor hands seems real. Already the peculiarities of the Histadrut's history have made some normal patterns of left-right politics inapplicable in Israel: thus, it is the parties of the center and right that want to nationalize certain services while the parties of the left resist, preferring to keep them in the Histadrut, under the Labor party's control. One of the first acts of the Likud government was to propose the establishment of national health insurance.

APPENDIX B

Knesset Election Results, 1949-1977

Compiled by Richard M. Scammon

Party	Votes	Percentage	Seats
Total eligible	2,236,293		
Total voting	1,771,726	79.2	
Invalid ballots	23,906	1.3	
Valid ballots	1,747,820		
Likud	583,075	33.4	43
Alignment (Labor)	430,023	24.6	32
Democratic Movement for Change	202,265	11.6	15
National Religious	160,787	9.2	12
Agudat Israel	58,652	3.4	4
Poalei Agudat Israel	23,956	1.4	1
Democratic Front	79,733	4.6	5
Shelli	27,281	1.6	2
Flatto-Sharon	35,049	2.0	1
Shlomzion (Sharon)	33,947	1.9	2
United Arab list	24,185	1.4	1
Independent Liberal	21,277	1.2	1
Citizens' Rights	20,621	1.2	1
Others	46,969	2.7	—
Total seats			120

SOURCE: Final official returns as released May 26, 1977.

TABLE TITLE: DISTRIBUTION OF SEATS, FIRST THROUGH THE NINTH KNESSETS, 1949–1977

Party	1st 1949	2nd 1951	3rd 1955	4th 1959	5th 1961	6th 1965	7th 1969	8th 1973	9th 1977
Mapai	46	45	40	47	42	45		Labor Alignment	
Achdut Ha'avoda			10	7	8				
Mapam	19	15	9	9	9	8	56	51	32
Rafi[a]						10			
Democratic Movement for Change									15
Herut	14	8	15	17	17	26	Gahal 26	Likud 39	43[b]
Liberal[c]	7	20	13	8	17				
Independent Liberal[d]	5	4	5	6		5	4	4	1
United Religious	16								
National Religious		10	11	12	12	11	12	10	12
Agudat Israel		5	6	6	6	4	4	5	4
Poalei Agudat Israel						2	2		1
Communist[e]	4	5	6	3	5	4	4	4	5
Citizens' Rights								3	1
Arab lists	2	5	5	5	4	4	4	3	1
Others	7	3				1	8		5

[a] Rafi was formed by David Ben-Gurion after he broke with Mapai in 1965. In 1968 the majority of its members joined the Labor Alignment.
[b] This figure rose to 45 shortly after the election, when Shlomzion (here included under "Others") joined the Likud.
[c] General Zionist through 1959.
[d] Progressive through 1959.

ᵃ The Communist figure represents Communist party seats in the First through the Fifth Knessets. In 1965 and 1969 the figure includes one seat for the "old" Jewish-oriented party (Maki) and three for the "new" Arab-oriented group (Rakah). In 1973 and 1977 the figure is for the latter only, in 1977 under the name Democratic Front for Peace and Equality. The left-wing parties Moked (1973) and Shelli (1977) are listed among "Others."

SOURCE: Through 1973, Central Bureau of Statistics, *Results of Elections to the Eighth Knesset and Local Authorities*, Special Series no. 461, Jerusalem, 1974; for 1977, final official returns as released May 26, 1977.

APPENDIX C Israeli Ballots, 1977

מחל

הליכוד

In the voting booth the Israeli voter is confronted with an array of pigeon holes containing stacks of ballots. Each stack is different, and there is one for each of the competing parties or lists. Blank write-in ballots are also available. The voter selects the ballot of the party for which he wishes to cast his vote and places it in an envelope, which he then seals. Emerging from the booth, he drops the envelope into the ballot box. In the 1977 Knesset election twenty-two different printed ballots were used, four of which are reproduced here. The Likud ballot above is shown its actual size, those on the next page are slightly reduced. Each ballot bears in large type the slogan or acronym associated with the list for purposes of the election and below it the party's name. The Alignment ballot also identifies several of the constituent parties.

This appendix was prepared with the assistance of Mordechai Pinkasovic.

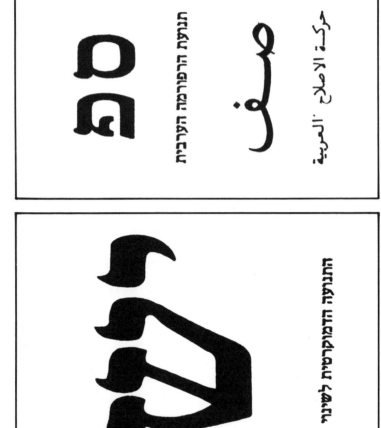

1977 ballots: from left to right, the Alignment, the Democratic Movement for Change, and the Arab Reform Movement.

314

GLOSSARY OF
POLITICAL PARTIES

AGUDAT ISRAEL. An ultraorthodox party which, prior to independence, opposed statehood and lived in self-imposed isolation from the mainstream of society. It has a strongly theocratic orientation and is governed by the decisions of a Rabbinical Council of Sages. It received four seats in the Ninth Knesset. Agudat Israel is a member of the Likud dominated coalition but is not a member of the government.

ACHDUT HA'AVODA. A socialist party with a strong base of support in the Kibbutz Hameuchad movement. Originally a faction within Mapai, it became independent in 1944. Then in 1948 it merged with Hashomer Hazaïr to form Mapam, from which it split off in 1954. It formed an electoral alignment with Mapai in 1965 and merged with Mapai and most of Rafi to form the Israel Labor party in 1968.

ALIGNMENT; MA'ARACH. The combined election list of the Labor party and Mapam which ran in the elections of 1969, 1973, and 1977. (In the 1965 election the same name was used for the joint list of Mapai and Achdut Ha'avoda.) The two component parties established institutions for mutual consultation. The Alignment lost one of the thirty-two seats it received in the Ninth Knesset when Moshe Dayan became an independent Knesset member, bringing the Alignment's total loss since the Eighth Knesset to twenty seats.

ARAB REFORM MOVEMENT. A list of local Arab dignitaries from the triangle region adjacent to the former border with Jordan. It received 5,695 votes (0.3 percent) in 1977.

BEIT YISRAEL. An ethnic list based in the Yemenite community which received 9,505 votes (0.5 percent) in 1977. This was a 0.2 percentage point improvement over the previous election, but was far short of the 1 percent of the vote required to win a seat in the Knesset.

BLACK PANTHERS; HOFESH. One of several splinter factions of a movement founded by young Israelis of North African origin which brought public attention to problems of social and economic inequality. By 1973 it had split into two factions which competed unsuccessfully for representation in the Knesset. Hofesh was one of several Panther off-shoots competing in 1977. Led by Shalom Cohen (a former associate of Uri Avneri) and Yehoshua Peretz (former leader of the Ashdod dock workers), it received 2,498 votes (0.14 percent) in 1977.

CITIZENS' RIGHTS MOVEMENT; RATZ. A group led by former Labor party member and civil rights activist Shulamit Alloni that capitalized on discontent with the Labor party and its conduct of the war in 1973. It won three seats in the Eighth Knesset but lost much of its support to the Democratic Movement for Change in 1977. The Citizens' Rights Movement succeeded in electing only one member, Alloni, to the Ninth Knesset.

COEXISTENCE WITH JUSTICE. A local list of Arab notables primarily from the Galilee area in northern Israel. It received 1,085 votes (0.06 percent) in 1977.

DEMOCRATIC FRONT FOR PEACE AND EQUALITY. A front created by Rakah, the Arab nationalist New Communist list, in order to broaden its appeal in 1977. The Democratic Front co-opted the non-Communist chairman of the influential organization of heads of Arab local councils as well as a former leader of the Black Panthers. It gained five seats in the Ninth Knesset (one more than Rakah in the Eighth) and has steadily increased its support among the growing proportion of younger and better educated Israeli Arabs.

DEMOCRATIC MOVEMENT FOR CHANGE. A new party formed through the merger of Yigael Yadin's Democratic Movement, with Change, the well-organized movement led by Amnon Rubinstein. The DMC (popularly known as Dash) absorbed Shmuel Tamir's Free Center movement, an offshoot of the Likud, and several prominent members of the Labor party, notably Meir Amit and David Golomb. Capitalizing on major discontent with the Labor party, it won fifteen seats in the Ninth Knesset and belatedly joined the Likud-led government without obtaining the major concessions for which it had held out. Immediately before the Camp David talks the DMC split in two: the Yadin-led Democratic Movement (including Tamir's group) remained in the government, while Rubinstein's group, the former Change movement and ex-Labor leaders, took the name Shai and joined the opposition.

FLATTO-SHARON. The one-man list of Shmuel Flatto-Sharon, a millionaire wanted by the French authorities in connection with allegations of illegal financial dealings. His active campaign won him sufficient votes for two seats in the Knesset. Since he was the only candidate on his list, the second seat was returned to the pool.

FREE CENTER. See Democratic Movement for Change and Likud.

GAHAL. The electoral alignment formed by Herut and the General Zionist wing of the Liberal party which competed in the elections in 1965 and in 1969. This alignment became the Likud in 1973.

GENERAL ZIONISTS. See Liberals.

GUSH EMUNIM. Literally the Bloc of the Faithful, a nonparty pressure group that came into being after the 1967 war. It is composed primarily of orthodox Jews whose main political concern is that all of historic Israel, especially Judea and Samaria, should be settled by Jews and incorporated into the state of Israel. It is supported by elements within the NRP and the Likud.

HAPOEL HAMIZRACHI. See National Religious party.

HERUT. Literally the "Freedom" party, founded by Menachem Begin in 1948 and led by him since then. Originally supported by members of the Revisionist Movement and the right-wing pre-state military organizations, it gained increasing support particularly among immigrants from Islamic countries and their children. It was the dominant faction in Gahal which in turn became the dominant force in the Likud.

HOFESH. See Black Panthers.

INDEPENDENT LIBERALS. The wing of the Liberal party that rejected the electoral alignment between the Liberals and Herut in 1965 and refused to join Gahal. Most of the Independent Liberals were former members of the Progressive party, formed in 1948, which had merged with the General Zionists in 1961 to create the Liberal party. A frequent coalition partner in Labor governments, the Independent Liberals lost three of their previous four seats in 1977.

KACH. A militantly nationalistic group headed by the former leader of the Jewish Defense League in the United States, Rabbi Meir Kahane. It received 4,396 votes (0.25 percent) in 1977.

LA'AM. An entity within the Likud formed toward the end of the term of the Eighth Knesset by the merger of three small factions, the State list, the Independent Center (that part of Shmuel Tamir's former Free Center that did not leave the Likud with Tamir), and the Land of Israel Movement.

LABOR; ISRAEL LABOR PARTY. A social democratic party formed in 1968 through the merger of Mapai, Rafi, and Achdut Ha'avoda. Labor, in its various guises, dominated Israeli politics from the earliest phase of the development of the society until the election of 1977 put it in the opposition. Led by Shimon Peres, Labor has only recently begun to recover from the shock of its loss of power and to take a more active role as the main opposition party in the Knesset. It provided the Begin government with its wide margin of approval for the Camp David agreements.

LIBERALS. Originally the group formed by the merger of the General Zionists and the Progressives in 1961. When the majority of the Liberals voted to join with Herut in forming the Gahal list in 1965, a minority group, who were mainly the former Progressives, split off to form the Independent Liberals. Thus, the remaining Liberals were essentially the former General Zionists. Led by the present minister of finance, Simcha Ehrlich, the Liberals are a key partner in the Likud and have primary influence in economic affairs.

LIKUD. The electoral bloc that won control of the government in the 1977 election. Established in 1973, the Likud joined together Gahal (Herut and the Liberal party), the State list, the Free Center (a group led by Shmuel Tamir which had left Herut in 1967), and many supporters of the Land of Israel Movement. In 1977 Shmuel Tamir led a group out of the Likud and later joined the Democratic Movement for Change, while Hillel Zeidel left the Independent Liberals and joined the Likud as the Achdut faction. After the election Ariel Sharon and his group, Shlomzion, which had just gained two seats in the

Knesset, joined Herut and thus entered the Likud. This brought the Likud's total to forty-five seats (six more than it had won in 1973). Its leader is Menachem Begin, prime minister under the present coalition government.

MAARACH. See Alignment.

MAPAI. A party formed in 1930 by the merger of Achdut Ha'avoda and Hapoel Hatzair. Mapai was the dominant factor in all governments from 1948 through 1977. It began to lose its internal dominance within the Labor party during the term of Yitzhak Rabin as prime minister.

MAPAM. A Marxist-Zionist party strongly supported by the Kibbutz Artzi movement. Mapam declined from being the second largest party with nineteen seats in the First Knesset to being a minor partner in the Labor Alignment. Only three of its members had winning positions on the Alignment list in 1977.

MIZRACHI. See National Religious party.

MOKED. See Shelli.

NATIONAL RELIGIOUS PARTY; MAFDAL. A party formed through the merger of two religious parties, Mizrachi and the labor-oriented Hapoel Hamizrachi. The NRP has been a coalition partner in every government of Israel since independence. Its religious goals are similar to those of Agudat Israel, but it has traditionally been less militant and more pragmatic in the means by which it attempts to achieve them. Increasingly dominated by the more militant Young Guard faction, it has moved closer to Herut in policies connected with settlements on the West Bank of the Jordan River. Having gained twelve seats in the Ninth Knesset (two more than in the Eighth), the NRP is a key member of the present governing coalition.

NEW GENERATION. An insignificant group that began activities in local elections in Tel Aviv. It received a total of 1,802 votes (0.1 percent) in 1977.

POALEI AGUDAT ISRAEL. A religious party that, on matters concerning the faith, adopts positions virtually identical to those of Agudat Israel. On social and economic issues it is closer to Labor, with which it has participated in coalitions. Its single member of the Ninth Knesset supports the Likud coalition government.

PROGRESSIVE PARTY. See Independent Liberals and Liberals.

RAFI. A party formed by David Ben-Gurion after he split off from Mapai in 1965. The majority of its members, led by Moshe Dayan and Shimon Peres, joined the Labor party in 1968. A more militant minority refused to join Labor and formed the State list, which joined the Likud in 1973.

RAKAH; NEW COMMUNIST LIST. An Arab nationalist faction that split away from the Israel Communist party in 1965 and became the Democratic Front for Peace and Equality in 1977.

RATZ. See Citizens' Rights Movement.

SHELLI. A left-wing Zionist party. Its name stands for Peace for Israel and Equality for Israel. Shelli was founded and led by several leading left-of-center politicians with different backgrounds and orientations. It had two M.K.s in the Ninth Knesset, Arieh Eliav, the former secretary-general of the Labor party, and Meir Pail, the sole representative of the former Moked (combined old Communist and new left) party in the previous Knesset. Third on the Shelli list was the editor of the weekly *Ha'olam Hazeh*, Uri Avneri, a former Knesset member. Fourth on the list was a leader of the former Black Panthers.

SHLOMZION. A small party led by Ariel Sharon, a former general whom many considered to have been a hero of the 1973 war. Sharon had been instrumental in establishing the Likud, which he subsequently left. After gaining two seats in the Ninth Knesset, Shlomzion joined the Herut wing of the Likud. Sharon (who had previously been affiliated with the Liberals) became minister of agriculture and chairman of the important Ministerial Committee on Settlements.

STATE LIST. A party established by former Rafi stalwarts who refused to join the Labor party in 1968. With David Ben-Gurion heading the list, it won four seats in the 1969 election. In 1973, after Ben-Gurion's death, it joined the Likud and eventually merged with two other small factions to form La'am within the Likud. As a member of the ruling government coalition, the State list strongly supported Prime Minister Begin's appointment of its former leader Moshe Dayan as minister of foreign affairs. Yigal Hurvitz, leader of the La'am faction and formerly of the State list, resigned as minister of industry, trade, and tourism in protest against the Camp David agreements. Eliezer Shostak, the second La'am minister, remained in the cabinet.

UNITED ARAB LIST. A consolidated list replacing the two Arab lists affiliated with Labor that had elected three members to the Eighth Knesset. The United Arab list gained only one seat in the Ninth Knesset. Composed mainly of older clan leaders, it lost much of its support to the Rakah-dominated Democratic Front for Peace and Equality. The Labor affiliated and independent Arab lists have relied primarily on patronage and clan loyalty, whereas the nationalistic appeals of Rakah have been increasingly successful among the growing proportion of younger voters in the Arab electorate.

WOMEN'S PARTY. A party influenced by the worldwide women's liberation movement. It failed to strike a chord among Israeli women and received only 5,674 votes (0.3 percent) in 1977.

ZIONIST PANTHERS. The least successful of the Panther lists competing in 1977. It received only 1,798 votes (0.1 percent).

ZIONIST AND SOCIALIST RENEWAL. A group led by former Labor party Knesset member Mordechai Ben-Porat. A devoted follower of Ben-Gurion and Moshe Dayan, Ben-Porat pitched his campaign primarily toward the Oriental communities and issued a call for the renewal of Zionist ideals. With 14,516 votes, he was only 0.2 percentage points short of the 1 percent of the vote required for representation in the Knesset.

Compiled by Myron J. Aronoff

CONTRIBUTORS

BENJAMIN AKZIN is professor emeritus at the Hebrew University, where he has taught political science and constitutional law since 1949. He was the founding president of Haifa University and has taught at major universities in the United States and Europe. In 1974 he became honorary president of the World Federation of United Nations Associations.

ASHER ARIAN is dean of the faculty of social sciences and professor of political science at Tel Aviv University. His books (many of them published under the name Alan Arian) include *The Choosing People*, a study of the Israeli electorate, and *Hopes and Fears of Israelis* (with Aaron Antonovsky).

MYRON J. ARONOFF is associate professor of political science at Livingston College, Rutgers University. He is the author of *Frontiertown: The Politics of Community Building in Israel* and *Power and Ritual in the Israel Labor Party* as well as editor of *Freedom and Constraint: A Memorial Tribute to Max Glukman.*

LEON BOIM was a professor of law in Poland before emigrating to Israel in the late 1950s. He continues to write on politics in Eastern Europe and is a leading student of the Israeli experiments with public financing of political parties and electoral campaigns. His essay on the early legislation in this area appeared in *The Elections in Israel—1969*, edited by Alan Arian.

AVRAHAM BRICHTA, a senior lecturer in political science at Haifa University, is the author of numerous articles on electoral systems and legislative recruitment in Israel, as well as a book on the 1977 Knesset elections, *Demokratia U'Bechirot*.

DANIEL J. ELAZAR is a professor of political science at Bar-Ilan and Temple Universities and editor of *Publius: The Journal of Federalism*. He is currently completing *Israel: Building a New Society* and a reader, *State and Society in Israel*.

JUDITH NEULANDER ELIZUR teaches international communications at the Communications Institute of the Hebrew University. Her special field of research is the image of Israel at home and abroad. She is the author of a policy study in commercial advertising on Israeli television.

ELIHU KATZ is director of the Communications Institute and professor of sociology at the Hebrew University. The founding director of Israel Television, he has written *The Secularization of Leisure Culture and Communication in Israel* (with Michael Guretvitch) and *Broadcasting in the Third World: Promise and Performance* (with E. G. Wedell).

BERNARD REICH is professor of political science at the George Washington University and a consultant to the Department of State on Middle Eastern affairs. His latest book is *Quest for Peace: United States-Israel Relations and the Arab-Israeli Conflict*.

ELYAKIM RUBINSTEIN is a member of the political science department at Bar-Ilan University and an assistant to the Israeli foreign minister. He has published books and articles on Jewish settlement in the Mandatory period, the supreme court in Israeli political history, and aspects of the Arab-Israeli conflict.

RICHARD SCAMMON, coauthor of *This U.S.A.* and *The Real Majority*, is director of the Elections Research Center in Washington, D.C. He has edited the biennial series *America Votes* since 1956.

EFRAIM TORGOVNIK is a member of the political science department at Tel Aviv University. He has written numerous articles on public administration and urban management as well as on Israeli politics.

INDEX

(Page numbers in italics designate tables.)

JQ 1825 .P365 I82
793129

Israel at the polls :

In add... ...hed by
the Ar... ...eries, a
collect... ...demo-
cratic...

Germa... Cerny,
  ed. ...

India... Weiner
  (15...

Irelan... niman,
  ed. ...

Italy... ...ard R.
  Pen...

Scand... ...orway,
  and... ...

Austr... R. Pen-
  nim...

Japan... Michael
  K. Blake...

Canada at... d R. Pen-
  niman, e...

France at... Ioward R.
  Pennima...

Britain at... Howard
  R. Penni...

This s... ...eferendum
on the Co...).

Studi... ...Australia,
and Spain... w Zealand.

DATE DUE

| | NOV 2 6 1981 | | |
| SEP 2 1 1989 | | | |

HIGHSMITH 45-220